Non-Legality in International Law

International lawyers typically start with the legal. What is a legal as opposed to a political question? How should international law adapt to the unforeseen? These are the routes by which international lawyers typically reason. This book begins, instead, with the non-legal. In a series of case studies, Fleur Johns examines what international lawyers cast outside or against law – as extra-legal, illegal, pre-legal or otherwise non-legal – and how this comes to shape political possibility. Non-legality is not merely the remainder of regulatory action. It is a key structuring device of contemporary global order. Constructions of non-legality are pivotal to debate in areas ranging from torture to foreign investment, and from climate change to natural disaster relief. Understandings of non-legality inform what international lawyers today do and what they refrain from doing. Tracing and potentially reimagining the non-legal in international legal work is, accordingly, both vital and pressing.

FLEUR JOHNS is an Associate Professor at the Sydney Law School, University of Sydney, and Co-Director of the Sydney Centre for International Law.

CAMBRIDGE STUDIES IN INTERNATIONAL AND COMPARATIVE LAW

Established in 1946, this series produces high quality scholarship in the fields of public and private international law and comparative law. Although these are distinct legal sub-disciplines, developments since 1946 confirm their interrelations.

Comparative law is increasingly used as a tool in the making of law at national, regional and international levels. Private international law is now often affected by international conventions, and the issues faced by classical conflicts rules are frequently dealt with by substantive harmonisation of law under international auspices. Mixed international arbitrations, especially those involving state economic activity, raise mixed questions of public and private international law, while in many fields (such as the protection of human rights and democratic standards, investment guarantees and international criminal law) international and national systems interact. National constitutional arrangements relating to 'foreign affairs', and to the implementation of international norms, are a focus of attention.

The series welcomes works of a theoretical or interdisciplinary character, and those focusing on the new approaches to international or comparative law or conflicts of law. Studies of particular institutions or problems are equally welcome, as are translations of the best work published in other languages.

A list of books in the series can be found at the end of this volume.

Non-Legality in International Law
Unruly Law

Fleur Johns

CAMBRIDGE
UNIVERSITY PRESS

CAMBRIDGE UNIVERSITY PRESS
Cambridge, New York, Melbourne, Madrid, Cape Town,
Singapore, São Paulo, Delhi, Mexico City

Cambridge University Press
The Edinburgh Building, Cambridge CB2 8RU, UK

Published in the United States of America by Cambridge University Press, New York

www.cambridge.org
Information on this title: www.cambridge.org/9781107014015

First published 2013

Printed and bound in the United Kingdom by the MPG Books Group

A catalogue record for this publication is available from the British Library

Library of Congress Cataloguing in Publication data
Johns, Fleur.
Non-legality in international law : unruly law / by Fleur Johns.
p. cm.
Includes bibliographical references and index.
ISBN 978-1-107-01401-5 (hardback)
1. International law. 2. Illegality. I. Title.
KZ3410.J64 2012
341'.1–dc23
2012029707

ISBN 978-1-107-01401-5 Hardback

For Pete

Contents

Foreword

It is an honour and pleasure to introduce Dr Fleur Johns' first book, with its intriguing title. My own first book, *The Creation of States in International Law*, was concerned with international lawyers making things with and through law, or at least participating in their making. In that respect, it shares a concern with Fleur Johns' book. Differing styles notwithstanding, the two have something else in common. *Creation of States* tackled phenomena commonly regarded as matters of 'fact' and not of law; it analysed material 'said to be "political" and, therefore, not a proper subject of legal analysis', as the late Professor Ian Brownlie remarked in introducing that text. In so doing, it probed fundamental concepts and considerations of legality in relation to various modes of illegal force and de facto situations.

In her book, Dr Johns likewise explores encounters of the legal and the non-legal across a wide range of settings marked by international legal argument. Many of these settings have elsewhere been characterised as wholly political creations (e.g. Guantánamo Bay) or scenarios in which international law's role is entirely reactive (e.g. the aftermath of natural disaster). By contrast, Dr Johns envisages international lawyers playing an active, constitutive role in each of these domains and asks that we bear a corresponding sense of responsibility.

The parallel between the two books naturally has its limits. My concern in *Creation of States* was to defend the formal coherence and completeness of international law as a system of law, as against the 'radical decentralization' that I there identified with nineteenth-century doctrine. That is not the goal of this book. Rather, Dr Johns' aspiration is, as she tells us, 'to make politically navigable and questionable' some aspects of international legal work previously unacknowledged, namely, work revolving around what are described in this book as international law's 'negative spaces'.

Across international legal fields and materials commonly seen as disparate, she traces some illuminating connections. Understandings of torture and counter-terrorist detention informed by international human rights law may have more to do with concepts of choice identified with international economic law than international legal scholarship has previously registered. Depictions of dead bodies, and work with them, in international policy manuals might owe something to patterns of thought discernible in scholarly writing on climate change. In these and other combinations, the repertoire of international legal thought and work manifest in this book is less cribbed than some accounts of contemporary international law would have us see. For all these reasons it is a welcome addition to Cambridge Studies in International and Comparative Law.

James Crawford
Lauterpacht Centre for International Law
University of Cambridge

Acknowledgements

The very earliest version of one chapter of this book was written in 2004, although the idea for such a book was then inchoate. Other chapters were written discontinuously between 2006 and 2012. Most were presented in varied forms before a range of audiences. In addition, I am fortunate to have received written commentary on published journal articles that formed the basis for a few of the chapters. Many people will, accordingly, have contributed to this work in ways that it is now beyond me to acknowledge. To all who have listened to me speak about some aspect of this work, referenced it in their own writing, and asked questions of or expressed interest in it, in one way or another, let me offer my thanks. At risk of unforgiveable omission, let me acknowledge in particular the input, feedback, insights and invitations of the following people in relation to various parts of this book: Mark Antaki, Irene Baghoomians, Katherine Biber, Edwin Bikundo, Selene Brett, Hilary Charlesworth, Davina Cooper, Mitchell Dean, Roshan DeSilva Wijeyeratne, Peter Fitzpatrick, Ben Golder, Richard Joyce, David Kinley, Karen Knop, Martti Koskenniemi, Euan Macdonald, Shaun McVeigh, Ralf Michaels, China Miéville, Stewart Motha, Jacqueline Mowbray, Pat O'Malley, Anne Orford, Sundhya Pahuja, Nikolas Rose, Kim Rubenstein, Wojciech Sadurski, Mehera San Roque, Ben Saul, Gerry Simpson, Tim Stephens, Mariana Valverde, Kevin Walton, Katie Young and Peer Zumbansen. I would also like to record particular thanks to four people who generously agreed to provide feedback on the book as it neared publication: David Kennedy, Susan Marks, Annelise Riles and Ralph Wilde. David Kennedy owes still further credit for being such an extraordinary teacher to me: first, in a formal sense, in the 1995–1996 Harvard LL.M. program, and in the years since that time, in many ways.

Throughout this book's lengthy gestation, I have been a member of faculty at Sydney Law School at the University of Sydney, an institution from which I have drawn support of many kinds. Of particular significance were two periods of leave from teaching afforded me by the Faculty's Special Studies Program and further research leave granted me through the University's Brown Fellowship Program. I am grateful to the former Dean, Professor Gillian Triggs, the current Acting Dean Greg Tolhurst, and the Deputy Vice-Chancellor (Research), Professor Jill Trewhella, for this support and to my colleagues at Sydney for innumerable acts of kindness, large and small. In the very earliest stages, research and writing towards this book was also assisted by the support of the Leverhulme Trust, which enabled me to visit Birkbeck School of Law in London under the generous auspices of Professor Peter Fitzpatrick.

Several talented research assistants have played a crucial role in the production of this book: Sadhana Abayasekara, Surya Gopalan and Richard Bailey. I am particularly indebted to Richard for the care and acumen he devoted to finalisation of the text. I have also benefited from the patience and encouragement of Nienke van Schaverbeke and Richard Woodham at Cambridge University Press, the efforts of Rob Wilkinson and Gail Welsh at Out of House Publishing, the guidance of Professor James Crawford, as Series Editor of Cambridge Studies in International and Comparative Law, and the valuable input of two anonymous reviewers.

For all these sources of help and stimulus, this would have remained a non-book about non-legality were it not for the unstinting support of my husband, Peter Hammond. I cannot here do justice to his warmth, wisdom, patience, generosity, creativity and unflagging faith in our collective ability to pull things off, whatever the complications; let the dedication of this book do what this deficient collection of nouns cannot. Also inadequate is any one-sentence acknowledgement of the contribution of my parents, Penelope and Murray Johns, and my sister, Diana Johns, each of whom has offered a cherished hand at critical moments. Elizabeth and Jim Hammond and all the Hammond, Harris, Savage and Warburton clans have similarly thrown lifelines of one sort or another on many an occasion, as have many of our wonderful friends. Since 2009, the skill and thoughtfulness of Monique Simmons has been absolutely invaluable. I am deeply grateful to them all. As for opening my eyes to the world anew and giving me boundless grounds for joy, I could not wish for three more extraordinary people than the three Johns-Hammonds who have happened upon us since 2005: Arlo, Claude and Ilka.

Finally, I would like to acknowledge the publications in which portions or earlier versions of some chapters of this book appeared: 'The Torture Memos' in Fleur Johns, Sundhya Pahuja and Richard Joyce (eds.), *Events: The Force of International Law* (London: Routledge-Cavendish, 2011), pp. 260–278; 'Financing as Governance' (2011) 31 *Oxford Journal of Legal Studies* 391–415; 'Performing Party Autonomy' (2008) 71 *Law & Contemporary Problems* 243–271; 'Performing Power: The Deal, Corporate Rule, and the Constitution of Global Legal Order' (2007) 34 *Journal of Law and Society* 116–138, reprinted in Stewart Motha (ed.), *Democracy's Empire: Sovereignty, Law, and Violence* (Oxford: Blackwell, 2007), pp. 116–138; and 'Guantanamo Bay and the Annihilation of the Exception' (2005) 16 *European Journal of International Law* 613–635.

1 Making non-legalities in international law

International lawyers make law as they go about their daily work, but they also make non-law. International lawyers, that is, routinely shape understandings of what stands opposed to or outside the reach of legal norms. This book is concerned with the latter dimension of international legal work. It aims to track how international lawyers have been shaping understandings of non-legal phenomena in some significant contemporary debates and what international lawyers have contributed to, or made of, those debates in the process. International lawyers' practice of making non-legalities entails the continual making and remaking of global political possibilities. Anyone concerned with global politics in the broadest sense must, accordingly, grapple with the patterns and implications of this work.

It will immediately be apparent that this book is making problematic something which has not been problematic for international legal scholarship to date. It does so following a rich tradition of problematisation – that is, of turning givens into questions – within the field of international law and in other scholarly fields.[1] Yet it does so in a vocabulary which international legal scholars do not currently use: a vocabulary of non-legalities (namely, illegality, extra-legality, pre- and post-legality, supra-legality and infra-legality). A sense of the would-be or could-be problem with which this book is concerned may, nonetheless, be gained from the following illustrative story: a short story

[1] On the history of international law as (in part) a history of making problems, see, for example, David Kennedy, 'The International Style in Postwar Law and Policy' (1994) *Utah Law Review* 7–104 at 27. See, more generally, Michel Foucault, 'Polemics, Politics, and Problematizations: An Interview with Michel Foucault' in Paul Rabinow (ed.), *Ethics: Subjectivity and Truth. The Essential Works of Michel Foucault 1954–1984*, Volume One (ed. James D. Faubion, trans. Robert Hurley, Baltimore: Penguin Books, 2000), pp. 109–119.

of drones, definitions and democracy. This is a story of international legal endeavours well-meaning, considered and commendable, yet also in some sense concerning. My interest in this story is not in targeted killings as such, but rather in the 'vacuums' that international legal thought creates around them.

In May 2010, the Special Rapporteur on extrajudicial, summary or arbitrary executions, Professor Philip Alston, reported to the United Nations Human Rights Council on recent state practices of targeted killing. That report framed targeted killing ('intentional, premeditated and deliberate use of lethal force, by States or their agents acting under colour of law, or by an organised armed group in armed conflict, against a specific individual who is not in the physical custody of the perpetrator') as a policy innovation associated with recent developments in technology – specifically, the introduction of armed drones into the armouries of at least eight states.[2] Targeted killing in this mode is not, according to the report, to be consigned to extra-legality in all circumstances. Rather, its legality depends on context, legally understood: that is, whether it was conducted in armed conflict, outside armed conflict, or in relation to the inter-state use of force. Repeated in the report were several versions of the phrase: '[t]argeted killing is only lawful when ...' or 'State killing is legal only if ...'.[3] The capacity for targeted killing was thus approached as a mutable, mobile force charged with prospects for illegality, except in so far as it may be tethered, here and there, to defined legal ground.

The tethering of this latent illegality that the report sought to enact was primarily procedural and the procedures in question await development. States should, the report recommended, 'publicly identify the rules of international law they consider to provide a basis for any targeted killings they undertake' and 'specify the procedural safeguards in place to ensure in advance of targeted killings that they comply with international law'.[4] In the case of killings carried out extra-territorially, the host state should 'publicly indicate whether it gave consent, and on what basis'. States should also, the report urged, 'make public the number of civilians collaterally killed in a targeted killing operation, and the measures in place to prevent such casualties'.[5] However, more work

[2] Philip Alston, *Report of the Special Rapporteur on Extrajudicial, Summary or Arbitrary Executions*, United Nations General Assembly, Human Rights Council, 28 May 2010, A/HRC/14/24/Add.6, www2.ohchr.org/english/bodies/hrcouncil/docs/14session/A.HRC.14.24.Add6.pdf (accessed 17 September 2012), paras. 2, 27.

[3] *Ibid.*, paras. 30, 31, 32, 33, 57, 70, 86.

[4] *Ibid.*, para. 93. [5] *Ibid.*

needs to be done to make such an accounting possible, the report made clear. It was, for instance, deemed necessary for the High Commissioner for Human Rights to convene a meeting of states, the International Committee for the Red Cross, and human rights and international humanitarian law experts to 'arrive at a broadly accepted definition of "direct participation in hostilities"'.[6]

Because targeted killings are, according to the report, taking place 'in times of peace as well as armed conflict'[7] and because states known to have carried out targeted killings have not made public the policies surrounding those operations, they occupy in the report's parlance an 'accountability vacuum'. That vacuum is presumably highly legalised: governed, for instance, by contractual arrangements between the United States' Central Intelligence Agency and its personnel, as well as corresponding contractual networks in other states and organisations involved. Yet the report offered no more than a glimpse of these: 'According to media accounts, the head of the CIA's clandestine services, or his deputy, generally gives the final approval for a strike.'[8]

The lack of accountability attributed to the terrain surrounding targeted killing was not expressed as a deficiency of legal rule per se. Rather that which is missing and remains to be exerted in or over this terrain was expressed in terms of broad, underlying, substantive value: States have failed to discharge generalised obligations to 'provide transparency and accountability' for targeted killings and to do so 'meaningful[ly]'.[9] This was characterised as a source of concern for international law irrespective of whether specific targeted killings may ultimately be shown to be legally compliant.

The deficiency with which targeted killings were surrounded in the report (even as their legality or illegality depended upon particularities

[6] *Ibid.* This is significant because civilians who 'directly participate' or take an 'active part' in hostilities lose the protection from attack they otherwise enjoy in armed conflict under international humanitarian law, by virtue of, inter alia, paragraph 1 of Common Article 3 of the Geneva Conventions, Article 51(3) of the First Additional Protocol to those Conventions and Articles 4(1) and 13(3) of the Second Additional Protocol to those Conventions. See, generally, International Committee of the Red Cross, 'Interpretive Guidance on the Notion of Direct Participation in Hostilities under International Humanitarian Law' (2008) 90 *International Review of the Red Cross* 991–1047, www.icrc.org/eng/assets/files/other/irrc-872-reports-documents.pdf (accessed 17 September 2012).

[7] Alston, *Report of the Special Rapporteur*, para 8.

[8] *Ibid.*, paras. 3, 20 (citing Jane Mayer, 'The Predator War', *The New Yorker*, 26 October 2009).

[9] *Ibid.*, paras. 87, 90.

of context) is to be matched by a latent legality still to be developed. The latter was expressed more as an aspiration for knowledge and meaning than legal rule as such. (Legal rules are to come later, once 'broad[ ] accept[ance]' of definitions can be engineered.)[10] In the report's account, the practice of targeted killing carried a 'problematic' capacity for 'blurring and expansion of the boundaries of the applicable legal frameworks'.[11] The countering legality that this is understood to demand is, accordingly, to be blurry and expansive: namely, a generalised call for 'disclosure', 'framework[s]' and 'procedures' identified with yet-to-be-enabled means of 'public investigation[ ]'.[12]

Embedded in this call is an implicit comparison with lethal practices presumed to reside squarely, stably and safely within the 'frameworks' of international law and to thereby remain accessible and accountable to the public. '[C]lear legal standards' have, the report indicated, been 'displace[d]' in the production of this particular 'vacuum'.[13] The 'basic legal rules' are, the report informed its readers, those of international humanitarian law and international human rights law. These are said to require transparency and to offer means by which 'the international community' may 'verify the legality of a killing ... confirm the authenticity or otherwise of intelligence relied upon, or ... ensure that unlawful targeted killings do not result in impunity'.[14] By implication, one might assume that they likewise resist 'blurring and expansion'.

One does not, however, have to look very far or think very hard to arrive at grave doubt about the capacity of international humanitarian law and/or international human rights law to deliver the sort of transparency and accountability to which the report aspires. Press briefings, embedded journalists and claims surrounding Wikileaks notwithstanding,[15] it is hard to identify any recent wartime exercise of lethal force the legality of which 'the international community' might have been in a position to 'verify' with any confidence in advance or, for that matter, in retrospect (witness the International Court of Justice's Advisory Opinion on Nuclear Weapons).[16] Even assuming a fully-fledged judicial or other public investigation in a

[10] *Ibid.*, para. 93. [11] *Ibid.*, para. 3. [12] *Ibid.*, para. 93.

[13] *Ibid.*, para. 3. [14] *Ibid.*, paras. 88, 92.

[15] See Yochai Benkler, 'A Free Irresponsible Press: Wikileaks and the Battle over the Soul of the Networked Fourth Estate' (2011) 46 *Harvard Civil Rights-Civil Liberties Law Review* 311–398.

[16] 'Advisory Opinion of 8 July 1996: Legality of the Threat or Use of Nuclear Weapons' (1996) *International Court of Justice Reports* 226–267, www.icj-cij.org/docket/files/95/7495.pdf (accessed 17 September 2012).

particular, controversial instance (and the overwhelming majority of wartime killings never provoke, nor would be expected to provoke, such investigation), all that one would hope to uncover in most cases would be whether attention was directed towards considerations of proportionality and necessity. That would hardly generate an experience of accountability, one imagines, for those with family members or close friends killed in the relevant incident or others like it, let alone for members of 'the international community' at greater remove.

Even imagining a scenario of uninhibited information-sharing, it is difficult to imagine the means by which 'the international community' might be put in a position to 'confirm the authenticity or otherwise of intelligence relied upon' when those collecting and relying upon global intelligence seem regularly unable to do so (witness the fiasco regarding Iraq's supposed stockpile of weapons of mass destruction). To suggest that international humanitarian law and/or international human rights law routinely ensure this level and type of 'accountability' in relation to states' exercise of lethal force outside the criminal justice system (or even within it) is to evoke fantasy.[17]

In this way, the report generates a mirage. That which seems to drive the report's indignation and hope is its projection of an as-yet-unimaginable prospect of direct communion between, on one hand, those mobilising lethal force in the name of a state and, on the other, a 'public', writ large and in unity as 'the international

[17] This fantasy is by no means benign. Jodi Dean has, for instance, written persuasively about the public aspiration to transparency as a feature of the ideology of technoculture. See Jodi Dean, 'Why the Net is not a Public Sphere' (2003) 10 *Constellations* 95–112 at 95, 101 and 110: ('If the public aspires to inclusivity, transparency, and reconciliation, then the secret holds open these aspirations via the promise that a democratic public is within reach – once all that is hidden has been revealed. Along with networked communications and practices of education and informatization, technologies of surveillance and practices of dissemination are installed to fulfil these promises, to bring everything before the gaze of the public. Publicity works through demands to disclose or reveal the secret and realize the public as the ideal self-identical subject/object of democracy … The politics of the public sphere has been based on the idea that power is always hidden and secret. But clearly this is not the case today… All sorts of horrible political processes are perfectly transparent today. The problem is that people don't seem to mind, that they are so enthralled by transparency that they have lost the will to fight … there is always more information available and … this availability is ultimately depoliticizing … [within] communicative capitalism's endless reflexive circuits of discussion').

community'. The vehicles for that communion are, in part, 'rules of international law' imagined as relatively clear and uncontested.[18] Yet just as important are numbers (a counting of civilians 'collaterally killed'), unspecified 'measures' (capable of 'control[ling] and limit[ing]' action by law enforcement officers), and 'system[s]' (for collection, analysis and dissemination of information necessary for the making of 'legal and accurate targeting decisions' and for displacing reliance on mere suspicion). The latest technology for automated killing is, it seems, to be matched by an equally obscure, remotely operated technology of control programmed to render transparent a power perpetually located elsewhere.

It may be too strong and premature a criticism to characterise the report on targeted killings as an instance of wholesale strategic failure on the part of international law or lawyers.[19] Its impacts remain to be assessed over the longer term. Nonetheless, certain features of the report do appear symptomatic of inattention to legal constructions of non-legality in international legal work and the problems to which this inattention may give rise.

For instance, the precise character of the 'vacuum' understood to surround targeted killings, especially those carried out by drone, escaped careful scrutiny in the report. The perception of a 'vacuum' surrounding targeted killings seemed to arise from a sense of power being exercised by decision-makers operating outside the purview of courts or other sources of independent check or balance. The report noted, for instance, that killing decisions may be taken wholly within the chain of command of the Central Intelligence Agency's clandestine services unit, by forces deployed at Russian presidential discretion, and in operations conducted by Israeli Defense Force personnel, without regard to judicially promulgated standards for their legality. The report's orientation towards judicial review (or the lack thereof) in this regard led it to neglect the detail of laws surrounding and structuring executive power in specific instances. Each of the aforementioned scenarios involves the invocation and deployment of executive power legally conferred. Yet the report failed to convey any sense of executive power having waxed and waned in the relevant jurisdictions

[18] Alston, *Report of the Special Rapporteur*, para. 93.

[19] In this instance, 'strategic' is used in the sense of 'strategy' suggested by Michel de Certeau rather than that suggested by Pierre Bourdieu. See below notes 71, 72, and 76 and related text.

and indeed globally, or to invite any consideration of factors informing these shifts in particular settings.[20]

Additional features of targeted killing by drone were highlighted in the report as particularly concerning. Disquiet about these seems to have reinforced the sense of a 'vacuum' on which the report relied and its apparent preoccupation with filling that vacuum with legal procedure. Among these is the capacity of drones to deploy lethal force without putting the perpetrator's forces at risk at the same time and in the same setting. Also of concern in the report is the risk of operators physically removed from the scene of their killing developing 'a "Playstation" mentality to killing', implying, presumably, a higher tolerance for or immunity to the trauma of causing human death. Both of these concerns revolve around a worry that decision-makers wielding lethal force now experience a heightened sense of freedom in exercising that force and, as a consequence, find it too easy to kill. The report's call for 'procedures' to ensure 'transparency and accountability' has, however, virtually nothing to say to or about this issue. It is entirely unclear how requirements of disclosure and vetting of the sort that the report advocated might play into the experience of liberty about which the report worries, since that experience is attributed to the geographic distance from a site of physical impact rather than distance from bureaucracy. Other than recommending an accounting of civilian deaths, the report had nothing to say about how the geographic gulf dividing decision-makers from the impact of their decisions might be narrowed or bridged, or if indeed it should be. (One could imagine an argument being made in favour of taking killing decisions away from the so-called 'fog of war', in the hope of cooler heads prevailing.) Moreover, beyond the throwaway Playstation analogy, no account was taken of the extent to which the technology in question – its coded architecture and associated user practices, as well as surrounding intellectual property and contractual norms – might regulate violence while enabling

[20] A sense of executive power's waxing and waning in legal and political terms in various jurisdictions may be drawn from accounts of executive power's changing intensity and status in the following texts: Harvey C. Mansfield Jr., *Taming the Prince: The Ambivalence of Modern Executive Power* (New York: The Free Press, 1989); Janet Maclean, 'Divergent Legal Conceptions of the State: Implications for Global Administrative Law' (2005) 68:3/4 *Law and Contemporary Problems* 167–188; Deirdre Curtin, *Executive Power of the European Union: Law, Practices and the Living Constitution* (Oxford University Press, 2009); Clement Fatovic, *Outside the Law: Emergency and Executive Power* (Baltimore: Johns Hopkins University Press, 2009).

it, might constitute the decision-makers in question, and might, given the impetus, do so otherwise.[21] In short, no account was taken of how regulated and regulable this 'vacuum' may already be.

Many things and forces come to occupy the sorts of 'vacuum' of international legal thought that is on display in the Alston report: instances, that is, of certain phenomena being characterised as outside law, lacking law or routinely opposed to law. This book maps a wide range of these 'vacuums' in international legal scholarship. Acts of torture and their scholarly reckoning; instances of extra-territorial counter-terrorist detention; lawyers' perceptions of economic choice in cross-border financial deal-making; the status of scientific knowledge in international legal analysis and argument surrounding climate change; international institutions' management of dead bodies after natural disaster. Like some which-one-is-the-odd-one-out riddle designed to reveal a previously unnoticed feature or pattern, this book pulls these disparate practices and fields of practice together. And despite the singular 'non-legal' of this book's title, the elements of this unlikely assemblage remain largely dissimilar. Legal professionals and others who wield the language of international law do, and seek to do, quite different things in these various settings. Understandings of what corresponds to or is distinctive about the work of 'international law' in each case vary accordingly.

Nonetheless, the argument of this book is that there *is* something common to the various fields of international legal practice mentioned in the preceding paragraph, namely, a tendency to try to confer upon international law some delimited time, space and subject matter for its 'proper' (albeit not autonomous) operation. In these divergent areas of practice, legal professionals (and other experts seeking or purporting to govern conduct on a global scale by lawful means) continually articulate, for and through international law, a jurisdiction bounded, as the case may be, by one or more before(s) and after(s), below(s) and above(s), against(s) and/or despite(s).

Wherever international law is invoked, we see created that which international law purports to stand against, beside, before or after. The insight that this occurs is not novel.[22] What is novel about this

[21] Cf. Lawrence Lessig, 'The Law of the Horse: What Cyberlaw Might Teach' (1999) 113 *Harvard Law Review* 501–549.

[22] See, for example, Martti Koskenniemi, *From Apology to Utopia: The Structure of International Legal Argument* (Cambridge University Press, 2005), p. 570: ('The law constructs its own field of application as it goes along, through a normative

book's contribution to international legal scholarship is its mapping of those parallel creations, their interrelationship, and the influence that they appear to exert in particular areas of international legal work. Whereas it is customary for works of scholarship in international law to orient themselves by reference to that which they work towards – a better way of addressing this or that problem, some enhancement of freedom or diminishment of suffering, the rise or the fall of something or other – this book is oriented around the before, the after, the below, the above, the against and the despite, which international legal work ceaselessly evokes. It is so oriented not in defence of some *status quo ante* or with a view to restoring some pre-existent referent. Rather, this book's goals are critical and cartographic.

In a series of case studies of work by legal professionals and others invoking norms and institutions of international law, this book juxtaposes received mappings of international law's limits and tethering points in particular areas with counter-mappings of international legal knowledge practices far more prevalent, unruly and uncabined. As will become apparent, the foil varies from case study to case study, but the goal in each chapter of this book is to make politically navigable and questionable some aspect(s) of international legal work previously, for the most part, un- or under-acknowledged. If international law and lawyers are shown to be complicit in constituting and/or entrenching that which they purport to stand against – forces of unsanctioned violence, say, or excesses of 'nature', human and otherwise – then attributions of responsibility and questions of reform might emerge that are different to those currently circulating in much contemporary international legal literature.

In relation to the practices of targeted killing discussed above, for instance, the case studies in this book suggest that somewhat less attention might be focused upon the promulgation of new norms to ensure 'transparency and accountability'. More attention might, instead, be directed towards those normative practices that already regulate critical decision-making surrounding targeted killing: the code-architecture of the relevant technologies and associated user practices; pertinent intellectual property and contractual norms; prevailing practices of modelling and prediction and the like. Rather than seeking the promulgation of new norms concerning targeted killing, it

language that highlights some aspects of the world while leaving other aspects in the dark').

might seem more pressing – or at least as pressing – to ask how those existing norms have developed and what sort of knowledge practices, experiences and tendencies they appear to be fostering.

The knowledge practices on which these case studies focus have been typologised in terms of the making of illegality, extra-legality, pre- or post-legality, supra-legality and infra-legality. Making *illegality*, in this context, denotes the legal crafting of that which exceeds suppression by, is forbidden by, or is defiant of, international law. The case study of the making of illegality in this book is the understanding of torture which legal professionals and others invoking international law have fostered of late – in particular, that identified with the notorious 'torture memos' written by lawyers serving the second Bush administration in the United States.

Making *extra-legality* here entails the legal construction of that which is understood to lie outside the province of international law. This book takes, as its case study of the making of extra-legality, styles of normative decision practised in and around the detention zone of Guantánamo Bay in the post-2001 period.

Making *pre-* or *post-legality* refers to the legal practice of making things – particular actions, agents or questions – come to stand immediately before the operation of international law, or in the wake of its operation. For a case study of the making of pre- or post-legality, this book looks to legal depictions of economic actors making determinative, autonomous choices either prior to law taking hold, or after lawful options have been laid before them, in the context of cross-border investment deals.

Making *supra-legality* is the name given here to the practice of consigning certain phenomena (political, biological, environmental, religious, etc.) to exogeneity in the sense of their surpassing international legal grasp or comprehension, rather than being carved out of or violative of international law. The case study of making supra-legality here focuses on international legal scholarship discussing the work of the Intergovernmental Panel on Climate Change, which is conferred in a number of ways with supra-legal status in that scholarship.

Finally, making *infra-legality* is the name which this book gives to the practice of relegating certain issues, experiences and elements to international law's margins, as the natural, the incidental, or the unworthy of direct notice. The case study of making infra-legality in this book examines literature surrounding international organisations' 'management' of dead bodies in the immediate aftermath of natural disaster.

Non-legality, this book argues, is more than the flip side or remainder of international legal work. Rather, non-legality is, in its own right, a central structuring device of international legal thought and work. Painstaking constructions of non-legality are pivotal in debates surrounding a range of phenomena from torture to foreign investment, and from climate change to natural disaster. In these debates, international lawyers are routinely involved in projecting and shaping conditions that they seem to experience as more political, environmental, economic or innate than legal (according to various understandings of legality). International lawyers then tend to approach these conditions as though they were exogenous to their work.

The characterisation of these various endeavours in terms of the making of non-legalities does, however, merit some clarification. 'Non-legality' is a rather obtuse term under which this book assembles a number of practices of legal professionals and others invoking international law. These practices share an orientation around behaviour or phenomena which seem (in international legal scholars' and practitioners' apparent estimation) not governed, or not governed effectively, by law. The making of illegality, extra-legality, pre- and post-legality, supra-legality and infra-legality in and around the norms and practices of international law is not, however, a matter of making or addressing things wholly other than law. Equally, these will not always be sites of some international legal blind spot. Illegality, for instance, is less a matter of neglect than a matter of preoccupation for international legal work. The classification of some action or condition as illegal is patently a quite deliberate outcome of legal imagination and endeavour.

The forays into non-legality on which this book focuses are, then, hardly ventures into clearly bounded fields of negation or emptiness. On the contrary, attention to the ways in which *some* kinds of legal technique, institution or analysis are understood to be lacking or inoperative in particular areas of international legal work (in other words, the sense that non-legality prevails) may render *other* legal norms and practices more visible or significant, as this book will show. Consider, for instance, the 'vacuum' of non-accountability surrounding targeted killing according to the Alston report discussed above. That 'vacuum' arose from the Alston report's sense of 'clear legal standards' and opportunities for legal review having been 'displace[d]'. Yet that 'vacuum' remained nonetheless structured by legal norms and normative practices to which Alston's report paid relatively little attention: technological code-architecture and user practices; intellectual property and contractual norms; norms governing executive power and decision; norm-governed and norm-making practices of modelling and prediction.

The idea of legality in which this book trades also warrants some explanation. As will become apparent over the course of the ensuing chapters, 'international law' is here somewhat of a moveable feast.[23] The adjective 'legal' and the nouns 'law' and 'legality' here denote normative practices of legal professionals. 'International' law indicates the projection of those normative practices on a global scale. Here international law, in short, is what legal professionals say and do in the course of a project of governing, or seeking to govern, globally.[24]

[23] Undoubtedly, the examination of explicitly non-legal forms of ordering within the purview of legal scholarly inquiry – and, further, the claim that phenomena understood as illegal, extra-legal or otherwise parallel to law be approached as artefacts of legal knowledge practice – may expose this book to the charge of 'folly' which Brian Tamanaha levels at legal pluralist scholarship, in light of an 'inability ... to locate an agreed definition of "law"' across that scholarship as a whole: Brian Z. Tamanaha, 'The Folly of the "Social Scientific" Concept of Legal Pluralism' (1993) 20 *Journal of Law and Society* 192–217 at 192. Provided, however, that the 'agglomeration' of law in question is 'disaggregated' and 'distinctions ... made that identify the provenance of rules and controls', as Sally Falk Moore has advocated, this seems a 'folly' one need not labour to expunge: Sally Falk Moore, 'Certainties Undone: Fifty Turbulent Years of Legal Anthropology, 1949-1999' in Sally Falk Moore (ed.), *Law and Anthropology: A Reader* (London: Blackwell, 2005), pp. 346–367 at p. 357. As Tamanaha himself later acknowledges, 'there are multiple uncoordinated, coexisting or overlapping bodies of law ... [and] there is diversity amongst them': Brian Z. Tamanaha, 'Understanding Legal Pluralism: Past to Present, Local to Global' (2008) 30 *Sydney Law Review* 375–411 at 375.

[24] Compare David Kennedy, 'One, Two, Three, Many Legal Orders: Legal Pluralism and the Cosmopolitan Dream' (2007) 31 *New York University Review of Law and Social Change* 641–660 at 650: ('International law is a group of *people* pursuing projects in a common professional language', emphasis in original); Martti Koskenniemi, 'Introduction' in M. Koskenniemi (ed.), *International Law* (Aldershot: Dartmouth, 1992), pp. xi–xxxii at p. xxvii: ('International law is a projection of what international lawyers think and do'); Martti Koskenniemi, 'Between Commitment and Cynicism: Outline for a Theory of International Law as Practice' in United Nations Office of Legal Affairs (ed.), *Collection of Essays by Legal Advisers of States, Legal Advisers of International Organizations and Practitioners in the Field of International Law* (New York: United Nations, 1999), pp. 495–523 at p. 523: ('International law is what international lawyers do and how they think'); Martti Koskenniemi, *The Gentle Civilizer of Nations: The Rise and Fall of International Law 1870–1960* (Cambridge University Press, 2001), p. 7: ('It may be too much to say that international law is *only* what international lawyers do and think. But at least it is that ... Like any social phenomenon, international law is a complex set of practices and ideas, as well as interpretations of those practices and ideas').

Beyond that, the 'international law' in each chapter varies. Chapters 2, 3 and 5 focus on the published writings of scholars who self-identify as specialists in the international legal field or otherwise make forays into debate concerning international law. Chapters 2 and 3 also 'find' international law in the records of international institutions (texts produced by the International Committee of the Red Cross) and in the statements of national military representatives about their cross-border work and the role of legal norms and processes in that work. Chapter 4 is oriented around the work of those who practise and advise on private international law: in this instance, corporate lawyers engaged in cross-border financing transactions. Chapter 6 focuses on 'soft law' promulgated by international and regional organisations and the work of independent experts, governmental employees, non-governmental organisations' staff, and volunteers operating apparently under its guidance.[25] In each case, the practices and texts in question are grouped together on the basis of their attention to a particular problem or episode and their framing of that problem or episode as an issue of global governance, at least in part.[26]

As noted at the outset, the link between the making of illegality, extra-legality, pre- and post-legality, supra-legality and infra-legality in these various modes and settings is not one that has been made before in international legal scholarship. Nevertheless, this book does build

[25] On 'soft law', see generally Anna di Robilant, 'Genealogies of Soft Law' (2006) 54 *The American Journal of Comparative Law* 499–554.

[26] Of course, as Jason Beckett observes, 'description must be normatively delimited' in that '[a] decision must be taken as to what is to count as legal data, or valid legal arguments': Jason Beckett, 'Rebel Without a Cause? Martti Koskenniemi and the Critical Legal Project' (2006) 7 *German Law Journal* 1045–1088 at 1077, 1083. To the extent possible, however, the chapters in this book seek to construct a sense of what 'count[s] as legal data' immanently, drawing from the fields of writing and practice with which each chapter is concerned. There is overlap, of course, between these (re)constructions of what counts. Moreover, one inevitably brings to the task of (re)construction a sense of what is likely to amount to international law in the argument(s) in question. Nonetheless, I disagree with Beckett to the extent that he argues that '[l]aw, to be understood or used at all, must be delimited and defined [and] must be separated from non-law' in advance of, and stably and consistently across, the terrain of argument, analysis and decision to which international legal professionals contribute: Beckett, 'Rebel Without a Cause?', at 1080. Just as descriptive method collapses into normative method in Beckett's account, so normative delimitation invariably entails description and ascription. As the chapters in this book show, the work of separating law from non-law descriptively and/or normatively remains ongoing across a number of distinct yet related fronts in international affairs. Such distinctions – and the effects that flow from them – are part of what is at stake in the work with which this book engages.

upon, and remain indebted to, prior work in the international legal field. In particular, it draws upon writings by Martti Koskenniemi and David Kennedy on governance projects lately pursued in the name of international law.[27]

After the fall: Koskenniemi and Kennedy on international legal managerialism

In a series of writings, and often in a key of lamentation, Martti Koskenniemi has recounted a more or less century-long effort of international law 'becoming technical'.[28] In place of prior centuries' efforts to translate inter-state diplomacy into the prudent and progressive administration of law on a global scale, Koskenniemi now plays witness to a pervasive, partly deformalised international law marked by seemingly endless negotiation and balance-striking among professional experts.[29] Koskenniemi attributes the predominance of international law in this mode to a complex range of influences, among them: the impact of French thought concerning international social administration spanning the late nineteenth to the mid twentieth centuries; interwar emigré lawyers' efforts to entrench a professionally administered cosmopolitan legal system modelled on the institutions of the liberal state; and the convergence of law and instrumentalism identified with the rise of the discipline of international relations in the United States after the Second World War.

[27] For the purposes of this introduction, important differences and disagreements across and between Koskenniemi's and Kennedy's work have been downplayed or set aside. Koskenniemi's 'recoil from the eclectic incoherence of postwar American legal thought' is, for instance, clearly distinguishable from Kennedy's insistence upon making critical forays more or less within that practice of thought (loosening its grip and/or sharpening its aim). I am quoting here from Kennedy's own brief, retrospective account of their alliance and divergence, in which Kennedy observes that he has 'never quite shared [Koskenniemi's] yearning for a "culture of formalism" which could redeem the promises of the liberal cosmopolitan vision he associates with the best in the European international law tradition': David Kennedy, 'The Last Treatise (Project and Person)' (2006) 7 *German Law Journal* 982–992 at 989.

[28] Martti Koskenniemi, 'The Fate of Public International Law: Between Technique and Polis' (2007) 70 *Modern Law Review* 1–30 at 1–2.

[29] *Ibid*. A story of this transformation is also told in Koskenniemi, *The Gentle Civilizer of Nations*, especially pp. 459–494 and 510–517 and, in highly abbreviated form, in Martti Koskenniemi, *From Apology to Utopia: The Structure of International Legal Argument*, Reissue with Epilogue (Cambridge University Press, 2005), pp. 612–615.

These and other factors have, in Koskenniemi's account, driven classical international law's 'fall'.[30] According to Koskenniemi, the advent of a 'deformalized concept of law' has left the 'interdisciplinary' international lawyer with two equally problematic temptations: 'to accept the self-image as an underlaborer to the policy agendas of (the American) international relations orthodoxy' or to 're-imagine [international] law's job as having to do with the resolution of the 3,000-year old enigma about objective morality'.[31]

Casting around (however ambivalently) for guidance, Koskenniemi has canvassed sociologies of law (understood in pluralist terms) and constitutionalism (recast as mindset or 'a programme of moral and political regeneration' rather than an architectural project).[32] He has found the former wanting even in respect of the modest goal of global sense-making, let alone any more ambitious political project.[33] The latter, on the other hand, offers promise in Koskenniemi's estimation. '[C]onstitutional vocabularies ... with all their historical thickness, contest the structural biases of present institutions and politicize what otherwise appears as routine administration', Koskenniemi has argued. A constitutional mindset is, he suggests, 'resistant, indeed opposed, to managerialism'.[34] Yet not even a constitutional mindset, in Koskenniemi's account, seems entirely up to the task of navigating, or counteracting the corrosive lap of that vast, 'shallow' inland sea which Koskenniemi names, pejoratively, the 'managerialist mindset'.[35] Worry over the managerialist 'takeover' of international law, and the associated 'transformation of the vocabularies of power' from the 'language of law' to that of 'amorphous "regulation" emerging from a heterogeneous variety of sources and actors', seems to have animated much of Koskenniemi's work over the past decade or so.[36]

Despite its potency in his work, Koskenniemi seems, for the most part, ill-inclined to map this managerialist expanse except in the broadest of strokes. This is noteworthy given the ambition and

[30] Koskenniemi, *The Gentle Civilizer of Nations*.

[31] *Ibid.*, pp. 484, 493–494.

[32] Koskenniemi, 'The Fate of Public International Law'; Martti Koskenniemi, 'Constitutionalism as Mindset: Reflections on Kantian Themes about International Law and Globalization' (2007) 8 *Theoretical Inquiries in Law* 9–36 at 18.

[33] Koskenniemi, 'The Fate of Public International Law', 20–24.

[34] Koskenniemi, 'Constitutionalism as Mindset', 34, 35.

[35] *Ibid.*, 9: ('[T]he effort to reimagine international law in purely managerial terms appears intellectually shallow and politically objectionable').

[36] *Ibid.*, 13.

tirelessness otherwise characteristic of his work. Managerialism is, in Koskenniemi's description, a 'view' or 'mindset' concerned with coordinating relations among transnational 'regimes' or fields of expertise while 'faithfully' refining and reproducing the logic of the regime or field of expert knowledge with which one primarily identifies. Its characteristic gestures are those of 'contextual deal-striking', balancing and adjusting. Its reading of freedom is as strategic interest-realisation.[37] Its preference is for 'informal "regimes"' rather than 'the formal aspects of the legal craft that it often sees as an obstacle for effective action'. Its fantasy is to counsel the prince towards 'concrete results' without much regard to normative analysis of those results; for managerialism, 'the objectives of institutional action are given'.[38] In managerialists' hands, according to Koskenniemi, international law has become a set of 'rules of thumb or soft standards that refer to the best judgement of the experts in the [sub-disciplinary] box' from which they emanate.[39]

Koskenniemi's painstaking study of the dynamics of international legal argument in *From Apology to Utopia* did include an exposition of characteristically modern appeals to politics, policies and ideals in international law, as identified with Hans Morgenthau, Myres McDougal and Alejandro Álvarez respectively.[40] Koskenniemi described, too, lawyers' 'constant movement' among these positions, based on recognition of each position's inability to sustain a 'positive programme'. He remarked, further, on the propensity of international lawyers to look 'beyond modern (liberal) doctrines' by reference to notions of justice or equitableness and to appeal to particular descriptions of social fact from which to infer corresponding readings of law. Yet this account seemed only partially to capture the practices to which Koskenniemi has later alluded in writing about managerialism. There is, for example, little if anything in *From Apology to Utopia* concerning the techniques of calibration and prediction on which international lawyers (alongside others) have come to rely, such as practices of financial or scientific model-making. Likewise, despite the promising trajectory his study would appear to set for such work, Koskenniemi has not traced

[37] Koskenniemi, 'The Fate of Public International Law', 1, 11–15, 26.

[38] Martti Koskenniemi, 'The Politics of International Law – 20 Years Later' (2009) 20 *European Journal of International Law* 7–19 at 14.

[39] Martti Koskenniemi, 'International Law: Constitutionalism, Managerialism and the Ethos of Legal Education' (2007) 1 *European Journal of Legal Studies* 1–18 at 8.

[40] Koskenniemi, *From Apology to Utopia*, pp. 197–223.

the patterns of mutual invocation, cross-reference and dependence between the 'boxes' he ascribes to the managerialist imagination.

More can, and has, been said of managerialism (as Koskenniemi names it) in international law. David Kennedy has for some time been producing maps more or less of this style, its proponents, its programmes and its politics, at least among 'legal internationalists' in the 'United Statesean' context.[41] Kennedy has explored the provenance of postwar legal internationalists' preoccupation with institutions.[42] He has examined the particular tenor of their historicism.[43] He has charted cycles of reform and re-affirmation in their work.[44] He has tracked postwar international law's shifting centres of gravity and some of its intra- and inter-disciplinary rivalries.[45] He has catalogued some of legal internationalists' preferred techniques of rule, highlighting their light and dark sides and the ambivalent impulses that may animate them.[46] He has probed the changed status of law in global warfare as it enables as much as it constrains.[47] For Kennedy's work, legal internationalists of the postwar era have performed more of an interlocutory role than those of rival or nemesis.[48] Kennedy has done much to shed light on the manoeuvres, mannerisms and multivalence of the disciplinary voice that Koskenniemi would have us hear, more or less univocally, as managerialism. Yet for all the richness of Kennedy's work, in this reader at least, there still lingers a worry that it might fail to engage the international legal sensibility of which it writes.

[41] David Kennedy, 'The Disciplines of International Law and Policy' (1999) 12 *Leiden Journal of International Law* 9–133 at 10.

[42] David Kennedy, 'The Move to Institutions' (1987) 8 *Cardozo Law Review* 841–988.

[43] David Kennedy, 'International Law in the Nineteenth Century: History of an Illusion' (1996) 65 *Nordic Journal of International Law* 385–420.

[44] David Kennedy, 'When Renewal Repeats: Thinking Against the Box' (2000) 32 *New York University Journal of International Law and Politics* 335–500.

[45] Kennedy, 'The Disciplines of International Law and Policy'; David Kennedy, 'New Approaches to Comparative Law: Comparativism and International Governance' (1997) 2 *Utah Law Review* 545–638.

[46] David Kennedy, *The Dark Sides of Virtue: Reassessing International Humanitarianism* (Princeton and Oxford: Princeton University Press, 2004); David Kennedy, 'Challenging Expert Rule: The Politics of Global Governance' (2005) 27 *Sydney Law Review* 5–28.

[47] David Kennedy, *Of War and Law* (Princeton University Press, 2006).

[48] David Kennedy, 'A New Stream of International Law Scholarship' (1988) 7 *Wisconsin International Law Journal* 1–49 at 2: ('Taken together, my own projects have been animated by a single interlocutory – the tragic voice of post-war, public law liberalism').

The elegant, readable essays that Kennedy has lately produced seem, in particular, to speak at too great a remove from the rather dense, self-referential practices of international legal technique.[49] Except, perhaps, as expert enactments of keynote speech writing, these essays refuse to belong to any sub-disciplinary speciality. They are less inter-disciplinary or intra-disciplinary than counter-disciplinary. They refuse to don the standard ornamentation of legal expertise (being, for instance, more or less stripped of footnotes). Even so, they move with great assurance over expansive historical and geographic ground. Adopting a tone of declamation, Kennedy seems to prefer pithy anecdote to detailed illustration, and capitalised surnames to exposition. Kennedy writes in the voice of a learned, thoughtful professional with friends in the right places. In his work on war law, for instance, he cites his participation in discussion at the Council on Foreign Relations, work as a civilian instructor for the Naval Justice School, and days spent as a visitor on board the USS *Independence* in the Persian Gulf in lieu of technical indicia of expertise.[50]

The project that Kennedy's essays enact – to expand perceptions of rule and associated experiences of responsibility among international lawyers and their cohorts – seems timely and important. And yet the responsibilities that he urges upon his readers seem, at once, too noble and too generalised to connect to the mundane work in which many international lawyers see themselves engaged today, whether they be mired in the politics of the academe or enmeshed in another institutional setting, public or private. For all their talk of struggle, there is something strikingly unruffled about Kennedy's most recent works.

It may be, of course, that this smooth, gliding, assured quality ensures the immanence of Kennedy's critique. Writing too strident, earnest or parochial would not articulate well to the mainstream of international legal scholarship or international legal practice. Nonetheless, there is something about the scale, tenor and resolute non-technicality of this work that could ready it for an all too rapid setting aside.[51] There is, after all, always so much more technical work to be done. Kennedy's Weberian call to experience politics as a vocation with an ethic of

[49] Kennedy, *Of War and Law* and *The Dark Sides of Virtue*.

[50] Kennedy, *Of War and Law*, pp. 32–33, 112, 139.

[51] There is, perhaps, a note of reflexive anxiety in this respect in Kennedy's parenthetical observation, of Koskenniemi's work, that, compared to Kennedy, Koskenniemi 'really does know a lot more about the doctrines and the history!': Kennedy, 'The Last Treatise', at 989.

responsibility – to take political action remaining mindful of its material consequences, but without regard to the service of social or ethically 'good' purposes as such – may resonate, if only momentarily, with those who envisage themselves as, or aspire to become, warrior leaders in the image of Weber's '*mature* man' who 'feels … responsibility with heart and soul'.[52] Yet for those who imagine themselves to be legal functionaries wholly taken up in carrying out plans, adhering to principles or working towards targets devised somewhere else, by someone else, at some other time, this calling may be difficult to heed.[53] In view of this concern, this book seeks to engage otherwise with the work of international law's 'managerialist' functionaries in a range of capacities.

How, then, might the 'engaging otherwise' enacted in this book relate to Koskenniemi's and Kennedy's work? In discussing the Alston report above, I derided the 'fantasy' that international law routinely affords 'transparency and accountability' in and for global legal order in all but a few darkened spaces of dysfunction or deviance.[54] In positioning this book in relation to Kennedy's and Koskenniemi's work, I indulge another fantasy (equally deserving of circumspection), namely the idea that one might – indeed, should seek to – work towards filling or remedying perceived gaps or weaknesses in the fabric of international legal scholarship. International legal scholarship does not, of course, comprise a seamless unfolding fabric, any more than the works of either Martti Koskenniemi or David Kennedy do. I have aired some worries about Koskenniemi's and Kennedy's recent writings. Even so, this book does not aspire to be corrective or completive of those writings in any conventional sense. Presented here are ethnographically

[52] Kennedy, *Of War and Law*, p. 172; Max Weber, 'Politics as a Vocation' in *From Max Weber: Essays in Sociology* (ed. H. H. Gerth and C. Wright Mills, Oxford University Press, 1946), pp. 77–128. For discussion of Weber's understanding of 'vocation' in comparison to that of the legal philosopher Rudolf von Ihering, see Stephen P. Turner and Regis A. Factor, *Max Weber: The Lawyer as Social Thinker* (London: Routledge, 1994), pp. 51–53.

[53] It is apparent, nonetheless, that Kennedy acknowledges the pervasiveness of this sense and is working against it. See Kennedy, *Of War and Law*, p. 164: ('Military and humanitarian professionals alike share the sense that somewhere else, outside or beyond their careful calculations, somebody *else* exercises political judgment and discretion').

[54] Susan Marks has referred to thinking along these lines as subscription to a 'myth of the dangerous dark': Susan Marks, 'Four Human Rights Myths', Remarks at the conference 'Human Rights: Old Dichotomies Revisited', Sydney Law School, 25–26 November 2011.

informed maps of what Koskenniemi might term managerialist technique. Yet this book is no more assured than Koskenniemi's and Kennedy's recent writing of engaging the various targets at which its chapters are levelled. This book's mapping exercise is experimental. The primary hunches and debts carried forward in this experiment are twofold.

First, I draw from Kennedy and Koskenniemi's work the insight that 'certainty-inducing rational demonstrations' of the coherence, autonomous closure and telic direction of international law often do not work to induce or sustain certainty in those who perform them and for or before whom they are performed.[55] In this book, this gets translated into a sense that efforts in the international legal field to distance or distinguish the terrain of legal negotiation and law-abiding conduct from the terrain of extra-legal politics, illegal violence, pre- or post-legal discretion, and supra-legal or infra-legal nature often don't work to sustain the distance or distinction in question.

Second, I take seriously Kennedy and Koskenniemi's repeated insistences that this insight, and the hypotheses with which it is associated, afford promising starting points rather than end points for work in the international legal field. Kennedy, for instance, has observed on many occasions that good maps are not yet available of the legal and political regimes of global governance and that, while fruitful experimentation in this direction has been ongoing for some time, there is call for much more.[56] This book has been particularly encouraged and inspired by ongoing research attentive to the technical dimensions of international legal work as practised or mobilised in a wide range of settings.[57] This explains its quasi-ethnographic orientation and its concern with practices, about which more will be said below.

To situate the quasi-ethnographic experiments that are undertaken in this book 'after the fall' (as in the heading to this sub-section) may be taken to imply that they are pursued in a relatively newly degraded or disillusioned field of international legal work. The fall from grace

[55] The phrase is from Duncan Kennedy, *A Critique of Adjudication (Fin de Siècle)* (Cambridge, MA: Harvard University Press, 1998), pp. 311–313, although as Kennedy observes, experiencing law as manipulable rhetoric is not the same as experiencing law as wrong or worthless.

[56] See, for example, Kennedy, 'The Last Treatise', at 990–991; Kennedy, 'When Renewal Repeats', at 500.

[57] See, for example, Annelise Riles, *Collateral Knowledge: Legal Reasoning in the Global Financial Markets* (Chicago and London: University of Chicago Press, 2011).

staged in different ways in Kennedy's and Koskenniemi's work could perhaps be imagined sequentially or historically. Koskenniemi's writing, in particular, suggests that degeneration may be identified with international law's postwar embrace of 'a political science-inspired language of "governance", "regulation", or "legitimacy"' and of 'informal "regimes"'.[58] To the extent that it may be extracted from Koskenniemi's work, this particular story of decline is not a narrative that I wish to endorse. This is not a book for, against or about the deformalisation of international law as such. The formal versus anti-formal distinction simply does not seem to me to be very telling for those who would seek to chart the dynamics and grasp the stakes of contemporary international legal work.[59] International lawyers have, as Kennedy observes, long exhibited awareness that 'tight rules can generate open-ended administrative or judicial discretion, just as broad standards can become routinized and predictable'.[60] In international law and in other legal fields, extra-legal normative codes (political, moral, religious, expedential, etc.) and related arguments have long been understood, at least some of the time, 'as … fully "inside" the practice of legal interpretation, rather than as external'.[61] Accordingly, in its variable accounts of work undertaken by legal professionals, this book will sidestep the question of whether international legal work has become more or less formal in style or content over time. The goals and concerns of this book lie elsewhere.

Quasi-ethnography – mode of inquiry and goals of this book

This book adopts what Harry Wolcott has characterised as an ethnographic way of seeing. That is a way of seeing identified with research that seeks to 'describe what the people in some particular place or status ordinarily do and the *meanings* they ascribe to the doing, under

[58] Koskenniemi, 'The Politics of International Law', at 15.

[59] There are no doubt good reasons to defend the relative autonomy of law with regard to international law, as Jan Klabbers has highlighted. However, as Klabbers acknowledges to some degree, it seems that this proverbial horse has already bolted: Jan Klabbers, 'The Relative Autonomy of International Law or The Forgotten Politics of Interdisciplinarity' (2005) 1 *Journal of International Law & International Relations* 35–48.

[60] See, for example, Kennedy, 'The Last Treatise', at 988.

[61] Duncan Kennedy, 'The Disenchantment of Logically Formal Legal Rationality, or Max Weber's Sociology in the Genealogy of the Contemporary Mode of Western Legal Thought' (2004) 55 *Hastings Law Journal* 1031–1076 at 1073.

ordinary or particular circumstances, presenting that description in a manner that draws attention to regularities that implicate cultural process'.[62] The chapters that follow borrow in a piecemeal fashion from ethnographic techniques, namely those of participant observation and archival research.

The prefix 'quasi-' is, however, added to the descriptor 'ethnographic' with respect to this book by way of concession that the mode of inquiry evident in it is not properly termed ethnographic. It does not, for instance, reflect the fieldwork technique commonly identified with ethnography.[63] No interviews were conducted in researching this book, despite interviewing being a staple of ethnographic research.[64] Moreover, participant observation can really only be said to have been conducted in the case of Chapter 4 and in that instance the participation in question (work as a corporate attorney in a New York law firm on various international project finance deals) predated the formulation of a related academic research agenda by several years. To the extent that this book's outlook is ethnographic, the ethnography in question is premised on an 'open-ended and speculative course of constructing subjects by simultaneously constructing the discontinuous contexts in which they act and are acted upon'.[65]

Through quasi-ethnographic inquiry of this sort, this book aims to shed light on how certain artefacts or assemblages of knowledge within the technical language and practice of contemporary international law come to be attributed to somewhere else, to someone else, or to some other time, other than the site, agent or time of international legal inquiry.[66] It aims, moreover, to elucidate relationships between

[62] Harry F. Wolcott, *Ethnography: A Way of Seeing*, Second Edition (Lanham: AltaMira Press, 2008), pp. 72–73 (emphasis in original). Compare Paloma Gay y Blasco and Huan Wardle, *How to Read Ethnography* (Abingdon and New York: Routledge, 2007), p. 5: ('Comparison, contextualisation of a life world, and an exposition of the relationships involved – these are the central prisms through which writers of ethnography look at the world').

[63] Wolcott, *Ethnography*, pp. 43–68.

[64] Karen O'Reilly, *Key Concepts in Ethnography* (London: Sage, 2009), pp. 125–131.

[65] George E. Marcus, *Ethnography Through Thick and Thin* (Princeton University Press, 1998), p. 82. For other inquiries indebted to Marcus' approach with respect to international (or rather 'transnational') law, see Sally Engle Merry, 'New Legal Realism and the Ethnography of Transnational Law' (2006) 31 *Law and Social Inquiry* 975–995.

[66] Consider, for instance, the attribution – in the Alston report discussed above – of more or less unfettered discretion to the military professionals involved in targeted killing: discretion supposedly exercised, without legal supervision or complicity,

a number of these tendencies of attribution and to shed light on their implications. It does so by beginning, not with particular international legal rules and institutions (as most technical works of international legal scholarship do), but with practices of reference, spatialisation and temporalisation through which international lawyers convey a sense of what may be opposed to international legal 'compliance'.[67]

In its orientation around practices of reference, spatialisation and temporalisation in international legal work of various types, this book enacts a 'turn to practice' of a sort ongoing within the humanities and social sciences in the study of social knowledge. As Camic *et al.* have observed, this turn to practice represents, to some degree, a turn away from what might be termed traditional approaches to social knowledge.[68] Camic *et al.* identify the latter with a tendency to focus on the ideas of a particular social thinker or group of social thinkers (as drawn from certain canonical documents) with a view to tracing those ideas to certain societal, cultural, economic, political or ideological 'macrofactors'. In contrast, an orientation towards knowledge practices is associated less with analysis of inputs and outputs, or causes and effects, than with immanent, critical investigation of the patterned activities and often mundane modes of work in which social knowledge-makers engage, whether intentionally or unintentionally. Such a 'turn' is discernible in contemporary international legal scholarship approaching international law as a form of social knowledge, albeit not to date widely or centrally so.[69]

at Playstation-like consoles in some undisclosed location. This sets the agenda for related international legal work in terms of its extension into terrain relatively uncharted in or by international law to ensure 'transparency and accountability'. That 'transparency and accountability' is, in turn, taken as given in relation to terrain more regularly traversed in and by international law.

67 On postwar international lawyers' preoccupation with 'compliance', see Koskenniemi, 'The Politics of International Law', at 15; Koskenniemi, *The Gentle Civilizer of Nations*, pp. 485, 495; Koskenniemi, 'Constitutionalism as Mindset', at 15–16.

68 Charles Camic, Neil Gross and Michèle Lamont, 'Introduction' in *Social Knowledge in the Making* (University of Chicago Press, 2011), pp. 1–40.

69 Again, one may look to the innovative work of Riles. See Riles, *Collateral Knowledge*; Annelise Riles, *The Network Inside Out* (Ann Arbor: University of Michigan Press, 2000). This turn to practice may be distinguished from a 'turn to interpretation' of the sort about which David Kennedy has written, although the two are not necessarily distinct: David Kennedy, 'The Turn to Interpretation' (1985) 58 *Southern California Law Review* 251–276. The point of difference, in this book at least, resides in the combination of a depiction of practice with intervention or 'tactical engagement' (discussed below) in some contemporary debates occupying

It is probably the case that many practices described in this book are also discernible in domestic legal work in at least some jurisdictions and areas of law. However, a parallel inquiry and foray into domestic lawyers' configurations of, and debates surrounding, non-legality, even in relation to one domestic legal system, could not be accomplished with any cogency within the confines of one book. So, the most important point of contrast here is not with domestic lawyers' work, but rather with international legal studies that seek to apply international law to a world cast in some sense as beyond that law (or vice versa), worry incessantly that international law is not law enough for the task of application (or absorption), and hence neglect to scrutinise and tactically engage with those aspects of international legal work that are constitutive of at least some dimensions of that beyond.

It matters that international lawyers disavow or downplay their role in constituting seemingly exogenous phenomena (and the role of those phenomena, legally construed, in constituting international law) because of the impact that this has upon agendas for international legal work. International lawyers often seem to feel entitled to leave to others – especially to professionals offering other forms of expertise – matters 'internal' to phenomena that they cast as non-legal. At the same time, international lawyers have often preferred to innovate within and extend their discipline by labouring to throw a normative net over one or other domain perceived as deficient of norms, rather than by engaging tactically in those domains. In both senses, perceptions of non-legality encourage international lawyers towards certain endeavours and away from others, even as those perceptions often go unscrutinised.

International lawyers' makings of non-legality (that is, in this book's terms, extra-legality, illegality, pre- and post-legality, supra-legality and infra-legality) also shape the content of international law, the ambit of possibility generated in international legal work, and the scope of the responsibilities that international lawyers assume in any one area. An international law framed as *responsive* to actions and agendas established elsewhere is likely to differ materially from an international law informed by a sense of legal complicity and immersion in those spheres of action and agenda-setting.

international lawyers. Paraphrasing Kennedy, '[t]he goal is to refuse, rather than to embrace, complicity in the management of [legality] and [non-legality], treating the apparent inevitability of their division and reconnection as a contingent social event': Kennedy, 'The Turn to Interpretation', at 275.

The international law on transnational narco-trafficking may exemplify both the aforementioned impacts of international lawyers' perceptions of non-legality. Many international legal instruments in this area seem based on an assumption that drug cartels operate (for the most part) outside or in defiance of law. The United Nations Convention against Illicit Traffic in Narcotic Drugs and Psychotropic Substances 1988, for instance, places greatest emphasis on the criminalisation of drug trafficking and related activities under state parties' domestic law and the establishment of corresponding criminal jurisdiction.

Consider how differently international law in this area could be formulated if it were based on recognition that many drug cartels assume and exercise quasi-sovereign functions (the provision of health care, etc.) and operate in complex interaction, and frequently through compliance, with domestic and international law. The writings of criminologists Alfredo Schulte-Bockholt and Enrique Desmond Arias present accounts of drug-traffickers' work that differ quite markedly from that suggested by the 1988 UN Convention.[70] Their scholarship may be read to challenge the wholesale consignment of narco-trafficking to the realm of illegality by showing how much narco-traffickers engage with and rely upon legal institutions and legal norms in order to accomplish their trafficking goals.

The contrast between these two depictions of narco-trafficking makes apparent how much tactical choice the making of illegality, and other forms of non-legality, may entail. The formulation of narco-trafficking as legally enabled invites international lawyers' tactical engagement in the processes and implications of that enabling. The characterisation of narco-trafficking as largely conducted through defiance or evasion of law invites an international legal disposition of righteous oversight and condemnation. It may turn out that righteous oversight and condemnation work well in particular instances. Nonetheless, my non-specialist intuition is that, to date, international law surrounding narco-trafficking might have relied rather too heavily on that approach. To the extent that a bias may be discernible in this regard (away from tactical engagement and towards righteous oversight in international law surrounding narco-trafficking), it is one to which the making of illegality likely contributes.

[70] Alfredo Schulte-Bockholt, *The Politics of Organized Crime and the Organized Crime of Politics: A Study in Criminal Power* (Lanham: Lexington Books, 2006); Enrique Desmond Arias, *Drugs and Democracy in Rio De Janeiro: Trafficking, Social Networks and Public Security* (Chapel Hill: The University of North Carolina Press, 2006).

I could, of course, be quite wrong both about the existence of a bias of this kind and the possibilities that could flow from its displacement. The point of the foregoing illustration is not to reveal how the international law on narco-trafficking might be made better, for all times and all places, by upending attributions of legality and illegality. Rather, the point is to show how unresolved and yet how significant these attributions may be. The role of illegality-making in international law in structuring priorities, dispositions and resource allocations with respect to narco-trafficking is precisely the sort of terrain-configuring work that this book seeks to open to international legal question and tactical engagement.

Tactical engagements

What, then, is meant by tactical engagement for the purposes of this book? What I have in mind is something other than an embrace of the 'strategic thinking' of security studies, international relations and foreign policy literature, with which international legal thought and practice have sometimes been contrasted and sometimes fused.[71] Tactical engagement, for this book's purposes, does not imply what strategic thinking is often taken to imply in international affairs – that is, the seizure of a power of 'conscious and individual choice, guided by rational calculation or by "ethical and affective" motivations' to ensure liberation from one or other 'constraint and ... collective norm'.[72] Rather, in this book, tactical engagement suggests what sociologist Pierre Bourdieu conceives of as reflexive engagement in and of 'more or less "automatic" strategies of the practical sense'. That is, it implies problematising that 'feel ... for a particular, historically determined game', gained and conveyed by 'socialized agents' through participation

[71] See, for example, Peter Margulies, 'When to Push the Envelope: Legal Ethics, the Rule of Law, and National Security Strategy' (2007) 30 *Fordham International Law Journal* 642–72, at 642: ('an unyielding respect for the letter of the law does not mix well with national security strategy'); Koskenniemi, *The Gentle Civilizer of Nations*, pp. 413–509 (recounting the merger of international legal professional practice with a rule scepticism and policy orientation identified with international relations as a consequence of which '[p]ublic international lawyers increasingly conceived international law from the perspective of a world power, whose leaders have "options" and routinely choose among alternative "strategies" in an ultimately hostile world' (p. 475)).

[72] Pierre Bourdieu, 'From Rules to Strategies' in *In Other Words: Essays Towards a Reflexive Sociology* (trans. Matthew Adamson, Stanford University Press, 1990), pp. 59–75 at p. 62.

in a wide range of social (and for our purposes, professional) activities. Neither this 'feel' nor the reflexive critique of it is synonymous with or reducible to 'the projects or calculations of any conscious mind'.[73]

To engage this 'practical sense' as a problem in and for international legal work is not to act in the hope of superseding it as false consciousness or otherwise. Rather, this engagement implies continuing to exercise its 'more or less "automatic" strategies' (from Bourdieu's account) while opening them to reflexive critique. In other words, the goal of this book's tactical engagement in contemporary international legal debates is not necessarily a comprehensive renewal of international legal architecture (although I would be happy for such renewal to be on the table). Rather, the aim of this book is to bring to the fore some problematic dimensions of the practical sense by which international legal work is daily animated.

The aspiration is not, furthermore, merely to describe and affirm existing practices of international legal thought. Instead, the goal is, first, to contribute to the delimitation of 'practices that have no discourse' within that thought (such as the practice of reproducing what are sometimes referred to as background norms, including those embedded in professional style) and, second, to contribute to the generation of discourse of and on these practices.[74] The idea, broadly speaking, is to enable readers to experience the international legal field afresh and, potentially, to acquire a new 'feel' for the political possibilities available within it.[75]

[73] *Ibid.*, pp. 62–64. This 'practical sense' is famously identified in Bourdieu's work with 'habitus' or that system of dispositions which is objectively constituted in the relationship between classifiable practices and a system of classification or between a field of possible forces and their manifestation in certain schemes of perception, appreciation and action. See generally Pierre Bourdieu, *Distinction: A Social Critique of the Judgment of Taste* (trans. Richard Nice, London: Routledge, 1984), pp. 169–177, 466–470; Pierre Bourdieu, *Outline of a Theory of Practice* (trans. Richard Nice, Cambridge University Press, 1977), pp. 1–30, 72–95.

[74] Michel de Certeau, *The Practice of Everyday Life* (trans. Steven Rendall, Berkeley: University of California Press, 1984), p. 46 (discussing Foucault's work). On 'background norms' see, for example, Kennedy, 'Challenging Expert Rule', 5.

[75] Foucault, 'Polemics, Politics, and Problematizations', p. 114: ('It is a question, then, of thinking about the relations of these different experiences [madness and mental illness; crime and punishment; sexuality] to politics, which doesn't mean that one will seek in politics the main constituent of these experiences or the solution that will definitively settle their fate'). Compare Emilios Christodoulidis' account of immanent critique: Emilios Christodoulidis, 'Strategies of Rupture' (2009) 20 *Law and Critique* 3–26 at 6–7.

If Pierre Bourdieu characterises the 'feel ... for a particular, historically determined game' - and political engagement in or with it - in terms of 'strategy', we might also think of such engagement in terms of 'tactics', with reference to the work of Michel de Certeau. Strategy, in de Certeau's account, presupposes delimitation of a subject attributed with will and power (unlike Bourdieu's understanding of the term). The archetypal corporate chooser who features in Chapter 4 of this book is one example. De Certeau suggests a business, an army, a city, a scientific institution by way of other examples. For strategic rationalisation to take place, such a subject must, de Certeau maintains, be envisaged in isolation, and in relation to an exteriority 'composed of targets or threats'. Again, de Certeau offers examples: customers, competitors, enemies, the country surrounding the city, objectives and objects of research. Strategic knowledge, for de Certeau, entails the deployment of such a wilful subject against targets or threats across plainly 'readable spaces'.[76]

Tactics, on the other hand, are for de Certeau 'calculated action[s]' presupposing 'the absence of a proper locus' such that those who engage in tactics 'play on and with a terrain' not solely or primarily of their own making. Tactics do not, in de Certeau's account, permit an agent 'the means to *keep to itself*, at a distance, in a position of withdrawal, foresight, and self-collection'.[77] Tactics are, moreover, identified as much with practices of consumption as with production. So, whereas strategy (contra Bourdieu) might be taken to imply some capacity to withdraw from the problems and shed the tendencies to which critical attention is drawn - to survey one's field from a distance, point out where wrong turns have been taken and chart a higher road that might yet be - tactics are deployed in a posture of immersion and complicity. In this book, tactical engagement in these terms entails drawing attention to some problematic effects of non-legality's representation in international legal work, without laying claim to a vantage point of rectitude or taintlessness.

An intuition pursued in this book is that opportunities for tactical engagement along these lines arise from time to time in and around precisely the sorts of 'vacuum' about which Alston worried in the

[76] De Certeau, *The Practice of Everyday Life*, pp. 35–37. This is patently not the sort of strategic knowledge of which Bourdieu wrote, but may be closer to popular understandings of strategic thinking and to those generally prevailing in international legal scholarship.

[77] *Ibid.*

report discussed in the opening pages of this introduction. These may go unnoticed by virtue of their frequently falling – or rather, being made to fall – within the ambit of the non-legal (that is, their being understood primarily in terms of their extra-legality, illegality, pre- or post-legality, supra-legality or infra-legality). How tactical engagement in Alston's 'vacuum' or in other comparable creations might play out is not something that this book will attempt to predict. One of the themes that will emerge from the ensuing chapters is a sense that international law is not an instrument readily subordinated to rational will in the singular; one must always be mindful of the unintended and unforeseen. Nonetheless, each of the following chapters redescribes terrain well trodden in international legal debate with a view to would-be debate participants experiencing that terrain anew and awry. In each instance, the relative coherence and convergence attributed to international lawyers' work arises from orientation around an eventful or episodic field of practice, even as the event or episode in question occasions the unmaking of international law in particular ways.[78]

In conclusion, the foil against which each of this book's tactical engagements is set – the argumentative terrain that each chapter would have readers experience anew – merits some more detailed elucidation. Chapter 2 revisits international legal responses to the sanctioning of abuse in the so-called 'torture memos' released between 2004 and 2009. Amid that chorus of condemnation and justification, it probes the generative functions of illegality in international legal thought. Recognition of the legalities of illegality (specifically, torture), this chapter suggests, could bring forth new prospects for agency and the remaking of legal subjectivities in a key of resistance.

Chapter 3 engages international legal scholarly representations of extra-legality in Guantánamo Bay, which are representations linked to international legal concern about emergency powers more generally. Here, a quasi-ethnographic study of decision-making surrounding Guantánamo Bay detainees reveals a hyper-proceduralism and rule-based banalisation of nominally extra-legal (and partially extra-judicial) power. This, in turn, implies a relationship of law and power more intertwined and mutually constitutive than often appears in accounts of the political derailing or circumvention of the legal norm at Guantánamo Bay. In this chapter's account, Guantánamo Bay is not

[78] Fleur Johns *et al.*, 'Introduction' in *Events: The Force of International Law* (London: Routledge-Cavendish, 2011), pp. 1–17.

a space in which international law has broken down or been wholly set aside. Rather, the detention camps of Guantánamo Bay are characterised here as works of legal representation and classification more or less coextensive with normalities of international legal practice.

Chapter 4 intervenes obliquely in debates concerning the use and misuse of power by transnational corporations in global development activities. International legal critics of transnational corporate action may, this chapter suggests, be somewhat misguided in their fixation on economic actors making determinative (and sometimes damaging) choices either prior to law, or in its wake. Far from being subordinate to autonomous choices made in some pre- or post-legal back room, lawyers are, in Chapter 4's account, centrally involved in the economic call-making to which they supposedly 'respond', including by helping to give shape and effect to apparently non-legal artefacts of knowledge: financial models, for instance.

In a related sense, Chapter 5 examines the legal construction of exogeneity in climate change debates. More specifically, it examines international legal scholars' depictions of the work and findings of the Intergovernmental Panel on Climate Change. What role, it asks, might international legal scholars have played in shaping perceptions of climate change – and surrounding policy debates – as supra-legal: that is, as phenomena open to political and/or scientific comprehension but otherwise so expansive or so entrenched as to surpass international lawyers' grasp? And what, moreover, may be the implications of this construction of supra-legality for creative actions concerning global climate change, international lawyers' actions in particular?

Finally, Chapter 6 makes a foray into international legal literature concerned with disaster management in the aftermath of natural disaster: that is, emergencies of environmental or physical rather than explicitly political provenance. Chapter 6 focuses, in particular, upon the 'management' of mass death resulting from natural disaster and the infra-legal conditioning of the dead bodies in question (that is, their marking as both marginal and crucial in international legal writing). Through close reading of some international organisations' manuals on the handling of dead bodies in disaster situations, this chapter explores the services which the dead bodies of disaster are called upon to perform in and around international organisational writing and practice. Whereas global commentary would often have us see international institutions' role in the wake of natural disaster as ameliorative or redemptive, this chapter focuses on ambivalent forces of governance that international institutions bring to bear through the medium of dead bodies.

Against these various foils, this book attempts a series of related experiments: to generate quasi-ethnographic (and, at the same time, quasi-fictional)[79] depictions of non-legalising tendencies in international law. International legal work as it has come to be known is made possible in part by practices of un-law- or non-law-making: practices of which this book's chapters offer a series of related compositions. Set against the various debates with which they intersect, these compositions are directed towards thinking and doing otherwise within the international legal field.

[79] This book's chapters are fictional in the specific sense suggested by Foucault, and hence quasi-fictional in that they are not fictional in the commonly understood sense of the term. See Michel Foucault, 'The History of Sexuality' in *Power/Knowledge: Selected Interviews and Other Writings 1972–1977* (ed. Colin Gordon, New York: Pantheon Books, 1980), p. 193: ('I have never written anything but fictions. I do not mean to say, however, that the truth is therefore absent … One "fictions" history on the basis of a political reality that makes it true, one "fictions" a politics not yet in existence on the basis of a historical truth'). As Timothy O'Leary notes, Foucault 'doesn't mean that they [his histories] aren't true, he means that they try (and sometimes succeed) in producing an effect that generates a new set of attitudes and new forms of practice': Timothy O'Leary, *Foucault and Fiction: The Experience Book* (London and New York: Continuum, 2009), p. 6.

2 Illegality and the torture memos

Of all the non-legalities with which this book deals, illegality is one of the main dancing partners of international legality and hence a good place to begin the task of thinking and doing otherwise in international legal work. Indeed, like other modes of non-legality, illegality *is* legality in international law. Illegality is a construction of law, internationally and otherwise. Illegality can only manifest itself as such in legality, yet is irreducible to legality. In that sense, illegality remains in perpetual retreat.[1] Illegality may also, at times, be a designation which international lawyers strive to have realised, but fail to yield 'for want of a competent instance'.[2] Whether in a posture of creation, response or aspiration, international legal work is provoked, captivated and sustained by illegality – both its realisation and its prospect.

[1] Compare Michel Foucault, *Madness and Civilization: A History of Insanity in the Age of Reason* (trans. Richard Howard, New York: Vintage Books, 1988), p. 107: ('Joining vision and blindness, image and judgment, hallucination and language, sleep and waking, day and night, madness is ultimately nothing, for it unites in them all that is negative. But the paradox of this *nothing* is to *manifest* itself, to explode in signs, in words, in gestures … For madness, if it is nothing, can manifest itself only by departing from itself, by assuming an appearance in the order of reason and thus becoming the contrary of itself. Which illuminates the paradoxes of the classical experience: madness is always absent, in a perpetual retreat where it is inaccessible, without phenomenal or positive character; and yet it is present and perfectly visible in the singular evidence of the madman … All that madness can say of itself is merely reason, though it is itself the negation of reason').

[2] Georges Abi-Saab, 'Namibia and International Law: An Overview' (1993) 1 *African Yearbook of International Law* 3–12 at 4: (Discussing the illegality of South Africa's mandate over 'South-West Africa', in relation to which it was the case that 'international law [could not], for want of proper means, directly act to undo illegality, [but] it [could] at least have the "passive virtue" of a "holding operation", in the face of an illegal but effective situation').

Illegality is not, of course, international law's sole or even primary source of sustenance; much international law is concerned with the promotion of social, political or economic agendas or the attainment of technical goals without apparent regard to the illegal as such. All illegality is not, moreover, equally objectionable or enthralling to international lawyers. Illegality may on occasions, as Francis Boyle once suggested, be 'treated as if it were a sin deserving of punishment and damnation'.[3] Yet in many instances, illegality is tolerated, even encouraged, by legal authorities, institutions and scholars.[4] Consider, for instance, the routinised illegality of cross-border trade in circumstances where bribery is regarded as necessary to trade any goods, be they legal or illegal.[5] Consider, alternatively, the marginal, incremental or confrontational illegality of the activist or envelope-pushing lawyer: enterprising lawyers who work with the 'smart kids' of global finance to skirt (and now and again slip over) the most vertiginous edges of legality, or the impassioned advocate who takes a higher road than mere lawfulness would permit. These figures of illegality meet with a very different reception in international law to the adrenalin-pumped fighter pilot who takes a military operation too far, the entrepreneurial narcotics dealer who employs needy youngsters as global mules, or, for that matter, the torturer.[6]

As Elaine Scarry famously observed, the intense physical pain inflicted in torture is 'language-destroying' even as torture 'is itself a language, an objectification, an acting out'.[7] The language of legality, in particular, is commonly understood to have been silenced or expelled at the site of torture. According to the 1984 Convention against Torture

[3] Francis A. Boyle, 'The Irrelevance of International Law: The Schism Between International Law and International Politics' (1980) 10 *California Western International Law Journal* 193–219 at 207.

[4] Josiah Heyman (ed.), *States and Illegal Practices* (Oxford: Berg, 1999).

[5] Akin Fadahunsi and Peter Rosa, 'Entrepreneurship and Illegality: Insights from the Nigerian Cross-Border Trade' (2002) 17 *Journal of Business Venturing* 397–429.

[6] In this regard, note Jack Goldsmith's characterisation of Bush administration decision-making surrounding counter-terrorist interrogation as a sometimes poorly executed exercise in navigating the edges of legality rather than a venture into illegality per se: Jack Goldsmith, *The Terror Presidency: Law and Judgment Inside the Bush Administration* (New York: W. W. Norton, 2007), p. 146: ('The administration's aim was to go right to the edge of what the torture law prohibited, to exploit every conceivable loophole in order to do everything legally possible to uncover information that might stop an attack').

[7] Elaine Scarry, *The Body in Pain: The Making and Unmaking of the World* (Oxford and New York: Oxford University Press, 1987), pp. 27, 35.

and Other Cruel, Inhuman or Degrading Treatment or Punishment (the 'Torture Convention'), a torturer may have his or her reasons and official functions. A torturer is not, however, presumed to be a font of legal argument, nor otherwise to lay claim to 'lawful sanctions':

> [T]orture means any act by which severe pain or suffering, whether physical or mental, is intentionally inflicted on a person for such purposes as obtaining from him or a third person information or a confession, punishing him for an act he or a third person has committed or is suspected of having committed, or intimidating or coercing him or a third person, or for any reason based on discrimination of any kind, when such pain or suffering is inflicted by or at the instigation of or with the consent or acquiescence of a public official or other person acting in an official capacity. It does not include pain or suffering arising only from, inherent in or incidental to lawful sanctions.[8]

In torture, then, one sometimes witnesses illegality cast as a void within law. Torture is more often understood to have arisen from primal or political impulses emerging in spite of law, than from the manipulation of legal language. What made the release of the so-called 'torture memos' so shocking and disruptive for international legal thought, this chapter will suggest, was their conflation of two senses of illegality in which international legal writing routinely trades. An illegality associated with the active expulsion of law – the illegality with which torture is typically ascribed – was collapsed into a far more mundane illegality; an illegality teeming with legality, and of a sort with which the international legal field is understood to be rife. This second sense of illegality is that of the 'aggressive' or 'creative' lawyer who makes legal arguments or takes interpretive positions that don't quite fly, a type of illegality by which international law is usually unperturbed outside conditions of moral panic.[9]

This chapter will focus on this uncomfortable convergence of illegalities within international legal scholarship associated with the release of the torture memos. The torture memos comprise many hundreds of pages of legal memoranda and correspondence produced by White House counsel, US Defense Department counsel, assistant Attorneys General and other officials and legal advisors of the US government and the US military

[8] Convention Against Torture and Other Cruel, Inhuman or Degrading Treatment or Punishment ('Torture Convention'), New York, 10 December 1984, in force 26 June 1987, 1465 UNTS 85, Art. 1.

[9] Goldsmith, *The Terror Presidency*, p. 167: (According to Goldsmith, in writing the torture memos, the Office of Legal Counsel 'pushed the envelope', and 'in pushing the envelope, [the] OLC took shortcuts in its opinion-writing procedures').

between 2002 and 2005.[10] The documents in question addressed the status of prisoners detained during US military operations in Afghanistan and Iraq, as well the lawfulness of certain counter-insurgency techniques used, or considered for possible use, in connection with anti-terrorism initiatives of the US administration. International legal commentators have focused particular attention on a few of these memoranda, especially one written in August 2002 that adopted a highly permissive reading of international legal prohibitions on torture.[11]

Media disclosure of some of these documents occurred in 2004, sparking a series of investigations, official and otherwise.[12] A further round of disclosures occurred in 2009, largely prompted by freedom-of-information requests made by the American Civil Liberties Union.[13] These documents circulated in the context of widespread allegations of detainee mistreatment and torture levelled at the United States and its allies; a number of these were substantiated in investigative reports.[14]

[10] Mark Danner, *Torture and Truth: America, Abu Ghraib, and the War on Terror* (New York Review of Books, 2004); Mark Danner, 'US Torture: Voices from the Black Sites', *The New York Review of Books*, 9 April 2009, www.nybooks.com/articles/archives/2009/apr/09/us-torture-voices-from-the-black-sites/?pagination=false (accessed 17 September 2012); Karen J. Greenberg and Joshua L. Dratel (eds.), *The Torture Papers: The Road to Abu Ghraib* (Cambridge University Press, 2005); Philippe Sands, *Torture Team: Rumsfeld's Memo and the Betrayal of American Values* (Hampshire: Palgrave Macmillan, 2008); American Civil Liberties Union, *Index of Bush-Era OLC Memoranda Relating to Interrogation, Detention, Rendition and/or Surveillance*, www.aclu.org/pdfs/safefree/olcmemos_2009_0305.pdf (accessed 17 September 2012).

[11] Jay S. Bybee, 'Memorandum for Alberto R. Gonzales, Counsel to the President, from Jay S. Bybee, Asst. Atty. General, Re: Standards of Conduct for Interrogation under 18 USC. 2340–2340A', 1 August 2002, reprinted in Greenberg and Dratel, *The Torture Papers*, pp. 172–217.

[12] Jess Bravin, 'Pentagon Report Set Framework for Use of Torture', *The Wall Street Journal*, 7 June 2004, www.informationclearinghouse.info/article6288.htm (accessed 17 September 2012); Jeffrey Rosen, 'The Nation; The Struggle Over the Torture Memos', *The New York Times*, 15 August 2004, www.nytimes.com/2004/08/15/weekinreview/15rose.html (accessed 17 September 2012).

[13] Mark Mazzetti and Scott Shane, 'Interrogation Memos Detail Harsh Tactics by the C.I.A.', *The New York Times*, 16 April 2009, www.nytimes.com/2009/04/17/us/politics/17detain.html?_r=1> (accessed 17 September 2012).

[14] International Committee of the Red Cross (ICRC), 'ICRC Report on the Treatment of Fourteen "High Value Detainees" in CIA Custody', Regional Delegation for the United States and Canada, Washington, 14 February 2007, WAS 07/76, www.nybooks.com/icrc-report.pdf (accessed 17 September 2012); 'Report of the International Committee of the Red Cross (ICRC) on the Treatment by the Coalition Forces of Prisoners of War and Other Protected Persons by the Geneva Conventions in Iraq During Arrest, Internment and Interrogation', February 2004,

In some accounts, a direct causal link was posited between the permissive legal (or illegal) architecture the torture memos asserted and the subjection of detainees to inhuman treatment.[15] Other accounts, however, pointed to incidents of alleged torture pre-dating the legal memoranda in question.[16] In either circumstance, international lawyers encountered their discipline anew in these memos, and found the encounter troubling. Of that encounter, and of the substance of these memos, much could be and has been written.[17] For its part, this chapter will 'fictionalise' the release of the torture memos as a moment calling forth, for international lawyers, an uneasy and ultimately unstable reckoning with illegality.[18] It is on the conditions and terms of that reckoning which this chapter will focus.

The chapter begins with a survey of some modes of illegality with which the discipline of international law frequently trades and grapples. Also considered are the modes in which international legal writing has tended to frame its 'encounters' with illegality. In this context,

www.globalsecurity.org/military/library/report/2004/icrc_report_iraq_feb2004.pdf (accessed 17 September 2012); Amnesty International, *Beyond Abu Ghraib: Detention and Torture in Iraq* (Amnesty International, 2006), www.amnesty.org/en/library/info/MDE14/001/2006 (accessed 17 September 2012); Human Rights Watch, 'By the Numbers: Findings of the Detainee Abuse and Accountability Project' (2006) 18 *Human Rights Watch* no. 2(G), hrw.org/reports/2006/ct0406/ (accessed 17 September 2012); Human Rights Watch, '"No Blood, No Foul": Soldiers' Accounts of Detainee Abuse in Iraq' (2006) 18 *Human Rights Watch* no. 3(G), www.hrw.org/reports/2006/us0706/ (accessed 17 September 2012); Physicians for Human Rights, 'Break Them Down: Systematic Use of Psychological Torture by US Forces' (authored by Gretchen Borchelt, Jonathan Fine and Christian Pross, Cambridge, MA: Physicians for Human Rights, 2005), www.williambowles.info/iraq/2005/psych_torture-1.pdf (accessed 17 September 2012); Major General Antonio M. Taguba, *Article 15-6 Investigation of the 800th Military Police Brigade*, www.npr.org/iraq/2004/prison_abuse_report.pdf (accessed 17 September 2012); Inspector General of the US Department of the Army, *Detainee Operations Inspection*, 21 July 2004, www.au.af.mil/au/awc/awcgate/army/ig_detainee_ops.pdf (accessed 17 September 2012).

15 Bravin, 'Pentagon Report'; Sands, *Torture Team*.

16 Jason Leopold, 'CIA Interrogation Tapes Predated Torture Memo', *The Public Record*, 11 April 2009, pubrecord.org/torture/264/cia-interrogation-tapes-predated-tortur e-memo (accessed 17 September 2012).

17 Jordan J. Paust, *Beyond the Law: The Bush Administration's Unlawful Responses in the 'War' on Terror* (New York: Cambridge University Press, 2007); Manfred Nowak, 'What Practices Constitute Torture? US and UN Standards' (2006) 28 *Human Rights Quarterly* 809–841.

18 See the discussion in Chapter 1 of this book's writing of 'quasi-fiction' and Michel Foucault, 'The History of Sexuality' in *Power/Knowledge: Selected Interviews and Other Writings 1972–1977* (ed. Colin Gordon, New York: Pantheon Books, 1980), p. 193; Timothy O'Leary, *Foucault and Fiction: The Experience Book* (London and New York: Continuum, 2009), p. 6.

it is argued, something like a disciplinary pleasure principle has tended to prevail.[19]

In an effort to go beyond the pleasure principle according to which international legal confrontations with illegality are commonly read, this chapter then depicts four moods through which international legal scholarship 'responding' to the torture memos has cycled erratically. Each of these narratives is, in part, a tale of illegality: as a source of hope; a deficiency awaiting correction and soliciting expertise; an unbonding from (and rallying point for) community; and an ambivalent call to conscience. Together, these narratives bring to light constitutive links between international law's breach or breakdown (or the perception thereof) in illegality and its force as legality. Here, illegality is as significant as compliance for the generation and shaping of international law.

Against the tendencies discernible in the aforementioned moods, the third part of this chapter explores the torture memos' release (and the release of other, related documents in that connection) as a breakdown in international law's customary representations of itself to itself through illegality. That is, the latter part of this chapter concerns the failure of the affirmational and representational claims outlined in this chapter's second part. That breakdown marks international law's openness to collective change unnameable as reformist programme. That opening has occurred especially at sites characterised in international legal terms as devoid of promise: around the unpresentable figure of the torture victim, for instance. There, law has been made in abundance. Further, detainees facing the prospect of torture or inhuman treatment are actively and combatively engaged in making and challenging legality at this site. Unlike the protagonists of the Torture Convention - a legally inarticulate torturer inflicting pain upon a victim rendered mute in the process - tortured and torturer alike generate, in this account, a profusion of legal and legalistic argument, each patently aware of the capacity of their words and actions to exert normative force beyond their immediate setting.

In this latter sense, legalities and illegalities apparently documented in, or authorised by, the torture memos and related documents are even now irresolute. Contra Lukács, illegality need not always entail a stance of opposition that accepts all the essentials of the existing

[19] Sigmund Freud, 'Beyond the Pleasure Principle' in *The Freud Reader* (ed. Peter Gay, London: Vintage, 1995), pp. 594–626.

legal order and invites continuance therein.[20] The torture memos may yet inscribe illegality as a site for intervention to enliven law-making subjectivities and possibilities that the international law concerning torture has otherwise often done its best to subdue; indeed, a site at which such interventions are already ongoing.

Illegalities in international law

Definitionally speaking, illegality connotes that which is contrary to or forbidden by law. It may also signify lawlessness or irregularity.[21] International legal doctrine stipulates that legality is to be presumed, absent specific international legal prohibition.[22] Illegality in international law would thus appear to follow the contours of international legal norms and to emerge from behind or around specific proscription.

Yet to the international legal advisor, illegality also corresponds to the darker or less credible gradations of the interpretive penumbra surrounding a particular norm – a point beyond which it would be ill-advisable to stray, as a matter of risk assessment and reputation. Hence, the focus on credibility, respectability and financial risk in advice given by the chief legal advisor of the UK Foreign and Commonwealth Office in August 2002 regarding military action in Iraq then being considered:

> I am not, at present, aware of facts which would provide a respectable legal basis for military action ... To act without a credible legal basis lays the United Kingdom open to claims for compensation, invoking our international responsibility.[23]

20 Georg Lukács, 'Legality and Illegality' in *History and Class Consciousness* (trans. Rodney Livingstone, London: Merlin Press, 1971), pp. 256–271.

21 *Oxford English Dictionary*, www.oed.com/viewdictionaryentry/Entry/91400 (accessed 17 September 2012).

22 The Case of the S.S. 'Lotus' (*France* v. *Turkey*) (1927) *Publications of the Permanent Court of International Justice*, Series A, No. 10, www.worldcourts.com/pcij/eng/decisions/1927.09.07_lotus.htm (accessed 17 September 2012).

23 'Letter from Michael Wood (Chief Legal Adviser of the UK Foreign and Commonwealth Office) to Stephen Wright (Deputy Under-Secretary of State for Foreign and Commonwealth Affairs) re Iraq: Legality of the Use of Force', 15 August 2002, declassified document presented in evidence to the UK Government Iraq Inquiry, www.iraqinquiry.org.uk/media/43499/doc_2010_01_26_11_02_28_403.pdf (accessed 17 September 2012).

Elsewhere, illegality may imply calling attention to legality's limitations and structural costs.[24] In a posture of political dissidence or 'conscientious lawbreaking' in the international legal field as elsewhere, illegality may entail a setting of legality against itself – an invocation of law's 'utopian content' against its positive content.[25]

Illegality is, therefore, more than international legality's underbelly or opposite. Rather, as Davina Cooper has argued of illegality in other settings, it is a 'significant structuring device in its own right'.[26] Cooper continues:

> I centre illegality as law's inevitable surplus – expelled, yet always present, constituted at the heart of law ... Not only does illegality generate its own effects in terms of practice and discursive rhetoric, but, as well, its terrain is always constituted in the production of legality. Thus, the formation and existence of illegality is as central to law's authority and efficacy as compliance.[27]

In international law, illegalities operate both as legal actions and calls to legal (and to social or political) action. Operative acts of international law may take the form of an action judged illegal more as a matter of instinct than considered professional assessment. 'Illegal!' may be a cry of protest or condemnation. Yet, given international law's customary dimension, such characterisations of illegality may be preliminary to a taking effect or remaking of legality, or its confinement within jurisdictional limits. Thomas Franck has observed, for instance (apropos of international customary law), that 'state practice, even when in violation of the law, may have the eventual effect of reforming the law'.[28] By way of example, Franck offered the Security Council's long-standing practice of not counting a permanent member's abstention as a veto, later confirmed by the International Court of Justice as a valid 'reinterpret[ation]' of Article 27(3) of the UN Charter. He tendered a second example as well: regional organisations'

[24] Martha Minow, 'Breaking the Law: Lawyers and Clients in Struggles for Social Change' (1991) 52 *University of Pittsburgh Law Review* 723–752.

[25] David Luban, 'Conscientious Lawyers for Conscientious Lawbreakers' (1991) 52 *University of Pittsburgh Law Review* 793–814.

[26] Davina Cooper, 'Institutional Illegality and Disobedience: Local Government Narratives' (1996) 16 *Oxford Journal of Legal Studies* 255–274 at 255.

[27] *Ibid.*, 255–256.

[28] Thomas M. Franck, 'After Austerlitz: The International System in the Age of Rampant American Unilateralism', (2003) 8 *Austrian Review of International and European Law* 35–48 at 41.

military actions only subsequently approved by the Security Council, contrary to the requirement, in Article 53 of the UN Charter, for prior approval.[29]

In a related sense, the influential treatise writer Ian Brownlie has observed that '[i]llegal conduct may produce a legal regime contingent on the existence of the conduct rather than its illegality'.[30] Hence, war commenced in breach of the UN Charter 'will nevertheless draw in its train most of, if not all, the rules governing the conduct of war'.[31] In other ways, 'illegal activity may produce valid results by the operation of prescription, acquiescence, and estoppel'.[32]

As to illegality's effects in international law, nearly as much turns on the *type* and *scope* of illegality, as the legality/illegality distinction per se. Actions in contravention of a peremptory or *jus cogens* norm of international law, for instance, may not form the basis of a change in customary law unless justified on the basis of another peremptory norm.[33] An illegal action's classification as such will, accordingly, be fatal to any attempt to change customary law through breach. Also, transforming the status of an action from illegal to legal may be easier to achieve if the (illegal-yet-would-be-legal) action in question is pitched at the level of regional or local custom, rather than that of general customary law.[34]

Illegality thus often figures as a trigger to international legal decision, be it adjudicative, repudiative, dismissive or ameliorative. Illegality may comprise, too, part of the doctrinal substance of decision, as rationale, excuse or identity-marker. In the latter context, the nomenclature of illegality may discourage action rather than summon it. Vast swathes of territory may be mapped illegal, as in the case of illegal occupation or 'informal' settlement. Likewise, masses of people may bear category markers of illegality: so-called illegal immigrants or unlawful combatants, for instance. In such circumstances, illegality often loses its dissident charge. Rather, a categorisation as illegal may confer seemingly permanent status: a matter more of being remaindered than being overtly suppressed. In such settings, illegality may mobilise bias[35] or sustain disinterest, inviting a decision not to act or to protest. Consider, for instance, widespread illegality cast as

[29] *Ibid.*

[30] Ian Brownlie, *Principles of Public International Law*, Seventh Edition (Oxford University Press, 2008), p. 508.

[31] *Ibid.* [32] *Ibid.* [33] *Ibid.*, p. 510. [34] *Ibid.*, p. 12.

[35] Cooper, 'Institutional Illegality and Disobedience', 271.

informality or cultural specificity on international law's peripheries, of which international law takes little or no notice.[36] Consider, also, the millions of 'illegal' migrants traversing the globe, often cast as ineluctable features of the physical world.[37] Consider, too, the unremarkable, contingent illegality of lower court or tribunal orders overturned by appellate ruling.

In the modes described in the preceding paragraph, illegality may be so entrenched, endemic or beneath notice as to spill over notions of illegality per se towards non-legalities discussed elsewhere in this book: the supra-legal or the infra-legal. Under such conditions, scholarly or activist intervention may prompt a resurfacing of these illegalities as such, bringing them into the centre of international law's disciplinary line of vision, as this chapter will later seek to show. Illustrating intervention to this effect (while exploring feminist theories of law-breaking), Kathleen Daly has written, for instance, of one woman announcing 'I am an offender, and I am proud to say that'.[38] There can be, however, no prior assurance of such interventions' success.

Carrying potential for novation and for unravelling, illegality is often a source of anxiety in international law. As if to contain this, in the International Law Commission's (ILC) Articles on Responsibility of States, illegality gets parsed and parcelled. An 'internationally wrongful act' may be established as such under a primary rule of international law[39] but the intensity, reach and effect of illegality's stain vary enormously. Illegality may be cured, in the event that a circumstance precluding wrongfulness is established.[40] Illegality may be categorised, with violations of 'peremptory norms' being invested with unique force.[41] Illegality may be centralised, dispersed, or offloaded from one agent or group of agents to another.[42] International illegality

[36] Xin He, 'Why Do They Not Comply with the Law? Illegality and Semi-Legality among Rural-Urban Migrant Entrepreneurs in Beijing' (2005) 39 *Law & Society Review* 527–562; Jane E. Larson, 'Informality, Illegality, and Inequality' (2002) 20 *Yale Law & Policy Review* 137–182.

[37] Laurie Berg, 'At the Border and between the Cracks: The Precarious Position of Irregular Migrant Workers Under International Human Rights Law' (2007) 8 *Melbourne Journal of International Law* 1–34.

[38] Kathleen Daly, 'Women's Pathways to Felony Court: Feminist Theories of Law-breaking and Problems of Representation' (1992) 2 *Southern Californian Review of Law and Women's Studies* 11–52 at 15.

[39] ILC, *The International Law Commission's Articles on Responsibility of States for Internationally Wrongful Acts: Introduction, Text and Commentaries* (ed. James Crawford, Cambridge University Press, 2002), Arts. 2, 3 and 12.

[40] *Ibid.*, Arts. 20–26. [41] *Ibid.*, Art. 26. [42] *Ibid.*, Arts. 4–11 and 16–18.

may override legality or illegality at other scales.[43] Illegality may also be a source of new legal obligation – the obligation to make reparation for instance, characterised as an 'essential principle contained in the actual notion of an illegal act'.[44] Illegality may be a condition precedent to legality, or a basis for the legitimation of violence, as in the context of countermeasures,[45] reprisals[46] or the coming to power of new governments.[47] For the purpose of giving one illegality a resting place, another illegality (illegality of origin, for example) may be erased. Hence, the ILC has observed that:

> No distinction should be made for the purposes of article 10 between different categories of movements on the basis of any international 'legitimacy' or of any illegality in respect of their establishment as a Government, despite the potential importance of such distinctions in other contexts. From the standpoint of the formulation of rules of law governing State responsibility, it is unnecessary and undesirable to exonerate a new Government or a new State from responsibility for the conduct of its personnel by reference to considerations of legitimacy or illegitimacy of its origin.[48]

'Responsibility' is charged with doing the work of reason in these settings, ensuring illegality's unruliness remains, for the most part, circumscribed.[49] Attribution of responsibility ensures illegality has an identifiable home and comprehensible voice, namely that of a state.[50] All unattributable illegality falls away, presumably to be dealt with otherwise, elsewhere, or not at all. Meanwhile, responsibility places illegality in time and space, as do its sensible siblings: obligation and knowledge.[51] So too they displace it, ensuring questions of illegality's precise 'origin or character' are set aside.[52] Related forces of control, reasonableness and will (consent) help to keep illegality from obstructing states' rational accommodation to 'circumstances'.[53]

In international law, then, the attribution of illegality is both permissive and prohibitive. It authorises and inaugurates as much as it de-legitimises. As Anne-Marie Slaughter has remarked of international

[43] *Ibid.*, Arts. 3 and 32.

[44] *Ibid.*, Arts. 34–38; *Factory at Chorzów (Germany v. Poland)* (Merits) (1928) *Publications of the Permanent Court of International Justice*, Series A, No. 17, 47.

[45] ILC, *Articles on Responsibility of States*, Arts. 49–54.

[46] Andrew D. Mitchell, 'Does One Illegality Merit Another? The Law of Belligerent Reprisals in International Law' (2001) 170 *Military Law Review* 155–177.

[47] ILC, *Articles on Responsibility of States*, Art. 10.

[48] *Ibid.*, Art. 10, Commentary para. 11. [49] *Ibid.*, Art. 1.

[50] *Ibid.*, Arts. 4–11. [51] *Ibid.*, Arts. 13–18.

[52] *Ibid.*, Art. 12. [53] *Ibid.*, Arts. 20–25.

law, 'breaking the law does not make the law disappear'.[54] Rather, one or more parties' apparent breaking of international law has often been a way of making international law appear or reappear, as both the authors of the torture memos and their (indirect) interlocutors, detainees, seemed to appreciate.

Even so, actions or advice many might dub instances of international illegality are rarely announced as such by their perpetrators or producers, in these mostly post-revolutionary days. Rather, they typically present as updated, progressive or circumstantially adapted legality. This was the case, for example, in the torture memos' argument for doing away with 'quaint' and 'obsolete' international humanitarian law rules.[55] In terms of illegality's disruptive potency, therefore, much depends on how an illegality is framed and the conditions of its framing.

Furthermore, as Lukács taught, the mere fact of an action's purported legality or illegality has rarely been revelatory of its likely strategic outcomes. To fetishise illegality, Lukács observed, has been as much a mistake as the maintenance of naïve confidence in the exclusive and enduring legality of one's own system of law. Indeed, Lukács suggested, a focus on the pursuit of revolutionary change through illegality for its own sake has sometimes undermined revolutionary forces' sense of their own capacity and legitimacy.[56]

Beyond international legality?

Whether as irregularity, breach, protest, prompt, margin-marker or distraction, illegality has featured in international legal writing as some type of unpleasure or excitation which, it is often presumed, international law is generally calculated to temper. An assumption along these lines appears to have informed the International Court of Justice's 1971 Advisory Opinion on Namibia (South West Africa):

> A binding determination made by a competent organ of the United Nations to the effect that a situation is illegal cannot remain without consequence. Once

[54] Anne-Marie Slaughter, 'Misreading the Record' in Edward C. Luck, Anne-Marie Slaughter and Ian Hurd, 'Stayin' Alive – The Rumors of the UN's Death Have Been Exaggerated *Response*' (2003) 82 *Foreign Affairs* 4, 201–205 at 203.

[55] Alberto R. Gonzales, 'Memorandum from Alberto R. Gonzales, Counsel to the President, to George W. Bush, President, Decision Re: Application of the Geneva Convention on Prisoners of War to the Conflict with Al-Qaeda and the Taliban', 25 January 2002, in Greenberg and Dratel, *The Torture Papers*, pp. 118–121.

[56] Lukács, 'Legality and Illegality'.

the Court is faced with such a situation, it would be failing in the discharge of its judicial functions if it did not declare that there is an obligation, especially upon Members of the United Nations, to bring that situation to an end.[57]

So, international legal writing has tended to adopt something like what Freud termed 'the pleasure principle': an assumption that 'the course taken by mental events … is invariably set in motion by an unpleasurable tension, and that it takes a direction such that its final outcome coincides with a lowering of that tension – that is, with an avoidance of unpleasure or a production of pleasure'.[58] Replace the preceding incidences of 'unpleasurable tension', 'tension' or 'unpleasure' with illegality, and that of 'pleasure' with legality, and one is left with something like the International Court of Justice's (ICJ's) account of the normality (or, in Freud's terms, the constancy) it 'cannot' but sustain.

Just as Freud ventured (however 'speculati[vely]') beyond the pleasure principle in psychoanalytic thought – positing the puzzling persistence and force of a compulsion to repeat and hence a regressive or death instinct[59] – so the preceding paragraphs suggest that international lawyers' drive for legality is neither dominant nor determinative. Rather, as in Freud's account of the 'instinctual' repetition of unpleasure, '[e]ach fresh repetition [of illegality] seems to strengthen the mastery they [for our purposes, writers of international law] are in search of', albeit through their own actual or threatened demise or the demise of their discipline.[60] Just as Freud speculated that the aim of organic life may be 'to cancel itself out' in death, so it may be speculated that the 'situation' that the ICJ felt compelled, in the extract above, to bring to an end may have been international *legality*, with a view perhaps to legal and/or other forms of authority 'being constantly created afresh'.[61] The paradoxical implications of this for international legal thought (centred on supposedly self-preserving states and other, like-minded legal decision-makers) were summarised by Freud some nine decades ago:

The hypothesis of self-preservative instincts, such as we attribute to all living beings, stands in marked opposition to the idea that instinctual life as a whole serves to bring about death. Seen in this light, the theoretical importance

[57] International Court of Justice, 'Legal Consequences for States of the Continued Presence of South Africa in Namibia (South West Africa) Notwithstanding Security Council Resolution 276 (1970)' (Advisory Opinion) (1971) *International Court of Justice Reports* 16–345 at 54.

[58] Freud, 'Beyond the Pleasure Principle', pp. 594–595.

[59] *Ibid.* [60] *Ibid.*, p. 611. [61] *Ibid.*, p. 613.

of the instincts of self-preservation, of self-assertion and of mastery greatly diminishes.[62]

Just as Freud's speculations called into question the status of 'self-preservative instincts' in psychoanalytic thought, so attention to the discipline's proclivities surrounding illegality might invite reconsideration of the idea that international law is overwhelmingly structured to sustain both the 'territorial integrity or political independence of ... state[s]' and states' sovereign mastery[63] and 'the principles of justice and international law'.[64] Perhaps, within international law, 'the theoretical importance of the instincts of self-preservation, of self-assertion and of mastery' (both discipline- and state-oriented) might be similarly 'diminishe[d]' having regard to the apparent orientation of international legal thought towards law's regenerative effacement in or through illegality.

What, then, are some possible implications of this brief co-option of Freud's notorious essay 'Beyond the Pleasure Principle'? In the context of this book, the analogy between Freud's death drive and a preoccupation ascribed to the discipline of international law with its own violation or exhaustion in illegality could be read in (at least) one of two ways.

Perhaps this borrowing from Freud could be equated with Freud's own problematic borrowings from biology, in the 1920 essay and related texts, towards the generation of a meta-theory inattentive to differences among social groups or across time and space.[65] That is, this analogy could be taken to postulate an internal structure or 'nature' for international law comparable to that 'of a psyche structured by a universal and eternal battle between noisy life and silent death'.[66] Such a reading of this analogy would, however, be in tension with at least some parts of Freud's essay itself. As Dufresne highlights, 'Freud's life/death dualism is not dialectical in any meaningful way';[67] it does not seem directed towards explanatory synthesis in one or other account of essential or transcendent nature.

[62] *Ibid.*, pp. 613–614.

[63] United Nations, Charter of the United Nations, San Francisco, 24 June 1945, in force 24 October 1945, 1 UNTS XVI, Art. 2(4).

[64] UN Charter, Art. 1(1).

[65] Frank J. Sulloway, *Freud, Biologist of the Mind: Beyond the Psychoanalytical Legend* (New York: Basic Books, 1979); Todd Dufresne, *Tales from the Freudian Crypt: The Death Drive in Text and Context* (Stanford University Press, 2000), pp. 43–65, 102.

[66] Dufresne, *Tales from the Freudian Crypt*, p. 44. [67] *Ibid.*, p. 93.

Rather, the compulsion to repeat which Freud takes to be emblematic of an impulse beyond the pleasure principle is a force which Freud must 'find courage to assume'.[68] It is posited in the mode of an 'as if'; Freud wrote: 'if a compulsion to repeat *does* operate in the mind, we should be glad to know … under what conditions it can emerge'.[69] Accordingly, it would be incumbent upon one seeking to make out such a parallel (between international law's orientation towards illegality and Freud's speculative death drive) to outline, in greater detail, the conditions under which such a parallel might emerge. This book could, then, be read as a study of the conditions under which such an 'as if' might emerge. That is, it could be read as a survey of practices on the basis of which one might contend that the trajectories of international legal thought and practice owe as much to impulses to destroy or surpass law than to a drive to uphold law. Or, more precisely, it could be read as an account of the ways in which prevailing international legalities depend on their writers' and practitioners' continued 'discovery' or evocation of threats to international law's existence as law.

Alternatively, one could read this brief analogy (as some have read Freud's essay) as part of a self-protective effort of self-erasure, or an attempt to do what one is describing in the course of its description.[70] Freud's account of the death instinct as a vehicle for the assertion of mastery foretells the death of his authority and that of psychoanalysis and thereby ensures that this expiration, in both instances, is read back into the fold of psychoanalytical explanation. So too one could read the foregoing analogy to Freud's essay as an attempt to script in advance the ubiquitous embarkation from one's discipline and to locate the destination of arrival already back within one's account of that discipline. Even as this book enacts a leaving behind of international law (by brief recourse to Freud in this chapter, and to Foucault and to others elsewhere), this analogy could be taken to ensure that the leaving behind is or will be consistent with the book's account of international law. It is (so the argument might run) as much an international legal tendency as a psychoanalytical one for a discipline to disavow itself, so each disavowal should be read as a return home.

In either case, the turn outside of international law made in this chapter is affirmative of (more) international law and affirmative, too,

[68] Freud, 'Beyond the Pleasure Principle', p. 605.

[69] *Ibid.*, p. 605.

[70] Jacques Derrida, *The Post Card: From Socrates to Freud and Beyond* (University of Chicago Press, 1987), p. 320.

of an account of law-making that regards the turn to non-law as crucial (such as this book's). At the same time, this chapter's turn outside of international law patently risks inadequacy for these purposes, both in its brevity and in its inattention to the whole that is comprised of Freud's complex and diverse body of work (therapeutic, analytical, institutional and philosophical), not to mention the related body of psychoanalytical work that 'continues to expand ever outward'.[71] Yet such are the risks entertained by a discipline that locates its sources amid such diverse locations, materials and practices, and plunders accordingly.[72] Here as elsewhere in international legal scholarship, the navigation of legalities/illegalities often occasions the opportunistic mining of non-legality of another sort (in this instance, through inter-disciplinary incursion) in circumstances where the latter non-legality more or less escapes scrutiny as such.

Upon the torture memos' release, there was a profusion of these illegalities to be cabined, enshrined or evoked anew, even as legality/illegality may sometimes have been beside the point. Yet to lessen international tension and to preserve or restore international legality have been only some of the aims towards which international legal scholarship on the torture memos appears to have worked. The next section of this chapter will examine the various ways in which the illegality of torture seems to have been generative of, or for, international legality in the literature surrounding the torture memos' release.

Generative illegality

Let us turn, now, away from Freud and Freudian literature to another ever-expanding body of work: the anxious outpouring of words

[71] Dufresne, *Tales from the Freudian Crypt*, p. 13.

[72] Friedrich Nietzsche warned that '[t]he worst readers are those who proceed like plundering soldiers: they pick up a few things they can use, soil and confuse the rest, and blaspheme the whole', *Basic Writings of Nietzsche* (trans. Walter Arnold Kaufmann, New York: The Modern Library, Random House, 2000), p. 155 (reproducing in translation Aphorism 137 from Friedrich Nietzsche, *Human All too Human. With a Supplement: Mixed Opinions and Maxims* (1879)). The first paragraph of Article 38 of the Statute of the International Court of Justice may be taken to authorise or affirm the anti-formal eclecticism long discernible in international legal reasoning: Statute of the International Court of Justice (26 June 1945) 961 UNTS 183, article 38(1). On 'mainstream eclecticism' and inter-disciplinary scavenging in legal scholarship and legal theory more broadly, see David Kennedy, 'A Rotation in Contemporary Legal Scholarship' in Christian Joerges and David M. Trubek (eds.), *Critical Legal Thought: An American-German Debate* (Baden Baden: Nomos Verlagsgesellschaft, 1989), pp. 358–363.

engendered by the torture memos' release. Among international lawyers, and others invoking international law, the unexpected public emergence of these documents, and the illegalities they were seen to embody, authorise and/or counter, provoked appeals to hope, correction, community and conscience. In a variety of ways, the writings in question have sought to reassert configurations of state/individual and law/violence familiar to the discipline in which they work: configurations in which the international lawyer has remained a central mediating figure. Yet at the same time, as explored below, international legal scholarship on the torture memos has repeatedly enacted the ritual immolation of this central figure, martyring itself in the name of disciplinary renewal.

To be fair, not all of the scholars whose writings are examined below would identify themselves as international lawyers or be regarded by others as such. Nonetheless, in publishing on the topic of the torture memos' release, these writers have contributed to work of legal reconstruction with particular significance for international law. Certainly, domestic legal, professional and ethical standards were also called into question by the torture memos' release. It may be that the effects that the torture memos' release might have had in relation to US military law, US criminal law, US conflicts of laws, and the regulation of professional conduct in the United States and in other jurisdictions differ markedly from those outlined here. To survey their impact in these various settings is beyond the scope of this chapter. Nonetheless, because the torture memos were widely read as synonymous with a 'crisis' of international legal (non-)compliance and endemic disregard for international law,[73] it seems plausible to co-opt much of the legal scholarly work specifically concerned with those memos into an international law-specific account of their impact.

The relevant point of comparison upon which implicit reliance is placed in this account is not with the torture memos' resonance in other areas of law (in relation to US rules of professional conduct, for instance). Rather, the tendencies attributed to scholarly writing on the torture memos (and, by extension, to international legal scholarship) are implicitly compared here to operations of international legal writing in other modes: when, for instance, international law understands itself to be tackling a novel technological problem. In the latter context, disavowals of international law's capacity or relevance may also

[73] For example, Michael P. Scharf, 'International Law and the Torture Memos' (2009) 42 *Case Western Reserve Journal of International Law* 321–358.

prove generative of its renewal.[74] Yet they are not so, I would venture to speculate, in precisely the same way as international law has lately been renewed and undone by the complex illegality of torture.

Hope

In describing abuse of his family by US prison guards, a disabled Iraqi man told US army investigators that guards pulled him around by his penis and then sodomised him with a water bottle.[75]

So begins one law review article on the torture memos. This is a familiar opening gesture from an international legal text. The sexualised body of a 'victim' is offered up for ritual consumption. That body is called upon to shock, to school and to inspire.[76]

It is, however, another sacrificial body that is offered up most regularly by the legal literature surrounding the torture memos: the body of the law. Throughout this literature, international lawyers and other legal writers critical of the torture memos and alarmed by the revelations of detainee mistreatment in related official reports have struggled to transpose international law itself onto the rack of moral trial and thereby to stage its deliverance. Consider the words of Scott Horton, chair of the Committee on International Law for the Association of the Bar of the City of New York:

> In the War on Terror, law and legal ethics have been sacrificed to a misguided notion of political expedience. We are suffering the consequences of those mistakes now, and our country is likely to suffer them for some time to come.[77]

International lawyers in the United States have hauled US Supreme Court Justice Louis Brandeis from the grave repeatedly to reissue a warning (from his dissent in the 1928 wire-tapping case of *Olmstead*

[74] Gamble and Ku's discussion of new actors, new technologies and their potential impact in or on international law is exemplary of international legal scholarship in another mode, in which renewal is associated with a 'shift in focus', mobilisation towards the realisation of 'opportunities' and the shedding of traditional 'letharg[y]': John K. Gamble and Charlotte Ku, 'International Law – New Actors and New Technologies: Centre Stage for NGOs?' (2000) 31 *Law and Policy in International Business* 221–262 at 221, 232, 237.

[75] Aaron R. Jackson, 'The White House Counsel Torture Memo: The Final Product of a Flawed System' (2006) 42 *California Western Law Review* 149–182 at 149.

[76] Anne Orford, 'Muscular Humanitarianism: Reading the Narratives of the New Interventionism' (1999) 10 *European Journal of International Law* 679–711 at 697.

[77] Scott Horton, 'Legal Ethics and the War on Terror: The Role of the Government Lawyer – Ethics Lawyers and the Torture Memoranda' (2005) 99 *American Society of International Law Proceedings* 301–306 at 301.

v. *United States*): that governmental contempt for law 'would bring terrible retribution'.[78] Theo van Boven, former UN Special Rapporteur on Torture, has worried about the effect on international human rights and humanitarian law of the United States attempting to 'argue[ ] away [its] real cornerstone[s]'.[79] Leila Sadat has warned of 'serious consequences … for the … stability of all the [international] institutions established … after the Second World War'.[80] And 'what will be the spiritual cost, the overall damage to the character of the nation?' lamented Karen Greenberg, co-editor of *The Torture Papers*.[81] Having marked with the stigma of illegality the torture memos' authors, and those who would act on their authority, international legal scholars would have those stigmata transferred to their discipline and themselves. Marks of infamy have been reshaped as marks of sanctity.

So framed, legal analysis of the illegality of torture, and of the torture memos themselves, has promised to perform one seventeenth-century sense of the term 'limit': to delineate the 'comely' contours of the human form.[82] As the torture memos purported to do away with pre-existing legal limits upon torture at the expense of mostly unnamed detainees, international legal scholars recorded the threat that they – and the illegal actions they authorised or condoned – posed as a danger to *themselves*: to the contours of their nation, their discipline, their profession and their faith. Jeremy Waldron's observation that the torture memos 'shook [his] faith in the integrity of the community of American jurists' seems characteristic of the reaction among international legal readers of these documents, both within and beyond the United States, even though Waldron was reading from the vantage point of another specialty.[83]

[78] Richard B. Bilder and Detlev F. Vagts, 'Speaking Law to Power: Lawyers and Torture' (2004) 98 *American Journal of International Law* 689–695 at 695; Richard B. Bilder, 'On Being an International Lawyer' (2006) 3 *Loyola International Law Review* 135–147 at 145.

[79] Theo van Boven, 'The Torture Papers: The Road to Abu Ghraib' (2006) 53 *Netherlands International Law Review* 149–152 at 151.

[80] Leila N. Sadat, 'Extraordinary Rendition, Torture and Other Nightmares from the War on Terror' (2007) 75 *George Washington Law Review* 1200–1248 at 1248.

[81] Karen J. Greenberg, 'From Fear to Torture', in Greenberg and Dratel, *The Torture Papers*, pp. xvii–xxi at p. xviiii.

[82] *Oxford English Dictionary*, www.oed.com/view/Entry/108477?rskey=q45e2T&result=1#eid (accessed 15 March 2012).

[83] Jeremy Waldron, 'Torture and Positive Law: Jurisprudence for the White House' (2005) 105 *Columbia Law Review* 1681–1750 at 1687.

Thus international lawyers, among others, have reacted to the degradation of international legal limits (and, only secondarily it seems, the degradation of detainee bodies) that they attribute to the torture memos by reinscribing the integrity of the human form in a number of metaphoric modes: as the body of the law, the body politic and the professional corps. Through this act of transposition, international lawyers' confrontation with what one commentator has termed law 'in the cause of evil' has offered many participants in the field hope.[84] In anticipation of the US Supreme Court's 2004 decision on Guantánamo Bay detainee claims in the consolidated case of *Rasul* v. *Bush*, George Fletcher invoked the corpus of the nation as a wellspring of hope:

> The hope remains that the Supreme Court will assert its judicial authority and redeem the American commitment to principles of liberty and individualised justice.[85]

Discussing, among other matters, the US government's 'use of cruel, inhuman and degrading interrogation methods at Abu Ghraib and elsewhere', Richard Bilder derived similar hope from the prospective realignment of a professional corps:

> Hopefully, international lawyers and others are succeeding in moving us gradually towards a better and more peaceful world – one in which law *does* speak to power.[86]

In each case, this hope stems, it seems, for a disentangling (correction), a rebinding (community) and a renewal of belief (conscience). Let us explore each of these further dimensions in turn.

Correction

For all the genuine expressions of horror and distress that they have provoked among international lawyers, the torture memos' publication, and the release of reports attributing responsibility for illegal torture and inhuman treatment to US and coalition forces, have elicited a thrill – a frisson palpable in international legal scholarly accounts of the

[84] Anthony Lewis, 'Introduction', in Greenberg and Dratel, *The Torture Papers*, pp. xiii–xvi at p. xiii.

[85] George P. Fletcher, 'Black Hole in Guantánamo Bay' (2004) 2 *Journal of International Criminal Justice* 121–232 at 132; see also Jamie Mayerfeld, 'Playing by Our Own Rules: How US Marginalization of International Human Rights Law Led to Torture' (2007) 20 *Harvard Human Rights Journal* 89–140 at 124.

[86] Bilder, 'On Being an International Lawyer', 146 (emphasis in original).

same. This, it seems, could be a Nuremberg moment for the noughties: a moment of clarity and distinction. Finally, it has appeared to many, international law's anti-formalism could be disentangled once and for all from the moral relativism it *knows* itself not to be. 'The constructive value of these memos and reports', Karen Greenberg wrote in the opening pages of *The Torture Papers*, 'is to enable open-minded reflection and self-correction'.[87] The 'self-correction' of which Greenberg has written is to proceed from a *redoubled* anti-formalism. The problem, we have been told, is not politics, but imprudence. Recall Scott Horton's words: the decomposition of law and legal ethics emanated from a '*misguided* notion of political expedience'.[88]

The answer, for many, is to do more or less what international legal pragmatists already do, only better. '[T]here is much these memos overlook', Greenberg has tutored, highlighting a number of legal, policy and strategic considerations missed.[89] Harold Koh has labelled the advice contained in the memos incompetent[90] and a 'stunning failure of lawyerly craft'.[91] Kathleen Clark has suggested that 'assertions about the state of the law [made in the 2002 Bybee memorandum] are so inaccurate that they seem to be arguments about what the authors (or the intended recipients) wanted the law to be rather than assessments of what the law actually is'.[92] Sometime political ally of the memo writers, Jack Goldsmith (former Assistant Attorney-General in the Office of Legal Counsel) has decried the 'errors' made in the memos as 'unusually worrisome'.[93] Philippe Sands has expressed horror at the 'awful' legal advice provided by one lawyer stationed at Guantánamo Bay.[94]

Indeed, even as he parses the substance of their advice, Sands enlarges the leaps and magnifies the errors made by the torture memos' authors,

87 Greenberg, 'From Fear to Torture', p. xx.

88 Horton, 'Legal Ethics and the War on Terror', 301 (emphasis added).

89 Greenberg, 'From Fear to Torture', p. xviii.

90 Mark Mazzetti and Scott Shane, 'Interrogation Memos Detail Harsh Tactics by the C.I.A.', *The New York Times*, 16 April 2009, www.nytimes.com/2009/04/17/us/politics/17detain.html?_r=1> (accessed 17 September 2012).

91 Harold Hongju Koh, 'A World Without Torture' (2005) 43 *Columbia Journal of Transnational Law* 641–662 at 649.

92 Kathleen Clark, 'Ethical Issues Raised by the OLC Torture Memorandum' (2005) 1 *Journal of National Security Law and Policy* 455–472 at 458.

93 Jack Goldsmith, *The Terror Presidency: Law and Judgment Inside the Bush Administration* (New York: W. W. Norton, 2007), p. 146.

94 Philippe Sands, 'Torture Team: The Responsibility of Lawyers for Abusive Interrogation' (2008) 9 *Melbourne Journal of International Law* 365–381 at 372.

distancing their work as far as possible from routine legalities/illegalities in which competent international lawyers daily trade. The problem, Sands suggests, was a combination of lack of expertise and the influence of a pernicious ideology distorting and derailing the 'normal' operations of international law:

> [R]eal responsibility centres on a small group of politically-appointed lawyers, adhering to a particular ideology as to America's place in the world and its relationship with norms of international law. The lawyers who knew the rules, who had lengthy experience on these issues, were circumvented. The military lawyers were cut out of the process … The normal checks and balances were avoided, with care and deliberation.[95]

Nonetheless, through careful effort, 'normality' might be restored, legal scholars report. 'Lawyers and public officials need to be instructed, in school and on the job, to be cognizant of the real-life consequences of their policy choices', Joshua Dratel has written.[96] The Office of Legal Counsel must return to the 'normal[ity]' of 'circulat[ing] its draft opinions to government agencies with relevant expertise', Jack Goldsmith has suggested.[97] Others provide instruction on the ways in which the office of the White House Counsel might be reformed.[98] New Zealand, Aaron Jackson has suggested, yields a useful example.[99] In this state of tropic inversion, international lawyers of the North must look to the South (albeit no further than the white Commonwealth) for tutelage in anti-corruption. Sounding an appeal for correction, illegality mobilises cross-border transfers of expertise and authority.

Community

Next comes the rebinding: there follows a call to courage and loyalty. 'American lawyers still honour … courage, integrity, and fidelity to the law', Richard Bilder and Detlev Vagts have insisted, citing noble lawyerly conduct against Watergate-era Nixon and among German military lawyers in the face of Nazi policy.[100] 'We as lawyers', Scott Horton

[95] *Ibid.*, 376.
[96] Joshua L. Dratel, 'The Legal Narrative', in Greenberg and Dratel, *The Torture Papers*, p. xxiii.
[97] Goldsmith, *The Terror Presidency*, p. 167.
[98] Jackson, 'The White House Counsel Memo'; Marisa Lopez, 'Professional Responsibility: Tortured Independence in the Office of Legal Counsel' (2005) 57 *Florida Law Review* 685–716.
[99] Jackson, 'The White House Counsel Memo', 153, 179–181.
[100] Bilder and Vagts, 'Speaking Law to Power', 695.

has written, 'have a sacred duty to ensure [the Nuremberg] legacy is upheld'.[101] So, international legal 'responses' to illegality in this context could be read as an effort to restore the sanctity of the human as such, after the fall and after a virtual (virtual for these commentators, that is) descent into hell. The lawyers responsible for the torture memos, Joshua Dratel wrote, 'all too willingly failed to act as a constitutional or moral compass that could brake their client's descent into unconscionable behaviour'.[102]

Yet the denouement in this morality tale has been not a scene of humanitarian triumph or ritual cleansing, but one of self-immolation. The culmination of *this* reformation is to be, as before, a reconnection with the commons.[103] There would be no miracles here. Bilder and Vagts have urged international lawyers to get back in touch with 'ordinary morality and common decency'.[104] They cited an American Bar Association committee report on the role of the government legal advisor as follows:

> Some members think that the international law community's good judgment and the public's common sense can generally be relied on to tell responsible arguments from those which are patently unfounded.[105]

In a similar vein, the publicly released *Lawyers' Statement on the Bush Administration's Torture Memos* looked to the 'public outcry' with which the torture memos' publication was greeted as confirmation of their 'original lawless[ness]'.[106]

Here, in this seemingly egalitarian gesture, one is reminded of the link between doctrines of equality and prohibitions on torture in the genealogy of liberalism. 'The same collective intelligence which brings in the doctrine of equality before the law ... will instantly put an end to torture', wrote the nineteenth-century anthropologist James Welling,

[101] Horton, 'Legal Ethics and the War on Terror', 305.

[102] Dratel, 'The Legal Narrative', at p. xxii.

[103] Philip J. Broadhead, 'Guildsmen, Religious Reform, and the Search for the Common Good: The Role of the Guilds in the Early Reformation in Augsburg' (1996) 39 *The Historical Journal* 577–597 at 584–587.

[104] Bilder and Vagts, 'Speaking Law to Power', 695.

[105] *Ibid.*, 694.

[106] Bruce Ackerman *et al.*, 'Lawyers' Statement on Bush Administration's Torture Memos, Open Letter Addressed to President George W. Bush, Vice President Richard B. Cheney, Secretary of Defense Donald Rumsfeld, Attorney General John Ashcroft and Members of Congress', 4 August 2004, www.sfcityattorney.org/Modules/ShowDocument.aspx?documentid=507 (accessed 17 September 2012).

for it was the 'mean and plebeian' who tended to be tortured.[107] John Langbein has suggested a historical connection between torture and egalitarianism of a more procedural kind.[108]

The problem, recent commentaries imply, was one of elevation and insulation. 'Hand-picked political appointees collaborated secretly on the Torture Memo', wrote Cornelia Pillard, 'driving directly to a desired bottom line'.[109] Philippe Sands suggested likewise in his reference to 'a small group of politically-appointed lawyers'.[110] Jack Goldsmith had a similar diagnosis: 'only a small handful of lawyers in the White House, Justice Department, and CIA were involved in drafting and reviewing the interrogation opinion, and few of them had a critical stance toward the opinion's interpretation of torture or the President's power'.[111] It is this elevation and insulation against which Bilder and Vagts have railed when insisting 'these memoranda cannot in themselves insulate or immunize persons engaging or complicit in torture' and against which Horton inveighed in warning '[t]here is no immunity for those who craft opinions'.[112] The turn these lawyers have attempted to take, by way of response, is outwards, towards transparency, weightlessness, dissolution.

The sensation of this turn is a vertiginous one: 'there may be no "safety net"', Bilder and Vagts have cautioned, 'other than these attorneys' own competence, care, integrity, and good faith'.[113] And yet there *is* a certain safety to be found in numbers, for the qualities cited are cast as professional qualities. Here is the rest of the Bilder and Vagts quote: 'it is only these professional qualities that protect against legal advice or advocacy that might undermine the national interest in respect for law, or subvert or erode the international legal order'.[114]

Appeals are made, again and again, to the public. Cornelia Pillard, for instance, lauds the salutary effects of publicity for legal

[107] James C. Welling, 'The Law of Torture: A Study in the Evolution of Law' (1892) 5 *American Anthropologist* 193–216 at 211.
[108] John H. Langbein, 'The Legal History of Torture' in Sanford Levinson (ed.), *Torture: A Collection* (Oxford and New York: Oxford University Press, 2004), pp. 93–104.
[109] Cornelia Pillard, 'Unitariness and Myopia: The Executive Branch, Legal Process, and Torture' (2006) 81 *Indiana Law Journal* 1297–1312 at 1297.
[110] Sands, 'Torture Team: The Responsibility of Lawyers for Abusive Interrogation', 376.
[111] Goldsmith, *The Terror Presidency*, p. 167.
[112] Bilder and Vagts, 'Speaking Law to Power', 694; Horton, 'Legal Ethics and the War on Terror', 303.
[113] Bilder and Vagts, 'Speaking Law to Power', 693. [114] *Ibid.*, 693.

decision-making: '[a]fter the public, the press, and other independent commentators had a chance to analyze and critique the executive's legal analysis, its flaws became clear', she writes.[115] Engagement of Congress in debate surrounding interrogation practices would, Jack Goldsmith suggests, 'have served an educative and legitimating function regardless of what emerged from the process'.[116]

Yet it is primarily to *each other* that international lawyers would be made transparent. The collectivity among whom legal judgment is to be dispersed, and from whom norms of 'common decency' are to be drawn anew, is a *professional* fraternity in most accounts. The 'professional obligations' of the torture memos' authors are those most frequently cited as the norms they violated, and by which they must be held to account.[117] As to the defensibility of the government attorneys' actions, Bilder and Vagts concluded that 'a final verdict on these matters is likely to emerge only out of the collective sentiment of the professional legal community'.[118]

The original substitution has been reinstated. It is the *discipline*, remember, that is suffering on the rack. It is the *profession* under thumbscrews. And it is the professional legal community (above all the community comprised of international law specialists) that is imagined to emerge all the worthier for the ordeal. The turn outwards has rapidly become an encircling or gathering in.

Conscience

The call to an ethical commons is, however, one chastened by a Hobbesian suspicion of antinomian conscience.[119] After all, critics have acknowledged that the lawyers concerned apparently believed themselves, and the cause for which they were working, to be right. Their affliction, those critics have reported, was not a lack of inwardness, but its excess. '[T]he torture debacle', Cornelia Pillard has written, was born in part of 'ideologically driven myopia'.[120] The policies inscribed

[115] Pillard, 'Unitariness and Myopia', 1301.

[116] Goldsmith, *The Terror Presidency*, p. 206.

[117] Carrie Johnson, 'Judge Invited to Testify about Role in Interrogation Memos', *The Washington Post*, 30 April 2009, A07; Koh, 'A World Without Torture', 654–655; Richard H. Weisberg, 'Loose Professionalism: Or Why Lawyers Take the Lead on Torture', in Levinson, *Torture: A Collection*, pp. 299–306 at p. 300.

[118] Bilder and Vagts, 'Speaking Law to Power', 694.

[119] Edward G. Andrew, 'Hobbes on Conscience Within The Law and Without' (1999) 32 *Canadian Journal of Political Science* 203–225 at 211–215.

[120] Pillard, 'Unitariness and Myopia', 1297–1298.

and endorsed in these memos were, according to Joshua Dratel, 'distorted by only a single, subjective point of view'[121] Their vice, in Bradley Wendel's account, was one of 'ethical solipsism'.[122] In Jack Goldsmith's view, a key problem afflicting the memos was their 'tendentious' and 'one-sided' tone.[123] These memos were written, it seems, by the men of Chapter Seven of *Leviathan*: 'men, vehemently in love with their own new opinions … and obstinately bent to maintain them, [that] gave those opinions also that reverenced name of conscience, as if they would have it seem unlawful, to change or speak against them'.[124]

So, for all their appeals to ethics, outraged international lawyers have sensed the way of (Protestant) conscience to be paved with peril for their rule of law. And the rule of law itself has inspired ambivalence in this context. For the shock of these memos, for some, is the diligence, competence and Ivy League provenance of those whose names they bear.[125] Absent careful readings emphasising their extremism, these memos' (il)legality could perhaps be unremarkable, even laudable. 'On the surface', Jack Goldsmith observes, 'the interrogation opinions seemed like typically thorough and scholarly OLC work'.[126] 'Th[e] men and women [of the Bush Administration] did not believe they were breaking the law, and indeed they took extraordinary steps to ensure that they didn't', Goldsmith reports.[127] Karen Greenberg recited the credentials of the authors in *The Torture Papers*: these were Harvard men, Yale men. Their writings 'do not', she has noted, 'overlook basic ethical and legal questions'. Rather, their memos evidenced a search for 'legally viable argument'.[128] These would-be torturers' accomplices, José Alvarez has observed, are 'distinguished, accomplished, highly credentialed … [and employed as] current or former professors of law at famous law schools'.[129] Their memos enacted some 'clever' manipulation of legal norms, it has been noted elsewhere.[130]

[121] Dratel, 'The Legal Narrative', p. xxiii.

[122] W. Bradley Wendel, 'Legal Ethics and the Separation of Law and Morals' (2005) 91 *Cornell Law Review* 67–128 at 126.

[123] Goldsmith, *The Terror Presidency*, pp. 150–152.

[124] Thomas Hobbes, *Leviathan: Parts I and II* (ed. A. P. Martinich, Peterborough, Ontario: Broadview Press 2005), p. 51.

[125] Weisberg, 'Loose Professionalism', p. 303.

[126] Goldsmith, *The Terror Presidency*, p. 144. [127] *Ibid.*, p. 69.

[128] Greenberg, 'From Fear to Torture', p. xvii.

[129] José E. Alvarez, 'Torturing the Law' (2006) 37 *Case Western Reserve Journal of International Law* 175–233 at 176.

[130] W. Bradley Wendel, 'Professionalism as Interpretation' (2005) 99 *Northwestern University Law Review* 1167–1234 at 1210.

International lawyers have long regarded as fraught the way of a legalism too 'punctilious' or 'excessively legalistic', as some commentators emphasised in relation to the memos.[131] Siding with legality against illegality in this context has not been easy or comfortable because of the diligent, familiar legalism in which these particular illegalities are set. Sensing these dangers, international lawyers draw the 'con' – the 'with' – of the conscience to which they would lay claim with circumspection.

So what would international lawyers invoking transparency against the 'darkness' of the torture memos have us see? What is the effect of the memos' 'original lawlessness' by which international law is to be so transported? What is to emerge, it seems, is a Hobbesian 'public conscience', hoarded as a professional cache.[132] Sensing both the dangers and the promises of quotidian illegality, international lawyers have struggled to remake their professional commonality anew. Faith *in* and *as* professionalism seeks to return law to its professional fold in order that it might be inoculated against excesses both of law and of conscience.

Witnessing torture, international lawyers respond with 'mineness', saying: let this suffering be mine that I might be saved.[133] Witnessing a destructive faculty seemingly in charge of its decisions – will-to-power worn as conscience – international lawyers respond by disavowing the mine, saying: let this be dispersed that we might be saved.[134] Witnessing legalism stinking of cruelty, international lawyers respond with a veil, saying: let this be utter lawlessness that we might be saved.[135] Witnessing the hordes rushing to judge, international lawyers respond with professionalism, saying: let us be the judges that we might not be judged.[136]

Hope, correction, community and conscience: in each mood, legal scholarly commentators writing about the torture memos and related reports have urged international law (or, in some writings, law in

131 Dratel, 'The Legal Narrative', p. xxii; Goldsmith, *The Terror Presidency*, p. 102.

132 Andrew, 'Hobbes on Conscience', 215–225.

133 Horton, 'Legal Ethics and the War on Terror', 301.

134 van Boven, 'The Torture Papers', 151.

135 Note Jack Goldsmith's characterisation of his decision to withdraw the terror memos authored by the Office of Legal Counsel – because of their 'egregious … error[s]' – as one taken 'under a veil of ignorance about government abuses or public perception': Goldsmith, *The Terror Presidency*, pp. 158–159.

136 For example, Bilder and Vagts, 'Speaking Law to Power'.

general) through an ambivalent encounter with illegality towards redemption. The route to redemption most favoured is one of learning to manage better international law's relation to that which it is not, or must not be: that is, to one or other quasi-naturalised domain 'outside' or 'beyond' international law, projected with awe and anxiety.[137] In many of the foregoing accounts, that outside is the world of 'the Washington policy makers' or their counterparts in the executive branches and defence departments of other governments.[138] Elsewhere, it is the secret, 'black[ened]' world of intelligence operatives and military personnel.[139] In many cases, these 'outside' worlds seem to have assumed such determinative or consuming force as to almost supersede questions of legality/illegality. The battle in which international legal scholars cast themselves as engaged is redolent with dangers of disciplinary death and lawyerly obsolescence.

In so doing, legal scholars have reordered the international legal field and its surrounds as if to structure every possible arrangement of its elements. In these narratives of illegality, the historico-social situation of international law is represented in apparent completeness. In the four different registers identified, the relationship of legal expertise to violence is to be stabilised through a restorative reconfiguration of illegalities.

Yet that which has only partially been refused by legal scholarship surrounding the torture memos' release is the unpresentable idea that the interactions between torturer and tortured of which the memos spoke might have been, or might yet be, law-making acts for international law. Tortured detainees have enacted their radical inconsistency with the international legal situation of which they would otherwise be presented as part. What has been evoked without containment by the torture memos' release is an errant illegality combining some of the most routine elements of legal reasoning and practice with extreme violence. Those elements converge, above all, in the figure of a legally enlivened yet still legally unpresentable terror-suspect detainee.

[137] For example, Paust, *Beyond the Law*.

[138] van Boven, 'The Torture Papers', 151; European Parliament, *Report on the Alleged Use of European Countries by the CIA for the Transportation and Illegal Detention of Prisoners*, 30 January 2007, European Parliament Document A6–0020/2007 www.europarl.europa.eu/sides/getDoc.do?type=REPORT&reference=A6-2007-0020&language=EN (accessed 17 September 2012).

[139] James Ross, 'Black Letter Abuse: The US Legal Response to Torture Since 9/11' (2007) 89 *International Review of the Red Cross* 561–590 at 587.

Errant illegality

For all the obsessive attention and regulatory fervour international lawyers and military policy-makers alike have devoted to the figure of the terror-suspect detainee in discussing the torture memos, this figure still seems to elude representation in international law. Despite the prevalence of the term in US domestic policy-making, international lawyers have repeatedly insisted that the identity 'unlawful combatant' does not belong in or to international humanitarian law.[140] Similarly, decades of debate in international legal circles have failed to yield global agreement on how to define terrorism or the terrorist for legal purposes.[141] Awareness of these doctrinal failures or resistances, plus the fact of such figures being afforded relatively limited access to judicial review, have loomed much larger in international lawyers' vision than the many, overlapping layers of transnational and national regulation deployed with a view to these figures' placement. International legal scholars' sense of such detainees as singularly and peculiarly lacking the benefits of law has also tended to impede those scholars' attentiveness to the numerous ways in which access to judicial review is routinely compromised elsewhere and otherwise (by plea bargaining, constraints upon publicly funded legal aid, three-strikes-and-you're-out laws and the like). As a result, the person of an 'unlawful combatant' or terror-suspect detainee – one of the globe's most intensely regulated sites – is still widely perceived as one whose belonging international law has so far failed to ensure.

It is tempting to read this incongruity, as I have elsewhere, as symptomatic of international law's deployment of the sort of law/non-law distinctions on which it routinely relies to affirm its renewability and its relevance.[142] That remains a part of the story here. This chapter, however, ventures another reading of international law's insistence upon this supposed vacuity. In their feature of not being amenable to stable arrangement or classification with other elements of the international legal order, the torture memos' involuntary protagonists suggest an emergent, law-making subjectivity that does not correspond to the traditional register of international legal subjects or would-be subjects.

140 Marco Sassòli, 'Is There a Status of "Unlawful Combatant"?' (2006) 80 *International Law Studies* 57–68; Shlomy Zachary, 'Between the Geneva Conventions: Where Does the Unlawful Combatant Belong?' (2005) 38 *Israeli Law Review* 378–419.

141 Ben Saul, *Defining Terrorism in International Law* (Oxford University Press, 2006).

142 Fleur Johns, 'Guantanamo Bay and the Annihilation of the Exception' (2005) 16 *European Journal of International Law* 613–635.

The incipience that may be evident at this site is not indicated by detainees' supposed non-representation in or by international law at a particular point in time (or the notion that they currently occupy a falsely fabricated legal category), but rather the persistence of their errancy in and for international law. The torture memos and scholarly commentary on those memos have inscribed terror-suspect detainees as more aberrant than is suggested by their status as unrepresented (or inadequately represented) in international law.

Those detained in the war on terror (unnamed doctrinally as well as routinely unnamed as a matter of military record) seem to occupy the absent centre of international legal debate surrounding torture, inhuman and degrading treatment practised in the name of the war on terror. Scholarly commentary on, and official military reactions to, the torture memos have sought to place the figure of the terror-suspect detainee in some reliable way, whether as a figure of abject, mute suffering or as 'a faceless enemy whose hatred of the United States knew no limits'.[143] Yet these efforts have failed.

International legal texts can draw near to the figure of the terror-suspect detainee in a posture of empathy, but cannot embrace him or her for fear of his or her agency; for fear, that is, of contamination by whatever deadly desires and faith-based motivations he or she might bring to bear. Hence, commentators vie to place themselves at the greatest possible remove from the prospect of aiding 'the' cause of terrorism. For international lawyers, it is those who would rewrite legal norms who risk conceding a 'victory for terrorism'.[144] So too, empathy is quickly redirected towards an embrace of, and lamentation for, the familiar: for Harold Koh, for instance, the 'American soldiers [at risk of being] tortured by foreign captors' and the 'soul' of the United States 'as a people'.[145] The 'world without torture' that Koh has sketched is, by implication, all the more reassuring by virtue of its banishment of the anxiety-producing figure of the tortured detainee.[146] Each drawing close to this figure triggers a drawing away, such that international law remains unable to redress the apparent unbonding from the international legal order that was, for international lawyers at least, one of

143 LTG Anthony R. Jones and MG George R. Fay, 'Article 15-6 Investigation of the Abu Ghraib Prison and 205th Military Intelligence Brigade', 23 August 2004, http://slate.com/features/whatistorture/pdfs/FayJonesReport.pdf (accessed 17 September 2012).

144 Ige Dekker, 'Declaration on the Fight Against Terrorism and the Protection of Human Rights – A Resolvable Conflict' (2003) 14 *Helsinki Monitor* 321–327 at 327.

145 Koh, 'A World Without Torture', 659, 661. 146 *Ibid.*

the most alarming aspects of the torture memos' release. The repeated attempts at substitution described above – seeking to transpose the law itself into the role of mute suffering intended for the terror-suspect detainee – indicate the profound and persistent unrecognisability of the latter for international law.

Similarly, for the international law on torture, inhuman and degrading treatment, the tortured must remain largely prostrate; needy of protection, *ex post facto* hearing as 'victims', and little else. In relation to torture, the limits of international legality have been designed for interpretative realisation above or around the body of the tortured, but that body is to remain inert in the process. The definition of torture set forth in the Torture Convention, for instance, concerns itself wholly with the purposes of the torturer and the official consent or instigation granted to the torturer. The tortured is vested indirectly with rights, but those rights' sum total is no more than the status of being recognised as the person upon whom torture has been inflicted. All that registers of that person is his or her 'severe pain or suffering, whether physical or mental'.[147]

That which emerged, however, at the site edged by the errant detainee of the torture memos was the possibility that some of international law's primary representations – its claims to stand opposed to unquestioned and unquestionable violence and to be capable of managing the processes of its own making – might not be sustainable. This was precisely what was signified by the torture memos' public release, an occurrence experienced as both exceptional and universal. The torture memos documented a process of law-making saturated with violence. Put in the reverse, they documented violence routinised through law: a practice of torture ('extreme' illegality) made continuous with mundane forms of legal work (routine illegality, or the recitation of viable or almost-viable legal argument in an envelope-pushing legal memorandum). Through the torture memos, international lawyers were invited to see sites of violent detention as loci of law-making and to see more or less routine practices of legal reasoning ('envelope-pushing') as pathways to those sites.

The torture memos revealed torture as a field of international legality/illegality within which detainees involved were far from inert. Rather, detainees were actively resistant to, and participating in, a process recognised by all involved as law-making: a violently embodied

[147] Torture Convention.

process entailing the promulgation of norms readied for application to other people and in other settings. Acting on contradictions latent within such categories as 'unlawful combatants', detainees have intervened to assume the posture of something like a detainee-law-maker. One such detainee, Abu Zubaydeh, reported the following:

> I collapsed and lost consciousness on several occasions. Eventually the torture was stopped by the intervention of the doctor. I was told during this period that I was one of the first to receive these interrogation techniques, so no rules applied. It felt like they were experimenting and trying out techniques to be used later on other people. At the end of this period two women and a man came to interrogate me. I was still naked and, because of this, I refused to answer any questions. So they again repeatedly slapped me in the face and smashed me against the wall using the towel around my neck.[148]

In Zubaydeh's account, he 'refuse[d] to answer any questions' out of protest at his continued deprivation of clothing, mindful that these were 'techniques to be used later on other people'. Elsewhere, reports reveal recurrent techniques of resistance, each marking an attempt to subvert and reorder the law-making routines and relations in which detainees were called to participate. Affidavits of those reporting violent abuse, for example, document the efforts of detainees to recall and record publicly each others' names as well as those of the soldiers occupying the sites of their abuse: efforts sometimes verging on the obsessive. The naming of names was, of course, vital to the evidence-gathering exercise in which detainees invited to give sworn statements understood themselves to be assisting.[149] Yet the ritual incantation of names in these statements seemed, at times, to exceed the requirements of evidentiary precision. By these methods, detainees sought, it seemed, to fill the space of their detention with a singularity and a collective agency that their captors would refuse them. The sworn statement of Nori Samir Gunbar Al-Yasseri is indicative in this respect:

> After this they make Hashim ... stand in front of me and they forced me to slap him in the face, but I refused cause [*sic*] he is my friend. After this they asked Hashim to hit me, so he punched my stomach. I asked him to do that so they don't beat him like they had beaten me when I refused to hit Hashim.

[148] ICRC, 'ICRC Report on the Treatment of Fourteen "High Value Detainees" in CIA Custody', p. 31.

[149] On the significance of detainees' naming as a site of struggle more generally, see Eric Schmitt, 'U.S. Shifts, Giving Detainee Names to the Red Cross', *The New York Times*, 22 August 2009, A1, www.nytimes.com/2009/08/23/world/middleeast/23detain.html (accessed 17 September 2012).

Nori Samir, Hussein, Mustafa Mahadi Saleh, Hashim, Hiadar, Hathem, Ahmed Sabri; those are the names of the people who were there at this night which felt like 1000 nights ... I don't know the soldiers names, but I know what one of them looks like and this was their supervisor. The reason why I know him [is] because I saw him every single night I spent there.[150]

Shalan Said Alsharoni's sworn statement revealed a similar insistence upon proper names as markers in a setting otherwise disorienting and lifted, as it were, out of time and space:

One of those days the guards tortured the prisoners. Those guards are Grainer, Davis and another man. First they tortured a man whose name is Amjid Iraqi ... And after that they beat up an Iraqi whose name is Assad ... Grainer beat up a man whose name is Ali the Syrian ... This is what I saw and what I remember to be true.[151]

Other statements recorded detainees straining publicly to register, with their every sensory power, the exact details of what was happening to them, including faint clues as to their locale, as though they might, by this means, have been able to undo the conditions of sensory deprivation and profound isolation to which they were subjected. A sworn statement provided by Kasim Mehaddi Hilas that detailed abuse to which he had been exposed as a detainee included the following statement: 'Not one night for all the time I was there passed without me seeing, hearing or feeling what was happening to me.'[152] Detainee Khaled Shaik Mohammed reported, of one location, that '[d]uring my time at this place of detention I could hear planes taking off and landing', which led him to suggest, 'I think the place was Bagram'.[153] Later in the same report he remarked:

I could see at one point that there was snow on the ground ... I think the country was Poland. I think this because on one occasion a water bottle was

150 Nori Samir Gunbar Al-Yasseri, 'Sworn Statement - Al-Yasseri, Nori Samir Gunbar taken at Baghdad Correctional Facility on 17 January 2004', media.washingtonpost.com/wp-srv/world/iraq/abughraib/7787.pdf (accessed 17 September 2012).

151 Shalan S. Alsharoni, 'Translation of Statement Provided by Shalan Said Alsharoni, Detainee # 150422 1630/17 Jan 04', Abu Ghraib Prison Complex, Abu Ghraib, Iraq, www.washingtonpost.com/wp-srv/world/iraq/abughraib/150422.pdf (accessed 17 September 2012).

152 Kasim M. Hilas, 'Translation of Statement Provided by Kasim Mehaddi Hilas, Detainee # 151108, 1300/ 18 Jan 04', media.washingtonpost.com/wp-srv/world/iraq/abughraib/151108.pdf (accessed 17 September 2012).

153 ICRC, 'ICRC Report on the Treatment of Fourteen "High Value Detainees" in CIA Custody', p. 33.

brought to me without the label removed. It had an email address ending in '.pl'. The central-heating system was an old style one that I would expect only to see in countries of the former communist system.[154]

Like other detainees, Khaled Shaik Mohammed also insisted upon assuming the power of naming and at least a nominal power of repositioning in his account:

It was here that the most intense interrogation occurred, led by three experienced CIA interrogators, all over 65 years old and all strong and well trained. They were '*emirs*'. Although of course they never revealed their own names, I gave them names by which I could refer to them, all beginning with 'Abu'. I think that 'Abu Captain' was of South American origin, whereas 'Abu Hannan' was perhaps of Moroccan origin and 'Abu White' was of Eastern European descent.[155]

Other techniques too were used to enact an incongruent, legal-illegal subject position within international law and thereby shift the register of the discipline. Through hunger strikes and suicide attempts, detainees reclaimed and reactivated bodies that international law would render torpid.[156]

For these detainees, the sites of their torture were not sites of simple or unitary illegality. That transnational norms surrounding their treatment and the treatment of others similarly categorised may have been violated was but a part of the claims they were making. Rather, they were engaged in a violent struggle over those norms' very formation, a struggle to which they brought every means of resistance and every possibility of reoccupation available to them. It was this violent, novatory, legal struggle that surfaced in the torture memos and rendered them supernumerary to that which international law surrounding torture was in the habit of counting. In seeking to assemble a novel legal regime around the sites of detainees' torture and abuse, the lawyers who wrote the torture memos were framing those sites in one sense just as the detainees quoted above had done: as sites for international law's profound remaking and violent reassertion. They were acknowledging, furthermore, that the processes of law-making ongoing at these sites were being vigorously contested and that, accordingly, they

[154] *Ibid.*, pp. 34–35. [155] *Ibid.*, p. 35.

[156] Avril McDonald, 'The Year in Review' (2005) 8 *Yearbook of International Humanitarian Law* 211–264 at 222–223.

were not processes over which either torturer or tortured (let alone the international law on sources as habitually known) had anything like complete control.

At the very point of their most insistent erasure by or within scholarly understandings of international legal order, detainees' legal-illegal agency seemed, at times, to puncture the surface of that order. Vital to that puncturing, it seemed, was the constitutive significance of illegality in international law combined with the relative inaccessibility of illegality's positive content. Here as elsewhere, illegality was associated with the making of law even as it had to become, in legality, the contrary of itself and vice versa. This generative yet absent dimension of torture's illegality was not mediated through understandings of what it could mean for those whom it may affect. (What, precisely, would it mean for a terror-suspect-detainee to be regarded as a law-maker? Is international law-making, in any event, predicated on meaningfulness?) It did not seem to arise from telic thinking. Rather, illegality's generative effect in this context arose from a failure of international legal meaning, namely that indicated by the unpresentability described above. It is in international law's unmaking, through legalised illegality, that the errant subjectivity of a detainee-law-maker has come to light.

Conclusion

International law is, conventionally, made of treaties, custom and general principles of law. Yet international law is also made of illegalities. Illegalities operate as limit concepts for international law (non-mathematically speaking). Illegalities encompass and domesticate happenstance: the idea that someone in the South China Sea, for instance, just decides, or is impelled by material circumstances, faith or some other factor, to take violent action that amounts to piracy. By characterising such action as international illegality, international law sets itself against the world. At the same time, this characterisation affirms the capacity of international law (and of people acting through international law) to be both world-making and of the world. International law says, in effect, this is not merely the worldly (or other-worldly) occurrence of violence, rationally explicable or otherwise. This act is to be experienced as an international crime, that is, as an offence concerning a public, in this instance, a public cast on a global scale.[157] This act must be understood to be about society, community, humanity or some other comparable unity posited on the plane of the international. This act is about and hence for *us*, however that human 'us' may be configured.

Illegalities also shadow international law and in that capacity they may bolster or undermine. As the nether side of envelope-pushing, international illegality stands at an infinitesimal remove from international legality (that is, at a remove both minuscule and infinitely divisible). In this mode, international illegality is international lawfulness but for the barest and yet the most significant of margins. For those doing international legal work, the prospect of tipping over this edge may terrify or inspire, paralyse or motivate. Others doing international legal work may consider this prospect only voyeuristically, if at all, assured of its remoteness from their particular version of the international legal mundane.

In the torture memos' release, and the scholarly commentary thereon, international law grappled at once with illegality at its most confrontational and illegality at its most diminutive. International legal envelope-pushing was seen to have a lethally sharp edge. Torture was seen to have an international legal paper trail both lengthy and, in some respects at least, unremarkable. At the same time, the paradoxical inaccessibility of these legalised illegalities surfaced in the international legal literature surrounding the torture memos. This may have been manifest most clearly in the difficulty of rendering the figure of the tortured or inhumanely treated detainee graspable by international law, notwithstanding the profusion of legal or quasi-legal words voiced by and about that figure. Subject only to articulation through legality, illegality, its agents and its products often elude representation in international law.

The difficulty of reconciling illegality with and within international law may, in part, have impelled the fervent efforts of restoration and delimitation described in the second part of this chapter relating to the torture memos' release. Those efforts may be understood as attempts at auto-erasure on the part of international law, combined with an aspiration for legality's renewal. Yet the incommensurability of illegality (and of torture, in particular) may also open international

[157] R. A. Duff, *Answering for Crime: Responsibility and Liability in the Criminal Law* (Oxford: Hart Publishing, 2007), pp. 141–2 (crime as a public wrong that is 'not a wrong that injures the public' but one that 'properly concerns the public').

law to the actions of a counter-disciplinary subjectivity, such as that of the norm-making detainee. In the actions, products and discomforts of illegality, contending claims to international lawfulness persist, indeed proliferate, just as they do in the domains of extra-legality to which the next chapter will turn.

3 Black holes and the outside within: extra-legality in international law

If illegality is international legality's shadow and its sometime propellant, then extra-legality is quite literally something else. Illegality may, at times, be intensified as extra-legal outlawry: through the expulsive designation of perpetrators of international crime as 'enemies of mankind', for instance.[1] Extra-legality is not, however, necessarily identified with the transgression of law. To give effect to extra-legality in international law is to give shape to a domain, situation or set of forces outside of law, whether temporarily or permanently. Extra-legal domains are, nonetheless, jurisdictions. That is, they are spaces from which the authority of law gets spoken or performed, albeit often in a register of disavowal or differentiation.[2] This chapter examines one particular rendering of such a jurisdiction in international legal practice and the dispositions that it engenders.

The focus of this chapter is the counter-terrorist detention facility at Guantánamo Bay, Cuba. In much of the international legal literature concerning this site, Guantánamo Bay has been characterised as an 'anomalous zone', a 'black hole', or an insurgence of 'utter lawlessness'.[3]

[1] Gerry Simpson, *Law, War and Crime: War Crimes Trials and the Reinvention of International Law* (Cambridge and Malden: Polity, 2007), pp. 159–171.

[2] Shaunnagh Dorsett and Shaun McVeigh, 'Questions of Jurisdiction' in Shaun McVeigh (ed.), *Jurisprudence of Jurisdiction* (Abingdon and New York: Routledge-Cavendish, 2007), pp. 3–18 at p. 3.

[3] These descriptors, often cited in international legal literature, are drawn from, respectively: Gerald Neuman, 'Anomalous Zones' (1996) 48 *Stanford Law Review* 1197–1234 at 1228–1233 (Neuman was, it must be noted, analysing the legal status of Guantánamo Bay at a time before it was turned over to usage as a counter-terrorist detention facility); *R (on the application of Abbasi et al)* v. *Secretary of State for Foreign and Commonwealth Affairs* [2002] EWCA Civ 1598 at para. 32; and Johan Steyn, 'Guantanamo Bay: The Legal Black Hole', 27th F. A. Mann Lecture, 25 November 2003, www.statewatch.org/news/2003/nov/guantanamo.pdf (accessed 17 September

Guantánamo Bay is, in these accounts, a space that international law 'proper' has failed to fill, whether due to the pre-existence of a terminal politics, or thanks to the pseudo-legal machinations of a renegade cadre of legal professionals. Guantánamo Bay's presence and persistence on the international legal scene, such accounts imply, represents a singular, grotesque instance of law's breakdown or its subordination to determinants outside itself.

This chapter begins, however, from a somewhat different starting point. Here, the plight of Guantánamo Bay detainees past and present is cast less as an outcome of the suspension, breakdown or subordination of international and domestic law than of elaborate regulatory efforts by a range of legal authorities. The detention camps of Guantánamo Bay are above all works of legal representation and classification. They are spaces where law and liberal proceduralism have been speaking and operating in excess.[4] In some respects, these efforts of representation and classification are more or less coextensive with normalities of international legal practice.

This chapter will develop this reading by examining legal practices constitutive of the jurisdictional order of the Guantánamo Bay Naval Base. These practices will be examined 'from without', as it were, by reference to the written work of international legal scholars writing about Guantánamo Bay. They will also be examined 'from within', by reference to some of the textually recorded experiences and techniques of decision-makers working in and around Guantánamo Bay.[5]

2012). David Dyzenhaus introduces the related yet distinct idea of a 'grey hole'. This is 'a legal space in which there are some legal constraints on executive action – it is not a lawless void – but the constraints are so insubstantial that they pretty well permit government to do as it pleases': David Dyzenhaus, 'Schmitt v. Dicey: Are States of Emergency Inside or Outside the Legal Order?' (2006) 27 *Cardozo Law Review* 2005–2040 at 2018. A grey hole, Dyzenhaus argues, 'is in substance a legal black hole, but it is worse because the procedural rights available to the detainee cloak the lack of substance' (at 2026). In his critique of the US Supreme Court's decision in *Hamdi* (at 2023–2026 and 2039), Dyzenhaus makes apparent that he regards Guantánamo Bay (where Hamdi was detained) as a grey hole that is in substance a black hole.

[4] *Contra* William Scheuerman, 'Globalization, Exceptional Powers, and the Erosion of Liberal Democracy' (1999) 93 *Radical Philosophy* 14–23.

[5] One of the implicit claims of this chapter, however, is that this 'without' and 'within' are mutually constitutive. That is, decision-makers at Guantánamo Bay seem to have acted (at least at times) with attention to the interpretation of their actions by 'external' critics, including international lawyers. At the same

The first part of this chapter presents a brief sketch of the jurisdictional order of the Guantánamo Bay Naval Base, as constructed primarily in the final decade of the twentieth century and the early part of the twenty-first. The second and third parts will examine the claims and characterisations of extra-legality made in respect of this order and otherwise, as these have circulated in international legal scholarship. This chapter will then turn to a quasi-ethnographic account of the legal regime operative at Guantánamo Bay, by reference to texts in the public arena. As this account will show, the jurisdiction of Guantánamo Bay is conditioned by extra-legalities, but these extra-legalities are, somewhat paradoxically, highly regularised through legal work and writing.

Finally, this chapter will explore what the extra-legalities so made may add to or withdraw from the possibilities of international law surrounding Guantánamo Bay and otherwise. Far from emboldening sovereign and non-sovereign forms of political agency under conditions of radical doubt, this chapter argues, the 'extra-legal' regime of Guantánamo Bay to which international legal scholarship has helped give shape seems dedicated to producing experiences of having no option, no doubt and no responsibility. For many who invoke international law in view of it, Guantánamo Bay seems to generate an experience of having their actions wholly and necessarily predetermined by norms, including norms surrounding the framing of extra-legality. Accordingly, what one sees traces of in the record surrounding Guantánamo Bay are successive attempts to domesticate the political possibilities occasioned by an experience of the exception – that is, an experience of operating under circumstances not wholly pre-codified by pre-existing norms. It is by reason of its effects in this respect, I would argue, that the legal regime of the Guantánamo Bay detention camps and its replication beyond Cuba merit interrogation and resistance.

time, international legal scholars have been among those 'outsiders' whose representations of Guantánamo Bay have helped to constitute the jurisdiction of the site. The distinction to which I am alluding here is not, therefore, strictly geographic or professional (military lawyers, for instance, have written as 'external' critics as well as in the capacity of Guantánamo Bay 'insiders'). Rather, the distinction is positional or political: some legal writers have positioned themselves as external critics of the decision-making apparatus concerned with Guantánamo Bay, while others tend to locate themselves – and to be located – within that apparatus.

The legal order of 'anomaly'

Guantánamo Bay is a forty-five square mile area of Cuba occupied by the United States pursuant to a perpetual lease agreement entered into in 1903.[6] Under that lease, the United States obtained the right to use the area for coaling and naval operations.[7] The text of the lease agreement provides inter alia that 'the United States shall exercise complete jurisdiction and control over and within such areas' while reserving to Cuba 'ultimate sovereignty'.[8] Accordingly, since December 1903, Guantánamo Bay has been operated as a US naval base, its area closed to private use, access and navigation without US authorisation.[9] The base maintains its own schools, power system, water supply and internal transportation system.[10] In one commentary, as of 2003, 'the base population ha[d] grown to 6,000, and ... in addition to McDonald's, there [were] now Pizza Hut, Subway and KFC [franchises]. Another gym [was] being built, and town houses, and a four-year college [was about to open] ... The base commander describe[d] it as "small-town America"'.[11] Having previously been dedicated wholly to military and related purposes, in the early 1990s this 'small town' was re-fashioned as a detention camp for those seeking asylum in the United States.[12]

[6] Agreement for the Lease to the United States of Lands in Cuba for Coaling and Naval Stations, February 23, 1903, US-Cuba T.S. No. 418. This agreement, as supplemented by a supplementary agreement of 2 July 1903, was confirmed in a treaty between the United States and Cuba, signed at Washington on 29 May 1934. See Treaty Between the United States of America and Cuba, 29 May 1934, US-Cuba T.S. No. 866, avalon.law.yale.edu/20th_century/dip_cuba001.asp (accessed 17 September 2012).

[7] On the legal status of the Guantánamo Bay Naval Base, see generally Gerald Neuman, 'Closing the Guantánamo Loophole' (2004) 50 *Loyola Law Review* 1–66 at 34–44.

[8] Agreement for the Lease to the United States of Lands in Cuba.

[9] By an executive order signed by the US President on 1 May 1941, Guantánamo Bay was declared a 'Naval Defensive Sea Area' and a 'Naval Air Space Reservation': Executive Order 8749 of May 1, 1941, 6 Fed. Reg. 2252 (3 May 1941). As such, it is an area closed to all vessels and aircraft other than public vessels of the United States, vessels engaged in Cuban trade, and public aircraft of the United States.

[10] Neuman, 'Anomalous Zones', 1228.

[11] Neuman, 'Closing the Guantánamo Loophole', 35 [footnotes omitted], quoting Nancy Gibbs, with Viveca Novak, 'Inside "the Wire"', *Time Magazine*, 30 November 2003, www.time.com/time/magazine/article/0,9171,552060,00.html (accessed 17 September 2012) and Carol Rosenberg, 'New Chief Brings Guantánamo Up to Date', *Miami Herald*, 25 October 2003, A15.

[12] For information – historical and current – published by the US navy about the naval base installed at Guantánamo Bay, see www.jtfgtmo.southcom.mil/ and www.cnic.navy.mil/Guantanamo/index.htm (both accessed 17 September 2012).

Between 1991 and 1996, more than 36,000 Haitian and more than 20,000 Cuban asylum-seekers were interned for varying periods in Guantánamo Bay, pursuant to US immigration policies of interdiction, administrative detention, offshore processing and, wherever possible, repatriation.[13] Thereafter, other than short-term operations in 1996 and 1997, the migrant processing operation at Guantánamo Bay was wound down. In January 2002, however, shortly after initiating a military campaign in Afghanistan, the United States began transferring hundreds of persons captured during military operations in Afghanistan to Guantánamo Bay. There they were held, for the most part without charge, as 'unlawful combatants'.[14] According to *The New York Times*, 779 persons were detained at Guantánamo Bay between 11 January 2002 and 11 September 2012.[15] As of 11 September 2012, the detainee population at Guantánamo Bay had declined to 151 due, primarily, to detainee transfers to other nations.[16]

In a 2001 Military Order and a series of subsequent orders issued by the Department of Defense, the US Executive constructed an elaborate legal regime surrounding these persons.[17] This regime was further elaborated by legislation, namely, the Detainee Treatment Act of 2005, the Military Commissions Act of 2006 and the Military Commissions

[13] See generally Harold Hongju Koh, 'America's Offshore Refugee Camps' (1994) 29 *University of Richmond Law Review* 139–174.

[14] The characterisation of detainees as 'unlawful combatants' or 'enemy combatants' rests, in part, on the claim that they do not satisfy the test for those engaged in the theatre of war (and thereby entitled to prisoner of war status) under Article 4(2) of the Third Geneva Convention. See, for example, *Hamdan v. Rumsfeld*, 126 S. Ct. 2749 (2006) at 2761, 2777, 2782, 2805 and 2832. The term 'unlawful combatant' is, however, taken from a 1942 (pre-Geneva Convention) US Supreme Court case: *US ex rel. Quirin v. Cox*, 317 US 1 (1942). In that case, the US Supreme Court upheld the use of military commissions for German saboteurs who were captured on US soil. This term has never been defined by an international agreement. See K. Elizabeth Dahlstrom, 'The Executive Policy Toward Detention and Trial of Foreign Citizens at Guantánamo Bay' (2003) 21 *Berkeley Journal of International Law* 662–682 at note 2.

[15] *The New York Times*, 'The Guantánamo Docket', http://projects.nytimes.com/guantanamo (ongoing, accessed 17 September 2012).

[16] *Ibid.*

[17] See Detention, Treatment, and Trial of Certain Non-Citizens in the War Against Terrorism, Military Order of November 13, 2001, 66 Fed. Reg. 57,833 (2001). For Department of Defense policies and fact sheets concerning Guantánamo Bay, see www.defense.gov/news/detainees.html (accessed 17 September 2012).

Act of 2009.[18] Since 2004, US federal court rulings have also played a significant role in reshaping aspects of this regime.[19]

The particular, tailored features of this regime have been justified, above all, by the detainees' unorthodox and peculiarly threatening status, namely, their compound illegality as 'unlawful combatants'. By recourse to this nomenclature, Guantánamo Bay detainees are cast both beyond the pale of non-violent political discourse and beyond the legal bounds of warfare. Yet although the terminology applied to the Guantánamo Bay detainees implies an extra-legal status, these detainees have, since the outset, been the focus of painstaking work of legal classification. By way of illustration, one might look to a press briefing given on 13 February 2004 by Paul Butler, Principal Deputy Assistant Secretary of Defense for Special Operations and Low Intensity Conflict. Mr Butler detailed an elaborate, multi-stage screening and evaluation process through which each detainee is passed. In Mr Butler's description, an 'integrated team of interrogators, analysts, behavioural scientists and regional experts' work alongside military lawyers and federal law enforcement officials to decipher and consider 'all relevant information'. '[W]e have a process', Mr Butler announced confidently, 'and ... that process will take its own course'.[20]

Thus, even before the June 2004 rulings of the US Supreme Court in *Hamdi* v. *Rumsfeld*[21] and *Rasul* v. *Bush*[22] affirmed the entitlement of Guantánamo Bay detainees to a 'meaningful opportunity to contest the factual basis for th[eir] detention before a neutral decisionmaker' and their capacity to invoke the jurisdiction of US federal courts,[23]

[18] Title XVIII of the National Defense Authorization Act for Fiscal Year 2010 (Military Commissions Act of 2009), Pub.L. 111–84, 123 Stat. 2190 (2009), codified at 10 USC §§ 1801–1807 (2009); Military Commissions Act of 2006, Pub.L. 109–366, 120 Stat. 2600 (2006), codified at 10 USC §§ 948–949 (2006); Detainee Treatment Act of 2005, Pub. L. No. 109–148, 119 Stat. 2739 (2005), codified at 10 USC §§ 1001–1006 (2005).

[19] See, in particular, *Hamdi* v. *Rumsfeld* 124 S. Ct. 2633 (2004); *Rasul* v. *Bush* 124 S. Ct. 2686 (2004); *Hamdan* v. *Rumsfeld* 126 S. Ct. 2749 (2006); *Boumediene* v. *Bush* 128 S. Ct. 2229 (2008). For an overview as of January 2010, see Benjamin Wittes, Robert Chesney and Rabea Benhalim, 'The Emerging Law of Detention: The Guantanamo Cases as Lawmaking', University of Texas Law, Public Law Research Paper No. 165, 22 January 2010, www.ssrn.com/abstract=1540601 (accessed 17 September 2012).

[20] Briefing on Detainee Operations at Guantánamo Bay, 13 February 2004, www.defense.gov/transcripts/transcript.aspx?transcriptid=2071 (accessed 17 September 2012).

[21] 124 S. Ct. 2633 (2004). [22] 124 S. Ct. 2686 (2004).

[23] *Hamdi* v. *Rumsfeld* 124 S. Ct. 2633 (2004) at 2635 (per O'Connor J for the Court, with whom Rehnquist CJ, Kennedy and Breyer JJ joined, Souter and Ginsburg JJ concurring in the judgment but dissenting with the reasoning in part, and Scalia, Stevens and Thomas JJ dissenting); *Rasul* v. *Bush* 124 S. Ct. 2686 (2004) at 2698 (per

the Department of Defense had produced a panoply of regulations concerning the handling of detainees. These included mechanisms for annual review (by an Administrative Review Board established in May 2004) of the grounds for each enemy combatant's continued detention or eligibility for transfer or release.[24] They also included provisions for detainees' trial before specially convened Military Commissions.[25]

After the US Supreme Court's June 2004 rulings, the normative and institutional network governing the 'process' at Guantánamo Bay became even denser. On 7 July 2004, the Deputy Secretary of Defense promulgated an order establishing a Combatant Status Review Tribunal. This Tribunal was charged with determining whether persons in the detention camps at Guantánamo Bay had been properly classified as enemy combatants.[26] This, alongside the Military Commissions and the Administrative Review Board, added a third body to the line-up of specialist legal institutions convened at Guantánamo Bay. Later in the same month, the Secretary of the Navy produced a lengthy

Stevens J for the Court, with whom Kennedy J concurred, Rehnquist CJ, Scalia and Thomas JJ dissenting).

[24] See Administrative Review Procedures for Enemy Combatants in the Custody of the Department of Defense at Guantánamo Bay Naval Base, Cuba, Deputy Secretary of Defense Order OSD 06942-04 of May 11, 2004.

[25] Following the Military Commissions' initial convening by 2001 Military Order (Military Order of November 13, 2001, 66 Fed. Reg. 57, 833 (2001)), Military Commission Instructions were issued by the Department of Defense in 2003 and 2004 (www.globalsecurity.org/security/library/policy/dod/mil-commission-instructions2003.htm, accessed 17 September 2012). Legislative enactments thereafter sought to restore the primacy of the Military Commission process in the face of a succession of Supreme Court rulings. Following the ruling in *Rasul* v. *Bush* 124 S. Ct. 2686 (2004) that federal judges had jurisdiction to review the executive's authority to employ military detention in particular cases and the process of detention employed, Congress enacted the Detainee Treatment Act of 2005. Following the ruling in *Hamdan* v. *Rumsfeld* 126 S. Ct. 2749 (2006) that, absent more specific congressional authorisation, military commissions lacked the power to proceed because their structure and procedures violated both the Uniform Code of Military Justice and the four Geneva Conventions signed in 1949, Congress passed the Military Commissions Act of 2006. Further modifications to the Military Commissions' procedures were introduced in the Military Commissions Act of 2009. Following both these 2006 and 2009 Acts, new regulations and manuals were issued to govern the Military Commission process. These are available at www.mc.mil/legalresources/MilitaryCommissionsDocuments.aspx (accessed 17 September 2012). Subsequent developments in relation to the Military Commissions are outlined below in notes 30 and 31 and related text.

[26] Deputy Secretary for Defense, Memorandum: Order Establishing Combatant Status Review Tribunal, 7 July 2004, www.defense.gov/news/jul2004/d20040707review.pdf (accessed 17 September 2012)

memorandum outlining procedures to govern this Tribunal's hearings, including (rather bizarrely) a standard form script for the conduct of a hearing.[27] Furthermore, by order of the Defense Secretary Donald Rumsfeld on 16 July 2004, a new Office of Detainee Affairs was created within the Pentagon to coordinate 'around 100 inquiries, investigations, or assessments' that were then said to be ongoing in respect of detainees' handling by US military police.[28]

For all its determination to close Guantánamo Bay, the Obama administration brought to this institutional architecture still further tweaks and crenellations.[29] In January 2009, Military Commission proceedings were suspended pursuant to Executive Order of the President pending review of US detention policy by two specially convened task forces.[30] A little over two years later, however, Military Commission proceedings were resumed in light of procedural changes (introduced by the Military Commissions Act of 2009 and related measures) and legislative obstruction of the transfer of Guantánamo detainees to the United States for prosecution.[31] At the same time, the Periodic Review

[27] Secretary of the Navy, Memorandum: Implementation of Combatant Status Review Tribunal Procedures for Enemy Combatants Detained at Guantánamo Bay Naval Base, Cuba, 29 July 2004, www.globalsecurity.org/security/library/news/2004/07/sec-040730-dod01.htm (accessed 17 September 2012).

[28] Jacquelyn S. Porth, 'Pentagon Creates New Policy Office to Review Detainee Issues', *Washington File*, Bureau of International Information Programs, U.S. Department of State, 16 July 2004, www.iwar.org.uk/news-archive/2004/07-16.htm (accessed 17 September 2012).

[29] By 22 January Executive Order, President Obama set out an intention to close Guantánamo Bay as soon as practicable, and no later than one year from the date of the order: See Executive Order 13492 of 22 January 2009, 'Review and Disposition of Individuals Detained at the Guantánamo Bay Naval Base and Closure of Detention Facilities', 74 Fed. Reg. 4897 (27 January 2009).

[30] *Ibid.* (inter alia directing military prosecutors to seek a suspension of legal proceedings before the Military Commissions pending review of the process). See Peter Finn, 'Obama Seeks Halt to Legal Proceedings at Guantánamo', *The Washington Post*, 21 January 2009, p. A.2. In connection with this measure, President Obama convened two task forces to review relevant aspects of US detention policy: the Special Task Force on Detainee Disposition and the Special Task Force on Interrogation and Transfer Policies. See Executive Order 13491 of 22 January 2009, 'Ensuring Lawful Interrogations', 74 Fed. Reg. 4893 (27 January 2009) and Executive Order 13493 of 22 January 2009, 'Review of Detention Policy Options', 74 Fed. Reg. 4901 (27 January 2009).

[31] See The White House, Office of the Press Secretary, 'Fact Sheet: New Actions on Guantánamo and Detainee Policy', 7 March 2011, www.whitehouse.gov/the-press-office/2011/03/07/fact-sheet-new-actions-guant-namo-and-detainee-policy (accessed 17 September 2012); Ed Pilkington, 'Obama Lifts Suspension on Military

Board was introduced in place of the Administrative Review Board and Combatant Status Review Tribunal to assess the continued detention of persons held at Guantánamo Bay without having been convicted of a crime or having formal charges pending against them.[32]

Far from a space of 'utter lawlessness' then, one finds in Guantánamo Bay a space filled to the brim with expertise, procedure, scrutiny and analysis. Amid the work of the Military Commissions and the Periodic Review Board (as well as that of the latter's predecessors, the Administrative Review Board and the Combatant Status Review Tribunal) and the other inquiries and task forces mentioned above, it is not upholding the rule of law that seems tricky. Rather, it is the possibility of encountering the yet-to-be-governed (extra-legal) exception that seems difficult to contemplate. Then again, extra-legality has always been difficult to place in international legal writing.

International legal scholarship and the assertion of extra-legality

Among the cartographies of legality that circulate in international legal scholarship, with respect to Guantánamo Bay and otherwise, renderings of extra-legality are numerous and varied. At times, these tend towards the dragon-filled.[33] Extra-legality is, in many accounts, identified with horror and dysfunction of one kind or another. This is the case even as efforts to access an extra-legal sphere, force or practice may remain highly legalistic. International legal scholars acknowledge, for instance, that 'states engage in legal interpretative dispute when

Terror Trials at Guantánamo Bay', *Guardian*, 7 March 2011, www.guardian.co.uk/world/2011/mar/07/guantanamo-military-terrorism-trials-resume (accessed 17 September 2012). For the legislative obstructions in question, see note 100 below.

[32] Executive Order 13567 of 7 March 2011, 'Periodic Review of Individuals Detained at Guantánamo Bay Naval Station Pursuant to Authorization to Use Military Force', 76 Fed. Reg. 13277 (10 March 2011). For discussion of the Periodic Review Board's relationship to pre-existing bodies, see Dick Jackson, 'Introductory Note to Executive Order 13567: Periodic Review of Individuals Detained at Guantánamo Bay Naval Station Pursuant to the Authorization for Use of Military Force and Accompanying Presidential Fact Sheet: New Actions on Guantánamo and Detainee Policy' (2011) 50 *International Legal Materials* 928–936.

[33] The Hunt-Lenox Globe (circa 1503–1507) in the New York Public Library famously features the phrase *hic sunt dracones* – 'here are dragons' – on an unmapped portion of its face. Elsewhere, dragons and monsters of various kinds feature pictorially and textually in medieval cartography, particularly on maps' southern and eastern margins. See generally Lorraine Daston and Katharine Park, *Wonders and the Order of Nature, 1150–1750* (New York: Zone Books, 1998), Chapter V.

seeking to escape international legality'.[34] Nonetheless, a recurrent feature of commentary on such efforts of 'escape' is the sense of an outside replete with death and disorder. Emergency suspensions of certain kinds of legal constraint are charged with 'ever-present danger ... [of] abuse'.[35] Escalating recourse to 'extra-legal methods of apprehending foreign suspects' is identified with the prospect of 'a Hobbesian state of nature ... replac[ing] our current notion of international criminal justice'.[36] International lawyers warn of 'prospect[s] both frightening and horrifying' the 'more freely and frequently' that international law is 'brushed aside' or 'declared to be inapplicable' through recourse to extra-legality.[37]

Elsewhere, the dragons recede and extra-legality signifies excess of other kinds. In some international legal scholarship, extra-legality is identified with a more ubiquitous multiplicity: that is, effusions of 'fact' or 'life' or 'context' of which international law must struggle to take account or which it must, as the case may be, translate, overcome, deflect or entrain. International legal literature abounds with references to 'barriers', 'pressures' and determining 'factors' arising extra-legally.[38] Even rights claims may be understood as '(predominantly) extra-legal' in their traceability to moral or political grounds.[39]

[34] Chin Leng Lim, 'Inter Arma Silent Leges? Black Hole Theories of the Laws of War' in Victor V. Ramraj (ed.), *Emergencies and the Limits of Legality* (Cambridge University Press, 2008), pp. 385–407, at pp. 406–407.

[35] Victor V. Ramraj, 'No Doctrine more Pernicious? Emergencies and the Limits of Legality' in Ramraj, *Emergencies and the Limits of Legality*, pp. 3–30, at p. 3.

[36] Abraham Abramovsky, 'Extraterritorial Abductions: America's "Catch and Snatch" Policy Run Amok' (1991) 31 *Virginia Journal of International Law* 151–210 at 155, 201: ('extra-legality' in this context is identified with extraterritoriality and an associated evasion of US judicial supervision, as in the case of extraterritorial abductions without recourse to the extradition process, with or without consultation with the state in which abduction takes place).

[37] Sarah Perrigo and Jim Whitman (eds.), *The Geneva Conventions Under Assault* (London: Pluto Press, 2010), p. 215.

[38] See, for example, Kelly Charles Crabbe, 'The Reality of Extra-legal Barriers to Mergers and Acquisitions in Japan' (1987) 21 *International Lawyer* 97–128; John Maton and Carolyn Maton, 'Independence Under Fire: Extra-Legal Pressures and Coalition Building in WTO Dispute Settlement' (2007) 10 *Journal of International Economic Law* 317–334; Colman Lynch, 'Indonesia's Use of Capital Punishment for Drug-Trafficking Crimes: Legal Obligations, Extra-legal Factors, and the Bali Nine Case' (2009) 40 *Columbia Human Rights Law Review* 523–594.

[39] Marie-Bénédicte Dembour, 'Human Rights Talk and Anthropological Ambivalence: The Particular Context of Universal Claims' in Olivia Harris (ed.), *Inside and Outside the Law: Anthropological Studies of Authority and Ambiguity* (London and New York: Routledge, 1996), pp. 19–40 at pp. 31–33.

Almost nowhere amid these narratives is the legal cast as broader, richer or more complex than the extra-legal.

Whether it represents death or life for legality, extra-legality remains difficult to pinpoint in international legal writing. In international legal accounts, extra-legal phenomena are sometimes a matter of vigorous assertion and sometimes 'just there'. But where are they, exactly, in relation to international law? As David Kennedy has observed, international lawyers 'seem unable to locate the extra-legal realm either temporally or spatially'.[40]

Nevertheless, as a matter of disciplinary disposition, international law often seems oriented towards conditions characterised in extra-legal terms. Even when operating in a mode of initiative or foundation (in the creation of international institutions, for instance), international law assumes the role of respondent, drawing impetus from forces and demands cast as external to international legality. Hence, the Agreement Establishing the World Trade Organization is positioned as a response to economic imperatives.[41] The UN Charter is characterised as a response to history, in particular the 'scourge of war'.[42] These preambles oppose law to the precipitants of material need and violence so that international legal action may afford a sense of moving beyond them. Yet the very creation of these agreements and institutions suggests that these precipitants are, at least in part, legal in structure and provenance, as are the future 'extra-legal' life conditions for which they are intended to make way. It would only make sense to 'respond' to history and economics with legal measures and institutions if law were understood to have exerted some determining force

[40] David Kennedy, 'Comparative Approaches to the Theory of International Law: Remarks' (1986) 80 *American Society of International Law Proceedings* 161–169 at 166. See further Austin Sarat and Thomas R. Kearns (eds.), *Law's Violence* (Ann Arbor: University of Michigan Press, 1992).

[41] Marrakesh Agreement Establishing the World Trade Organization, 15 April 1994, in force 1 January 1995, 1867 UNTS 154, 33 ILM 1144 (1994). In the Preamble, the Parties to the Agreement recognise that 'their relations in the field of trade and economic endeavour *should* be conducted with a view to raising standards of living, ensuring full employment and a large and steadily growing volume of real income and effective demand' (emphasis added). Likewise, they recognise 'that there is *need* for positive efforts designed to ensure that developing countries, and especially the least developed among them, secure a share in the growth in international trade commensurate with the needs of their economic development' (emphasis added).

[42] Charter of the United Nations, San Francisco, 24 June 1945, in force 24 October 1945, 1 UNTS XVI. The 'peoples' of the United Nations affirm, in the Preamble, their 'determin[ation]' to 'save succeeding generations from the scourge of war, which twice in our lifetime has brought untold sorrow to mankind'.

on the historical and economic phenomena in question. In this way and others, the 'extra-legal' is continually drawn into international law to be managed, parsed and tempered.

The particular parsing of extra-legality with which this chapter is concerned is, as already noted, the constitution of a distinct jurisdictional sphere which, in its relation to national and international legal orders, is understood as extra-legal. To many commentators, the extraordinary characteristics of the legal institutions installed at Guantánamo Bay rendered Guantánamo Bay Naval Base effectively 'a prison outside the law' (to quote the petitioners in *Rasul* v. *Bush*)[43] or at least outside the pre-existing order of legality.[44] Before exploring further the legal make-up of this particular exteriority, its representation within international legal scholarship merits some further elucidation.

Extra-legality from 'without': Guantánamo as exception

For more than a decade, public international lawyers have voiced concern about procedural deficiencies afflicting decision-making and

[43] Petitioners' Brief on the Merits in *Rasul* v. *Bush*; *Al Odah* v. *Bush* (US Supreme Court Nos. 03-334, 03-343) (2004) at 16.

[44] See, for example, *R ex rel. Abbasi* v. *Sec'y of State for Foreign & Commonwealth Affairs* [2002] EWCA Civ 1598 at para. 64 (a 'legal black-hole'); International Committee of the Red Cross, 'Guantanamo Bay: Overview of the ICRC's Work for Internees', 30 January 2004 Operational Update, www.icrc.org/eng/resources/documents/misc/5qrc5v.htm (accessed 17 September 2012) (stating 'that the US authorities have placed the internees beyond the law'). For popular endorsement of this characterisation in the press, see Henry Weinstein, 'Prisoners May Face "Legal Black Hole"', *Los Angeles Times*, 1 December 2002, at p. A1, articles.latimes.com/2002/dec/01/nation/na-detainees1 (accessed 17 September 2012); Neil Lewis, 'Detainees from the Afghan War Remain in a Legal Limbo in Cuba', *The New York Times*, 24 April 2003, p. A1, www.nytimes.com/2003/04/24/us/aftereffects-prisoners-detainees-afghan-war-remain-legal-limbo-cuba.html?pagewanted=all&src=pm (accessed 17 September 2012); Augusta Conchiglia, 'Dans le trou noir de Guantanamo', *Le Monde Diplomatique*, January 2004, pp. 1, 20 and 23, www.monde-diplomatique.fr/2004/01/CONCHIGLIA/10996 (accessed 17 September 2012); Clive Stafford Smith, 'America's Legal Black Hole', *Los Angeles Times*, 5 October 2007, available at articles.latimes.com/2007/oct/05/opinion/oe-smith5 (accessed 17 September 2012); Robert Verkaik, 'Exclusive: Caught in America's Legal Black Hole', *Independent*, 9 August 2010, www.independent.co.uk/news/world/americas/exclusive-caught-in-americas-legal-black-hole-2047307.html (accessed 17 September 2012); George Williams, 'Guantánamo: Legal Black Hole', 30 November 2010, www.amnesty.org.au/hrs/comments/24286/ (accessed 17 September 2012); *The New York Times*, 'The Prison that Won't Go Away', 8 March 2011, Editorial, www.nytimes.com/2011/03/09/opinion/09wed2.html (accessed 17 September 2012) (stating that '[t]he prison at

review at Guantánamo Bay. The Military Commissions have been the focus of particular criticism for their 'fail[ure] to deliver justice that the world at large will find credible' by 'authoriz[ing] the [US] Department of Defense to dispense with the basic procedural guarantees required by the Bill of Rights, the International Covenant on Civil and Political Rights (ICCPR) and the Third Geneva Convention of 1949'.[45] Criticism in this vein was most intense in respect of the Military Commissions' original design, under a 2001 military order. Nonetheless, after their 2006 legislative modification (in light of *Hamdan* v. *Rumsfeld*), the Commissions were still 'fatally flawed' in many accounts.[46] This remained the case, according to some international legal critics, even after their further legislative overhaul in 2009.[47]

The extra-legal status of decision-making at the Guantánamo Bay Naval Base has been a recurring theme of international legal critiques of the internment, interrogation and review practices that have been put into effect there. In international legal literature, development of this theme has typically entailed a two-part discursive move. First, the regime of Guantánamo Bay Naval Base is isolated and distanced from the ambit of routine legality. By expressly disavowing

Guantánamo Bay, Cuba, has long been the embodiment of Bush-era arrogance and lawlessness').

45 Harold Hongju Koh, 'The Case Against Military Commissions' (2002) 96 *American Journal of International Law* 337–344 at 338–339. See also Daryl Mundis, 'The Use of Military Commissions to Prosecute Individuals Accused of Terrorist Acts' (2002) 96 *American Journal of International Law* 320–328 at 328 (arguing that 'the use of military commissions will be difficult to reconcile with the US obligations under the Geneva Convention'). Contra Ruth Wedgwood, 'Al Qaeda, Terrorism and Military Commissions' (2002) 96 *American Journal of International Law* 328–337 at 332 and 334 (arguing that '[t]he [US] president's proposal for military commissions to try Al Qaeda suspects conforms to international law and does not represent any usurpation of civilian jurisdiction', that 'the jurisdiction of military commissions has been set by the bounds of international law directly incorporated within American law' and 'the jurisdiction of military commissions is defined by the norms of the customary law of nations, namely, the law of war').

46 Mark P. Denbeaux and Jonathan Hafetz (eds.), *The Guantánamo Lawyers: Inside a Prison Outside the Law* (New York and London: New York University Press, 2009), p. 169. See further David W. Glazier, 'A Self-Inflicted Wound: A Half-Dozen Years of Turmoil over the Guantánamo Military Commissions' (2008) 12 *Lewis & Clark Law Review* 131–204.

47 David W. Glazier, 'Still a Bad Idea: Military Commissions Under the Obama Administration', Loyola-LA Legal Studies Paper No. 2010-32, www.ssrn.com/abstract=1658590 (accessed 6 February 2012); Devon Chaffee, 'Military Commissions Revived: Persisting Problems of Perception' (2011) 9 *University of New Hampshire Law Review* 237–260.

the entitlement of detainees to certain due process guarantees enshrined in international law and US constitutional law, the US executive has, it is said, created an abomination: a 'legal no man's land';[48] a place 'beyond the rule of law'.[49] Guantánamo has been cast as a 'law-free zon[e]' in which 'law-free persons' are brought before 'law-free courts'.[50] Judgments there are said to have been 'based on politics, not legal norms'.[51] To many, Guantánamo Bay is, legally, a 'black hole'. 'The nature of th[at] black hole', it has been suggested, 'is that there is no way out, except through the good grace of the military'.[52]

Next, this severance of Guantánamo Bay from the prevailing legal order – or the normative emptying out of this jurisdiction, ostensibly to make way for the political – is identified per se as a critical source of concern. As one scholar has observed, '[h]uman rights law abhors a vacuum'.[53] Horror is directed as much towards the apparent refutation of international law's claim to completeness as it is towards the perceived effects of this, namely, the inability to subject detainees' indefinite detention, torture and degradation to third-party question or constraint. Thus, Professor Jordan Paust has insisted 'under international law, no locale is immune from the reach of relevant international law'.[54] 'Despite claims that certain persons, including "enemy combatants" or so-called "unlawful combatants", have no rights', Paust has argued, 'no human being is without protection under international

[48] Jordan J. Paust, 'Post-9/11 Overreaction and Fallacies Regarding War and Defense, Guantánamo, The Status of Persons, Treatment, Judicial Review of Detention, and Due Process in Military Commissions' (2004) 79 *Notre Dame Law Review* 1335–1364 at 1346.

[49] David Hope, 'Torture' (2004) 53 *International and Comparative Law Quarterly* 807–832 at 807: ('The place where the detainees are being held is beyond the rule of law').

[50] Harold Hongju Koh, 'The Future of Lou Henkin's Human Rights Movement' (2007) 38 *Columbia Human Rights Law Review* 487–498 at 492. See also Harold Hongju Koh, 'On American Exceptionalism' (2003) 55 *Stanford Law Review* 1479–1528 at 1498 (arguing that 'the administration has opted … for a two-pronged strategy of creating extra-legal zones, most prominently the US Naval Base at Guantánamo Bay, Cuba, where scores of security detainees are held without legal recourse, and *extra-legal persons* … are effectively accorded no recognized legal avenue', emphasis in original) and at 1509 (referring to an 'exceptional "rights-free zone" on Guantánamo').

[51] Koh, 'The Case Against Military Commissions', 341.

[52] George Fletcher, 'Black Hole in Guantánamo Bay' (2004) 2 *Journal of International Criminal Justice* 121–232 at 123.

[53] Dianne Marie Amann, 'Guantánamo' (2004) 42 *Columbia Journal of Transnational Law* 263–348 at 315.

[54] Paust, 'Post-9/11 Overreaction and Fallacies', 1346.

law ... in every circumstance, every human being has some forms of protection under human rights law'.[55]

The notion of a domain from which law has withdrawn, or where it has been forced into exile, is thus first generated as a definitive diagnosis of the Guantánamo Bay 'problem', then cast as intolerable. The encounter with this prospect has, in turn, occasioned two main types of response, each dedicated to affirming the comprehensiveness of the systemic order of national-international legality.

One response among legal critics has been to appeal to a variety of legal institutions to subject Guantánamo Bay Naval Base to their purview, under the rubric of existing law and institutional procedures. Thus, while some advocated congressional action within the United States, international lawyers and others instigated litigation, mobilised complaint procedures and sought to inform mechanisms of review in a wide range of settings around the world. These extended from the US and UK courts to the Inter-American Commission on Human Rights, the United Nations Working Group on Arbitrary Detention, the United Nations Human Rights Council and the United Nations Committee Against Torture.[56] Others turned to the law review as a forum in which to avow the breadth of international law's reach and the pertinence and inviolability of its precepts.[57] The exceptional circumstances of

[55] *Ibid.*, at 1350–1351.

[56] See *Hamdi* v. *Rumsfeld*, 124 S. Ct. 2633 (2004); *Boumediene* v. *Bush*, 128 S. Ct. 2229 (2008); *Hamdan* v. *Rumsfeld*, 126 S. Ct. 2749 (2006); *Rasul* v. *Bush*; *Al Odah* v. *United States*, 124 S. Ct. 2686 (2004); *Rumsfeld* v. *Padilla*, 124 S. Ct. 2711 (2004); *R ex rel. Abbasi* v. *Secretary of State for Foreign and Commonwealth Affairs* [2002] E.W.C.A. Civ. 1598; *R (Binyam Mohamed)* v. *Secretary of State for Foreign and Commonwealth Affairs (No 6)* [2009] E.W.C.A. Civ. 65; [2010] 3 WLR 554; *Al Rawi and Others* v. *Security Service and Others* [2010] E.W.C.A. Civ. 482; Inter-American Commission on Human Rights, 'Adoption of Precautionary Measures, Detainees in Guantánamo Bay, Cuba', Working Group on Arbitrary Detention, Opinion No. 21/2002, 13 March 2002, E/CN.4/2003/8/Add.1, www1.umn.edu/humanrts/iachr/guantanamomeasures2002.html (accessed 17 September 2012); Inter-American Commission on Human Rights, Resolution 2/06, 28 July 2006; Inter-American Commission on Human Rights, Resolution 2/11, 22 July 2011; Working Group on Arbitrary Detention, Opinion No. 21/2002 (United States of America) (E/CN.4/2003/8/Add.1); UN Human Rights Council (Special Procedures), Joint Report on the Situation of Detainees at Guantánamo Bay, 27 February 2006, (E/CN.4/2006/120); United Nations Committee Against Torture, Concluding Observations (United States of America), CAT/C/USA/CO/2, 25 July 2006, at para. 22.

[57] See, for example, Paust, 'Post-9/11 Overreaction and Fallacies'; Derek Jinks and David Sloss, 'Is the President Bound by the Geneva Conventions?' (2004) 90 *Cornell Law Review* 97–202 (arguing that the US president is indeed bound by the Geneva Conventions, formally and effectively); Luigi Condorelli and Pasquale De Sena,

state or executive overreach at Guantánamo Bay and elsewhere have been said to demand exceptional efforts of re-enclosure by a global array of institutions.

A second approach among legal scholars (constitutional lawyers especially) has been to insist upon the necessity of reshaping the law – domestic US law in particular – to fit the ostensibly novel phenomena thrown up by the events of 11 September 2001, including the demand for indefinite detention of those suspected of terrorist allegiances at Guantánamo Bay and elsewhere. This too is based upon the invocation of extra-legality in the mode of emergency or exceptional circumstances. The emergency here is not identified with exceptional political overreach; it is attributed to a newly resurgent and proximate terrorist threat. 'Terrorist attacks', US constitutional law scholar Bruce Ackerman has written, 'will be a recurring part of our future'. In view of this, Ackerman goes on to propose 'a newly fashioned emergency regime' so as to permit 'short-term emergency measures[,] but draw[ing] the line against permanent restrictions', thereby 'rescu[ing] the concept [of emergency power] from fascist thinkers like Carl Schmitt, who used it as a battering ram against liberal democracy'.[58]

Oren Gross has similarly demanded that law be reformulated in profound ways to take account of recent confrontations with 'acute exigency'. 'Taken together, the panoply of counterterrorism measures put in place since September 11th has created', he has written, '"an alternate system of justice" aimed at dealing with suspected terrorists'.[59] Gross, however, diverges from Ackerman in the following respect. Although, according to Gross, '[s]eparation between normalcy and emergency along geographic lines has once again been resorted to' and 'the anomalous nature of Guantánamo … has been invoked once again', those juridical mechanisms designed to keep emergency and normalcy

'The Relevance of the Obligations Flowing from the UN Covenant on Civil and Political Rights to US Courts Dealing with Guantánamo Detainees' (2004) 2 *Journal of International Criminal Justice* 107–120.

[58] Bruce Ackerman, 'The Emergency Constitution?' (2004) 113 *Yale Law Journal* 1029–1093 at 1029, 1030–1031 and 1044. For criticism of Ackerman's proposals, see David Cole, 'The Priority of Morality: The Emergency Constitution's Blind Spot' (2004) 113 *Yale Law Journal* 1753–1801 and Laurence H. Tribe and Patrick O. Gudridge, 'The Anti-Emergency Constitution' (2004) 113 *Yale Law Journal* 1801–1870; Dyzenhaus, 'Schmitt v. Dicey', 2015–2018; Oren Gross, 'Extra-Legality and the Ethic of Political Responsibility' in Ramraj, *Emergencies and the Limits of Legality*, pp. 60–94 at pp. 84–90.

[59] Oren Gross, 'Chaos and Rules: Should Responses to Violent Crises Always be Constitutional?' (2003) 112 *Yale Law Journal* 1011–1134 at 1016–1017, 1076.

separate have, in Gross' view, repeatedly broken down.[60] '[T]he exception has merged with the rule', in Gross' account, such that 'belief in our ability to separate emergency from normalcy … is misguided and dangerous'.[61] The time has come, in Gross' account, to normalise extra-legal decision-making by recourse to an 'extra-legal measures' model of emergency powers, one which permits *ex post* evaluation of emergency action by reference to both legal and non-legal norms.[62]

While purporting to reject a normalcy–emergency distinction, Gross reinstates it in the form a division between, on one hand, 'extremely grave … dangers' such as require 'extra-legal' adventures and, on the other, conditions under which such adventures are not justifiable. Gross argues that accommodating such extra-legal adventures will serve the ultimate goal of 'preserv[ing] enduring fidelity to the law' by fostering a combination of frank political self-explanation on the part of government officials and open and informed public evaluation, accompanied by powers of *ex post* legal and non-legal sanction.[63]

Among international lawyers, as opposed to constitutional lawyers, reform discussions tracing their impetus to emergency – and touching Guantánamo Bay in particular – have tended to focus on the question of international humanitarian law's possible obsolescence.[64] On

[60] *Ibid.*, at 1076.

[61] *Ibid.*, at 1022, 1089. For Gross' reading of Schmitt's theory of the exception, see Oren Gross, 'The Normless and Exceptionless Exception: Carl Schmitt's Theory of Emergency Powers and the "Norm-Exception" Dichotomy' (2000) 21 *Cardozo Law Review* 1825–1868. Curiously, Gross later claims that the goal of his extra-legal measures model is 'to keep the ordinary legal system distinct from the dirty and messy reality of emergency so as to prevent the perversion of that system in order to give answers to the hard exceptional cases': Gross, 'Extra-Legality', p. 92.

[62] Gross, 'Chaos and Rules'; Oren Gross and Fionnuala Ní Aoláin, *Law in Times of Crisis: Emergency Powers in Theory and Practice* (Cambridge University Press, 2006), pp. 110–170; Gross, 'Extra-Legality'.

[63] Gross, 'Chaos and Rules', 1097.

[64] See, for example, 'White House Memorandum for the President from Alberto R. Gonzales, Decision Re Application of the Geneva Convention on Prisoners of War to the Conflict with Al Qaeda and the Taliban', 25 January 2002, www.hereinreality.com/alberto_gonzales_torture_memo.html (accessed 17 September 2012): ('[T]he war against terrorism is a new kind of war. It is not the traditional clash between nations adhering to the laws of war … In my judgment, this new paradigm renders obsolete Geneva's strict limitations on questioning of enemy prisoners and renders quaint some of its provisions'). For discussion of this argument, see Luisa Vierucci, 'Is the Geneva Convention on Prisoners of War Obsolete? – The Views of the Counsel to the US President on the Application of International Law to the Afghan Conflict' (2004) 2 *Journal of International Criminal Justice* 866–871; Jordan J. Paust, 'War

the whole, however, international lawyers have seemed reluctant to engage in the sort of thought experiments in which Ackerman, Gross and others have been trading, that is, to entertain the prospect of international law's wholesale reconfiguration to accommodate the apparent exigencies of recent times.

Regardless of the divergence in proposals that have emerged from the foregoing writings, international legal scholarly characterisations of Guantánamo Bay have overwhelmingly relied on the archetype of extra-legality, taking an apparent play-off between legal and political power as their starting point. According to one characteristic account, 'the situation of the detainees in Guantánamo cried out for the application of that body of law [comprised of international human rights law, humanitarian law (the law of war), and international criminal law] as well as other international norms'.[65]

Some practices at Guantánamo Bay - indefinite detention without criminal charge, preventative detention without international humanitarian law grounds, detention of the verifiably innocent, and conduct amounting to torture or inhuman or degrading treatment - have also been characterised as *illegal* in international legal commentary. The attribution of extra-legality to Guantánamo Bay, however, has an effect over and above this characterisation. Illegality may, as discussed in the prior chapter, attach to relatively routine activities within international legal order. Troubling connections are maintained between 'extreme' illegality (the illegality of torture for instance) and illegality of a more incidental nature (such as the illegality attending a legal submission that has been rejected or overruled). In contrast, the denotation of extra-legality usually entails an attempt to sever such connections.[66]

Extra-legality as a descriptor of Guantánamo Bay emphasises distance between the order of conduct, decision and review to which people at Guantánamo Bay - detainers and their associates, as well as

and Enemy Status After 9/11: Attacks on the Laws of War' (2003) 28 *Yale Journal of International Law* 325–336. See generally Sarah Perrigo and Jim Whitman (eds.), *The Geneva Conventions Under Assault* (London and New York: Pluto Press, 2010).

65 Richard J. Wilson, 'A Long, Strange Trip: Guantanamo and the Scarcity of International Law', WCL Research Paper No. 2009-12, American University, ssrn.com/abstract=1368420 (accessed 17 September 2012).

66 In David Dyzenhaus' account, for example, extra-legality is identified with an 'extreme kind of illegality' amounting to the 'unlegalisable': phenomena which can only 'be dealt with on a highly individual basis' and never afford an apt foundation for rule-of-law models: David Dyzenhaus, 'The Compulsion of Legality' in Ramraj, *Emergencies and the Limits of Legality*, pp. 33–59 at pp. 52–53.

detainees – are subject, and legal orders to which those persons may be subject at other times and in other places. It stresses, in particular, that order's purported incommensurability with a rational, peaceable normalcy with which international legality is otherwise attributed. Extra-legal descriptors of Guantánamo Bay also convey a view about causal determinants underpinning that order: namely, the idea that practices at Guantánamo Bay have resulted from the subordination of law to politics, ideology or something else opposable to law.

Extra-legality thus signifies a much more forceful effort of expulsion or sequestration from international legal order than illegality. Legal claims arising from an extra-legal sphere or regime are difficult for many international legal scholars to engage absent an equally forceful act of reincorporation, enclosure or calling-to-account. Hence the copious guidelines and standards to which Guantánamo Bay's decision-makers refer have not assuaged critics' insistence that the procedures surrounding Guantánamo Bay are substantively lawless. No 'bad apples' argument suffices in this context as it often seems to do in the case of illegality; that is, rooting out a few malevolent individuals is rarely if ever expected to 'cure' the extra-legality in question. US Defense Secretary Robert Gates suggested in 2009 that Guantánamo Bay was 'one of the best prisons in the world today, because of all the things that have been done to change it and improve it'. Yet even he accepted that it would 'forever be tainted' and therefore 'need[ed] to be closed'.[67] The expulsive characterisation of extra-legality permits few if any concessions of the legitimacy of, or strategic potential within, the extant legal order of extra-legality.

With respect to Guantánamo Bay, the act of expulsion investing it with extra-legal status tends to be attributed in international legal literature to the executive branch of the US federal government, primarily under the second Bush administration. Less frequently, it is attributed to a longer series of executive actions and practices of administrative detention.[68] Yet international legal literature may itself bear some responsibility for this expulsive understanding of the Guantánamo Bay legal order, in view of the recurrent evocations of international

[67] Remarks by Secretary Gates at a Meeting of the Economic Club of Chicago, 16 July 2009, www.defense.gov/Transcripts/Transcript.aspx?TranscriptID=4445 (accessed 17 September 2012).

[68] Nasser Hussain, *The Jurisprudence of Emergency: Colonialism and the Rule of Law* (Ann Arbor: University of Michigan Press, 2006).

law's 'twilight' on one small stretch of the Cuban shoreline.[69] After all, as Gayatri Chakravorty Spivak reminds us, '[a] response not only supposes and produces a constructed subject of response, it also constructs its object'.[70]

By assuming or being attributed with the frame of extra-legality, the normative order of Guantánamo Bay has soaked up critical energies. It is, after all, the exceptional and the extra-legal that ring liberal alarm bells. Accordingly, the focus has fallen on the relatively small number of persons who have passed through Guantánamo Bay detention camps, rather than upon the millions subjected to endemic sexual, physical and substance abuse in prisons across the democratic world. In a similar way, attention is captured by the violation of rights of asylum-seekers in administrative detention, rather than by the over-representation of immigrants in the most informal and vulnerable sectors of the contemporary economy.[71]

For those concerned about violence and domination in and around Guantánamo Bay, the extra-legal frame makes some strategic options available and obscures others. In its fixation on the figure of the detainee in extra-legal isolation, rather than upon detainees as part of a highly regulated and potentially solidary group, international legal scholarship has tended to elicit humanitarian rather than political impulses.[72] As far as Guantánamo detainees are concerned, international legal scholarship does not invite collaborative action on questions surrounding

[69] Mark Drumbl writes of the 'rather sudden twilight of law' emerging in and around Guantánamo Bay 'with only the occasional intervention by the judiciary stalling a sunset'. This he attributes to a view having taken hold within the executive branch of the US Government that 'too much law … is dangerous insofar as it threatens United States national security interests by bogging down the rapidity and effectiveness of counterterrorist initiatives': Mark Drumbl, 'Guantánamo, Rasul, and the Twilight of Law' (2004–2005) 53 *Drake Law Review* 897–922 at 909. Nathaniel Berman refers to the 'US government's seeming desire to keep unprivileged combatants in a legal twilight zone' even as his analysis reveals that zone to be thick with unresolved 'legal construction[s]': Nathaniel Berman, 'Privileging Combat? Contemporary Conflict and the Legal Construction of War' (2004–2005) 43 *Columbia Journal of Transnational Law* 1–72 at 57.

[70] Gayatri Chakravorty Spivak, 'Terror: A Speech After 9–11' (2004) 31:2 *Boundary 2* 81–111, at 82.

[71] Cf. David Kennedy, *The Dark Sides of Virtue: Reassessing International Humanitarianism* (Princeton and Oxford: Princeton University Press, 2004), p. 300: ('Occupying the field, the humanitarian vocabulary can channel attention to a limited range of questions').

[72] On the separation between humanitarianism and politics, drawing on Hannah Arendt, see Giorgio Agamben, *Homo Sacer: Sovereign Power and Bare Life* (trans. Daniel Heller-Roazen, Stanford University Press, 1998), pp. 126–135.

the attribution and exercise of power globally. The 'rightful' response towards detainees and detainee experiences that this scholarship has most commonly sought to evoke is one combining a measure of sympathy with a measure of disgust. In this respect, the extra-legality of Guantánamo Bay owes much to the ambivalence surrounding illegal torture discussed in the preceding chapter.

As in the case of 'extreme' illegality, the encounter with extra-legality so cast – and the imminent demise of international law it is often taken to signify – is understood to demand some effort of conquest or accommodation on the part of law and lawyers, so as to close the circle of international legal systematicity once more. That effort has for the most part been directed at overcoming the extra-legal sequestration upon which so much emphasis had been placed. Yet a further sequestration nonetheless persists. But for the aforementioned efforts towards conquest (and but for a few significant exceptions, namely those who have directly advised the Bush administration), international law and lawyers are imagined to stand well apart from events at the Guantánamo Bay Naval Base over the past decade, and to remain exempt from responsibility for conditions there.

A schematic of extra-legality along these lines – and with these ethical, political and material effects – has taken firm hold in international legal scholarship on Guantánamo Bay. As we have seen, emphasis has consistently been placed upon the site's extraordinariness and its normative parchedness. Yet, this is not the only characterisation of Guantánamo Bay that the written record invites. For those charged with maintaining it on a day-to-day basis, the 'extra-legality' of Guantánamo Bay may owe more to the norm than the exception.

Extra-legality from 'within': annihilation of the exception?

As framed by Carl Schmitt (primarily in his 1922 work, *Political Theology*), the exception is that domain within juristic order in which decision-making 'cannot be subsumed' by existing norms.[73]

[73] Carl Schmitt, *Political Theology: Four Chapters on the Concept of Sovereignty* (trans. George Schwab, Cambridge, MA: MIT Press, 1985), p. 13. For discussion of the exception as framed in Schmitt's *Political Theology* in relation to its framing in the earlier *Die Diktatur* (1921), subsequent editions of the same, as well as in the later *Der Hüter der Verfassung* (1931) and *Legalität und Legitimität* (1932) and subsequent editions of those works, see John McCormick, 'The Dilemmas of Dictatorship: Carl Schmitt and Constitutional Emergency Powers' (1997) 10 *Canadian Journal of Law and Jurisprudence* 163–188.

Even though 'order in the juristic sense still prevails' in the space or moment of the exception, programmes of norm-implementation and norm-compliance cease to govern action and decision-making.[74] In the exception, norms are held open to suspension or transformation. For Schmitt, the exception is synonymous with the attempt to exercise momentarily decisive agency or, as Schmitt put it, 'principally unlimited authority'.[75] The exception 'cannot be circumscribed factually and made to conform to a preformed law'.[76] The decision on and in the exception cannot, accordingly, be derived from the content of any code or norm, nor can responsibility for its taking be deflected; it is 'a decision in the true sense of the word'.[77] For all the 'extra-legality' of Guantánamo Bay, the legal regime of Guantánamo Bay is designed to negate rather than enable an experience of the exception in Schmitt's terms.[78]

In so arguing, it is important to acknowledge the extent to which the legal order of Guantánamo Bay often *looks* and *sounds* like a domain operating as one of 'pure' sovereign discretion and thus exceptionalism in Schmittian terms. Lawyers for the US Justice Department have asserted that the US president has unlimited discretion to determine the appropriate means for interrogating enemy combatants detained at Guantánamo Bay and elsewhere.[79] Likewise, counsel for the US government contended, before the US Supreme Court, that '[a] commander's wartime determination that an individual is an enemy combatant is a quintessentially military judgment, representing a core exercise of the Commander-in-Chief authority'.[80] Even after a decade of litigation,

[74] Schmitt, *Political Theology*, p. 12. [75] *Ibid.*

[76] *Ibid.*, p. 6. [77] *Ibid.*

[78] Cf. Frédéric Mégret's discussion of the mobilisation of the rhetoric of war – that which Mégret characterises as 'Schmittian posturing' – as a means by which 'the sovereign [may] rejuvenate its constituent power' such that 'on the heroic altar of sacrifice, liberalism can be saved from itself and its inherent meekness, and the way paved for the banal functioning of technocratic rules': Frédéric Mégret, '"War?" Legal Semantics and the Move to Violence' (2002) 13 *European Journal of International Law* 361–399.

[79] Jay S. Bybee, 'Memorandum for Alberto R. Gonzales, Counsel to the President, from Jay S. Bybee, Asst. Atty. General, Re: Standards of Conduct for Interrogation under 18 USC. 2340–2340A', 1 August 2002, http://news.findlaw.com/wp/docs/doj/bybee80102mem.pdf (accessed 17 September 2012) at 39: ('Any effort by Congress to regulate the interrogation of battlefield combatants would violate the Constitution's sole vesting of the Commander-in-Chief authority in the President').

[80] Brief for the Respondents, *Hamdi* v. *Rumsfeld*, 124 S. Ct. 2633; 159 L. Ed. 2d 578 (2004) (No. 03–6696) at 25.

assertions of extra-legal discretion at Guantánamo have persisted. In March 2011, an Executive Order signed by President Obama acknowledged 'the executive branch's continued, discretionary exercise of existing detention authority' at Guantánamo Bay and established a process for its 'discretionary' review. In so doing, it made clear that '[t]he process established under this order does not address the legality of any detainee's law of war detention' which could still be 'call[ed] into question' at 'any time'.[81]

For detention decisions taken at Guantánamo Bay to correspond to Schmitt's understanding of the exception, however, '[t]he precondition as well as the content of jurisdictional competence in such a case must necessarily be unlimited. From the liberal constitutional point of view', Schmitt wrote, 'there would be no jurisdictional competence at all. The most guidance the constitution can provide is to indicate who can act in such a case'.[82] Yet in respect of Guantánamo Bay, both the content and competence of the US executive is repeatedly cast as pre-codified in presidential and governmental statements. At times, the 'code' is said to be that of 'freedom', 'democracy' or 'justice'.[83] Elsewhere, it is a 'matrix' of coordinated bureaucracy.[84] At other times, it is the code of

[81] Executive Order 13567 of 7 March 2011, 76 Fed. Reg. 13277 (10 March 2011).

[82] Schmitt, *Political Theology*, p. 7.

[83] See, for example, Press Release, 'President Speaks to the United Nations General Assembly', Office of the Press Secretary, 21 September 2004, http://georgewbush-whitehouse.archives.gov/news/releases/2004/09/20040921-3.html (accessed 17 September 2012): ('Freedom is finding a way in Iraq and Afghanistan – and we must continue to show our commitment to democracies in those nations ... I have faith in the transforming power of freedom'); Press Release, 'Remarks by the President at "ask President Bush" Event', Office of the Press Secretary, 30 August 2004, http://georgewbush-whitehouse.archives.gov/news/releases/2004/08/20040830-4.html (accessed 17 September 2012): ('The Taliban can't stop this movement toward liberty because freedom is universal. Freedom is inherent in people's souls ... Freedom is powerful in this world ... Liberty is a powerful, powerful agent of change'); Press Release, 'President Discusses Progress in the War on Terror', Office of the Press Secretary, 12 July 2004, http://georgewbush-whitehouse.archives.gov/news/releases/2004/07/20040712-5.html (accessed 17 September 2012): ('[W]e are extending the peace by supporting the rise of democracy, and the hope and progress that democracy brings, as the alternative to hatred and terror in the broader Middle East'); Press Release, 'President Signs Defense Appropriations Bill', Office of the Press Secretary, 10 January 2002, http://georgewbush-whitehouse.archives.gov/news/releases/2002/01/20020110-5.html (accessed 17 September 2012): ('This cause is noble, and this cause is just. And we will stay on this cause until we have achieved our objective. You're delivering justice; not revenge, but justice, to agents of terror').

[84] See, for example, Daniel F. McCallum, 'Why GTMO?', National Security Strategy Process Research Paper, National War College Report, National Defense University,

God.[85] On still further occasions, constitutional norms are invoked to frame a decision.[86] The acts of the would-be sovereign, in each case, are characterised by repeated references to some higher source of competence and direction, overt deference to a predetermined programme in the course of implementation, and insistence upon the conduit or vessel-like status of executive or military authority.

Secretary of the Navy Gordon England, speaking about the annual administrative review process then in effect at a press briefing on 23 June 2004, conceded: '[T]here's no question there's judgment involved. I doubt if many of these are black and white cases. I would expect most are going to be gray.' When pressed to define his role in the process, he confirmed that he was the one who would, at that point in time, be making the final decision regarding release, transfer or continued detention of each detainee, in the wake of an Administrative Review Board assessment. 'I operate and oversee, organise the process, and I also make the ultimate decision', he stated.[87]

Secretary England went on, however, to convey an impression of this judgment as one cabined by broad policy directives, notions of reasonableness and the institutional demand for standardisation: '[W]e do have some guidelines ... the boards do have some guidelines', he assured the audience, '[e]very board doesn't have a different standard'. He continued: '[I]t will be a judgment based on facts, data available ... the best decision a reasonable person can make in this situation ... [I]t's what is the situation today and going forward in terms of a threat to America. And that is what we will decide, and that's what the decision will be based on.'[88]

2003, www.dtic.mil/cgi-bin/GetTRDoc?AD=ADA442074%27&Location=U2&doc=GetTRDoc.pdf (accessed 17 September 2012) (outlining 'the interagency decision process that selected the US Naval Station, Guantánamo Bay, Cuba, as the location to detain the "illegal combatants" from the Global War on Terrorism').

85 Press Release, 'Remarks by the President at "ask President Bush" Event': ('Freedom is not America's gift to the world; freedom is the Almighty God's gift to each man and woman in this world'). For discussion of Bush's invocations of a divine mandate, see Alan Cooperman, 'Bush's References to God Defended by Speechwriter: President Does Not Claim Divinity is on His Side, Gerson Contends', *The Washington Post*, 12 December 2004, p. A.06.

86 See, for example, John C. Yoo, 'War and the Constitutional Text' (2002) 69 *University of Chicago Law Review* 1639–1684.

87 'Special Defense Department Briefing with Secretary of the Navy Gordon England', 23 June 2004, www.defense.gov/transcripts/transcript.aspx?transcriptid=3349 (accessed 17 September 2012).

88 *Ibid.*

From expressing the decision he would be taking in personal, case-specific terms, Secretary England thus moved rapidly into the mode of generalisation, depersonalisation and necessity. 'His' decision became 'the' decision of the reasonable person, made not to assess the individual detainee's responsibility, but rather to assess his or her proximity to a generalised 'threat to America'. In Secretary England's case, this may be attributable in part to the effects of military discipline. Yet this sense of pre-codification had significance and impact beyond military personnel as well.

Such an approach is also discernible in the Military Order issued by President Bush in 2001, pursuant to which the Military Commissions were convened before which Guantánamo Bay detainees were initially tried.[89] The 'findings' upon which the jurisdiction created by that order was predicated cast the steps taken thereby as inexorable reactions to a state of affairs of immeasurable proportions and persistent duration. Attacks by international terrorists were said to have 'created a state of armed conflict that *requires* the use of the United States Armed Forces'.[90] Likewise, it was said to be '*necessary* for individuals subject to [the] order ... to be detained', just as the issuance of the order itself is stated to be '*necessary* to meet the emergency'.[91] Although expressed in terms of 'an extraordinary emergency', this order framed the presidential decisions embodied in its text as matters of exigency – in other words, as non-decisions – dictated by a 'state of armed conflict'. The only acknowledgement of discretion was buried in the final paragraph of the order's 'findings', where the president is said to have 'determined that an extraordinary emergency exists for national defense purposes'. The exercise of sovereign discretion was, accordingly, cast as a derivative matter: a question of classification after the fact.

One could, of course, read these claims as exercises in public relations, designed to cloak the deployment of unfettered sovereign power in the guise of liberal proceduralism.[92] Yet regardless of how one might

89 Detention, Treatment, and Trial of Certain Non-Citizens in the War Against Terrorism, Military Order of November 13, 2001, 66 Fed. Reg. 57,833 (2001).

90 *Ibid.*, Section 1(a) [emphasis added].

91 *Ibid.*, Section 1(e) and 1(g) [emphasis added].

92 This is the sort of assessment that has been made by many scholarly commentators. See, for instance, Perrigo and Whitman, *The Geneva Conventions Under Assault*, pp. 208–214. It is also an assessment made by those directly engaged in Guantánamo Bay legal processes: see, for example, remarks of Muneer I. Ahmad in Denbeaux and Hafetz, *The Guantánamo Lawyers*, pp. 176–178: ('The commissions

characterise or seek to access the 'real' intent behind the military mandates governing Guantánamo Bay, the experience of decision-making reported by figures such as Secretary England seems, to a significant degree, to be one of disavowing prerogative power. In England's account, it is as though his job were more a matter of implementation than decision. Speaking of the determination, by the Combatant Status Review Tribunal, that one of the first thirty detainees to be heard by the Tribunal was not, in fact, an 'enemy combatant', Secretary England explained:

> [I]n this case we – we set up a process, we're following that process, we're looking at all the data … Determinations were made he was an enemy combatant. We now have set up another process; more data is available. Time has gone by … I believe the process is doing what we asked the process to do, which is to look at the data as unbiased as you can, from a reasonable person point of view … and I believe the process is working.[93]

This is not the language of Schmittian exceptionalism. Rather, it is suggestive of efforts to construct a series of normatively airtight spaces in which the prospect of agonising over an impossible decision may be delimited and, wherever possible, avoided. As such, the jurisdiction created at Guantánamo Bay is constituted, in Schmittian terms, in the liberal register of the norm (indeed, an overdetermined version thereof).[94]

In January 2009, a further sovereign decision – to close Guantánamo Bay and take certain related steps – was expressed by Executive Order.[95] By this measure, President Obama demanded 'prompt and appropriate disposition of the individuals currently detained at Guantánamo'. Announcing delivery of his report into conditions of confinement at Guantánamo Bay (one of the requirements of the relevant Executive Order), Admiral Patrick M. Walsh celebrated the relative freedom he

masqueraded as law – indeed, we were told to refer to the ever-changing body of rules as "Commission Law" … Our consistent argument was that the trappings of law – gavels and blue velvet curtains – were substituting for a truly fair system').

93 'Special Defense Department Briefing with Secretary of the Navy Gordon England'.

94 On 'overdetermination', from which the foregoing usage is extrapolated, see Sigmund Freud, 'The Aetiology of Hysteria' in *The Freud Reader* (ed. Peter Gay, London: Vintage, 1995), p. 108; Sigmund Freud, 'Fragment of an Analysis of a Case of Hysteria ("Dora")', in *The Freud Reader*, p. 203; Louis Althusser, 'Contradiction and Overdetermination' in *For Marx* (trans. Ben Brewster, London and New York: Verso, 1977), pp. 87–128.

95 Executive Order 13492 of 22 January 2009, 74 Fed. Reg. 4897 (27 January 2009).

had been afforded by the president's directives.[96] '[T]he benefit of having this review is that I come into this unconstrained. There's no limitations placed in terms of – from leadership to me, in terms of what to look at or where to put our emphasis', he observed. Likewise, the Joint Detention Group commander at Guantánamo, Walsh reported, was 'mak[ing] … decision[s] moment-to-moment' about detention conditions.[97]

As his remarks continued, however, Walsh seemed to place far less emphasis on the freedom-of-action and decisive capacity of the executive, the military and their agents than upon the 'limitations' to which they were subject. Considerations of 'risk management', Walsh cautioned, meant that certain detention arrangements were 'not practical'. Other 'limitations' flowed from the requirements of a 'governance model of compliance' directed towards detainee behaviour modification through reward. These requirements, read against the physical circumstances of Guantánamo, left only 'very limited and very narrow' options available to the Joint Detention Group commander. There was, moreover, the problem of handling the sheer mass of paper and words in which decision-makers seemed to see themselves entangled: 'what we're talking about is accumulating more evidence', Walsh remarked, 'so just the ability to store, to archive, to file and be able to track all of that is one of the limitations'.[98]

In light of his anticipation of 'necessary technical, fiscal, legal review of some of [the] ideas [put forth in his report]' and the extent to which implementation of those ideas may be 'resource-driven, or … manpower-limited or … technically-limited', Walsh's 'unconstrained' review soon came to seem quite pinched. '[G]iven the history of what's in the public domain about Guantánamo', Walsh offered plaintively, 'I think all parties would be well served if we figure out a way to get through the technical limitations'. His report would, however, ultimately be little more than a 'part of the dialogue'.[99]

So densely codified was the 'extra-legality' of Guantánamo Bay that even its much-heralded return to the fold of lawfulness under President Obama has thus been subject to endless deferrals. This appeared to be the case, in Admiral Walsh's reported experience for instance, even

[96] 'DoD News Briefing With Adm. Walsh From The Pentagon', US Defense Department News Briefing, 23 February 2009, www.defense.gov/Transcripts/Transcript.aspx?TranscriptID=4359 (accessed 17 September 2012).

[97] *Ibid.* [98] *Ibid.* [99] *Ibid.*

before legislative obstacles were placed in the way of President Obama's programme of camp closure.[100] Since its reopening for wartime and counter-terrorist detention in 2002, Guantánamo Bay has been a site of intense normative productivity. Yet everyone concerned directly and mundanely with Guantánamo Bay seems to regard themselves as implementing norms promulgated elsewhere or at some other time.

To some, it may be immaterial that decision-makers in and around Guantánamo Bay seem to experience themselves as norm-implementers rather than as actors taking decisions in the Schmittian sense. Could the more important questions be precisely which norms those decision-makers elect or are acculturated to implement and which they have set aside, disregarded or distorted and which legal norms or approaches underpin those tendencies in turn? These have certainly been among the questions that international legal scholars have posed.[101] By and large, however, international legal scholarship has not tended to frame debate and analysis concerning Guantánamo Bay around the question of which legal norms are serving to facilitate and sustain ongoing detention. For the most part, practices at Guantánamo Bay have not been characterised as instances of lawyers simply picking up the wrong tool from the international legal toolbox or using a more or less valid tool incorrectly. Again and again, decision-making in and around Guantánamo Bay has been attributed to people having thrown the international legal toolbox away altogether or hidden it deeply under their political bedclothes.

Others would maintain that the operative distinction in relation to Guantánamo Bay is that between 'rule by law, where as long as there is a legal warrant for what government does, government will

[100] Ike Skelton National Defense Authorization Act for Fiscal Year 2011, Pub. L. No. 111–383, §§ 1302 and 1304, 124 Stat. 4137, 4406 (2011) (prohibiting the use of Department of Defense funds for the transfer of Guantánamo Bay detainees to the United States or to construct or modify existing facilities to enable Guantánamo detainees to be held in military custody on US soil). This prohibition was extended to Fiscal Year 2012 through the National Defense Authorization Act for Fiscal Year 2012, Pub. L. No. 112–81 (2011), §§ 1026 and 1027. For further illustration of pre-existing legality arguably standing in the way of Guantánamo's closure, see the argument of Kyndra Rotunda that 'President Obama's decision to halt Guantánamo trials, over the objection of the presiding military judge (Colonel Pohl), may have violated governing law': Kyndra Rotunda, 'Halting Military Trials in Guantánamo Bay: Can the President Call a Time-Out?' (2010) 19 *Michigan State University College of Law Journal of International Law* 95–104.

[101] See, for example, Kal Raustiala, 'The Geography of Justice' (2005) 73 *Fordham Law Review* 2501–2560.

be considered to be in compliance with the rule of law' and 'rule of law, understood as rule by substantive principles'.[102] Only in the former sense would David Dyzenhaus, for instance, likely concede that legal rule prevails at Guantánamo Bay. Yet the promise afforded by appeal to this distinction seems forever to recede. In the case of Guantánamo Bay, neither the 'rough restoration of ... constitutionalism's discursive boundaries' in the series of US Supreme Court decisions since *Hamdan*, nor the 'finding of constitutional infirmity' introduced in *Boumediene*, has permitted unease about extra-legal determinants to fall away in most legal commentators' accounts.[103] An apparent shift from rule by law to an order acknowledged as the rule of law in relation to Guantánamo Bay does not seem to have eliminated a prevailing sense that the jurisdiction is irredeemably despoiled by extra-legal factors.

Consider, for instance, the effect of the 2008 decision of the US Supreme Court in *Boumediene*.[104] To some, this represented an expression of judicial discontent with the resolution of detainees' fate by political branches of government and a reassertion of substantive legal principle against that possibility.[105] Yet *Boumediene* is acknowledged to have 'left open' much of importance, affording 'murky standards and silences' within which decisions are thereafter to be taken.[106] Courts have since 'struggled' and 'labored' with the 'persistent ... uncertainty' generated by the Supreme Court's ruling.[107] Debate about what may lawfully be done to detainees continues to be displaced onto debate about where to do it (New York? Guantánamo Bay? At sea?).[108] And, as one commentator remarked in 2011, 'nine years after the first

[102] Dyzenhaus, 'Schmitt v. Dicey', 2018.

[103] David Dyzenhaus, 'The Puzzle of Martial Law' (2009) 59 *University of Toronto Law Journal* 1–64 at 48 (quoting John Fabian Witt, 'Book Review: Anglo-American Empire and the Crisis of the Legal Frame (Will the Real British Empire Please Stand up?)' (2007) 120 *Harvard Law Review* 754–798 at 796); Scott Sullivan and Joshua Colangelo-Bryan, 'Closing the Loop on Guantánamo' (2010) 19 *Tulane Journal of International & Comparative Law* 247–260 at 254.

[104] *Boumediene* v. *Bush*.

[105] See, for example, Sullivan and Colangelo-Bryan, 'Closing the Loop', 254.

[106] Robert M. Chesney, 'Boumediene v. Bush' (2008) 102 *American Journal of International Law* 848–853 at 852; Sullivan and Colangelo-Bryan, 'Closing the Loop', 260.

[107] Joshua Alexander Geltzer, 'Decisions Detained: The Courts' Embrace of Complexity in Guantánamo-Related Litigation' (2011) 29 *Berkeley Journal of International Law* 94–131 at 94–95.

[108] See, for example, Julian E. Barnes and Evan Perez, 'Clarity Sought on Detainees', *The Wall Street Journal*, 12 August 2011, www.online.wsj.com/article/SB10001424053111904823804576502331882663322.html (accessed 17 September 2012); Raustiala, 'The Geography of Justice', 2501–2503.

detainees arrived at Guantánamo, dozens of detainees remain there, and the basic contours of detention policy remain set by the political branches'.[109] The spectre of extra-legality persists, in endless dissimulation, amid the 'formless rumbling', the 'streaming' and the 'waiting' of legal language.[110]

If the experience of extra-legal or exceptional decision evoked by Schmitt's work has been in retreat in and around Guantánamo Bay, then what might its critical resurgence suggest? Or rather, what could the reinvigoration of a more defrocked and wayward sense of the exceptional than Schmitt's work promotes imply for resistance to initiatives undertaken at Guantánamo Bay and related initiatives underway elsewhere? These are the questions to which this chapter will now turn.

On exception, decision and resistance

According to Schmitt's formulation, the taking of an exceptional decision in or about Guantánamo Bay would entail a 'think[ing] [of] the general with intense passion', with the decision-maker thereby 'becom[ing] instantly independent of argumentative substantiation'.[111] 'The exception in jurisprudence is', Schmitt maintains, 'analogous to the miracle in theology'; both are brought about by 'direct intervention' – in the former case, 'the sovereign's direct intervention in a valid legal order'.[112] The exception is, accordingly, incommensurable with democracy, since '[d]emocracy is the expression of a political relativism and a scientific orientation that are liberated from miracles … and based on human understanding and critical doubt'.[113]

[109] Geltzer, 'Decisions Detained', 128.

[110] Michel Foucault, 'Maurice Blanchot: The Thought from Outside' in Michel Foucault and Maurice Blanchot, *Foucault/Blanchot* (trans. Jeffrey Mehlman and Brian Massumi, New York: Zone Books, 1987), pp. 7–60 at p. 57: ('For a long time it was thought that language had mastery over time … it was also thought that in its sovereignty it could bring to light the eternal and visible body of truth; it was thought that its essence resided in the form of words or in the breath that made them vibrate. In fact, it is only a formless rumbling, a streaming … and the transparent emptiness of waiting').

[111] Schmitt, *Political Theology*, pp. 15, 31 (in the first instance, quoting Søren Kierkegaard, *Repetition: An Essay in Experimental Psychology* (trans. Walter Lowrie, Princeton University Press, 1946)).

[112] *Ibid.*, pp. 36–37.

[113] *Ibid.*, p. 42. The exception, in Schmitt's account, cleaves close to the extra-legal because of Schmitt's insistence upon its independence from the norm. Note, however, that the exception is not always understood in these terms

In Schmitt's account, as noted above, the exception occasioning a decision in these terms 'cannot be circumscribed factually and made to conform to a preformed law'.[114] Schmitt, nevertheless, attempted to do precisely this. Insisting on the correspondence of the decisional space of the exception with an absolute, indivisible sovereignty, Schmitt sought to anchor the exception to a preformed law of political order.[115] Accordingly, the prospect of sovereignty operating as 'a play between two [or more] parties' was, in Schmitt's assessment, 'contrary to all reason and all law'.[116] The 'law' in this latter context apparently referred to some predetermined mandate higher than the law of liberal constitutionalism – a mandate seemingly (against Schmitt's own account of 'law' elsewhere) immune to suspension or question. Schmitt wrote: '[T]here is no irresistible highest or greatest power that operates according to the certainty of natural law.'[117] Yet an 'irresistible highest or greatest power' was smuggled in nonetheless in Schmitt's univocal account of the exception.

Schmitt's insistence upon this higher 'law' was undoubtedly bound up with his critique of the pluralism of the Weimar Republic and his hopes for a state order beyond it.[118] Bonnie Honig has observed how

jurisprudentially. Frederick Schauer, for example, casts exceptions as products of linguistic fortuity or indications of mismatch between a particular law's purposes and the 'pre-legal social and categorical structure on which it operates'. In each case, Schauer would have us see 'rules and their exceptions occupy[ing] the same plane', such that the power to create exceptions is no greater, no lesser and of no more significance than the power to change rules: Frederick Schauer, 'Exceptions' (1991) 58 *University of Chicago Law Review* 871–900 at 871. For a critique of Schauer that insists on the 'reality' of exceptions by reference to their extra-legality – the idea that exceptions sometimes represent a step outside the bounds of legal rule or principle by reason of political or personal expediency and hence 'the exercise of power unfettered by any pre-existing legal constraint' – see Jeremy B. Stein, 'The Necessary Language of Exceptions: A Response to Frederick Schauer's "Exceptions"' (2007) 63 *New York University Annual Survey of American Law* 99–138.

114 Schmitt, *Political Theology*, p. 6.

115 *Ibid.*, p. 7. Nasser Hussain makes a somewhat comparable observation when he notes 'how much the decision on the exception, which cannot be codified in advance, and normatively, "seems to emerge out of nothingness," is nonetheless linked to very specific and actual conditions' in Schmitt's work: Hussain, *The Jurisprudence of Emergency*, p. 19.

116 Schmitt, *Political Theology*, p. 9. 117 *Ibid.*, p. 17.

118 For a helpful critique of Schmitt's reliance on the political givens of a unified people, identified with a unified state (one which, at the same time, takes seriously Schmitt's critique of liberal democracy), see Chantal Mouffe, 'Carl Schmitt and the Paradox of Liberal Democracy' (1997) 10 *Canadian Journal of Law and Jurisprudence* 21–34.

'secure' Schmitt's account of the exception sought to make political sovereignty through its grounding in metaphor:

> Schmitt turns to political theology to find a way to secure political sovereignty, something he thinks modern constitutionalism fails to do ... Metaphor posits its plural, contested ground ('miracle', in this instance) as an apparently uncontroversial simple (miracle simply means sovereign suspension of law) and presents as the problem for scrutiny its effect or figure ... Thus, the miracle of metaphor is its naturalization of its ground, its removal of its ground for scrutiny. In this instance, in Schmitt's political theology, that means theology's concepts are treated as if they possess clear and univocal meanings – we *know* what miracle is – such that they can serve as the ground for unclear and contested political concepts that we are unclear about: like the state of exception ... The fraught nature of the concept [of miracle] is hidden from view when Schmitt presses miracle into service as the ground of his metaphor. This is one of the miracles of metaphor.[119]

Yet, as Honig goes on to argue in other ways, one need not follow the suggestive perplexities of Schmitt's exception down this particular centralising and securing route.[120] Were authority to decide on the exception already known to be monopolised, then the exception would no longer embody 'the power of real life [to] break[ ] through the crust of a mechanism that has become torpid by repetition': that is, the crust of acceptance of what presents as normality or, what Kierkegaard termed 'comfortable superficiality'.[121] Indeed, Schmitt himself wrote: '[a] distinctive determination of which individual person or which concrete body can assume [the authority to decide] cannot be derived from the mere legal quality of a maxim'.[122]

Acknowledgement of the impossibility of any sovereign or sovereign state retaining a monopoly on decision might allow the exception to retain its exceptional character, albeit not exactly in Schmitt's miraculous terms. Instead of envisaging the exception 'emanat[ing] from nothingness',[123] one could identify the absence of pre-codification characteristic of the exception with immersion in the ubiquity of power. Only when the following questions – who decides, or plays a

[119] Bonnie Honig, 'The Miracle of Metaphor: Rethinking the State of Exception with Rosenzweig and Schmitt' (2007) 37:2–3 *Diacritics* 78–102 at 79.

[120] Honig argues for likening the state of exception to Franz Rosenzweig's version of the miracle – one which, in Honig's reading, 'points ... towards popular receptivity and interpretation' – rather than Schmitt's. *Ibid.*, p. 80.

[121] Schmitt, *Political Theology*, p. 15 (quoting Søren Kierkegaard, *Repetition*).

[122] *Ibid.*, p. 31. [123] *Ibid.*, p. 32.

role in decision; where and when is there occasion for exercising prerogative; and how should that prerogative be exercised? – form part of the 'concrete case that [the law] cannot factually determine in any definitive manner' is the potential of the exception to 'confound the unity and order of the rationalist scheme' held open, as Schmitt contemplated.[124]

Schmitt's exception, accordingly, evokes an experience of politico-legal decision-making that is amenable to de-linking from Schmitt's fetishism of the state and the person of the sovereign ruler. The exception, in this de-linked sense, arises from the vertiginous combination of, on one hand, responsibility assumed and, on the other, faith in one's determinative authority relinquished amid the omnipresence of both power and legality. In this mode, I believe, it offers scope for resistance to the 'extra-legal' normative order of Guantánamo Bay.

To de-link the experience of deciding on/in the exception from the sovereign state is not to deny Schmitt's claim that every decision involves a would-be exclusion.[125] Nor is it to configure the state as 'an association that competes with other associations', the sort of competitive pluralism targeted by Schmitt in *The Concept of the Political*.[126] Rather, it is to argue that appeals to the exception are not necessarily contingent upon an insistence upon the state's (or any self-sustaining sovereign's) monopolisation of all political decisions.[127] Nor, for that matter, are they contingent upon any predetermination of the structure of the political order per se (whatever Schmitt might say).[128] Rather, it is

[124] *Ibid.*, pp. 9–10.

[125] Carl Schmitt, *The Concept of the Political*, Expanded Edition (trans. George Schwab, John P. McCormick and J. Harvey Lomax, Chicago and London: University of Chicago Press, 1996), p. 37. For discussion of this 'moment of closure' in the context of a Schmitt-inspired critique of deliberative democracy, see Mouffe, 'Carl Schmitt and the Paradox of Liberal Democracy', 26–28.

[126] Schmitt, *The Concept of the Political*, p. 44.

[127] Here one might return to Foucault and, in particular, to the force of diffusion in his writing. See, for example, Michel Foucault, *The History of Sexuality, Volume I: An Introduction* (trans. Robert Hurley, New York: Random House, 1978), pp. 136–137: ('This death that was based on the right of the sovereign is now manifested as simply the reverse of the right of the social body to ensure, maintain, or develop its life … [T]his formidable power of death … now presents itself as the counterpart of a power that exerts a positive influence on life, that endeavours to administer, optimize, and multiply it, subjecting it to precise controls and comprehensive regulations. Wars are no longer waged in the name of a sovereign who must be defended; they are waged on behalf of the existence of everyone; entire populations are mobilized').

[128] Schmitt would surely have resisted such a contention. See, for example, Schmitt, *The Concept of the Political*, at 45, 47: ('To the state as an essentially political entity

possible to conceive as both political and exceptional (at least in part) a much broader range of decisions, approached by or among a much broader range of agents and aggregations, than those which Schmitt entertained as such.

To do so, one could, as Honig does, look to the plural, contested understandings of the political theology on which Schmitt sought to rely. By recourse to Franz Rosenzweig's theology (produced around the time of Schmitt's work), Honig is drawn by Schmitt's metaphor for the state of exception to 'very different conclusions' to those reached by Schmitt – towards recognition of the 'vulnerability' of a 'so-called state of exception … to democratic action and resistance'. In Honig's reading, the 'metaphor of miracle, normally taken to mark extraordinary ruptural, or inaugurative politics' might 'license instead a turn to the ordinary', albeit an ordinary which 'can also be ruptural' in an immanent sense.[129]

Yet one does not necessarily need to make yet another extra-legal foray (reaching towards, say, Honig's political theory and the philosophical theology of Rosenzweig) in order to enact a 'turn to the ordinary' of this kind. The legal record of everyday decision-making surrounding the legalised extra-legality of Guantánamo Bay affords material amenable to reading more or less in this way. That is, it carries traces of a much more pervasive and unresolved exceptionalism than Schmitt (or, for that matter, most legal scholars worried about the resurgence of Schmitt's extra-legal 'battering ram' at Guantánamo Bay) would have us see.

In the anxious appeals to rule and reasonableness made by Secretary of the Navy Gordon England, for instance, one may discern an active worry about getting each decision on a detainee's fate 'right'. Admiral Patrick Walsh's fretful deferral to 'limitations' alongside his celebration of being 'unconstrained' sound a somewhat similar note. That worrying might be taken to suggest some awareness of an imminent prospect of getting even the most seemingly routine of those decisions wrong, or that others facing such decisions might justifiably take a different tack.

belongs … the real possibility of deciding in a concrete situation upon the enemy … A human group which renounces these consequences of a political entity ceases to be a political group, because it thereby renounces the possibility of deciding whom it considers to be the enemy and how he should be treated').

129 Honig, 'The Miracle of Metaphor', 78.

England's and Walsh's remarks in this vein are not the pronouncements of people who perceive themselves to be seized with unfettered decisive power. Yet they are also not the words of people invested with a definite sense of what normative compliance might entail. Their words suggest, rather, some manifestation of what Karl Llewellyn drew attention to when he characterised the work or practice of law as a series of doings premised on 'the greatest of doubts as to *how far* that supposed certainty in decision which derives merely from the presence of accepted rules really goes'.[130]

It is possible to read some agonism into Secretary England's and Admiral Walsh's accounts of their decision-making around Guantánamo Bay. And with that reading comes a suggestion that the conditions of Guantánamo Bay might not have resulted just or even primarily from the downward imposition of extra-legal sovereign power. Rather, those conditions were and are the outcome of a far more diffuse and mundane interplay of invitations and acceptances and, for that matter, refusals.

After all, people have not all performed alike under the conditions with which Secretary England and Admiral Walsh were grappling. Military employees clashed with superiors over detention conditions.[131] Information was leaked from within the military in aid of detainees' legal claims and associated lobbying.[132] One panellist on the Combatant Status Review Tribunal spoke publicly with and alongside lawyers representing detainees about the Tribunal's workings and provided a sworn declaration in support of their claims.[133] The force of the largely state-sponsored opposition with which actions such as

[130] Karl Llewellyn, 'Some Realism About Realism – Responding to Dean Pound' (1931) 44 *Harvard Law Review* 1222–1264 (emphasis in original).

[131] John Mintz, 'Chaplain Clashed with Officials over Guantánamo Detainees', *The Washington Post*, 24 October 2003, community.seattletimes.nwsource.com/archive/?date=20031024&slug=chaplain24 (accessed 17 September 2012).

[132] Erik Saar and Viveca Novack, *Inside the Wire: A Military Intelligence Soldier's Eyewitness Account of Life at Guantánamo* (New York: Penguin Press, 2005); David Leigh, James Ball, Ian Cobain and Jason Burke, 'Guantánamo Leaks Lift Lid on World's Most Controversial Prison', *Guardian*, 25 April 2011, www.guardian.co.uk/world/2011/apr/25/guantanamo-files-lift-lid-prison (accessed 17 September 2012); Lt. Cmdr. Matthew Diaz, 'Ex-Navy Lawyer Explains Guantanamo Leak', *All Things Considered*, National Public Radio broadcast interview transcript, 10 April 2008, www.npr.org/templates/story/story.php?storyId=89538109 (accessed 17 September 2012); Tim Golden, 'Naming Names at Gitmo', *The New York Times Magazine*, 21 October 2007, www.nytimes.com/2007/10/21/magazine/21Diaz-t.html?pagewanted=all (accessed 17 September 2012).

[133] Denbeaux and Hafetz, *The Guantánamo Lawyers*, pp. 222–225.

these have been met is not to be underestimated.[134] Nonetheless, as experienced detainee defence lawyer Clive Stafford Smith has written, '[t]here is always something you can do'.[135]

Lawyers, their detainee clients and others have engaged in a myriad of tactical ways with the rule-bound 'extra-legal' world of Guantánamo Bay, with variable effects.[136] Sometimes their appeals to norms have had some effect.[137] Elsewhere, invocations of some exception seem to have worked.[138] At other times, actions taken do not seem to fall squarely on a norm-to-exception spectrum.[139] Amid the dense thicket of legality comprising Guantánamo Bay's extra-legality (as we have come to know it), a range of actions could still be, and have been, taken. The designation 'extra-legal', however, often seems to make that full range of possible action – and both tensions and

[134] David Luban, 'Lawfare and Legal Ethics in Guantánamo' (2008) 60 *Stanford Law Review* 1981–2026 at 1985: ('[M]illions of dollars of resources, and the attention of some of the highest officials of government, have been devoted to capturing, imprisoning, isolating, interrogating, and in some cases torturing a few hundred men and boys').

[135] Clive Stafford Smith, *Bad Men: Guantánamo Bay and The Secret Prisons* (London: Weidenfeld & Nicolson, 2007) pp. 296–297.

[136] Denbeaux and Hafetz, *The Guantánamo Lawyers*; Luban, 'Lawfare and Legal Ethics'.

[137] Aside from the record of litigation surrounding Guantánamo, another instance of appealing to legal norms that apparently had some effect (in the view of those who adopted the strategy) was the practice of writing 'lawyers letters': 'open letters to members of Congress – essentially petitions – urging preservation of habeas corpus': Gary Isaac in Denbeaux and Hafetz, *The Guantánamo Lawyers*, pp. 200–218. In Isaac's account, such letters permitted him and his colleagues to come 'excruciatingly close' to their goals in lobbying against the Military Commissions Act of 2006 and ultimately 'became an organizing tool … to garner support for Obama … Our work felt validated as we moved forward', Isaac writes, 'since Obama campaign staff sought the advice of habeas counsel as they devised policy regarding Guantánamo, a stark contrast with the outgoing administration'.

[138] Thomas B. Wilner recounts, for instance, the surprising success of his and Neil Koslowe's efforts, on behalf of their detainee clients, to have the Supreme Court reverse its own prior decision to deny the writ of certiarori in the *Boumediene* and *Al Odah* cases, something which the Court eventually did for the first time in fifty years: quoted in Mark P. Denbeaux and Jonathan Hafetz, 'Red Tape and Kangaroo Courts' in *The Guantánamo Lawyers*, pp. 109–227 at 221–223.

[139] The practice of putting oneself on a hunger strike, as many detainees did, does not, for instance, readily translate into either norm-enforcement or the assertion of exceptionalism, although it may embody an indirect argument for outcomes of either type: Mark P. Denbeaux and Jonathan Hafetz, 'Tortured' in *The Guantánamo Lawyers*, pp. 229–288 at 265–280: ('Many prisoners were willing to risk dying rather than silently endure the injustices of Guantánamo'). See further Mark P. Denbeaux and Jonathan Hafetz, 'Alternative Forms of Advocacy' in *The Guantánamo Lawyers*, pp. 289–312.

complicities that arise between different tactics – hard to appreciate and evaluate.

Conclusion

Extra-legality introduces a particular type of legality. Above all, that legality revolves around expulsion and re-enclosure. In opting for extra-legality as a lens through which to view Guantánamo Bay, international legal scholarship has focused attention on relatively recent beginnings and relatively narrow ends. Accordingly, the act of reopening Guantánamo Bay in early 2002 for wartime and counter-terrorist detention and the ever-receding prospect of closing it down, once and for all, as a facility used for that purpose have loomed largest in recent debate. Other actions, possibilities and questions, meanwhile, have tended to recede. For instance, the ongoing significance of Cuban-American relations for Guantánamo Bay's contemporary usage has not received much recent attention.[140] Practices of administrative detention cultivated and refined in colonial settings and in the context of immigration policy have mostly escaped critical engagement with regard to Guantánamo Bay's legal underpinnings, at least in so far as public advocacy is concerned.[141] Likewise, the reliance of executive

[140] For important counter-examples from outside international legal scholarship, see Amy Kaplan, 'Where is Guantánamo?' (2005) 57 *American Quarterly* 831–858 (surveying the 'long imperial history' of 'the "legal black hole" of Guantánamo'); Simon Reid-Henry, 'Exceptional Sovereignty? Guantánamo Bay and the Re-colonial Present' (2007) 39 *Antipode* 627–648; Jana K. Lipman, *Guantánamo: A Working-Class History Between Empire and Revolution* (Berkeley and Los Angeles: University of California Press, 2008). For an insight into legal and political possibilities that seemed to legal scholars to be available at an earlier time, see Robert L. Montague III, 'A Brief Study of Some of the International Legal and Political Aspects of the Guantánamo Bay Problem' (1962) 50 *Kentucky Law Review* 459–523 (providing an overview of the 'legal, historical and diplomatic background facts and policies' in order 'to position the Guantánamo problem in the larger perspective of Cuban and Latin American affairs of which it is an integral part' and analysing 'some of the arguments which Cuba might develop should she seek to bring the Guantánamo Bay lease before the International Court of Justice').

[141] For important counter-examples, see Hussain, *The Jurisprudence of Emergency*, p. 3: ('drawing out and delineating how questions of law and emergency shaped the conceptualization and practice of colonial rule' in India from the late eighteenth to the early twentieth century, 'and how these concepts in turn affected the development of Western legality'); Neuman, 'Closing the Guantánamo Loophole' (highlighting the relationship between legal understandings of Guantánamo Bay and jurisprudence concerning non-citizens more generally); Raustiala, 'The Geography of Justice' (placing governmental attitudes towards Guantánamo Bay

and/or military mandates in contemporary secular democracies upon an implicit or explicit sense of religious righteousness has not been at the forefront of critical commentary surrounding Guantánamo Bay.[142]

Were Guantánamo Bay instead approached as a product of legal work in large part (as it sometimes has been), then the criss-crossing and far-reaching routes traversed by lawyers and others in shaping its jurisdictional features could arguably be made more visible. Legal work concerned with the various modes of normativity at work in and around Guantánamo would likely entail the tracing and unpicking of some of these routes more forensically than work concerned with the conquest of extra-legality. As the preceding chapter showed, illegality tends to get parcelled and graded in international law and its generative force is more readily acknowledged. Broken down in these ways, the extra-legality of Guantánamo Bay might appear more navigable to those who would seek to unravel, obstruct and/or redirect actions being taken under its auspices.

At the same time, representing Guantánamo Bay in the language of legality or ordinary illegality may have downsides as well. In its proximity to the routine, such a representation of this jurisdiction might lack the resonance and impact that extra-legality has brought to public conversation surrounding Guantánamo Bay. Neither extra-legality nor legality can offer a 'right' way of understanding Guantánamo Bay for all time and for all purposes. The point is, rather, that the framing of its non-legality matters and merits critical and strategic attention.

International lawyers, activists and commentators appealing to the frame of extra-legality have laid claim to the juridical phenomenon of Guantánamo Bay by way of invoking a code and seeking to follow that code to a predetermined exit point and/or point of origination.

in the context of a 'strictly territorial approach' to non-citizens' constitutional status maintained over the past century, in tension with a 'progressive relaxing of legal spatiality' within US jurisprudence more generally); Joseph C. Sweeney, 'Guantánamo and US Law' (2007) 30 *Fordham International Law Journal* 673–779 (tracking 'the nature of the jurisdiction exercised … by the United States' at Guantánamo Bay since its acquisition 'as an imperial outpost in a time of great empires').

142 The relationship between understandings and expectations of the executive in modern democracies (especially presidential democracies) and religiously inspired ideas of kingship has received quite extensive treatment in scholarly writing. See, for example, William Scheuerman, 'American Kingship? Monarchical Origins of Modern Presidentialism' (2005) 37 *Polity* 24–53. This relationship and the questions which it provokes have not, however, surfaced in debate surrounding Guantánamo Bay, to my knowledge.

If only, these accounts suggest, there could be more law at or about Guantánamo Bay, then the mortal politics at play there – unleashed by the executive withdrawal of judicial oversight – might be overcome once and for all. In so far as it propagates this narrative and pursues these ends, the effect of international legal commentary is often to compound efforts to curtail the experience of deciding on or in the exception – deciding, that is, amid 'the greatest of doubts' of Karl Llewellyn's description. As we have seen, these efforts of curtailment have already long been under way at Guantánamo Bay. For notwithstanding all the liberal heartache that they provoke, the law and legal institutions of Guantánamo Bay are working to negate the exception in tandem with, rather than in opposition to, what Schmitt identified as '[t]he tendency of liberal constitutionalism to regulate the exception as precisely as possible'.[143]

To corrode the experience of the exception in this way is to eviscerate or avoid the experience of deciding in circumstances where no person or rule offers assurance that the decision that one takes will be the right one or, indeed, whether one does in fact exert the decisive authority that one envisages oneself to hold. Even when stripped of Schmittian univocalism, the exception poses 'a case of extreme peril' because it permits both righteousness and self-knowledge to be placed at risk; because the decision which the exception demands remains 'independent of the correctness of its content'.[144] Notwithstanding all the talk of threats that surrounds Guantánamo Bay, it is this sense of peril that may be lacking within its legal order. Moreover, it may be, in part, the absence of such peril that has contributed to the often tenuously founded assurance demonstrated by people like Secretary England in announcing, as he did at a press briefing on 8 September 2004, 'we have a lot of very bad people' in detention at Guantánamo Bay.[145]

It is, therefore, to a renewed, diffused sense of the exception within law, rather than to a vehement insistence upon the norm in all circumstances, that this chapter suggests turning in order to raise further doubts about the work of the 'good' people of Guantánamo Bay.

[143] Schmitt, *Political Theology*, p. 14.

[144] *Ibid.*, p. 31.

[145] US Defense Department News Briefing, 8 September 2004, transcript available at www.iwar.org.uk/news-archive/2004/09-08-4.htm (accessed 17 September 2012). On the often tenuous foundations for this assurance, see David Leigh *et al.*, 'Guantánamo Leaks Lift Lid'.

By understanding the legal workings of Guantánamo Bay over the past decade as dedicated as much to the annihilation or codification of the exception as to the assertion of exceptional extra-legality, we may come to appreciate better the scope for action within such a juristic zone and how that has been enlarged or diminished in various peoples' experience.

The exception in this context need not be that which 'emanate[s] from nothingness',[146] as Schmitt's work would have us believe. The turn to exceptionalism need not be identified with would-be-sovereign Gullivers struggling to be free of pesky, lawyerly Lilliputians.[147] Exceptions emerge on all scales throughout legality. The exception is not, moreover, the sole repository of politics, discretion or strategic potential within legality.

Nonetheless, by recognising in herself or himself an exceptional decision-maker, the functionary implementing a programme might come to experience that programme as a field of decisional possibility and impossibility, with all the danger and difference that that implies, and to do so without necessary recourse to the miracle of extra-legality. It is precisely this experience that critics of the Guantánamo Bay programme might strive to evoke in officials at all levels upon whose concrete decisions that programme still depends, as well as in the audiences with which they – critics and officials alike – perpetually dance.

Routine recourse to terminal extra-legality risks shutting down such decisional dances, this chapter has argued, and confirming the inevitability of one or other programme. Yet routine recourse to exceptional autonomy in decision carries similar risks. It is to the latter risks – the perils of an international legal orientation around untethered choice – that the next chapter will now turn.

[146] Schmitt, *Political Theology*, p. 32.

[147] This damning, Swiftian image of 'lawfare' is drawn from Luban, 'Lawfare and Legal Ethics', 2020. See also Jack Goldsmith, *The Terror Presidency: Law and Judgment Inside the Bush Administration* (New York: W. W. Norton, 2007), p. 68.

4 Doing deals: pre- and post-legal choice in transnational financing

Preceding chapters have dealt with legality's transgression or apparent expulsion in international law. This chapter, in contrast, envisages legality in a relatively smooth, well-functioning mode. The legality in question here is that of private international law in the context of transnational cross-border financing. The non-legality with which we are here concerned is that of an imaginative domain immediately preceding legal analysis (pre-legality) or opening in its aftermath (post-legality) in which the autonomous exercise of choice is understood to predominate.

When international lawyers look around the global marketplace, as it were, they see choosers. Private international law is framed accordingly. Private international law is said largely to be determined by the spontaneous, personal preferences of non-governmental legal or natural persons (which states are called upon to implement or temper). These preferences are understood to drive, for instance, contractual choices of law or forum. A choice of law is the decision to subject one's actions and agreements in a particular transaction or field to the law of one jurisdiction (or, less commonly, selected aspects of more than one jurisdictions' laws), typically expressed by contractual provision. A choice of forum is a stipulation (again, by contractual provision) that any lawsuit between contracting parties arising from their contract or other legal dealings shall be litigated before a particular court or in a particular jurisdiction. Inevitably, these also entail a decision to try to rule out subjection to the tribunals or laws of any jurisdiction(s) that might otherwise be available or applicable. Such an application and exclusion of law will, however, only be effective to the extent that it is legally recognisable in any jurisdiction in which the parties might thereafter be called to account.

Choices of law and forum are envisaged in international legal literature in both pre-legal and post-legal terms. In pre-legal terms, persons are imagined formulating views about economic and strategic commercial objectives, risks and risk appetites from which their subsequent choices of law and forum are understood to flow. In post-legal terms, persons are envisaged surveying the possibilities made available to them by regulation and precedent and thereafter deciding among them. From either direction, scholarly analysis in international law tends to proceed from the moment of a choice already having been made, or towards the possibility of its making. The act of choice itself remains curiously unreadable in terms of its legal dimensions or the role of lawyers in its making. It is in this sense that this chapter approaches the idea of autonomous choice in private international law as a form of non-legality.

More specifically, this chapter is concerned with transnational corporate agents and with a prevailing tendency to frame their power as wholly resolved pre- or post-legally. Legal principle and scholarship concerning contractual choice of law and forum tend to be framed as either a direct expression of the power of choice, or its necessary antithesis. This configuration merits question because it anticipates – and, as it were, guarantees – the unalterable necessity of that with which it sometimes purports to contend: private (corporate) rule. The effect is at least partially akin to that described by Judith Butler in relation to gender: '[W]hat we take to be an "internal" feature of ourselves [or, in this case, of the global legal order] is one that we anticipate and produce through certain ... acts.'[1]

Scholarly and doctrinal projections of choices of law and forum as deliberate, measured and coherent decisions, upon which normative constraints become operative only in anticipation or after the fact, sit rather uneasily with this writer's experience of transnational legal practice. This unease is particularly acute in relation to the corporate enactment of 'autonomous' choice. The limits of the traditional conception of contracting as a spontaneous meeting of minds have long been highlighted in studies of standard-form,[2] or boilerplate,[3]

[1] Judith Butler, *Gender Trouble: Feminism and the Subversion of Identity* (New York and London: Routledge, 2006), pp. xv–xvi.

[2] See, for example, Stephen J. Choi and G. Mitu Gulati, 'Contract as Statute' (2006) 104 *Michigan Law Review* 1129–1174; Friedrich Kessler, 'Contracts of Adhesion – Some Thoughts About Freedom of Contract' (1943) 43 *Columbia Law Review* 629–642.

[3] The contemporary sense of the term boilerplate is derived from the nineteenth-century practice of stamping or casting units of text onto large, flat

contracting.[4] Yet it is arguable that corporate parties' 'autonomous' choice in explicitly negotiated contracts and contractual provisions may be just as fictional as the 'meeting of minds' supposed to underpin standardised contractual provisions. Indeed, much recent work in the social sciences has highlighted the potential pitfalls of contractarian approaches to economic relations, institutions and knowledge practices.[5] Even when projections of corporate autonomy are framed as necessary or convenient fictions (as they are by some leading commentators on private international law),[6] these fictions remain problematic by virtue of the types of inquiry and points of negotiation they foreclose. Accordingly, it is this 'interior' – the terrain of autonomous choice-making – on which this chapter focuses.

In this chapter, the name given to the patterned emplacement of corporate parties' autonomous choices is 'the deal'. In the parlance of practitioners and industry rags concerned with cross-border commercial investment, the deal is a summary term for an assemblage of private law contracts, public law permits and concessions, equity investments, loans, bonds, security interests, insurance policies, rating agency grades, debt pricing and terms, national economic and political agendas, construction plans, environmental impacts, professional

metal plates (of the kind otherwise used in making steam boilers), then distributing these prepared plates to newspapers throughout the United States as 'filler' for their respective editions. Carol Bast, 'A Short History of Boilerplate' (1994) 5 *Scribes Journal of Legal Writing* 155–157 at 155–156.

4 Annelise Riles, 'The Anti-Network: Private Global Governance, Legal Knowledge, and the Legitimacy of the State' (2008) 56 *American Journal of Comparative Law* 605–630 at 624–629; Annelise Riles, *Collateral Knowledge: Legal Reasoning in the Global Financial Markets* (Chicago and London: University of Chicago Press, 2011), pp. 57–64.

5 See, for example, Justin A. Elardo and Al Campbell, 'Choice and the Substantivist/Formalist Debate: A Formal Presentation of Three Substantivist Criticisms' in Donald C. Wood (ed.), *Choice in Economic Contexts: Ethnographic and Theoretical Enquiries* (Oxford, Amsterdam and San Diego: Elsevier JAI, 2007), pp. 267–284; Ash Amin and Patrick Cohendet, *Architectures of Knowledge: Firms, Capabilities, and Communities* (Oxford University Press, 2004) (observing, at p. 39, that '[a] significant body of research located in different disciplines … has grown seriously to question the traditional contractarian vision of the firm … It views the firm as a social institution, the main characteristic of which is to know (well) how to do certain things … In this approach, the firm is conceived of as an institution where competences are continuously built, shaped, maintained, and protected').

6 See, for example, *ibid.*; Michael J. Whincop and Mary Keyes, *Policy and Pragmatism in the Conflict of Laws* (Aldershot: Ashgate/Dartmouth Publishing, 2001), p. 167 (observing that 'corporations are accorded legal personality [recognised as a reification] for pragmatic reasons, not ontological ones').

identities and industry 'firsts' (or revisited precedents).[7] One might also think of the deal as an abode, a workplace, or a polity divided in and against itself. The making of parties' contractual choices, for a given state or non-state law and a state or non-state dispute-resolution forum, is recast here as one enacted in, by and for the deal. The story told here is of the performance of choices of law and forum from the perspective of corporate lawyers working 'in' and 'on' a cross-border deal.

If the autonomous choice of corporate parties is read as the product of a deal, and the deal is read as a site already saturated with legality and regularised quasi-legality, then questions arise before the question of when or whether those parties may be governed by non-state norms (particularly merchant law or usage, or *lex mercatoria*), in preference to norms prescribed by state institutions (courts and legislatures).[8] Such

[7] See, for example, *Project Finance Magazine*, 'Latin American Oil & Gas Deal of the Year 2007', 1 February 2008. Cf. Doreen McBarnet, 'Transnational Transactions: Legal Work, Cross-Border Commerce and Global Regulation', in Michael Likosky (ed.), *Transnational Legal Processes: Globalisation and Power Disparities* (London: Butterworths, 2002), pp. 98–133 at pp. 98–99 ('turn[ing] the spotlight on the legal construction of global deals … from the pragmatic perspective of practising lawyers working for specific clients') and Victor Fleischer, 'Deals: Bringing Corporate Transactions into the Law School Classroom' (2002) *Columbia Business Law Review* 475–498.

[8] This issue is a central preoccupation of private international law literature. For scholarship supportive of affording parties the option of subjecting commercial contracts to *lex mercatoria*, see, for example, Thomas E. Carbonneau, 'The Remaking of Arbitration: Design and Destiny' in *Lex Mercatoria and Arbitration: A Discussion of the New Law Merchant*, Revised Edition (New York: Juris Publishing, 1998), pp. 23–42 at p. 23; Andreas Lowenfeld, 'Lex Mercatoria: An Arbitrator's View' in Carbonneau, *Lex Mercatoria*, pp. 71–92 at p. 71; Friedrich K. Juenger, 'American Conflicts Scholarship and the New Law Merchant' (1995) 28 *Vanderbilt Journal of Transnational Law* 487–502; Friedrich K. Juenger, 'The Lex Mercatoria and Private International Law' (2000) 60 *Louisiana Law Review* 1133–1150. For reservations about this prospect, see, for example, Okezie Chukwumerije, *Choice of Law in International Commercial Arbitration* (Westport: Quorum Books, 1994), p. 130 (observing that national courts' deference to the customary norms of the 'new' law merchant would 'grant arbitrators the power to dictate which rules of national laws would be applied in the national arena, a rather strange prospect'); William W. Park, 'Control Mechanisms in the Development of a Modern Lex Mercatoria' in Carbonneau, *Lex Mercatoria*, pp. 143–172 at p. 143 (querying whether *lex mercatoria* might be 'a fig leaf to hide an unauthorized substitution of [arbitrators'] private normative preferences in place of the parties' shared expectations under the properly applicable law'); Symeon C. Symeonides, 'Contracts Subject to Non-State Norms' (2006) 54 (Supplement) *American Journal of Comparative Law* 209–232 at 224–227 (expressing concern that non-state norms' selection might authorise the exploitation of relatively unsophisticated or weak parties and worry as to the uncertain, imprecise content of the *lex mercatoria*). See generally Michael Joachim Bonell, 'Soft Law and Party Autonomy: The Case of the UNIDROIT Principles' (2005) 51 *Loyola Law Review* 229–252; Jan H. Dalhuisen, 'Legal

questions include the following: to what extent, how and with what effects does deal-constraint get effaced by deal-freedom in scholarly representations of 'autonomous', pre- or post-legal decision-making concerning choices of law and forum? What norms or blind spots are enacted in this supposedly freedom-heavy configuration of choice in international commercial transactions? What gets ruled in and ruled out when one locates determinative choices before or after but not so much *in* the legal deal? What are the implications of an overdetermination of the pre- or post-legal arena of choice for the presumed link between party autonomy and political and economic liberalism? In other words, what might be some implications of envisaging the pre- and post-legal arena from which parties' autonomous preferences are understood to emanate as crosshatched with lawyers' tracks? These are the sorts of questions that this chapter considers or introduces for further consideration.

By way of launching an investigation into these questions, the first part of this chapter summarily compares the pre- or post-legality of the sphere from which autonomous choice is understood to emanate to the illegality and extra-legality addressed in the preceding chapters. Brief explanation will then be given of the significance of party autonomy in private international law scholarship and doctrine.

Claiming that the 'non-legal' sphere in which autonomous choice is said to be performed in private international law comprises an under-interrogated backdrop to private international law scholarship, this chapter then proceeds to replace this seamless backdrop with another scene. It redescribes corporate parties' choices of law and forum in terms of a quasi-ethnographic rendering of their making in the course of a deal, drawing attention to the role of lawyers and legal work in that process. In the course of this redescription, the following arguments are made: first, the 'non-legal' exercise of 'autonomous choice' in selecting a contract's applicable law and dispute-resolution forum in an international corporate transaction is, in practice, normatively overdetermined.[9] That is, the factors shaping the enactment of choice in a

Orders and Their Manifestation: The Operation of the International Commercial and Financial Legal Order and its Lex Mercatoria' (2006) 24 *Berkeley Journal of International Law* 129–191; Abul F. M. Maniruzzaman, 'The Lex Mercatoria and International Contracts: A Challenge for International Commercial Arbitration?' (1999) 14 *American University International Law Review* 657–734.

[9] On 'overdetermination', from which the foregoing and later usages in this chapter are extrapolated, see Louis Althusser, 'Contradiction and Overdetermination' in *For*

complex corporate transaction remain normatively irreducible either to the apparently determined 'non-legal' choices attributed to those entities that are parties to each contract in question, or to the principles of private international law that purport to uphold or constrain those choices. Second, corporate parties' enactments of 'non-legal' autonomous preference in market transactions tend to be structured in particular, patterned ways, including through deal architecture and financial modelling. These recurrent structures or patterns – and the contributions that lawyers make to their production and reproduction – merit as much questioning as is levelled at the private international law principles by which parties' choices are understood to be circumscribed in advance or after the fact. The final part of this chapter highlights some possible implications of a line of questioning directed at those structures and patterns that constitute the non-legal 'private' of private international law.

Non-legalities compared

In preceding chapters' accounts, international legal scholarship has been enlivened and threatened by the persistent trace of non-legality. Illegalities, we have seen, operate as both triggers to action and justifications for inaction. Accordingly, as emerged from the discussion of torture, international legal scholarship expresses some ambivalence about illegality. Both illegality's intimate relation to legal creativity, and its potential to draw international law into modes of violence and domination to which it customarily sees itself opposed, meet with uneasy acknowledgement. Illegality suggests for international law both an ever-present capacity for novation and an ever-present risk of unravelling.

Extra-legality, explored in relation to Guantánamo Bay, also orients international legal scholarship towards inauguration. In contrast to discussion surrounding illegality, however, discussion surrounding extra-legality appears less concerned with professional refinement, temperance and improvement than with keeping political insurgence

Marx (trans. Ben Brewster, London and New York: Verso, 1977), pp. 87–128; Sigmund Freud, 'The Aetiology of Hysteria' in *The Freud Reader* (ed. Peter Gay, London: Vintage, 1995), pp. 96–110 at p. 108; Sigmund Freud, 'Fragment of an Analysis of a Case of Hysteria ("Dora")' in *The Freud Reader*, pp. 172–238 at p. 203. On the implications of 'overdetermination' in Althusser's work, and the export (and transformation) of the term, see William S. Lewis, 'The Under-Theorization of Overdetermination in *Hegemony and Socialist Strategy*' (2005) 4:2 *Borderlands E-Journal*, www.borderlands.net.au/vol4no2_2005/lewis_overdetermination.htm (accessed 17 September 2012).

and over-take at bay. Whereas the denotation 'illegal' seems to invite a laborious tending to legality (lamenting its wounding, subduing its errancy), the denotation 'extra-legal' seems to elicit legality's frantic elevation and to prompt institutional and scholarly mobilisation towards the task of re-conquest or re-enclosure.

In their effects within international legal work, pre- and post-legal imaginative domains share something with both illegality and extra-legality. Each of these modes of non-legality generates some justification, direction and purpose for current and ongoing international legal work. Pre- and post-legality tend, however, to cleave much more smoothly than illegality or extra-legality to the characteristic operations of international law. The relation of pre- or post-legality to legality seems often to be cast as one of flows; pre- and post-legal actions and choices are understood to be in continuous communion with, and endlessly translatable into, the making and unmaking of law.[10] It is from its configuration of pre- and post-legal terrain in this respect that international legality draws a sense of its capacity both to constitute and to curtail freedom.

In the case of pre- or post-legality identified with personal or corporate contractual choice, for instance, non-legality mediates some of the tensions at play in the idea of a global, secular rule of law. The anchorage of international law in human choice affirms the secular origins of law, rather than its traceability to any divine source. The location of that choice in a moment, an action or a space regarded as non-legal (predominantly in terms of economic choice, for example) affords international law a basis for its own observation; it confers, upon international law that is, some 'external' basis for asserting positive facticity in the world. Finally, by focusing attention on the act of subjection to legal jurisdiction (through choices of law and forum), international law maintains a link between non-legal choice and the effective legality to which it is said to give rise. The maintenance of a close proximity – but not a fusion – between the pre- or post-legal on one hand and the legal on the other, and the insistence upon their flowing continuously into one other, ensures, in other words, that international law is traceable, but not entirely reducible, to personal, national or corporate preference. This helps sustain a sense that human freedom – specifically, freedom of individual, state or corporate choice – is answerable, but not entirely subordinate, to prevailing international legality.

[10] On the limits of this translatability, see Riles, 'The Anti-Network', 623–629.

Party autonomy as pre- or post-legality in private international law: doctrinal and legal realist accounts

The sense that private international law is properly referable to the 'private' (read: personal, familial and commercial) desires of individual persons (be they natural or legal persons) both pre-existing and post-dating their legal expression is encapsulated, in particular, by legal doctrine concerning party autonomy in contractual choice of law and choice of forum.[11] In private international law, 'party autonomy' in relation to contract is generally taken to refer to the entitlement of parties to select the law under which their contractual terms will be interpreted and the jurisdiction in which those terms will, in the event of dispute, be enforced.[12] In contracts with indicia of internationalism, an actual or inferred choice on questions of applicable law and forum is supposed to bring clarity and certainty to the confusion posed by multijurisdictional overlap, allowing at least some regulatory rubber to meet the parties' chosen road.

The influence borne by an idea of party autonomy in private international law is discernible not only in doctrinal argument that explicitly favours or frets about the prioritisation of private choices. It is evident too in how contractual choices are depicted in private international law scholarship. Both in scholarship celebratory of party autonomy and in scholarship anxious about its impact in private international law, the negotiated enactment of contractual choice is, as already noted, envisaged as a pre-regulatory or post-regulatory moment. Parties are presumed more or less capable of standing back from the laws and jurisdictions with which they are potentially engaged, assessing the likely outcomes of those engagements, and contracting around the impacts they wish to avoid.[13]

[11] See, for example, Michael Whincop and Mary Keyes, 'Putting the "Private" Back into Private International Law: Default Rules and the Proper Law of the Contract' (1997) 21 *Melbourne University Law Review* 515–543 at 542: ('We consciously endorse … an approach [that is] most consistent with the normative principle of party autonomy, and most supportive of private ordering and exchange facilitation. As our title suggests, it is a way to put the "private" back into private international law').

[12] Peter E. Nygh, *Autonomy in International Contracts* (Oxford and New York: Clarendon Press and Oxford University Press, 1999), pp. 1, 13.

[13] As Annelise Riles points out, this capacity for disengaged choice is also assumed by much legal-realist scholarship on private international law in its 'technoscientific' mode. Annelise Riles, 'A New Agenda for the Cultural Study of Law: Taking on the Technicalities' (2005) 53 *Buffalo Law Review* 973–1024 at 1007–1008.

Moreover, for the purposes of choosing law and forum, each contracting party is gathered more or less into a single consciousness, vested with coherence, preferences and directive vision understood to pre-exist their legal engagement. Even those who rail against the rise and abuse of private power seem to take the seamless, pre- or post-legal interiority of each 'autonomous' party more or less for granted. Likewise, as a matter of private international law doctrine, provided that a written choice of law or forum is deemed the true choice of a given party (free from duress, *mala fides* or fraud), the actual making of a contractual choice of law or forum becomes virtually unreadable.[14]

Legal devolution to 'non-legal' party preference in private international law has long provoked concerns about regulatory evasion, the subversion of sovereign authority, and disregard for the legitimate interests of governments.[15] Accordingly, the delineation of the proper ambit of party autonomy, and the extent to which it should be subordinated to mandatory law or public-policy principles, preoccupies much private international law scholarship.[16] In recent decades, scholarly attention to the scope of party autonomy in contractual matters has been particularly intense regarding contract-making by transnational corporations,[17] the scenario on which this chapter focuses.

[14] See generally Nygh, *Autonomy in International Contracts*, pp. 66–71, 92–97, 104–121. Nygh rationalises private international law's tunnel vision in this respect as follows: ('The reason for the ... exclusion of evidence of pre- and post-contractual behaviour is certainty, a policy which is understandable where the agreement between the parties has been reduced to writing'): p. 112.

[15] See, for example, *E. Gerli & Co.* v. *Cunard S. S. Co.*, 48 F. 2d 115, 117 (2d Cir. 1931): ('People cannot by agreement substitute the law of another place; they may of course incorporate any provisions they wish into their agreements – a statute like anything else – and when they do, courts will try to make sense out of the whole, so far as they can. But ... [s]ome law must impose the obligation, and the parties have nothing whatever to do with that'). See also Ernest Rabel, *The Conflict of Laws: A Comparative Study*, Second Edition (Michigan: Michigan Legal Studies, 1960), pp. 359–431.

[16] See, for example, Ama S. Bekoe, 'The Illusory Choice: Examining the Illusion of "Choice" in Choice of Law Provisions – A Country Study Exploring One Aspect of Foreign Investment in the Caribbean' (1999) 42 *Howard Law Journal* 505–534 at 511: ('[T]he success of any choice of law system[ ] can and should be measured by the degree of autonomy that contracting parties have to determine which law would govern their cross border contracts'). See generally Andreas F. Lowenfeld, 'International Litigation and the Quest for Reasonableness' (1994) 245 *Recueil des Cours* 9–320 at 255–291. Lowenfeld is among those sceptical of 'viewing private controversies as if they involved deep-seated national interests': p. 291.

[17] See, for example, Tai-Heng Cheng, 'Power, Authority and International Investment Law' (2005) 20 *American University International Law Review* 465–520 at 505; Robert

Written accounts abound of the nineteenth-century enthronement of private parties – including corporate parties – as primary 'legislators' for their contractual relations.[18] Peter Nygh has observed that '[w]hereas originally [a contract] was seen as an obligation imposed on the parties by the general law arising out of their transaction, it came to be seen as an obligation created by the parties themselves'.[19] Nygh regarded it as one consequence of this shift that private international law in most Anglo-Commonwealth, North American and Western European jurisdictions came to authorise parties to 'exit' the realm of an otherwise applicable legal regime, and the purview of an otherwise competent court, as a matter of contractual choice. Thus, in 1999, Nygh wrote: 'Today the freedom of the parties to an international contract to choose the applicable law and its corollary, to choose the forum, judicial or arbitral, for the settlement of their disputes arising out of such contract is almost universally acknowledged.'[20]

Equally well-documented, however, is the late nineteenth- and early twentieth-century assault, by legal-realist scholars, on the idea of liberty upon which the foregoing configuration of contractual autonomy relies.[21] Robert Hale, among others, argued that freely negotiated, voluntary, contractual exchanges amounted to complex networks of mutual coercion. In Hale's work, as Warren Samuels has observed, 'decisions made [by corporations, for instance] are a function of the decision-making structure, [such that] that structure becomes the critical, if not always conspicuous, policy issue'.[22] Parties' contractual choices, Hale showed, were conditioned by the unavailability of alternative choices.[23]

Wai, 'Transnational Liftoff and Juridical Touchdown: The Regulatory Function of Private International Law in an Era of Globalization' (2002) 40 *Columbia Journal of Transnational Law* 209–274 at 219–220.

18 See, for example, Patrick S. Atiyah, *The Rise and Fall of Freedom of Contract* (Oxford University Press, 1979).

19 Nygh, *Autonomy in International Contracts*, p. 7 (footnote omitted).

20 *Ibid.*, p. 13.

21 See generally William W. Fisher III *et al.* (eds.), *American Legal Realism* (New York: Oxford University Press, 1993), pp. 76–120; Barbara H. Fried, *The Progressive Assault on Laissez Faire: Robert Hale and the First Law and Economics Movement* (Cambridge, MA: Harvard University Press, 1998), pp. 29–70.

22 Warren J. Samuels, 'The Economy as a System of Power and its Legal Bases: The Legal Economics of Robert Lee Hale' (1973) 27 *University of Miami Law Review* 261–371 at 351.

23 Robert L. Hale, 'Value and Vested Rights' (1927) 27 *Columbia Law Review* 523–529 at 524–525: ('The law places on the staff no legal duty to work for this employer ... but it does impose various other restrictions on their liberty which have an indirect effect of making them seek jobs ... The legal restraints on their conduct ...

The availability or unavailability of such alternatives was a consequence, in part, of the law of contract's (among other laws') unevenly disbursing entitlements.[24] Accordingly, the free-market system of contractual freedom was, according to Hale, 'not a system of liberty at all, but a complicated network of restraints, imposed in part by individuals, but very largely by the government itself at the behest of some individuals on the freedom of others, and at the behest of others on the freedom of the "some"'.[25] '[I]n a sense', Hale argued, 'each party to [a] contract, by the threat to call on the government to enforce his power over the liberty of the other, *imposes* the terms of the contract on the other'.[26] That parties' contractual choices were not generally experienced by the parties themselves as products of coercion was, Hale contended, solely a matter of social convention.[27] Of this 'system', Hale concluded:

> What in fact distinguishes this counterfeit system of '*laissez-faire*' from paternalism is not the absence of restraint, but the absence of any conscious purpose on the part of the officials who administer the restraint, and of any responsibility or unanimity on the part of the numerous [property] owners [or holders of other tangible or intangible entitlements] at whose discretion the restraint is administered.[28]

All that could be extrapolated from the principle of party autonomy in contractual matters, according to Hale's reading, was a conscious or unconscious normative commitment on the part of law-makers (public and private) to maintain, as far as possible, the existing distribution of background constraints and entitlements. Given the ubiquity

constitute the indirect sanction which drives them into the employ of the particular factory owner').

[24] Robert L. Hale, 'Labor Legislation as an Enlargement of Individual Liberty' (1925) 15 *American Labor Legislation Review* 155–160 at 156–157 (attacking '[t]he idea … that at common law we all have equal rights, whether of personal liberty or of property' with the observation that '[t]he common law interferes with liberty by imposing legal duties and these duties are not the same for all … [T]he institution of ownership constitutes for everyone both a curtailment of some sort of liberty and an enlargement of some other sort of liberty').

[25] Fried, *The Progressive Assault on Laissez Faire*, p. 50 (quoting Robert Hale, 'Economic Nationalism Versus Representative Government', unpublished manuscript).

[26] Robert L. Hale, 'Law Making by Unofficial Minorities' (1920) 20 *Columbia Law Review* 451–456 at 452.

[27] Robert L. Hale, 'Our Equivocal Constitutional Guaranties' (1939) 39 *Columbia Law Review* 563–594 at 577.

[28] Fried, *The Progressive Assault on Laissez Faire*, p. 50 (quoting Robert Hale, 'Economic Nationalism Versus Representative Government', unpublished manuscript; Fried's bracketed edits removed).

of unacknowledged coercion, the extant regime of legal rights and prohibitions could not be deduced from any plausible notion of party autonomy in the abstract.

Legal-realist critiques of deductive legal reasoning in general, and contractual freedom in particular, were extended into the private international law field by Walter Wheeler Cook.[29] Like Hale, Cook set out to demonstrate the inadequacy of generic explanations for decisions at which courts arrived in particular instances. Focusing on decisions made by courts, rather than on the reasons given for those decisions, Cook argued that US case law on private international law issues could not be reconciled with a theory of law's essentially territorial character nor with any other general principle delineating the scope of sovereign jurisdiction.[30] According to Cook, notions of 'right' and other hypostatisations of legal relations ('party autonomy' included) had no more effect in law than as predictions of the probable behaviour of certain officials in a particular case.[31] Cook maintained that judicial behaviour in any one case was better understood as 'a practical result based upon … reasons of policy'.[32]

Cook has often been read as one more advocate of doctrinal deference to autonomous choice.[33] Cook's interest in parties' choices of law and forum, however, merits reading in the context of his interest in exploring the effect and limits of private 'legislation'.[34] By Cook's

[29] See generally Walter Wheeler Cook, *The Logical and Legal Bases of the Conflict of Laws* (Cambridge, MA: Harvard University Press, 1942); Walter Wheeler Cook, 'The Logical and Legal Bases of the Conflict of Laws' (1924) 33 *Yale Law Journal* 457–488.

[30] Cook, *The Logical and Legal Bases of the Conflict of Laws*, pp. 3–68.

[31] *Ibid.*, pp. 30–31. Hence Cook's observations that 'th[e] arbitrariness of [parties'] choice is usually concealed by confusing the occurrence of the factual events with the attachment of legal obligation' and that 'an unconscious preference [on the part of the forum court] for the domestic rule of the forum may lead to a "presumption" that that "law" is the one the parties "intended" to govern': pp. 414, 416.

[32] *Ibid.*, p. 480.

[33] For such a reading, see Roger C. Cramton *et al.* (eds.), *Conflict of Laws: Cases, Comments, Questions*, Third Edition (Minnesota: West Publishing Company, 1981), p. 155: ('The rule permitting parties to select the law to govern the validity of a contract has many adherents, including Cook'); Symeon C. Symeonides, 'The American Choice of Law Revolution in the Courts: Today and Tomorrow' (2002) 298 *Recueil des Cours* 9–448 at 37: ('Cook thought of the choice-of-law problem as one of choosing between competing rules').

[34] See Cook, *The Logical and Legal Bases of the Conflict of Laws*, pp. 393–398 (challenging the argument attributed to Professors Ernest Lorenzen, Joseph Beale and Herbert Goodrich that 'this kind of "legislation" – if one calls it that – is never permitted under our legal system'). In so far as Cook did endorse giving effect to parties' 'intention' with respect to choices of law and forum (and Cook always couched the word 'intention' in scare quotes as if to alert readers to its constructed nature),

reading, when, at the behest of a contractual choice of law clause, a forum court purported to apply foreign law, that court was disavowing the law-creating dimension of its finding that foreign law applied. 'The most practical and simple statement' of what courts do in such instances, Cook contended, 'appears to be that the forum always "enforces rights" created by its own "law" and never "foreign law" or "foreign rights"'.[35]

Similarly, when a forum court determined to uphold an express choice of another jurisdiction set forth in a contract, Cook argued, it was not abstaining from law-making or permitting an evasion of forum law. Rather, the court was making a determination that, having regard to public policy in the forum and the reasonableness of the parties' choice in the circumstances, the law of the forum was, for purposes of the transaction in question, identical to the rules of the jurisdiction chosen by the parties, as the forum court understood them.[36]

Accordingly, Cook described courts' refusal to give effect to parties' choice of law, in certain cases, as 'purely practical', a decision taken in recognition of risks and inconveniences posed by parties litigating in jurisdictions to which their dispute bore little or no connection.[37] In Cook's view, '[n]o attempt should be made to state a single, comprehensive rule or brief set of rules, to be applied more or less mechanically to all types of contracts', such as a rule or rules requiring deference to parties' expressed or presumed intention in contractual choice of law, subject to certain conditions.[38] Instead, Cook concluded, 'The "conflict-of-laws" problems in the field of "contracts" need[ed] to be

he contended that choice should be limited to the law of some state with which the transaction in question has some substantial connection, and warned that the public-policy test to which this 'intention' must further be subject must be 'kept constantly in mind': pp. 412, 418. Note also that Cook's endorsement of a rule deferring to the expressed intention of the parties was always expressed as relative to the more problematic (as he saw it) 'place of contracting' theory. Cook conditioned this endorsement further by suggesting that it would be meaningful only '[i]f such a brief set of rules is thought desirable': p. 419. As Annelise Riles notes, Cook himself had little interest in producing or validating a brief set of rules: Riles, 'A New Agenda for the Cultural Study of Law', 1030.

35 Cook, *The Logical and Legal Bases of the Conflict of Laws*, p. 478.

36 Walter Wheeler Cook, '"Contracts" and the Conflict of Laws: "Intention" of the Parties' (1938) 32 *Illinois Law Review* 899–920 (hereinafter Cook, 'Contracts I'). See also Walter Wheeler Cook, '"Contracts" and the Conflict of Laws: "Intention" of the Parties: Some Further Remarks' (1939) 34 *Illinois Law Review* 423–432 (hereinafter Cook, 'Contracts II').

37 Cook, 'Contracts I', 920. 38 *Ibid.*

broken down so that different types of social, economic, and business problems may receive separate consideration'.[39]

The legal-realist critique of, on one hand, the idea that contractual choices of law and forum properly arise from the unfettered will of contracting parties deployed pre- and post-legally and, on the other, the idea that a principled commitment to uphold 'party autonomy' yields predictable outcomes across private international law cases was rigorous and compelling. Nonetheless, each of these ideas still retains considerable purchase in private international law today.[40] These ideas prevail, moreover, both as a matter of legal doctrine and scholarly analysis. In 2008, for example, the European Parliament and the Council of Europe adopted a regulation proposed by the Commission of the European Community to clarify and 'modernise' the Rome Convention of 1980 on the Law Applicable to Contractual Relations, while transforming it into an instrument of the European Community.[41] Article 3.1 of the Rome Convention already provided that '[a] contract shall be governed by the law chosen by the parties'.[42] The 2008 Regulation sought to 'further boost the impact of the parties' will' in relation to choice of law and choice of forum, permitting, for example, parties' selection of codified bodies of non-state law to govern their contractual relations.[43] At the same time, scholars in many jurisdictions continue to champion the cause of party autonomy. Invoking economic-efficiency arguments and political-rights criteria, commentators have rallied periodically to contest the perceived winding-back of parties' freedom under mandatory rules of private international law.[44]

[39] *Ibid.* That the generic characterisation of 'social', 'economic' or 'business' problems could itself be subjected to Cook's critique was not a point taken up in his work.

[40] For a study of the status and effects of party autonomy in contractual choice of law in US private international law, see Louis C. James, 'Effects of the Autonomy of the Parties on Conflict of Laws Contracts' (1959) 36 *Chicago-Kent Law Review* 34–59.

[41] Law Applicable to Contractual Obligations (hereafter 'Rome 1'), Council Regulation 593/2008, OJ 2008 No. L177, p. 6.

[42] Convention of the Law Applicable to Contractual Obligations (hereafter 'Rome Convention'), Rome, 19 June 1980, in force 1 April 1991, 19 I. L. M. 1492; OJ L 266.

[43] Article 13, Rome 1. The Hague Choice of Court Convention seeks to effect a similar change: see Louise Ellen Teitz, 'The Hague Choice of Court Convention: Validating Party Autonomy and Providing an Alternative to Arbitration' (2005) 53 *American Journal of Comparative Law* 543–558.

[44] See, for example, Whincop and Keyes, *Policy and Pragmatism*, p. 67: ('Contractual freedom has been substantially wound back by mandatory rules'); p. 22: ('Efficiency generally requires that parties should be able to agree to the law that should

There are, of course, a wide variety of ways in which courts across the common-law world can and do avoid application of the law and devolution to the forum expressly chosen by contracting parties. Courts may find that the contract at issue was so formed as to exclude a clause setting forth that choice, that the choice was not bona fide, not legally permissible, or was contrary to forum public policy, or that the choice of a law or forum unconnected with the contract was otherwise indefensible.[45]

As noted above, the concern of this chapter is not with the question of whether arguments framed in terms of party autonomy hold sway in private international law disputes as a doctrinal matter. Rather, its objective is to highlight the background-structuring effects of the notion of party autonomy exercised in a pre- or post-legal sphere. In other words, regardless of whether parties' explicit choices of law and forum always prevail in litigation or arbitration, it is *itself* politically significant that a contracting party presumed to be vested with, or assertive of, autonomy arising independently of law serves as a touchstone for scholarly debate and norm development in private international law. It is in light of the persistence of this touchstone in recent literature that one may observe that the autonomous party has weathered the legal-realist squall remarkably well.

In public international law literature, the sometime conceptual counterpart to the contracting party, the autonomous sovereign state,

apply to their [contractual] relation, subject to the usual, uncontroversial limits on contractual freedom, such as incapacity and duress'); Lea Brilmayer 'Rights, Fairness, and Choice of Law' (1989) 98 *Yale Law Journal* 1277–1320 at 1297–1298 (arguing that the application of law and the extension of jurisdiction under private international law principles must be defensible as a matter of political theory and that a subject's consent to be subjected to a particular rule of law is a paradigmatic indicator of the legitimacy of its application); Erin A. O'Hara and Larry E. Ribstein, 'From Politics to Efficiency in Choice of Law' (2000) 67 *University of Chicago Law Review* 1151–1232 at 1151: ('To the extent practicable, parties should be able to choose their governing law, subject to possible procedural protections designed to ensure that the choice is real. In the absence of an explicit agreement, courts should apply rules that facilitate party choice or that select the law the parties likely would have contracted for – that is, the law of the state with the comparative regulatory advantage').

45 See generally Nygh, *Autonomy in International Contracts*, pp. 66–71 (discussing, inter alia, *Carnival Cruise Lines Inc.* v. *Shute*, 499 US 585 (1991); *Bremen* v. *Zapata Off-Shore Co.*, 407 US 1 (1972); *Oceanic Sun Line Special Shipping Co., Inc.* v. *Fay* (1988) 165 C. L. R. 197; *Messageries Maritimes* v. *Wilson* (1954) 94 C. L. R. 577; *Vita Foods, Inc.* v. *Unus Shipping Co.* (1939) A. C. 277; *Golden Acres, Ltd.* v. *Queensland Estates Pty. Ltd* (1969) Q. R. 378).

has been subject to successive rounds of disaggregation.[46] The corporation contracting internationally has confronted similar indignities, most notably in the decomposition of the enterprise into a 'nexus of contracts' in law-and-economics literature.[47] Legal scholarship has also, from time to time, adopted a thicker, transaction-specific frame for the analysis of corporate contracting, dispensing with contract law's customary preoccupation with written indicia of intent.[48] The legal literature on transaction costs and third-party externalities has, on occasion, pointed towards the moment and mode of the parties' choice.[49] Public-choice literature has sought to redescribe legal decision-making in terms attentive to 'rent-seeking', framing parties' autonomous preferences within networks of influence and interest.[50] Behavioural law

[46] See, for example, David Kennedy, 'A New World Order: Yesterday, Today, and Tomorrow' (1994) 4 *Transnational Law and Contemporary Problems* 329–376.

[47] Richard A. Posner, *Economic Analysis of Law*, Second Edition (Boston and Toronto: Little Brown & Co., 1977). See also Steven N. S. Cheung, 'The Contractual Nature of the Firm' (1983) 26 *Journal of Law and Economics* 1–22; Melvin A. Eisenberg, 'The Conception that the Corporation is a Nexus of Contracts, and the Dual Nature of the Firm' (1999) 24 *Journal of Corporation Law* 819–836. For an overview and critique of this literature, see generally Victor Brudney, 'Corporate Governance, Agency Costs, and the Rhetoric of Contract' (1985) 85 *Columbia Law Review* 1403–1444. For further efforts to 'crack open … the black box of the corporation' in relation to contracting behaviour, see Marcel Kahan and Michael Klausner, 'Standardization and Innovation in Corporate Contracting (or "The Economics of Boilerplate")' (1997) 83 *Virginia Law Review* 713–770 at 716.

[48] Victor Fleischer's recent contributions are both exemplary of this inclination and indicative of the impact of socio-legal critiques of the myopia of 'doctrinal' contract-law scholarship. See Victor Fleischer, 'Brand New Deal: The Branding Effect of Corporate Deal Structures' (2006) 104 *Michigan Law Review* 1581–1638; Fleischer, 'Deals: Bringing Corporate Transactions into the Law School Classroom'. Sociologists have also weighed in on the 'debate' between 'doctrinal' approaches to contract law and more 'context-attentive' versions of the discipline. See, for example, Mark C. Suchman, 'The Contract as Social Artifact' (2003) 37 *Law and Society Review* 91–142 at 96: ('The key finding here is that "Contract Law", as the doctrinalists study it, exerts remarkably little influence on a remarkably wide range of transactions'); see also Jeffrey M. Lipshaw, 'Contingency and Contracts: A Philosophy of Complex Business Transactions' (2005) 54 *DePaul Law Review* 1077–1146 at 1077–1078: ('The behavior of lawyers and business people in the course of complex commercial transactions and relationships suggest *homo economicus* is not the only model of human behavior, even in economic relationships').

[49] See, for example, Kahan and Klausner, 'Standardization and Innovation'; Michael Klausner, 'Corporations, Corporate Law, and Networks of Contracts' (1995) 81 *Virginia Law Review* 757–852.

[50] See, for example, Bruce L. Hay, 'Conflicts of Law and State Competition in the Product Liability System' (1992) 80 *Georgetown Law Journal* 617–652 at 639–642 (exploring the 'structural incentive[s]' that states face to circumscribe parties' choice of law); Erin A. O'Hara, 'Opting Out of Regulation: A Public Choice Analysis of Contractual Choice of Law' (2000) 53 *Vanderbilt Law Review* 1549–1604 at 1572–1586.

and economics has inserted insights about actual human behaviour into the modelling of choice.[51] Sociologically informed studies of contract law have replaced 'elegant models' of contract practice with complex, empirical pictures.[52]

The contributions of this work have been enormous.[53] However, to the extent that these approaches have been deployed in relation to private international law, the concern of their proponents has generally been to invest that law with greater accuracy, predictability or efficiency.[54] Literature of this kind seeks, in other words, to consolidate the non-legal facticity and integrity with which acts of choice – and the so-called autonomous parties that make them – are already invested, albeit in a more sophisticated fashion. 'Law-in-action' scholarship on corporate contracting (international and domestic) has tended to relocate the search for a stable, impartial principle governing legal decision to the domain of context, guiding philosophy or institutional identity.

Despite tracing or attributing corporate legal action to a 'nexus of contracts',[55] 'a bureaucratic hierarchical organization',[56] a tightly-woven network of 'thick personal relationships',[57] or the 'culture' of a firm

[51] See, for example, Christine Jolls, Cass R. Sunstein and Richard Thaler, 'A Behavioral Approach to Law and Economics' (1998) 50 *Stanford Law Review* 1593–1608. Reza Dibadj argues for the extension of these insights into an 'organizational behavioral economics' of the corporate firm; Reza Dibadj, 'Reconceiving the Firm' (2005) 26 *Cardozo Law Review* 1459–1534 at 1459.

[52] See, for example, Stewart Macaulay, 'Elegant Models, Empirical Pictures, and the Complexities of Contract' (1977) 11 *Law and Society Review* 507–528 at 508–512 (contrasting a 'classical model' of contracting that 'starts with the assumption that entrepreneurs need to plan and deal with risk' and that '[t]hey do so by carefully drafting contracts, which they understand and agree to' with an empirical picture that 'shows that business people in all societies compromise differences rather than invoke contract norms').

[53] For a discussion of some of the implications of socio-legal scholarship for public and private international law, see generally Paul Schiff Berman, 'From International Law to Law and Globalization' (2005) 43 *Columbia Journal of Transnational Law* 485–556.

[54] See, for example, Stephen J. Choi and G. Mitu Gulati, 'Contract as Statute' (2006) 104 *Michigan Law Review* 1129–1174 at 1172: ('[T]o recognize the reality of how these documents evolve and how certain terms can get forgotten but nevertheless [be] retained in the contracts will help courts reach a more accurate understanding of the reality of what the contract is intended to mean'); O'Hara and Ribstein, 'From Politics to Efficiency'.

[55] Eisenberg, 'The Conception that the Corporation is a Nexus of Contracts', 836.

[56] *Ibid.*, 829 (emphasis omitted).

[57] Volkmar Gessner *et al.*, 'Introduction: The Legal Culture of Global Business Transactions' in Richard P. Appelbaum *et al.* (eds.), *Rules and Networks: The Legal Culture of Global Business Transactions* (Oxford: Hart Publishing, 2001), pp. 1–38 at pp. 1–2.

or an industry,[58] 'post-doctrinal' contract, corporate and private international law scholarship has tended to reproduce, at a different scale and with richer embroidery, more or less the very meeting-of-minds-between-autonomous-parties structure that it was ostensibly concerned to surpass.[59] Instead of offer and acceptance between discrete agents, we are presented with a confluence of 'corporate systems' and the like, each system, organisation, community or culture attributed with more or less the coherence, univocality and interiority that private international law has traditionally attributed to contracting parties (and to states) in the pre- and post-legal sphere.[60] As Judith Butler has reminded us, recourse to context in lieu of subjectivity often amounts to recourse to yet another 'posited unit[y]'.[61]

The next part of this chapter works against the tendency to take the pre- or post-legal 'interiors' of transnational corporate contracting for granted in assessing decisions concerning contractual choice of law and forum. Those decisions by which corporations are presumed, by many, to arrive at the most cost-effective or transaction-suited choices of law and forum are, in this chapter's account, decisions

[58] Harry Arthurs, 'The Role of Global Law Firms in Constructing or Obstructing a Traditional Regime of Labour Law' in Applebaum *et al.*, *Rules and Networks*, pp. 273–300 at pp. 273–274.

[59] For illustrative incarnations of the subjectivity of corporate contracting parties in these various modes, see Gessner *et al.*, 'Introduction' p. 2; Eisenberg, 'The Conception that the Corporation is a Nexus of Contracts'; Michael C. Jensen and William H. Meckling, 'The Theory of the Firm: Managerial Behavior, Agency Costs, and Ownership Structure' (1976) 3 *Journal of Financial Economics* 305–360 at 310–311. As Victor Brudney observes, 'the vision that informs the "nexus of contracts" concept approaches the classical mode [of contracting, premised on the presumption of autonomy] more closely than it does … [an] approach that is sensitive to information asymmetries, duress, incapacity, and lack of "good faith" in performance, and that encourages judicial intervention to protect those thus disadvantaged': Brudney, 'Corporate Governance', 1405.

[60] See, for example, Eisenberg, 'The Conception that the Corporation is a Nexus of Contracts', 836. Contra Ralf Michaels, 'The Re-state-ment of Non-State Law: The State, Choice of Law, and the Challenge from Global Legal Pluralism' (2005) 51 *Wayne Law Review* 1209–1260 at 1247: ('Once the state no longer serves as the formal criterion distinguishing law from non-law, no other criterion seems to do the job … [W]e cannot stop arbitrarily at the thin criterion of "community"').

[61] Butler, *Gender Trouble*, p. xxii. Butler here makes a point that has been much more fully elaborated elsewhere, including in anthropological writing on the search for an ethnographic 'real' and the making of scientific fact. See, for example, James Clifford, *The Predicament Of Culture: Twentieth-Century Ethnography, Literature and Art* (Cambridge, MA: Harvard University Press, 1998), pp. 117–151; Bruno Latour and Steve Woolgar, *Laboratory Life: The Social Construction of Scientific Facts* (Princeton University Press, 1979).

that emanate from an unwieldy normative thicket. The normative dimensions of this thicket are, moreover, neither well captured nor best rendered critically negotiable by recourse to the 'convenience' of party autonomy (whether to celebrate or attack it). Envisaging one or more personified corporations to be acting autonomously in pre- or post-legal choices of law and forum, whether in a straightforward transactional mode or in a more complex 'nexus of contracts' or similar arrangement, tends to mischaracterise the stakes and participants operating in this field and the forces at work therein. Accordingly, critical attention should be given to some of the decision-making dynamics and structures that might otherwise be written out of view by that approach.

Overdetermination and overflow in autonomous choice

The critique of pre- or post-legal party autonomy developed in this chapter proceeds from a stylised account of how corporate lawyers arrive at contractual choices of law and forum in transnational corporate deals. Contrary to the impression generated by standard scholarly renderings of transnational corporate agency, experiences of corporate transactional work yield no sullied corporate 'soul' amenable to liberation or circumscription on a disciplinary, organisational or individual level.[62] Whereas Michael Hardt and Antonio Negri have insisted in their widely read book *Empire* that there is 'no more outside' to the reign of global capital,[63] this chapter proceeds in the opposite direction, towards a claim that there may be no inside or no a priori to transnational corporate deal-making that resolutely determines every performance of 'autonomous' choice, however unassailable certain systemic or subjective properties may appear. The following sketch of corporate dealing suggests that there may be more irresolution to, and a denser array of legal influences upon, 'non-legal', private decision-making than much

[62] See, for example, Fleischer, 'Brand New Deal', 1585: ('[T]he legal infrastructure of deals provides … a window through which [one] can view, or imagine, the soul of the company'). Contra Friedrich Nietzsche, *Writings from the Late Notebooks* (trans. Kate Sturge, ed. Rudiger Bittner, Cambridge University Press, 2003), p. 27: ('Supposing that "the *soul*" was an attractive and mysterious idea which philosophers, rightly, gave up only with reluctance – perhaps what they're now learning to exchange for it is even more attractive … life and corporeality' (emphasis in original)).

[63] Michael Hardt and Antonio Negri, *Empire* (Cambridge, MA: Harvard University Press, 2000), p. 186.

recent critical scholarship would have us believe.[64] Experiences of transnational corporate dealing instead register a sense of those decisions that private international law invests with pre- and post-legal autonomy as decisions 'overflowing with the performative' and a performative legality at that.[65]

This chapter seeks to evoke an experience of this performative overflow, with a view to recapturing a sense of some of the myriad legal and policy issues in contention within the pre- and post-legal architecture of 'party autonomy' and the range of people who contribute to working out those issues. It is, however, a starting point for the account that follows that the redescription of transnational corporate power does not render that power up for regulatory grabs, any more than the preferences expressed by transnational corporate decision-makers will always prevail. The deal is not, in this account, entirely pre-codified in either direction, even as it is patently not a domain of pure freedom. Rather, this chapter is intended to evoke an experience of corporate decision-making on contractual choices of law and forum in which both the predictability *and* the pliability of those decisions may be experienced anew.

Importantly, the redescription that follows is not metaphoric. Here, the deal is not intended as a stand-in for anything but that which it presents: haphazardly recorded notes from days spent as a corporate lawyer. Moreover, this record does not purport to erase autonomous personhood in favour of some 'improved' explanatory points of reference for private international law: a now-routine gesture that often serves to enshrine a revised version of the very subjectivity it claims to disaggregate or surpass. The discussion that follows here is concerned with 'how' rather than 'what' questions: in particular, how does the

[64] See, for example, A. Claire Cutler, *Private Power and Global Authority: Transnational Merchant Law in the Global Political Economy* (New York: Cambridge University Press, 2003) pp. 180–182, 237–238. The transnational corporations and the 'global mercatocracy' of which they are a part feature in Cutler's account as 'united', directive, and largely autonomous protagonists of contemporary processes of global restructuring.

[65] Jacques Derrida, 'Force of Law: The "Mystical Foundation of Authority"', in *Acts of Religion* (ed. Gil Anidjar, New York: Routledge Press, 2002), pp. 228–298 at pp. 228, 256. Cf. Duncan Kennedy, 'Freedom and Constraint in Adjudication: A Critical Phenomenology' (1986) 36 *Journal of Legal Education* 518–562 at 518–519 (attempting to 'describe the process of legal reasoning as [Kennedy] imagine[s] [he] might do it if [he] were a judge' and thereby 'looking at law as a person who will have to apply it, interpret it, change it, defy it, or whatever' such that 'the experience of legality may well be different according to the character of the "I want" that opposes "the law"').

necessity of transnational corporations prevailing across the global legal order get produced through 'freely' negotiated transactions? The ensuing account implies that the idea of a corporate actor as a coherent, will-bearing subject (the economic properties and preferences of which pre-exist law or operate independently in law's wake) is one medium for that necessity's production. Moreover, even self-consciously contingent versions of such an identity work rather well in that capacity.[66]

In short, it is not contended here that, in the rabbit warren of a deal, one might (or should seek to) outrun coercion or constraint and recapture a more 'authentic' pre- or post-legal autonomy. Rather, this brief sketch of choice-making in a cross-border deal is undertaken towards continued excavation (and, potentially, critical mobilisation) of some of the innumerable background 'rules' by which 'non-legal' choosers and choices are shaped, circumscribed and empowered. As indicated earlier, the work of legal-realist scholars such as Robert Hale and Walter Wheeler Cook taught us much about how the apparent inevitabilities of corporate domination are produced, day by day, decision by decision, deal by deal. It is in debt to their studies of the regulatory power borne by 'unofficial minorities', the ubiquity of coercion, and the endowments of intangible privilege as well as tangible property, that the daily life of a deal is now sketched.

Doing deals: the vocabulary of the market

When corporate lawyers engaged in the 'American mode of production of law'[67] talk to each other about international transactional work in which they are engaged, they use the nomenclature of the deal. 'We just won a mining deal in Chile.' 'I know [X] from that deal we did last year.' 'I can't do [Y] until this deal closes.' Among legal elites dedicated to transactional work in the international financial sector, these are the terms in which lives are punctuated. Whereas scholarship concerning transnational corporate contracting has tended to prefer the vocabulary of agreements, regulations, firms and institutions (with important exceptions),[68] industry rags announce 'deals of the year'. Under the

[66] Contra Meir Dan-Cohen, 'Responsibility and the Boundaries of the Self' (1992) 105 *Harvard Law Review* 959–1003.

[67] David M. Trubek *et al.*, 'Global Restructuring and the Law: Studies of the Internationalization of Legal Fields and the Creation of Transnational Arenas' (1994) 44 *Case Western Reserve Law Review* 407–498 at 413, 419–426.

[68] See, for example, Thomas W. Waelde and George Ndi, 'Stabilizing International Investment Commitments: International Law Versus Contract Interpretation' (1996) 31 *Texas International Law Journal* 215–268; Jeswald W. Salacuse, 'Renegotiating

banner of a deal, as noted above, industry publications summarise an assemblage of legal and non-legal arrangements among participants public and private.[69]

Documenting all of the arrangements between the parties involved in a deal, and their authority to enter into those arrangements, is the responsibility of lawyers. For the lawyers concerned with transnational financing, 'getting the deal done' will mean, at a minimum, getting those documents prepared, negotiated and signed, so that money (debt and/or equity) may start to move. Included in that task will be the satisfaction of a litany of legal and non-legal conditions precedent to financing. The issues to be negotiated to that end are numerous and often fraught. In the project finance context, for example, they typically revolve around the entitlement of foreign lenders to oversee a project's day-to-day financial and technical management and, should problems arise, to step in and take over. This is the sort of scene being evoked here: a complex transaction, presenting an array of multijurisdictional, multidisciplinary issues for negotiation, in which sizeable amounts of money and, in many cases, the provision of basic public services (via energy infrastructure, for example) are at issue.

Performing (corporate) power: pace, place and projected returns

Corporate agents' capacity to choose among available legal possibilities in complex deals is highly conditioned. Some of the conditions to which it is effectively subject are menial and mechanistic: questions of scheduling and venue often left to junior or non-professional staff. To locate at this level arrangements colouring the making of 'substantive' legal decisions, including choices of law and forum, is to stress that power is ubiquitous across the deal's formulation as such (a point made, in relation to economic relations generally, by Robert Hale).[70]

Typically, the first step in embarking upon a complex cross-border deal is for the sponsors' (or equity investors') legal or financial advisors to convene an 'all hands' meeting. So begin the successive rounds of meetings and conference calls that comprise the daily life of the deal.

International Business Transactions: The Continuing Struggle of Life Against Form' (2001) 35 *International Lawyer* 1507–1542. But see Lipshaw, 'Contingency and Contracts', 1077–78; Suchman, 'The Contract as Social Artifact', 96.

69 See, for example, *Project Finance Magazine*, 'Latin American Oil and Gas Deal of the Year 2011: OSX 2'.

70 Robert L. Hale, 'Bargaining, Duress, and Economic Liberty' (1943) 43 *Columbia Law Review* 603–628 at 626.

Each of these will be oriented around a draft document, pending-issue list and/or logistical concerns. They are interspersed with periods of feverish document preparation on the part of lawyers and occasional lulls in activity. The tempo of the deal tends towards this faltering rhythm. Time drags in the long, air-conditioned hours of a multi-party meeting. Then, periodically, it gets compressed and caffeinated – pushed against the railing of a deadline.

Each time that a lawyer gets called upon to make a decision, however significant, its making will be inflected in some way by this discontinuous temporality.[71] Engineering the reduction of transaction costs is supposedly the lawyers' broader mandate, a mandate discharged, in part, by identifying a choice of law and jurisdiction considered 'optimal' for the parties' selection, in terms of the economic and other advantages that may flow therefrom.[72] This is how, it has been claimed, lawyers 'create value'.[73] Yet neither identification of the 'costs' of each available choice, nor the 'value-creating' processes of their comparison and elimination, is independent of the cadence of their performance.[74]

Another action typically taken early in corporate deal-making is the gathering of precedents.[75] Having reviewed publicly available documents and firm files (containing documents from prior deals in which the firm participated), each of the major law firms involved in a deal will assemble disclosure documents, contracts and legal opinions pertaining to comparable deals. These may be selected for their industry relationship to the current deal, geographic proximity or structural

[71] This temporality is too erratic and deal-specific to be amenable to modelling in terms of time-inconsistent preferences. But see Manuel A. Utset, 'A Model of Time-Inconsistent Misconduct: The Case of Lawyer Misconduct' (2005) 74 *Fordham Law Review* 1319–1352.

[72] See, for example, Larry E. Ribstein, 'Choosing Law by Contract' (1993) 18 *Journal of Corporation Law* 245–300 at 246: (Choice-of-law 'clauses provide standard terms and are a powerful way of avoiding inefficient mandatory rules ... [thereby] minimizing transaction costs').

[73] See Ronald J. Gilson, 'Value Creation by Business Lawyers: Legal Skills and Asset Pricing' (1984) 94 *Yale Law Journal* 239–313; Steven L. Schwarcz, 'Explaining the Value of Transactional Lawyering' (2007) 12 *Stanford Journal of Law, Business and Finance* 486–535.

[74] '[T]empo', wrote Nietzsche, 'is as significant a power in the development of peoples as in music': Friedrich Nietzsche, *The Gay Science: With a Prelude in German Rhymes and an Appendix of Songs* (trans. Josefine Nauckhoff and Adrian Del Caro, New York: Cambridge University Press, 2001), p. 36.

[75] Kahan and Klausner outline, in terms of 'learning benefits' and 'network benefits', some of the factors influencing lawyers' use of precedents: Kahan and Klausner, 'Standardization and Innovation', 719–729.

similarities. Any prior agreements to which current deal participants have been a party in somewhat similar circumstances will also be gathered for the evidence that they provide about terms previously accepted by those parties, and hence the range of negotiating possibilities potentially available.

In addition, drafting responsibilities will be allocated, at an early stage, among the lawyers involved in the deal. This allocation may be made, in part, on the basis of the deal experience (and, by extension, the depth and range of precedents) that one or another law firm can boast. It will also depend upon the style of lawyering favoured by the persons in question. Some lawyers insist, wherever possible, on controlling the document (and hence, to some degree, the negotiating agenda) in their clients' interests.[76] Others prefer to weigh in on the drafting process in a commentator role.

Among the terms commonly subject to standardisation in corporate practice (terms conveyed from contract to contract with minimal alteration, often referred to as boilerplate provisions)[77] are the choice of law and choice of forum provisions. Accordingly, the starting point for the negotiation of applicable law and jurisdiction for a contract will often depend upon which law firm has assumed responsibility for drafting that contract and hence the institutional origin of the guiding precedent for that exercise. Thereafter, the ease with which non-drafting deal participants accept the drafting firm's boilerplate may depend on a range of factors, from the volume of documentation those concerned are called upon to review (and the time afforded to do so), to the confidence that deal participants have come to place in the lawyers responsible for the drafting task in question. The fact that choice of law and forum selection clauses, along with other boilerplate provisions, typically appear at the back of a contract also ensures that they often receive less critical attention than they otherwise might.[78]

[76] On the disproportionate power that may be enjoyed by the 'party with the pen', see Lawrence M. Solan, 'The Written Contract as Safe Harbor for Dishonest Conduct' (2001) 77 *Chicago-Kent Law Review* 87–120 at 92.

[77] For the meaning of 'boilerplate' in this context, see Bast, 'A Short History of Boilerplate'.

[78] Tina Stark has observed that '[d]eal lawyers most frequently come into contact with boilerplate provisions at 2:00am, after the business portions of the contract have been hammered out or reviewed – hardly a propitious time to begin extensive, critical analysis': Tina L. Stark, *Negotiating and Drafting Contract Boilerplate* (New York: ALM Publishing, 2003), p. 6.

Thus, notwithstanding the emphasis often placed, retrospectively, on the positive, independent 'truth' of each party's consent to a clause stipulating a choice of law or jurisdiction,[79] the actual enactment of choice in relation to these terms is frequently, to some degree, a matter of compound inertia. Those negotiating a contract may be unwilling to query that which presents as routine (or accepted market practice) in a competent draft. Implicit reliance might also be placed on the received 'wisdom' of well-credentialled, experienced lawyers – wisdom presumed to be embedded in a given firm's chosen precedents.[80]

Where contract negotiation meetings occur is also a matter bearing, potentially, on the substance and scope of parties' contractual choices of applicable law and forum. Typically, 'high level' strategic meetings will be convened in the principal financing venue, where the preponderance of a deal's international personnel are likely based. Somewhat more mechanical and project-specific matters, such as regulatory filings, due diligence and the negotiation of operational and technical agreements, will usually be dealt with 'locally', in the country of investment. These latter meetings will often involve junior lawyers, who are frequently those with the strongest language skills within international firms. Through the navigation and staffing of deal-making locales, the deal is given a significant scalar dimension. Through the type of meetings convened in each locale, the country of investment is typically cast as the particularised ground to or from which deracinated 'internationals' seek both a knowing proximity (in the sense of 'having one's ear close to the ground') and the safety of distance (so as to be able to project a generalised business sense, attuned to the 'needs' of the global market).[81]

[79] See, for example, *I. P. Metal Ltd. v. Ruote Oz SpA*, 1994 WL 1060817 (Cal. Civ. Div.), [1994] 2 Lloyd's Rep. 560 (considering, as a question of fact, 'whether or not the parties concerned *truly* consented or agreed to a special jurisdiction clause to govern any disputes between them', emphasis added). But see Lake Avery, 1996 WL 1093659 (QBD (Adm. Ct.), [1997] C. L. C. 683, [1997] 1 Lloyd's Rep. 540 (requiring only a 'good arguable case' that the parties agreed to a contract governed by UK law).

[80] Kahan and Klausner have observed that '[a]necdotal evidence suggests that [the] copying [of precedent documents] is sometimes based on the drafter's faith that prior users have eliminated formulation errors, rather than on [an] independent understanding and assessment of [each] standard term': Kahan and Klausner, 'Standardization and Innovation', 721 (n. 16).

[81] See Annelise Riles, 'The View From the International Plane: Perspective and Scale in the Architecture of Colonial International Law' (1995) 6 *Law and Critique* 39–54.

This scalar dimension feeds into the range of legal possibility experienced within the deal, including in relation to choices of law and forum. Consider, for instance, the choice of arbitration venue for disputes arising under a material contract for an emerging-market project financing.[82] International counsel would commonly advise that the market norm is to convene such arbitration in a major international capital home to none of the potential disputants, in which some or all parties are presumed capable of feeling at home, while being insulated from unseemly, parochial influences.[83] In the interests of national pride, or for other practical or strategic reasons, local sponsors and their counsel might argue for arbitration to be seated at a local or regional centre for international commercial arbitration.[84] The former argument most frequently prevails, in part because of the interests of all persons concerned in presenting as being fluent in the dispassionate language of global commerce.[85] However, where a local party has been able to secure the attendance of senior 'internationals' at meetings in the project's home country (housed in the protective bubble of a suitably generic corporate office), it might seem more plausible to international lenders and equity investors to accept, say, International Chamber of Commerce (ICC) arbitration in the project region, in the event of dispute under one of the deal's key agreements.[86] Aside from the implications of this arrangement for any resulting dispute, such a concession may take deal negotiation in a rather different direction. Struggles over schedule and venue function as struggles over authority within and over the deal and, obliquely, over its material outcomes.

[82] See Filip De Ly, 'The Place of Arbitration in the Conflict of Laws of International Commercial Arbitration: An Exercise in Arbitration Planning' (1991) 12 *Northwestern Journal of International Law and Business* 48–85.

[83] See, for example, Stefano E. Cirielli, 'Arbitration, Financial Markets, and Banking Disputes' (2003) 14 *American Review of International Arbitration* 243–284 at 249.

[84] On the establishment of centres for international commercial arbitration in Asia, Africa and the Islamic world in the late 1970s, see Charles N. Brower and Jeremy K. Sharpe, 'International Arbitration and the Islamic World: The Third Phase' (2003) 97 *American Journal of International Law* 643–655 at 653–654.

[85] Judge Keba Mbaye (then of the International Court of Justice) observed that developing countries are rarely the venue of international arbitration. See Fali S. Nariman, 'Courts and Arbitrators: Paradigms of Arbitral Autonomy' (1997) 15 *Boston University International Law Journal* 185–190 at 189–190.

[86] The Arbitration Rules of the ICC provide that the place of arbitration shall be chosen by the parties or, in the absence of parties' choice, fixed by the Paris-based Court of the ICC: Rules of the Court of Arbitration of the International Chamber of Commerce, in force 1 January 2012, Article 18, www.iccwbo.org/products-and-services/arbitration-and-adr/arbitration/icc-rules-of-arbitration (accessed 17 September 2012).

Of such quotidian, routine stuff are 'autonomous choices' made and remade.

At this discontinuous tempo and at these various sites, deal participants perform pre- and post-legal 'choice', in part, as an enactment of deal-specific identities. These identities invariably shift. Among lawyers, for instance, one may speak or write as representative of another ('my client has instructed me to …'); as a principal (drafting an opinion of one's firm, for instance); and/or as employee or employer (when, for instance, lawyers within a firm speak to one another about the deal, partner-to-associate). Here one may speak as the most senior lawyer in the room; there one may be the most junior lawyer; at another time, one may talk as a lawyer to a non-lawyer (imparting advice to a non-lawyer client, instructing an administrative staff person, or receiving information from an expert in another field). Learning by observation and imitation, lawyers acquire facility in these various roles. The lawyer-role that one is performing at any given moment sets a bearing for the legal advice which one gives, including in relation to choices of law and forum.

Other identities are also enacted that may wreak havoc with assigned roles and formal hierarchies. On a certain deal, a particular lawyer might be the quiet one, the belligerent one, the old hand, the young gun, the workhorse or the 'rain-maker' (that is, the one whose particular gift appears to be bringing profitable new deals through the door). A lawyer may also circulate through these roles over the life of the deal. He who performed as sexy and charismatic at the first meeting may present as lumpish and withdrawn at another. She who seemed compliant on one occasion might later become the recalcitrant one. How one does a deal, in a particular instance, will be informed by an implicit loyalty to the role that one assumes within the socio-political life of the deal. If I am the young one on this deal, I may defer to my older counterparty on a particular negotiating point, or I may fight it to the death. If I am the funny one, I may be ill-inclined to rock one or another negotiating boat, for fear of losing my likeability. Conventionally, atomism and anomie are supposed to result from sustained engagement in the work of capital.[87] At close range, however, one finds that it is often through the cultivation and repetitive performance of 'personal' idiosyncrasies – and the

[87] The classic account is Herbert Marcuse, *One-Dimensional Man* (Boston: Beacon Press, 1964). This thesis is attributable in more general terms to Emile Durkheim, *Suicide: A Study in Sociology*, Second Edition (London: Routledge, 2002).

momentum and loyalties generated thereby – that choices are made and deals shaped.[88]

Deal tempo, deal locales and deal-contingent personalities: these are among the patterns that inform and condition the 'free' exercise of choice to which legal work and lawyers contribute. Ready-made scripts are received and sent on, including through legal work, and these are often framed in terms of economic or strategic goals. Those in the role of investors typically understand themselves to be seeking a return on their respective investments: lenders, through the payment of interest; equity investors, through the sale of goods or services at a profit, after debt repayment. The parties concerned may also have other objectives in engaging in a deal. One investor might be seeking particular tax or accounting treatment for an investment, to improve its balance sheet. Another might be pursuing vertical integration by, for example, extending a portfolio of downstream energy investments upstream. Among lenders, a project might complement an existing investment portfolio (spreading risk in terms of industry or geography), or it may be responsive to client demand for access to certain types of investment opportunity. In relation to choices of law and jurisdiction, as well as other matters, legal counsel will understand themselves to be charged with helping to articulate these subjective goals as well as ensuring that they are met and/or reconciled to the extent of conflict.

In pursuing such goals, deal participants tend to understand themselves to be assuming a particular posture towards, or maintaining a certain relationship to, risk, including the risk of illegality. This often folds into yet another dimension of corporate identity – the variability of risk appetites. Fleischer maintains that '[c]ontract design helps form the identity of the firm'.[89] One firm may be more 'aggressive' or 'push the envelope' more than another. Whatever the institutional identity they are performing or helping others to perform, lawyers engaged in cross-border transactional investment typically envisage themselves engaged in site-specific navigation of a matrix of risks.[90]

[88] Consider, for example, the vivid portraits colouring the deal memories of a US corporate lawyer, in Lawrence Lederman, *Tombstones: A Lawyer's Tales from the Takeover Decades* (New York: Farrar, Straus and Giroux, 1992), pp. 77, 189.

[89] Fleischer, 'Brand New Deal', 1588.

[90] See, for example, Fleischer, 'Deals: Bringing Corporate Transactions into the Law School Classroom', 478; John Flood, 'Doing Business: The Management of Uncertainty in Lawyers' Work' (1991) 25 *Law and Society Review* 41–72; Arturo Olvera

Perceptions of and appetites for risk cannot, however, wholly pre- or post-date their legal expression. 'Risk allocation' is engineered into the detail of deal agreements, including in choices of law and forum for deal-related contracts. Practices surrounding jurisdictional choice afford an illustration. Foreign investors' lawyers commonly favour selection of their 'home' forum and corresponding law, understanding that selection to mitigate the risk that their clients' contractual rights might prove unenforceable in the event of default. An argument will often be made that the home jurisdiction (or another investor-favoured jurisdiction) is more accustomed to handling disputes arising under contracts of the type in question and, by reason of the accumulation of judicial precedent in comparable matters, is more likely to arrive at carefully considered and relatively predictable decisions for the benefit of all parties. Alternatively, foreign investors might wish to secure the support of a host government for a particular deal in order to mitigate the risk of asset nationalisation or expropriation. In pursuit of this second risk-mitigation objective, those investors might elect to make a concession on contractual forum selection – acceding to choice of the host government's preferred forum in relation to certain contracts – as a sign of respect, trust and positive engagement. In so doing, the lawyers concerned would likely understand their clients to be taking a calculated risk, balancing one risk (unenforceability of foreign investors' contractual rights in a particular jurisdiction) against another (nationalisation or expropriation). Lawyers representing a host state will be expected to make a similar calibration of legal and non-legal risk from the other side of this imagined equation.

However measured their expression, these goal- and risk-oriented subjectivities retain some inherent volatility. One cannot be sure whether one's goal-oriented performance will arrive at its destination, so to speak. Yesterday's visionary is often today's cowboy.[91] Moreover, the promise of projected returns depends in part upon an embrace of the risk that those returns might not come about. Accordingly, for all the labours of risk calibration across a deal, risk

Vega, 'Risk Allocation in Infrastructure Financing' (1997) 3:2 *Journal of Project Finance* 38–42.

[91] The contrast between pre-bankruptcy and post-bankruptcy portrayals of Enron's top management is illustrative. See Craig S. Lerner, 'Calling a Truce in the Culture

analysis and mitigation are continually perceived as incomplete.[92] Risk proliferates. Risk cannot be contained.

One discerns, among corporate transactional lawyers, at once an anxiety about risk and a belief in its centrality to legal work.[93] Among such lawyers, contingency (for example, the danger of pre-legal choice proving non-translatable into law) is often perceived as a life-giving and bountiful force.[94] With risk comes the promise of return for the client and the invigorating sense that one is acting beyond the realm of precedent.[95]

It is perhaps this sense of proximity to risk that evokes such efforts of choreography among transactional lawyers. It is a dedication to the choreographic endeavour that one discerns, above all, in the daily work of transactional lawyering: a persistent effort to ensure everyone involved in the deal has a designated role and to have them perform it more or less to script. This commitment to orchestration extends well beyond the production of legal documents. Transactional lawyers tend to agonise as much over menus as they do over covenants. Logistical planning, project management and hospitality may occupy transactional lawyers' time almost as much as technical legal work. Whereas private international law scholarship on contractual choice of law tends to cast transnational corporate power as supreme,[96] those engaged in the doing of a deal often seem scrupulously attentive to its fragility.

Wars: From Enron to the CIA' (2006) 17 *Stanford Law and Policy Review* 277–302 at 291–292.

[92] See, for example, Robert E. Ebel, 'Politics Before Business: A Study in Risk Analysis by a Multinational Corporation' (1989) 11 *University of Pennsylvania Journal of International Business Law* 453–468: ('Country risk analysis is strictly subjective, and there is no alternative'); Michael P. Malloy, 'International Project Finance: Risk Analysis and Regulatory Concerns' (2004) 18 *Transnational Lawyer* 89–106 at 105: ('The current regulatory rules for the supervision of risk are not sophisticated enough to reflect the actual degree of risk in a particular transaction accurately').

[93] See Roy Kreitner, 'Speculations on Contract, or How Contract Law Stopped Worrying and Learned to Love Risk' (2000) 100 *Columbia Law Review* 1096–1138 at 1132–1133; Lipshaw, 'Contingency and Contracts', 1082–1100.

[94] Lipshaw observes that 'dealmakers live with contingency, but they do not necessarily invoke the law to control it': Lipshaw, 'Contingency and Contracts', 1092.

[95] See, for example, James C. Freund, *Lawyering: A Realistic Approach to Legal Practice* (New York: Law Journal Seminars-Press, 1979), p. 3: ('For want of a better term, I consider myself an activist lawyer – I believe that … the practitioner must at all times be alert, reach out and *accomplish*', emphasis in original).

[96] See, for example, Bekoe, 'The Illusory Choice', 511: ('[I]n the context of foreign investment into developing countries, weaker parties are consistently stripped of the ability to choose the law that will govern their contracts in any meaningful way').

This hazard-riddled deal landscape is terraced, in part, in terms of 'what the law requires' in the various jurisdictions concerned and the post-legal choices consequently available. Lawyers delineate the range of permissible action under relevant national and international laws and tinker with the deal accordingly. If a state-owned company is involved in the deal, lawyers will focus on the range of post-legal choices in which that entity is permitted to engage, under applicable national laws (including private international law) and prior contractual commitments. Having regard to the treaty commitments of the relevant states, and the past practice of their courts in private international law disputes, lawyers assess prospects for contract-enforcement and foreign-judgment recognition in this or that jurisdiction. And so on and so forth, the legal analyses continue. The implication of any such analysis is that capital must bend post-legally to the 'will' of the law or of legal institutions.

The deal is also demarcated, from time to time, in terms of 'what the market requires' and the pre-legal choices reconcilable with those requirements. It may be understood, for example, that the market 'requires' that withholding or other tax not attach to debt repayments to foreign lenders or to dividends paid to foreign equity holders. Counsel would then dedicate themselves to devising a funds-flow and contractual structure to achieve that result, one dimension of which may be an attempt to 'relocate' the transaction wholly offshore, excising it from the taxing jurisdiction. In such a scenario, the selection of the law or submission to the jurisdiction of the taxing state may be ruled out at the behest of 'the market'. Each legal issue open for negotiation within a deal will be discussed (at least in part) in terms of market norms. The implication of any such discussion is that the law must bend to the pre-legal 'will' of capital and its drive to accumulate.

Yet the promise of capital accumulation is, as already noted, one only ever expressed in forecast terms. Likewise, the assurance of lawfulness will become increasingly tentative the more that a deal is seen as breaking new ground (an alluring prospect for deal participants vested in affirming their own creativity). Among the risks with which deal participants will understand themselves to be intimate is the risk that their deal-specific approximation of either 'what the law requires' in a post-legal context or 'what the market requires' in a pre-legal setting might be controverted from somewhere beyond the deal. It might turn out that the lawyers' reading of pertinent private international law authorities does not conform to an appellate court's subsequent pronouncement on the same. The market's appetite for the product being produced by the borrower might wane. Thus, the deal hovers between deal-specific projections of two horizons of possibility – the pre-legal ('what the market requires') and the post-legal ('what the law requires') – each one often as unsettled as the other.

The model as mute master: deal as commodity

If the pre- and post-legal undecidedness of a complex, cross-border deal acquires an objective existence for its participants (including legal professionals), it is more or less encapsulated by the financial model that in-house and external financial advisors usually produce in the course of its planning. Literally, the model is a set of interlocking spreadsheets in which economic relationships are established between simulated variables in an attempt to calibrate the economic consequences of particular future scenarios.[97] The model represents an attempt to cultivate a master narrative of uncertainty for the deal: both to entrain risk and to give the deal over to risk. Lawyers rarely engage with the details of the financial model, but nonetheless tend to regard it, if only obliquely, as an expression of the deal's central animus and purpose. Its very impenetrability (for all but the few financial types who work on it) seems to augment the model's talismanic force.[98]

The model also expresses another sense in which the deal tends to be experienced by deal participants: as a work of art or industry operating independently of any would-be authors.[99] In the more or less automated unity of the model, one gains an impression of the deal as the work of many, yet belonging to no one. Transactional lawyers tend, accordingly, to experience the deal as a collaborative, creative work, at one remove from the grubby brawls in which their litigation colleagues engage.[100]

[97] The Monte Carlo class of computational algorithms is often used for this purpose, the name of which signals their incorporation of randomness and repetition. See Sawakis Savvides, 'Risk Analysis in Investment Appraisal' (1994) 9 *Project Appraisal Journal* 3–18.

[98] Miyazaki and Riles rightly warn against overemphasising the mystique of such financial artifacts, which are more often than not treated with disinterest (beyond certain fundamental features and outputs) except by their designated keepers: Hirokazu Miyazaki and Annelise Riles, 'Failure as an Endpoint', in Aihwa Ong and Stephen J. Collier (eds.), *Global Assemblages: Technology, Politics, and Ethics as Anthropological Problems* (Oxford: Blackwell, 2005), pp. 320–332 at pp. 320–321.

[99] Fleischer casts deal structure as a product or advertising medium, the effects of which remain 'ethereal': Fleischer, 'Brand New Deal', 1586.

[100] See, for example, Freund, *Lawyering*, p. 35.

This sense of the deal (and the model by which the deal is represented) may exert a pacifying effect on employer–employee relations, as well as on disputes that might otherwise arise over forum selection and choice of law. The law firm associate handed yet another urgent, late-night assignment may understand *the deal* to be doing this to her, not the partner communicating the demand. Similarly, particular choices of law and forum may be framed as dictates of the deal. The choice of a jurisdiction perceived to be particularly 'investor friendly' may be experienced as a consequence, not of contestable, subjective legal preference, but rather of the compulsion to render a deal 'saleable' as an economic and risk package (of which the model is, for many, the highest or most refined expression). Through the deal's modelling and circulation as collective work, friction is assuaged, available choices eliminated, and points of possible resistance smoothed away.

After closing, the autonomy with which the deal is invested (in part, through modelling) subsists in the commodified mode of a precedent. A particular deal structure gets invested with a brand value independent of the institutional or jurisdictional sites of its making.[101] As noted above, lawyers embarking on a new deal will often begin by collecting publicly available accounts of past deals bearing some connection to their yet-to-be-created work, from which a new deal is assembled like some Dadaist collage. In so doing, they insert their new deal into a deal-lineage associated with 'success'; associative value is purloined, reputation bolstered and anxiety about uncertainty of outcome allayed.

The deal-commodity's circulation fosters reproduction of the very '*stylized repetition of acts*' or 'knowledge practices' by which deal-specific pre- and post-legal 'choices' are produced.[102] The deal evokes a collective allegiance among deal participants that sets it apart from relations among them, however fraught. Accordingly, the instability arising from the 'performativity' of the deal and these choices gets cast outwards (as market uncertainty or as a variable response to generalised, systemic, non-legal demands) rather than inwards (as, say, employer–employee or investor–state conflict). When concerns get raised about corporate practices and their impacts, the standard scholarly rejoinder has been to redouble that movement away from the deal's performative terrain: to plumb the global market's non-legal 'interior', ascribing

[101] See generally Fleischer, 'Brand New Deal', 1582, 1628; D. Gordon Smith, 'The "Branding Effect" of Contracts' (2007) 12 *Harvard Negotiation Law Review* 189–200.

[102] Butler, *Gender Trouble*, p. 191 (emphasis in original). See also Riles, 'A New Agenda for the Cultural Study of Law', 1030.

determinative force to a latent bias or culture within this entity or that. The foregoing account suggests the potential fruitfulness of a different engagement – moving *through* the substance of the market, the law, the corporation or Empire,[103] and into the mêlée of those intensely legalised performances that comprise their properties, powers and choices.

Revisiting pre- and post-legal autonomy in private international law

What questions arise from the foregoing redescription of the exercise of pre- and post-legal choice in international contracting that may be salient for current debates in private international law? And what might an appreciation of the regularised 'interiors' of pre- and post-legality add to our understanding of the role of non-legality in international legal work, including in debates with which preceding and succeeding chapters are concerned? To address the first of those questions, one might consider the controversy ongoing in private international law scholarship concerning the selection of non-state law (contemporary incarnations of the so-called *lex mercatoria*) as the governing law in commercial contracts.

Legal scholars' and practitioners' endorsement of *lex mercatoria* amounts, in one account, to 'a new political movement, aimed at replacing the national regulation of foreign trade with a transnational, customary law'.[104] 'Partisans of [the] "new" *lex mercatoria*', according to Stephen Sachs, 'look forward to a day when arbitrators will be free to decide cases according to the custom of merchants, relaxing a national regulation when it is "not fit for international trade"'.[105] Supporters of this 'movement' justify recourse to *lex mercatoria* by reason of its responsiveness to contemporary demands arising primarily from outside law, particularly the 'need' for law to be commercially effective. Thus, Jean-Pierre Dupuy has written:

> [Forms of international trade] have created a phenomenon whose principal characteristic is that it is *spontaneous* and has been established by the creation of new rules or by the adaptation of existing legal rules and practice to the requirements

[103] See generally Hardt and Negri, *Empire*.

[104] Stephen E. Sachs, 'From St. Ives to Cyberspace: The Modern Distortion of the Medieval "Law Merchant"' (2006) 21 *American University International Law Review* 685–812 at 808 (noting also that use of a supposed medieval notion of the 'law merchant' as a model for corporate self-regulation has attracted some criticism).

[105] *Ibid.*

of contemporary international economy. Its origin is the *need for effectiveness* pursued by the various economic agents across, or in defiance of, frontiers.[106]

Some commentators also stress that allowing parties' recourse to *lex mercatoria* is consistent with private international law's declared respect for party autonomy and consonant with private international law's pursuit of certainty and predictability.[107] In the surrounding debate, partisans and recalcitrants alike assume that the trade-off to be made, through the medium of *lex mercatoria*, is one between state law-making power (attributable to formal, politico-legal investiture) and private law-making power (attributable to economic clout), or between traditional 'statist' and supposedly more innovative 'pluralist' approaches to private international law.[108]

To some extent, the foregoing restaging of pre- and post-legal choice could be read as raising questions about the collapse of law into raw power, and the abuse of power, that will be familiar to any reader of this debate, or indeed of contemporary international law scholarship more broadly. Stephen Toope maintains, for instance, that 'the so-called *lex mercatoria* is largely an effort to legitimise as "law" the economic interests of Western corporations'.[109] Ralf Michaels highlights, further, that this worry is not assuaged by the prospect of states embracing non-state law-making under a 'cosmopolitan' private international law: 'The apotheosis of legal pluralism collapses back into crude international relations realism in which each community determines what is best for itself.'[110] Further, states' legal recognition

106 Jean-Pierre Dupuy, Legal Opinion to Aminoil para. 26, in Aminoil Pleadings, *Kuwait v. Aminoil* (1982) 21 I. L. M. 976, quoted in Maniruzzaman, 'The Lex Mercatoria and International Contracts', 667 (emphasis in original).

107 Lowenfeld, 'Lex Mercatoria: An Arbitrator's View', pp. 71, 75–76 (Lowenfeld quotes, with approval, Professor Ole Lando's observation that '[b]y choosing the *lex mercatoria* the parties oust the technicalities of national legal systems and they avoid rules which are unfit for international contract' (Ole Lando, 'The Lex Mercatoria in International Commercial Arbitration' (1985) 34 *International and Comparative Law Quarterly* 747–768 at 748). Lowenfeld notes further that in response to 'plea[s] for certainty and predictability', Lando might say, that 'the general principles of the law merchant offer at least as much predictability as the (often unexpected) law of a given country, particularly a law not selected by the parties'. Again quoting Lando, Lowenfeld attributes the binding force of *lex mercatoria* to its recognition 'as an autonomous norm system by the business community' (Lando, *ibid.*, at 752).

108 See, for example, Dalhuisen, 'Legal Orders and their Manifestation', 133–134. For a more nuanced account of 'statist' and 'pluralist' positions and their interaction, see Michaels, 'The Re-state-ment of Non-State Law'.

109 Stephen J. Toope, *Mixed International Arbitration: Studies in Arbitration Between States and Private Persons* (Cambridge: Grotius Publications, 1990), p. 96.

110 Michaels, 'The Re-state-ment of Non-State Law', 1255, 1258 (footnote omitted).

of non-state law 'becomes the opposite of recognition – it becomes a "violent appropriation"'.[111] Perhaps sensitivity to the concentration of power in private hands (with or without state 'recognition' or 'appropriation' thereof) should be felt all the more acutely when one takes account of the myriad, barely perceptible ways that power, vested unevenly through and within legal deal-making, operates to condition pre- and post-legal 'choice'?

The point of the foregoing discussion, however, has *not* been to defend law against private coercion or conditioning. Rather, the concern of this narrative has been to suggest the difficulty of pitting law against non-legal (economic or political) power, or of pitting freely (privately) chosen outcomes against legislatively (publicly) mandated outcomes, in relation to contractual choices of law and forum. That difficulty arises from the mutually constitutive nature or the inseparability of legality and non-legality, private choice and public interest, as played out in the tangled web of a deal. In this sense, the analysis here sideswipes and disrupts, rather than replicates, the structure of the *lex mercatoria* debate (to the extent that it can be attributed with *a* structure). The line of questioning that this chapter is intended to provoke can perhaps best be illustrated by reverting to one of the questions posed at the outset of this chapter: what gets ruled in and ruled out when one locates determinative choices before or after but not so much in the legal deal (and thereby de-emphasises the role of legal work in conditioning that 'before' and 'after')?

One possibility apparently ruled out of the *lex mercatoria* debate is the prospect that the stakes at issue in this debate (or at least some incarnations thereof) may be relatively inconsequential. By focusing attention on the contractual designation of *lex mercatoria* and its (positive or negative) public-policy implications, private international lawyers may be buying into the very 'statist' fictions many rail so hard against. That is, to worry about whether national laws expressly permit corporations to subject their dealings to *lex mercatoria* is to reaffirm that the private power about which one must be most circumspect is that which explicitly co-opts 'public' legal functions, such as law-making in an overt, legislative mode. Assumptions that may be embedded in this worry include the following: that public (state) power and private (corporate) power routinely offset (rather than support) each other, that they

[111] *Ibid.*

ordinarily occupy distinct (legal versus non-legal) spheres of influence, and that (non-legal) coercive power corresponding to private parties gets ramped up to a noteworthy or question-begging degree only when it visibly enters a (legal) domain properly reserved to the state. In their reliance on something approaching these assumptions, both sides of the *lex mercatoria* debate may be read to occupy more or less the same ground, so that this controversy might begin to sound less like debate and more like quibbling between compatriots.

The *lex mercatoria* 'debate' might thus be foreclosed in favour of a partial understanding of law–power and legal–non-legal relations before it even gets underway. If, however, one regards these shared understandings as politically or empirically questionable, then the pragmatic question for private international law becomes not *whether* private rule (as opposed to public rule), but *how* and *with what effects* power gets produced and allocated in and through legal decision-making in particular instances, including in the supposed domains of pre- and post-legal choice, and how and with what effects might it be allocated differently.[112] The latter are by no means new questions, but they are ones that rarely seem to get asked when private international law scholars debate the permissibility of contracting under *lex mercatoria*.

A second possibility that may be ruled out of the *lex mercatoria* debate through the insulation of pre- and post-legal deal dynamics from critical purview is the prospect that crucial 'conflicts' in conflict of laws (as private international law is sometimes called) might be located *elsewhere* than that debate's most commonly drawn front lines, namely the line between insatiable global capital and an ever-more-emasculated state, that between one nation state and another (often, a 'developed' nation and a 'developing' one), the line between non-legal (political or economic) power and legal power, and that between the mercatocratic elite and the rest. To reread the vagaries of a transnational corporate deal is to recall that fault lines periodically open within the 'autonomous personhood' of a corporate party, just as they frequently do within the 'autonomous personhood' of any one member of the

[112] Questions so posed remain loyal or immanent to the pragmatic sensibility that is the default posture of private international law today. For discussion and illustration of pragmatic tendencies prevailing in private international law scholarship, see Joseph William Singer, 'A Pragmatic Guide to Conflicts' (1990) 70 *Boston University Law Review* 731–820; Symeonides, 'The American Choice of Law Revolution', 413–415.

mercatocracy. Consider conflicts between, say, an associate and a partner, fellow associates, or a lawyer and an administrative assistant. Consider conflicts within the elite in a particular city, and between elites from different professions and geographic settings, vested with different types and degrees of elitism. Consider conflicts within the personhood of the lawyer or those internal to the styles of business or corporate lawyering. These conflicts, often consigned to a pre- or post-legal sphere, may be as or more material to the realisation or frustration of corporate 'choice' than those that private international law customarily addresses. And the tensions at work in these conflicts may operate in defiance of conventional mappings of core and periphery, freedom and constraint, law and politics, legality and non-legality.[113] To locate questions surrounding party autonomy before or after the legal terrain of the deal is to negate the manoeuvrability of these conflicts and their materiality in the constitution and consolidation of 'autonomous' positions.

Yet, for all the blind spots borne by private international law, perhaps commentators and practitioners might yet amplify – perhaps even make pragmatic use of – its inclination to register and approach conflict. Where a public international lawyer is more inclined to see a 'higher' commonality or 'mere' politics, the private international lawyer tends to see difference – difference that is not always amenable to being managed or massaged away. Might a disinclination to avoid conflict per se get ruled *in* when we approach an issue as a private international law matter?[114] If so, this predilection, combined with the richness of the legal-realist legacy, may yet equip private international lawyers to navigate better some of the banal and complex pre- and post-legal 'interiors' of party autonomy in a corporate context. Private international law scholars, lamenting the demise of their discipline

[113] One way of coming to grips with such conflicts in methodological terms is offered by Holmes and Marcus, who seek to track the production of 'illicit, marginal social thought' within technocratic milieu in terms of a 'para-ethnographic dimension' of domains of expertise: Douglas R. Holmes and George E. Marcus, 'Cultures of Expertise and the Management of Globalization: Toward the Re-Functioning of Ethnography' in Ong and Collier, *Global Assemblages*, pp. 235–252 at pp. 235–237.

[114] Indeed, as Michaels highlights, private international law issues can even inspire political passion at times: Ralf Michaels, 'EU Law as Private International Law? Reconceptualising the Country-of-Origin Principle as Vested-Rights Theory' (2006) 2 *Journal of Private International Law* 195–242 at 195 (noting that 'people all over Europe took to the streets to protest against a proposed norm of private international law – the "country-of-origin" principle stated in Article 16 of the proposed services directive').

in the face of legislative and treaty harmonisation,[115] may yet find in the architecture of autonomous choice a plethora of material conflicts in which lawyers are already active. These may not be of a kind amenable to codification, litigation or reform in conventional terms. Nevertheless, private international lawyers could still ask, in and of these domains, the sort of pragmatic questions that they most readily ask of private international law's judicial and legislative development: what is the price of 'autonomy' in contractual choice of law; which costs or interests should matter in the assessment of that price; and who pays that price in each instance?

A confluence of non-legalities

The potential significance of rereading the regularised 'interiors' of pre- and post-legal choice is not, however, restricted to private international law scholarship and controversies within that field. This form of non-legality also informs international legal understandings of illegality and extra-legality discussed earlier and those explored in later chapters. The practices and writings surveyed in the two preceding chapters depend not only upon an ambivalent sense of torture's illegality under international law or a sense of Guantánamo Bay's extra-legal remoteness from the legally mundane. Also significant in both contexts is a vision of military and intelligence leaders as innovators or entrepreneurs, inevitably (and indeed properly) making decisions before or beyond the reach of any explicit legal assessment or directive.

In relation to torture, the notion of command-in-the-field put forward in the Fay-Jones Report, for example (issued in August 2004 after an investigation by Army Major General George Fay and Lieutenant General Anthony R. Jones into detainee torture and mistreatment at Abu Ghraib), seemed structured in significant ways by the expectation of pre- or post-legal choice.[116] Decisions concerning detainee abuse were

[115] See, for example, C. G. J. Morse, 'Making English Private International Law' in James Fawcett (ed.), *Reform and Development of Private International Law: Essays in Honour of Sir Peter North* (Oxford University Press, 2002), pp. 273–302 (on legislative developments); Hans Ulrich Jessurun d'Oliveira, 'The EU and a Metamorphosis of Private International Law' in Fawcett, *Reform and Development of Private International Law*, pp. 111–136 (on the effect of EC treaty-based law).

[116] LTG Anthony R. Jones and MG George R. Fay, 'Article 15-6 Investigation of the Abu Ghraib Prison and 205th Military Intelligence Brigade', 23 August 2004, http://slate.msn.com/features/whatistorture/pdfs/FayJonesReport.pdf (accessed 17 September 2012) (the 'Fay-Jones Report').

taken, according to this Report, in a sphere resolutely non-regularised by military doctrine. So, Lieutenant General Jones cautioned that '[d]octrine could not provide quick solutions for all the situations that confronted [Combined Joint Task-Force-7 (CJTF), the interim military formation that directed the US effort in Iraq between June 2003 and May 2004]. In many cases, the situation, mission, and environment dictated the decisions and the actions taken by the CJTF leadership ... Rarely does war follow the pre-planned strategy'.[117] 'Doctrine allows leaders at all levels to adapt', Jones continued, 'to the different environments and situations that their units may encounter ... doctrine does not replace the inherent responsibilities of commanders to execute their missions ... An overarching doctrine allows commanders the latitude to develop tactics, techniques and procedures ... to focus Soldier and unit operations'.[118]

According to the Fay-Jones Report, military leaders were expected to bring pre-legal preferences (informed by conditions, training, experience and 'non-negotiable' professional values) together with a post-legal selection from among, and adaptation of, available (legal) options in order to exercise their 'inherent responsibilities [as] commanders'.[119] Only through a clearing of doctrine from the field or instance of decision – a rendering of commanders' decisions as fundamentally set apart from applicable regulation – could the 'inherent responsibilities' and freedoms of military command be recognised and realised as such, or so it seemed. Little by way of narrative guidance emerged from the Fay-Jones Report for the exercise

[117] *Ibid.*, at p. 13.

[118] *Ibid.*, at p. 19. Note that the term 'doctrine' used in the Fay-Jones Report does not correspond to legal doctrine. Rather, 'doctrine' in this context implies military doctrine, that is, '[f]undamental principles by which the military forces guide their actions in support of objectives'; a framework that is 'authoritative but requires judgement in application': NATO Glossary of Terms and Definitions, AAP-6 (2010), available at www.dtic.mil/doctrine/doctrine/other/aap6.pdf (accessed 17 September 2012) p. 2–0–9. Nonetheless, for the purposes of this book, the Fay-Jones Report's imagining of the arena of decision as more or less doctrine-free is analogous to international legal scholarship's imagining of the domain of economic choice as pre- or post-legal.

[119] Fay-Jones Report, p. 22: ('Our values are non-negotiable for members of our profession. They are what a professional military force represents to the world ... leaders need rigorous training to be able to adapt to this level of complexity ... Leaders must be trained for certainty and educated for uncertainty').

of responsible decision within the irresolute, doctrine-riddled mêlée of contemporary warfare.[120]

International legal scholarship critical of contemporary torture and detention practices has often revolved around a comparable vision of pre- and post-legal choice. In Craig Forcese's description, for example, torture is an outcome of decisions by individuals selecting among clear choices arrayed before them. The most that international law can hope to do is to rule out some of the options among which officials choose.[121] A similar scenario gets played out in international legal literature surrounding Guantánamo Bay. According to Peter Margulies, for instance, '[a] narrow vision of efficiency drove the Bush administration's establishment of the [counter-terrorist detention] facility' at Guantánamo Bay: thus, a 'narrow' economic calculus lay at the root of this elaborate legal architecture.[122]

The expectation of 'non-legal' choice being determinative in these settings – an expectation seemingly common to both decision-makers at relevant military sites and by their international legal critics – owes much to the characterisation of 'choosers' in transnational financing contexts such as those depicted in this chapter. Illegal and extra-legal action on the part of the US military has been attributed to military leaders not adapting innovatively to prevailing risks in their pursuit of subjectively defined goals, more or less as financiers are expected to innovate in the face of global uncertainty. It is true that '[t]he military does not want military personnel to "get creative" with prisoners'.[123] Nonetheless, contemporary military doctrine does promote an ideal

120 Cf. David Kennedy, *Of War and Law* (Princeton University Press, 2006), pp. 6–7: ('The military, like other public and private bureaucracies today, operates in war and peace against the background of innumerable local, national, and international rules ... Today's military is also itself a complex bureaucracy whose managers discipline their forces and organize their operations with rules ... law today shapes the politics, as well as the practice, of warfare').

121 Craig Forcese, 'The Myth of the Virtuous Torturer: Two Defences of the Absolute Ban on Torture' (2008) 46 *Osgoode Hall Law Journal* 853–870 at 853, 869–70: ('Law codifies a choice. In practice, that choice is to ban torture and thereby bear the risk even in circumstances where torture may defuse a ticking bomb. International law – and if properly implemented, domestic law – makes torture a violation that can never be justified ... Even if, in the cold light of hindsight, the bomb was defused only through torture, the consequences of that decision fall on the individual').

122 Peter Margulies, 'Putting Guantanamo in the Rear-View Mirror: The Political Economy of Detention Policy' (2010) 32 *Western New England Law Review* 339–372 at 339, 343.

123 Jessica Wolfendale, *Torture and the Military Profession* (Basingstoke and New York: Palgrave Macmillan, 2007), p. 160.

of flexible, entrepreneurial soldiering. In the Fay-Jones Report, for example, detainee abuse at Abu Ghraib was explained in part as a failure of some military leaders to 'adapt' fast enough 'to a new complex operational environment' and 'a complex, adaptive enemy'.[124]

This cross-pollination of non-legalities across the political and economic fields is not, moreover, peculiar to the settings of Abu Ghraib or Guantanámo Bay or the international legal scholarship surrounding them. In a 2002 speech at the National Defense University, then US Secretary of Defense Donald Rumsfeld called for members of the armed forces to 'behave somewhat less like bureaucrats and more like venture capitalists', arguing for promotion of 'a more entrepreneurial approach to developing military capabilities'.[125] As Pat O'Malley has observed of a 'revised liberal military ethos' across a number of liberal democracies, 'new forms of agency are required and expected of troops, in a constantly adaptable military with fewer chains of command in military hierarchies ... troops [are] required to a far greater extent to be innovative, to show initiative and act as informed decision-makers ... the model to be adopted by military governance is that of the successful business enterprise'.[126]

The entrepreneurial, self-governing warrior evoked in recent accounts of torture (as a warrior capable of straddling the knife edge of legality–illegality surrounding detainee interrogation on ground nominally cleared of doctrine) is thus a close cousin of the transnational deal-maker depicted in this chapter whose choices are understood 'properly' to take place in a pre- or post-legal sphere. Likewise, the Guantánamo Bay decision-maker represented in international legal scholarship, making extraordinary choices delinked from routine legality, exercises an intensified version of that deal-maker's pre- and post-legal autonomy. At the same time, the capacity for overweening, determinative force commonly attributed to transnational corporations in global economic affairs might borrow something from the

[124] The Fay-Jones Report, pp. 8, 22: ('They were in a counter-insurgency operation with a complex, adaptive enemy'; 'In Iraq, leaders had to adapt to a new complex operational environment. Some of our leaders adapted faster than others').

[125] Donald Rumsfeld, 'Remarks on "21st Century Transformation of U.S. Armed Forces"', National Defense University, Fort McNair, Washington, D.C., 31 January 2002, available at www.defense.gov/speeches/speech.aspx?speechid=183 (accessed 17 September 2012) and quoted in Pat O'Malley, 'Resilient Subjects: Uncertainty, Warfare and Liberalism' (2010) 39 *Economy and Society* 488–509 at 502–503.

[126] O'Malley, 'Resilient Subjects', 502–503.

traditional model of a militarised state translating its will into law, in part through violence or the threat of violence.[127]

Viewing these settings together, through the lens of international legal scholarship – the administration of torture at US military-run sites, official decision-making at Guantánamo Bay, and the 'unfettered' exercise of choice in transnational financing – enables one to see confluence between the governing non-legalities discussed so far. It seems possible for Guantánamo Bay to appear as extra-legal in international legal scholarship because we are accustomed to envisioning decisive agents standing behind law, and maintaining a coherent identity apart from law, as in the context of pre- and post-legality. Continuous flow between pre- and post-legal choice and the emergence or deployment of law in transnational financing becomes conceivable in part because international lawyers are used to looking to illegal acts for generative potential and forever parsing them into regulable and non-regulable forms. Ambivalence about illegal conduct (such as torture) as both a source of creativity and a harbinger of violent domination may be traceable, to some degree, to ambivalence about enshrining the unfettered, autonomous, self-directing chooser (state, individual or corporate) as the primary repository of freedom within contemporary international law.

Conclusion

To enliven the pre- and post-legal 'private' of private international law as a matter for international legal inquiry is to probe what is at stake in international law seeking to depict, consolidate, validate, redistribute, augment, co-opt or circumscribe power in non-legal terms. This chapter has highlighted that there are significant stakes at issue *before* the question of what private international lawyers should do in the face of question-begging concentrations of non-legal power. In their vital role in the framing and enactment of that power, lawyers advising on private international law issues have been and continue to be already engaged in the contentious business of allocating resources and authority. The mode of that engagement is mostly far removed from measured weighing and balancing.

[127] Robert Weisberg explores the 'analogy between public legal authority and private remedial violence': Robert Weisberg, 'Private Violence as Moral Action' in Austin Sarat and Thomas R. Kearns (eds.), *Law's Violence* (Ann Arbor: University of Michigan Press, 1992), pp. 175–210 at p. 175.

Drawing inspiration from the work of Robert Hale and Walter Wheeler Cook, among others, this chapter has cautioned against the reading of 'autonomous' legal decisions by multinational corporations as instances of congealed, pre- or post-legal power in private international law. In the stylised setting of a cross-border deal, this chapter has instead depicted the performative enactment of autonomous choice in all its tawdry, collective, highly legalised routinisation. In so doing, it has suggested establishing as both politically significant and worthy of legal scholarly attention the mundane, technical terms in which pre- and post-legal 'choices' are formulated and articulated as such, and to recapture some sense of the persistent undecidedness of that articulation.

Persistent undecidedness is not, however, a sensation which international lawyers commonly aspire to generate in themselves or others. That may be for good reason. As the next chapter will show, in its examination of international legal scholarly representations of the Intergovernmental Panel on Climate Change, uncongealed power rarely remains so for long. Many in the field of climate change law and policy – and in the parallel, nemesistic field of climate change scepticism – are already working to reset prevailing international legal coordinates, in part through new re-combinations of the legal and the non-legal (that is, the political, the economic and the scientific). And the hybrid creatures of these narratives can be as monstrous as they may be marvellous.

5 Receiving climate change: law, science and supra-legality

The Intergovernmental Panel on Climate Change (IPCC) represents, for some, 'the greatest ever feat of global scientific cooperation' performed by a 'lodestar' for our times.[1] Some regard it as 'the most extensive and carefully constructed intergovernmental advisory process ever known in international relations'.[2] To others it is remarkable less for its greatness than for its 'mess[iness]' - its embeddedness in, and expression of, trans-disciplinary global 'conflict' and 'controversy'.[3] Yet, for all its prominence in policy debate and media reporting surrounding climate change (or perhaps because of that prominence and associated controversies) the work of the IPCC is typically not central in international legal writing on climate change.

International legal scholars frequently characterise the IPCC and its work as exogenous to the international legal field by reference to the scientific work and personages underpinning them. The work of the IPCC is also externalised in international legal scholarship as political craft. Whether for their scientific or their political character (or some combination of the two), the IPCC and its Assessment Reports

[1] Damian Carrington, 'In Defence of the IPCC: Critics Ignore the Real Scandal', *Damian Carrington's Environment Blog*, 28 July 2011, *Guardian*, www.guardian.co.uk/environment/damian-carrington-blog/2011/jul/28/ipcc-climate-change-science-pachauri (accessed 17 September 2012); Peter Stanford, 'Can Prof Rajendra Pachauri Really Survive "Glaciergate"? The Head of the UN Panel on Climate Change, Prof Rajendra Pachauri, is Still Adamant that One Famously Exaggerated Report Should Not Cost Him His Job', *The Daily Telegraph* (UK), 26 July 2011, www.telegraph.co.uk/earth/environment/climatechange/8660714/Can-Prof-Rajendra-Pachauri-really-survive-Glaciergate.html (accessed 17 September 2012).

[2] Ari Bessendorf, 'Games in the Hothouse: Theoretical Dimensions in Climate Change' (2005) 28 *Suffolk Transnational Law Review* 325–357 at 326, n. 14.

[3] *The Economist*, 'A Climate of Conflict: A New Row about the IPCC', 25 June 2011, p. 72.

are emblematic, in much international legal scholarship in which they appear, of an idea that certain normatively significant practices are so expansive or so endemic as to surpass international law's and lawyers' grasp or engagement as such – a notion to which I give the name supra-legality.[4]

The non-legalities so far discussed are generally situated on the same scale as international lawyers' field of work. A shift from legality to illegality in the international legal field, for instance, is generally conceived in terms of a slippage sideways, across some contestable line marking the limits of international legality. In contrast, supra-legality is a mode of non-legality (or extraordinary normativity) posited on a surpassing scale. Supra-legal phenomena are understood to enliven, elicit or constrain international legal doings from a plane above or beyond the terrain of international legal work. The work of the IPCC is often so configured in international legal scholarship.

The problem that this chapter seeks to put in play, however, is not the architecture of supra-legality per se. There may be good reasons for international law to approach the IPCC's work from a distance: this may, for instance, encourage attention to be paid to the specificities of this work. The problem, rather, is the relative inattention paid, as a consequence, to the various dimensions of governance work in which the IPCC is engaged. Also problematic is the related reading down of international legal work in the climate change field and the possibilities and responsibilities associated with that work. The way in which

[4] According to the *Oxford English Dictionary*, the prefix supra- signifies 'above, beyond, in addition (to), before in time': 'supra-, prefix': *Oxford English Dictionary Online*, www.oed.com (accessed 17 September 2012). Probably the most common invocation of the prefix in international legal writing is in relation to the 'supranational' status of the European Community and the law governing European integration on which theme there is an 'abundant' scholarship: René Barents, *The Autonomy of Community Law* (The Hague: Kluwer Law International, 2004), p. 23. In legal scholarship broadly, 'supra-legal' is a term of art given a range of meanings not necessarily in line with its usage in this chapter. Richard Greenstein suggests, for instance, that '[e]xamples of supralegal norms include natural, divine and customary norms': Richard K. Greenstein, 'Why the Rule of Law?' (2005) 66 *Louisiana Law Review* 63–94 at 64, n. 11. As far as international lawyers are concerned, however, customary norms would not qualify as supra-legal to the extent that they are understood to have satisfied the requirements of sources doctrine. See generally David Kennedy, 'The Sources of International Law' (1987) 2 *American University Journal of International Law and Policy* 1–96. The concern of this chapter is with the attribution of certain normative knowledge practices to some 'higher' realm in international legal scholarship, regardless of the reach or limits of sources doctrine.

the work of the IPCC has become known in and through international legal writing helps to foster certain kinds of intuition, certain kinds of analyses and certain kinds of argument concerning climate change, while discouraging others.

Performed in a reactive posture (in relation to one or other supra-legal a priori), international legal work on global climate change tends to be imagined, in large part, as a conveyor belt operation: a matter of shepherding the transmission, the global scaling up, or the pragmatic scaling down of naturalised imperatives generated elsewhere.[5] Moreover, the demands upon international legal work so 'received' tend to conform to a standard array: international law must deliver a global accord or, failing that, generalised, exhortative inputs for national legislative implementation and/or litigious mobilisation. Also recurring is the aspiration to resolve, once and for all, the fit between 'law' and 'science' or between 'law' and 'politics' on a global scale – a preoccupation attended, often, by frustration and despair. In short, when most or all critical agents of climate change related knowledge practice are understood to lie outside international law's field of work, international legal repertoires in this area can appear rather cribbed.[6] It is this cribbing of international legal work with which this chapter is concerned, rather than the merits or demerits of any one climate change related programme or initiative.

Argument along these lines will be familiar from other chapters of this book. Chapter 2 argued that collective inattention to the generative force of illegality in and for international legal work may have led international lawyers concerned about recent practices of torture to de-emphasise the role of law in enabling illegal violence and the contributions of illegal norm-makers (such as detainees subjected to torture or mistreatment). Chapter 3 presented a related critique of normative decision-making at and surrounding Guantánamo Bay and the misreading of that site as an instance of an extra-legal intensification of exceptional sovereign power. An argument was made for better critical tracing of the continuities between the anomalous legal order of Guantánamo Bay and unexceptional legal orders around the world.

[5] See generally Karen Knop, 'Here and There: International Law in Domestic Courts?' (2000) 32 *New York University Journal of International Law and Politics* 501–535 at 505.

[6] The difficulties, generalisations, fantasies and reductions attendant upon attributing a single gaze or cast of mind to the discipline or practice of international law are highlighted elsewhere in this book and persist unabated throughout. See, for instance, Chapter 1 note 17 and Chapter 6 note 8.

Chapter 4 then focused on one recurrent version of the figure of the exceptional decision-maker that Chapter 3 might be taken to elicit: the wilful chooser occupying pre- or post-legal terrain within a multijurisdictional regulatory complex and acting, within that complex, more or less like a shopper selecting possibilities off a shelf. In Chapter 4's account, that chooser brought along her own cautionary tales. Haphazard recollections of transnational corporate practice recorded in that chapter suggested that the exercise of 'autonomous' choice in corporate settings is more an outcome than an origin of deal-specific structuring, routinisation and conditioning. To the extent that there might be call for more freedom in global economic negotiations – including, say, freedom from the apparent inevitabilities of multinational corporate choice – Chapter 4 suggested that such freedom might be better pursued within the persistent undecidedness of one or other global regulatory tangle than by recourse to some magical, decisionist clearing-in-the-woods.

This chapter recalls, nonetheless, that no such regulatory tangle will ever comprise a level playing field. Unevenness persists; some elements will be harder to question or engage than others. One of the factors contributing to that unevenness is the construction of supra-legal scaffolding around certain sites and institutions. In order to explore how such supra-legal scaffolding is made in particular instances, and possibilities that may be attendant upon its remaking, this chapter looks to international legal scholarly representations of the IPCC and its work.

Envisaging the IPCC's work supra-legally has been one way for international lawyers to manage what is often seen as a generalisable problem of fit or interface between domains of science or politics, on one hand, and law, on the other, in global affairs. After introducing (and then bypassing) this problem and surveying the provenance and work practices of the IPCC, this chapter describes three ways in which supra-legality has been conferred upon its work in international legal scholarship: as a supervening catalyst; as a source of super-probative evidence; and/or as an expression of consensus among persons understood to comprise a more or less unitary, supra-legal global community. Finally, the chapter highlights some dimensions of ongoing international legal work on climate change that may be sidelined in these renditions of the IPCC and its work. In so doing, it draws upon and contributes to contemporary scholarship on relations between legal and scientific thought, while taking portions of that scholarship as its foil.

Making the supra-legal

To the extent that global policy-makers' expert knowledge and 'good sense' prevail in many policy settings today, that prevalence depends upon 'hard work'.[7] The shaping of knowledge architecture through law comprises a significant dimension of that work, as other chapters in this book have shown. International legal scholars recognise this; the importance of properly configuring objects of study or regulatory attention is widely acknowledged. In this vein, international legal scholars often worry about the question of fit between law and the science.[8]

Sometimes the problem of fit is expressed as one of reduction or under-inclusion: the expansive, messy world of legal and policy decision gets 'reduced to matters of science', with an associated 'sacrific[e]' of interests, nuance, understanding or participatory potential: so Jacqueline Peel has argued in writing about the role of science in 'international risk regulation'.[9] Elsewhere, the problem is rendered more or less in inverse terms: pressing legal questions get lost or muddied amid 'a wealth of impressive sounding information', much of it subject to dispute among those generating it: so Robin Feldman has cautioned in relation to courts' and legal scholars' deference to scientists.[10] In the first instance, the corrective may entail 'recasting' science so that it seems larger, more flexible or more accommodating, perhaps by 'melding scientific knowledge with other inputs'.[11] In the latter context, the remedy is likely to involve cutting science down for legal purposes: recognising the 'limitations' of scientific knowledge, affording it a strictly 'supportive' role in legal decision-making, and insisting upon its expression in plain language terms.[12]

To direct attention towards the making of supra-legality in international law is, however, to take a step back from generalised problems

[7] Sheila Jasanoff, 'The Practices of Objectivity in Regulatory Science' in Charles Camic *et al.* (eds.), *Social Knowledge in the Making* (University of Chicago Press, 2011), pp. 307–338 at pp. 307–308.

[8] See generally Sheila Jasanoff, 'The Intersections of Science and Law' in Sheila Jasanoff, *Science at the Bar: Law, Science, and Technology in America* (Cambridge, MA and London: Harvard University Press, 1995), pp. 1–23.

[9] Jacqueline Peel, *Science and Risk Regulation in International Law* (Cambridge University Press, 2010), pp. 11, 383 (in the latter context, seeking ways to assure 'those exposed to risk that their interests have not been sacrificed on the altar of impossible scientific certainty').

[10] Robin Feldman, *The Role of Science in Law* (Oxford University Press, 2009), pp. 41, 46.

[11] Peel, *Science and Risk Regulation*, pp. 383–384.

[12] Feldman, *Science in Law*, pp. 140, 159, 176.

of fit in a science–law 'interface'.[13] In order for the sorts of dilemmas and correctives on which Peel and Feldman focus to arise, one has first to buy into what Sheila Jasanoff has derided, with reference to US policy-making and courtroom practice, as an 'untenab[ly] firm[ ] … boundary' between science and law. To learn from Jasanoff's argument (made in relation to US regulatory and judicial practice), that 'cultures of law and science are in fact mutually constitutive', is to recognise that the making and remaking of that boundary in particular settings is a matter of critical interest.[14] It becomes important to explore, for instance, how the sense of a scientific or a political arena 'interfacing' with international law from afar is sustained in particular legal knowledge practices (to the extent that it is) as well as some possible effects of its maintenance as such.[15] This is a different inquiry to that addressing 'fit'; the question becomes less one of how international law should relate to science or politics (or vice versa) in some general and enduring sense than how this sort of worry shapes international legal work. As already signalled, this chapter takes up the latter question with reference to the work of the IPCC.

The IPCC

The IPCC is an inter-governmental organisation established in 1988 in order to generate comprehensive, 'internationally co-ordinated

[13] Shaw and Robinson's reference to 'science-policy interface' seems representative of the way in which a relationship between 'science' and 'law' (and/or 'policy') tends to be configured in related scholarship: Alison Shaw and John Robinson, 'Relevant but not Prescriptive? Science Policy Models within the IPCC' (2004) 48: Supplement *Philosophy Today* 84–95.

[14] Jasanoff, *Science at the Bar*, pp. 7–8. This argument is not Jasanoff's alone. It owes much to the social study of science and technology by Bruno Latour and many others. See, for example, Bruno Latour, *We Have Never Been Modern* (trans. Catherine Porter, Cambridge, MA: Harvard University Press, 1993). For an IPCC-specific illustration of dangers of co-production (in this instance, science and politics' co-production), see Clark Miller's discussion of the role played by the IPCC's 'boundary work' (affirming the separability of science and politics) in facilitating the US' unilateral exit from the Kyoto Protocol: Clark A. Miller, 'Climate Science and the Making of Global Political Order' in Sheila Jasanoff (ed.), *States of Knowledge: The Co-Production of Science and the Social Order* (London: Routledge, 2004), pp. 46–66 at pp. 59–60, 63.

[15] Consider, for instance, Donald MacKenzie's claim that a 'key "subpolitical" matter' for the IPCC is, 'paradoxically, preserving the boundary between "science" and "politics", since that boundary is precisely what is needed to facilitate political action, because it matters that action can be seen as based upon "sound science"':

scientific assessments of the magnitude, timing and potential environmental and socio-economic impact of climate change and realistic response strategies'.[16] Formed under the joint auspices of the World Meteorological Organization (WMO) and the United Nations Environment Programme (UNEP), the IPCC has attracted broad governmental involvement: it had 195 state members as of September 2012.[17]

IPCC work is conducted at three main levels: in plenary session of the IPCC among government representatives (with environment and industry groups enjoying observer status); in the process of assembling and planning the undertakings of Working Groups and Task Forces (involving nomination of experts by governments, international, intergovernmental and non-governmental organisations); and at the level of individual Working Groups and Task Forces populated by 'scientific experts' (assisted by their respective Chairs, Vice-Chairs and Technical Support Units and by the IPCC Bureau).[18] The work of the IPCC is also shaped by its interaction with activities ongoing under the auspices of the United Nations Framework Convention on Climate Change (UNFCCC), principally through the IPCC/UNFCCC Joint Working Group.[19]

Donald MacKenzie, 'Making Things the Same: Gas, Emission Rights and the Politics of Carbon Markets' (2009) 34 *Accounting, Organizations and Society* 440–455 at 453.

16 UN General Assembly Resolution A/RES/43/53, 6 December 1988, www.un.org/documents/ga/res/43/a43r053.htm (accessed 17 September 2012). In this resolution, the General Assembly endorsed the action of the World Meteorological Organization and the United Nations Environment Programme in jointly establishing the IPCC.

17 www.ipcc.ch/organization/organization.shtml (accessed 17 September 2012).

18 Shardul Agrawala, 'Structural and Process History of the Intergovernmental Panel on Climate Change' (1998) 39 *Climactic Change* 621–642 at 623. According to guidance issued by the IPCC Secretariat, '[t]he IPCC aims to select the best available scientific experts representing a range of disciplines, views and geographical balance' including 'appropriate representation of experts from developing and developed countries and countries with economies in transition'. These experts are nominated by the governments of IPCC member countries and by international, inter-governmental and non-governmental organisations. See IPCC Secretariat, 'Guidance Document for IPCC Government Focal Points on the Nomination of Potential Lead Authors, Coordinating Lead Authors and Review Editors' (January 2010), www.ipcc.ch/pdf/ar5/ar5-fp-guidance.pdf (accessed 17 September 2012). On 'legitimacy concerns' surrounding the extent of developing country representation on IPCC bodies and participation in IPCC processes, see Daniel Bodansky, 'The Legitimacy of International Governance: A Coming Challenge for International Governance' (1999) 93 *American Journal of International Law* 596–624 at 617.

19 UNFCCC, 'A Guide to the Climate Change Convention Process (Preliminary 2nd edition)', Climate Change Secretariat: Bonn, 2002, www.unfccc.int/resource/process/guideprocess-p.pdf (accessed 17 September 2012).

Among the most significant aspects of the IPCC's work has been its production of Assessment Reports every five-to-seven years. These Reports seek to 'evaluate the overall state of knowledge' on climate change, its impacts and possible response strategies, drawing from multidisciplinary literatures.[20] Each is a combined output of the entire organisation involving peer review by scientific experts as well as review by IPCC member governments.[21] Each is, moreover, comprised of a separate report from each of the IPCC's three Working Groups as well as a Synthesis Report, the latter including an intensely negotiated Summary for Policymakers.[22]

The IPCC acknowledges that it deals (in its Assessment Reports and otherwise) with 'scientific, technical and socio-economic factors relevant to the application of particular policies'.[23] The register in which the organisation does so, however, varies from body to body - variation which tends to get elided in the solidary representation of IPCC work that so frequently appears in international legal scholarship. Each of the IPCC's three Working Groups has a distinct mandate. IPCC Working Group I (WGI) assesses the 'physical scientific aspects of the climate system and climate change'. IPCC Working Group II (WGII) assesses the 'vulnerability of socio-economic and natural systems to climate change, negative and positive consequences of climate change, and options for adapting to it', assessing information by sector (water resources; ecosystems; food and forests; coastal systems; industry; human health) and region (Africa; Asia; Australia and New Zealand; Europe; Latin America; North America; Polar Regions; Small Islands). IPCC Working Group III (WGIII) assesses 'options for mitigating climate change through limiting or preventing greenhouse gas emissions and enhancing activities that remove them from the atmosphere', seeking to 'take[ ] into account' the 'main economic sectors' of energy, transport,

[20] Shaw and Robinson, 'Relevant but not Prescriptive?', 92.

[21] *Ibid.*; Agrawala, 'Structural and Process History', 623–628. For an overview of the 'internal dynamics that lead to the final product', see Bernd Siebenhüner, 'The Changing Role of Nation States in International Environmental Assessments - The Case of the IPCC' (2003) 13 *Global Environmental Change* 113–123.

[22] For insights into the process, see Agrawala, 'Structure and Process History', 623–628; Bernd Siebenhüner, 'How do Scientific Assessments Learn? Part 1. Conceptual Framework and Case Study of the IPCC' (2002) 5 *Global Environmental Change* 411–420 at 415–419.

[23] Principles Governing IPCC Work, Approved at the Fourteenth Session of the IPCC, Vienna, 1 October 1998 (as amended), www.ipcc-wg1.unibe.ch/procedures/procedures.html (accessed 17 September 2012) (hereafter IPCC Principles).

buildings, industry, agriculture, forestry and waste management 'both in a near-term and in a long-term perspective'.[24] As Shardul Agrawala observes, the three IPCC Working Groups cater 'to very different communities with vastly differing levels of disciplinary cohesion'.[25]

Irrespective of the significant divergences among their respective areas of focus, all IPCC bodies are subject to the IPCC governing principles' stipulation that they handle 'scientific, technical and socio-economic' factors 'objectively' while remaining 'neutral with respect to policy'.[26] This is the case even though the IPCC's design and work processes are said to be the outcome of 'an intensely political process within the US and the UN system' at their inception, not to mention later political wrangling.[27] According to Agrawala (a widely referenced chronicler of the organisation's development), 'it is somewhat of a paradox that the IPCC has managed to attract and sustain the participation of high calibre *scientists* and has consistently produced reports that carry credibility in scientific circles' given its acutely political provenance.[28]

Two themes emerge in Agrawala's writing that carry over into much international legal scholarship in which the IPCC and its work are represented. The first theme that emerges is the sense of the IPCC as a scientific body identified more with the natural sciences rather than with the social sciences. The second theme is the location of that scientific body within a complex and expansive political firmament of which it is understood to comprise a part, albeit a distinctively 'scientific' part. In Agrawala's account, as in other accounts of the IPCC in social science scholarship, understandings of the organisation as, on one hand, an artefact and maker of science and, on the other, as a product of and contributor to global politics have variously given rise to perceptions of the IPCC as a hybridising or boundary organisation.[29] In international legal scholarship, however, depictions of the IPCC as

[24] www.ipcc.ch/working_groups/working_groups.shtml (accessed 17 September 2012).

[25] Agrawala, 'Structural and Process History', 624.

[26] IPCC Principles.

[27] Shardul Agrawala, 'Context and Early Origins of the Intergovernmental Panel on Climate Change' (1998) 39 *Climactic Change* 605–620 at 617.

[28] *Ibid.* (emphasis in original).

[29] Clark A. Miller, 'Hybrid Management: Boundary Organizations, Science Policy, and Environmental Governance in the Climate Regime' (2001) 26 *Science Technology Human Values* 478–500; Jane Hunt and Simon Shackley, 'Reconceiving Science and Policy: Academic, Fiducial and Bureaucratic Knowledge' (1999) 37 *Minerva* 141–164 at 149; Simon Shackley, 'The Intergovernmental Panel on Climate Change: Consensual Knowledge and Global Politics' (1997) 7 *Global Environmental Change* 77–79; Paul N. Edwards and Stephen H. Schneider, 'Self-Governance and Peer Review in

a hybridising or boundary organisation have not been prominent. The arena of scientific knowledge of a sort with which the IPCC is typically identified tends to be kept apart from the legal knowledge field in international legal writing, such that the 'balancing' of these fields' respective authority, or the greater 'assimilat[ion]' of the legal to the scientific, are quite common scholarly goals.[30]

Reflecting this sense of separability, two prominent international legal scholars have characterised the IPCC's 2007 Fourth Assessment Report as having 'injected a new sense of urgency into' states' negotiations concerning an international agreement towards emission reduction.[31] This sense of the IPCC 'inject[ing]' material, energy, facts and ideas into the international legal arena from somewhere outside that arena is representative of much international legal scholarship in which the IPCC appears, as will be discussed further below. This is the case even though the IPCC could be regarded as much a product of international law as it is a creature of global politics and scientific method.

The IPCC owes its existence and status to legal enactments by international organisations (WMO and UNEP).[32] Its work is carried out in large part through the promulgation of international norms, guidelines and standards.[33] The IPCC helps to regulate what constitutes 'policy relevant scientific information' in the climate change context and

Science-for-Policy: The Case of the IPCC Second Assessment Report' in Clark A. Miller and Paul N. Edwards (eds.), *Changing the Atmosphere: Expert Knowledge and Environmental Governance* (Cambridge, MA: MIT Press, 2001), pp. 219–246.

30 See, for example, Peel, *Science and Risk Regulation*, p. 384, (arguing for 'solutions … to be worked out on a case-by-case basis' that result in 'acceptable ways of balancing conventional and non-standard knowledges, expertise and politics, science and democracy'). See further Jasanoff, *Science at the Bar*, p. 7 (characterising a 'strikingly recurrent' theme in legal writing about science in general as the claim that 'the culture of law should strive as far as possible to assimilate itself to the culture of science').

31 Jutta Brunée and Stephen J. Toope, *Legitimacy and Legality in International Law: An Interactional Account* (Cambridge University Press, 2010), p. 138.

32 Resolution 4 (EC-XL) of the Fortieth Session of the Executive Council of the World Meteorological Organization, Geneva, 7–10 June, 1988, reproduced in World Meteorological Organization, Resolutions of Congress and the Executive Council (WMO-No. 508) (2010), A.II-27, www.wmo.int/pages/governance/policy/index_en.html (accessed 17 September 2012); United Nations Environment Programme: Report of the Governing Council on the Work of its 14th Session, 8–19 June, 1987, UN Doc. A/42/25, p. 71 (Resolution 14/20, 18 June 1987).

33 See, for example, Simon Eggleston, Leandro Buendia, Kyoko Miwa, Todd Ngara and Kiyoto Tanabe (eds.), *2006 IPCC Guidelines for National Greenhouse Gas Inventories* (Hayama, Japan: Institute for Global Environmental Strategies, 2006), www.ipcc-nggip.iges.or.jp/public/2006gl/index.html (accessed 17 September 2012).

how that should be generated and communicated.[34] It has played a vital role in constituting matters of global regulatory concern and has guided the corresponding allocation of research funds worldwide.[35] It has also played a crucial role in defining global regulatory objectives. The Council of the European Union's determination that the global annual mean surface temperature increase should not exceed two degrees above pre-industrial levels and the Copenhagen Accord's adoption of a target to the same effect are, for instance, traceable directly to IPCC Assessment Reports.[36] In these and related ways, the IPCC is an artefact of international law doing governance work on a global scale.

Yet even as scientific experts comparable to those working within the IPCC are recognised as 'entrenched in … global governance networks and relevant international institutions',[37] the sense persists in international legal scholarship that the science that is the IPCC's domain is something to which international law struggles (or should struggle) to reach out, and vice versa. The IPCC Assessment Reports' status, as works of science, works of politics, and/or hybridisations of the two, seems to render them above and beyond the terrain of international legal argument, even as they are understood to exert normative force within that terrain. It is in this sense that the IPCC Assessment Reports are made supra-legal in

34 Shaw and Robinson, 'Relevant but not Prescriptive?', 84.

35 Sonja Boehmer-Christiansen argues that '[c]reating concern has a similar function as a lobbying tool': Sonja Boehmer-Christiansen, 'Global Climate Protection Policy: The Limits of Scientific Advice (Part 2)' (1994) 4 *Global Environmental Change* 185–200 at 198. One does not need to subscribe to Boehmer-Christiansen's rather conspiratorial account of the IPCC leadership making 'skilful use of the world political context and available allies' (at 195) in order to recognise the IPCC's impact in these respects. According to Richard Tol, the IPCC has 'use[d] its brand to branch out into areas outside its core mandate' including in relation to 'scenario building … standard setting … monitoring, and research funding': Richard S. J. Tol, 'Regulating Knowledge Monopolies: The Case of the IPCC' (2011) 108 *Climactic Change* 827–839 at 830. In the latter regard, see the IPCC's scholarship programme explained at www.ipcc.ch/ipcc-scholarship-programme/ipcc_scholarshipprogramme.shtml (accessed 17 September 2012).

36 Hans-Holger Rogner *et al.*, 'Introduction' in Intergovernmental Panel on Climate Change, *Climate Change 2007: Mitigation of Climate Change: Contribution of Working Group III to the Fourth Assessment Report of the Intergovernmental Panel on Climate Change* (Bert Metz *et al.* (eds.), Cambridge and New York: Cambridge University Press, 2007), pp. 95–116 at pp. 99–116, 99–100; Report of the Conference of the Parties on its fifteenth session, Copenhagen, 7–19 December 2009, Addendum, Part Two: Action taken by the Conference of the Parties at its fifteenth session, Decision 2/CP. 15, FCCC/CP/2009/11/Add.1, p. 4, http://unfccc.int/meetings/copenhagen_dec_2009/items/5262.php (accessed 17 September 2012). I am indebted to Tim Stephens for highlighting the provenance of this target.

37 Peel, *Science and Risk Regulation*, p. 108.

international legal scholarship. Before elaborating upon this claim, however, a few preliminary words of clarification are required.

The claim that international legal scholars' supra-legal rendering of IPCC work helps to shape prevailing views of that work and the questions, intuitions and possibilities to which it gives rise should not be confused for a claim that expert views about anthropogenically enhanced climate change are 'just' political and therefore wide open to refutation by anyone with an opinion.[38] One can argue, as this chapter does, that: (a) international legal scholars participate (deliberately, often) in knowledge politics surrounding the work of the IPCC in ways that matter; and (b) there is potential for reconfiguration in international legal understandings or representations of IPCC work, without arguing that what a climate scientist and an international lawyer do in their professional lives is interchangeable (or should be so regarded) or that climate science is up for grabs to the extent that some so-called climate change sceptics might suggest.[39]

Furthermore, to argue that the IPCC Assessment Reports are given supra-legal effect in international legal writing is not to claim that, but for this tendency, those Reports would be indistinguishable from any other output of inter-governmental processes or any other artefact of international legal knowledge. The point is not to suggest a pre-existing sameness or unity which gets unnaturally disrupted by reference to science-law or politics-law distinctions, any more than it is to affirm a sense of unbridgeable distance between the two sides of those hyphenated terms. Rather, the goal of this chapter is to bring into the foreground of international legal scholarship the potential significance of that scholarship's making of both similarity and difference (or proximity and remoteness) along science-law and politics-law axes, with specific reference to the IPCC.

[38] Compare Shackley and Skodvin's contention that the 'scientific knowledge base represented by the IPCC is itself a product of negotiation, as is the portrayal of uncertainty in its assessments', and that there is an important role for the interpretative social scientist in the global environmental change field, alongside which they still argue stridently for advancement of processes 'to mitigate anthropogenically enhanced climate change': Simon Shackley and Tora Skodvin, 'IPCC Gazing and the Interpretative Social Sciences' (1995) 5 *Global Environmental Change* 175–180 at 178 and 180.

[39] Cf. the 'findings' of '40 citizen auditors from 12 countries' in Donna Laframboise, 'Findings of the Citizen Audit of the 2007 Intergovernmental Panel on Climate Change (IPCC) Report' (14 April 2010), www.heartland.org/sites/all/modules/custom/heartland_migration/files/pdfs/27686.pdf (accessed 17 September 2012).

Consider, by way of preliminary illustration, international legal scholarly characterisation of the IPCC as more alike the International Council for Science (ICSU) than other global advisory bodies to which it might arguably be just as comparable; the International Council on Monuments and Sites (ICOMOS) for example. The ICSU is an organisation founded in 1931 to 'promote international scientific activity in the different branches of science and its application for the benefit of humanity'.[40] In the past, it has been characterised as 'the most significant nongovernmental organisation [working on] the climate change issue' by reason of its convening of the seminal 1985 Villach scientific conference on greenhouse gases and its participation in the World Climate Program created in 1979.[41] ICOMOS, on the other hand, is a 'network of experts' established in 1964 who are 'dedicated to promoting the application of theory, methodology, and scientific techniques to the conservation of the architectural and archaeological heritage'.[42]

Among the constellation of scientific advisory bodies represented in international legal accounts, there is cause to align the IPCC more closely with the ICSU than with ICOMOS based on the former bodies' sustained attention to climate change.[43] With regard to their respective

[40] The International Council for Science (ICSU) has a global membership of national scientific bodies and International Scientific Unions that seeks 'to strengthen international science for the benefit of society': www.icsu.org/ (accessed 17 September 2012). The ICSU acted as principal scientific advisor to the United Nations Conference on Environment and Development (UNCED) in Rio de Janeiro in 1992 and, again in 2002, to the World Summit on Sustainable Development and has convened a number of meetings on this theme: www.icsu.org/about-icsu/about-us/a-brief-history (accessed 17 September 2012).

[41] Glen Plant, 'Institutional and Legal Responses to Global Warming' in Robin Churchill and David Freestone (eds.), *International Law and Global Climate Change* (London and Boston: Graham & Trotman/Martinus Nijhoff, 1991), pp. 165–181 at pp. 168, 171. On the role of the ICSU and the relationship between the Villach 1985 workshop and the creation of the IPCC, see Agrawala, 'Context and Early Origins of the [IPCC]'.

[42] ICOMOS is a 'global non-government organisation' comprised of individual members, national committees and international scientific committees which was established pursuant to a resolution of the Second Congress of Architects and Specialists of Historic Buildings in 1964 (known as the International Charter for the Conservation and Restoration of Monuments and Sites or the Venice Charter) and is named in the 1972 UNESCO World Heritage Convention as one of the three formal advisory bodies to the World Heritage Committee: www.icomos.org/ (accessed 17 September 2012).

[43] The IPCC and the ICSU are grouped together without explanation in Peel's analysis (although the ICSU's establishment of an Advisory Group on Greenhouse Gases in 1985, prior to the IPCC's creation, is acknowledged as one point of direct

institutional structures, work processes or products, however, the IPCC could just as easily be aligned with ICOMOS. It would seem open to international legal scholars, for instance, to underline the relative similarity of IPCC Assessment Reports to ICOMOS Thematic Studies. Like IPCC Assessment Reports, ICOMOS Thematic Studies 'do not entail new research. Rather, they present a synthesis of existing research on a specific theme at a given time'. They 'support' international treaty action by states (namely, tentative listings and nominations under the World Heritage Convention) by 'summarising available evidence', but strive not to 'compromise' those subsequent processes.[44] The IPCC and ICOMOS institutions could potentially be regarded as exemplary of relatively similar forms of international legal knowledge practice: carrying out a particular variant of 'soft' governance work on the part of international organisations.[45]

The tendency of international legal scholarship to group the IPCC with the ICSU, rather than with ICOMOS (for instance) or other international institutions with which comparable connections might be made, may depend upon a presumption of the necessary confluence and relative status of certain types of scientific work. The alignment of

relation). Meanwhile, Peel argues elsewhere that greater account needs to be taken of variability among the tasks that scientists are called by international law to undertake: Peel, *Science and Risk Regulation*, pp. 73, 322–323, 377, 380–383. Peel is not alone in aligning the IPCC with the ICSU rather than with other intergovernmental bodies providing scientific or other expert advice to governments. Sonja Boehmer-Christiansen, for instance, has positioned the IPCC and ICSU together in 'an interlocking system of national-international scientific bureaucracies' allegedly coordinating the global climate change research agenda: Sonja Boehmer-Christiansen, 'Global Climate Protection Policy: The Limits of Scientific Advice (Part 1)' (1994) 4 *Global Environmental Change* 140–159 at 143. For a counter-narrative to Boehmer-Christiansen's (albeit not explicitly in relation to the IPCC–ICSU alignment), see Shackley and Skodvin, 'IPCC Gazing'.

[44] Ian Lilley (Coordinator), *Early Human Expansion and Innovation in the Pacific: ICOMOS Thematic Study* (Paris: International Council on Monuments and Sites, 2010), www.international.icomos.org/world_heritage/TS_Pacific_20101210_final.pdf (accessed 17 September 2012), p. 3. Compare www.ipcc.ch (accessed 17 September 2012): in the IPCC Assessment Reports and otherwise, the IPCC 'reviews and assesses the most recent scientific, technical and socio-economic information produced worldwide relevant to the understanding of climate change' but 'does not conduct any research nor … monitor climate related data or parameters'.

[45] On 'soft' governance, see generally Anna di Robilant, 'Genealogies of Soft Law' (2006) 54 *The American Journal of Comparative Law* 499–554; Dinah Shelton (ed.), *Commitment and Compliance: The Role of Non-binding Norms in the International Legal System* (New York and Oxford: Oxford University Press, 2000), pp. 10–17.

the IPCC with the ICSU rather than with the more social scientifically- and humanities-oriented ICOMOS helps to de-emphasise the IPCC's economic and social scientific work (especially evident in the work of WGII and WGIII) in favour of its natural science analyses and claims (at the forefront of the work of WGI). This is the case even as 'the social sciences are being represented at, and integrated into the IPCC process' across all Working Groups.[46]

Representations of the IPCC as emblematic of climate-related work in the natural sciences (rather than, say, global governance or social science work) may also depend on an idea of scientific method as more or less coherent in particular scientific disciplines, in certain research areas, or even across the physical sciences in general.[47] In addition, such representations might be taken to imply that participants' adherence to scientific method is determinative of, or at least pre-eminent in determining, a particular institution's governance role.

These assumptions are among those relevant to the global reception of the IPCC's work which international legal scholarship plays some small part in reproducing. They are, accordingly, perceptions which international legal inquiry could, if so inclined, play some small part in opening to challenge. Yet the IPCC tends to be consigned to a different world in international legal scholarship to that occupied by most other international institutions (ICOMOS included). As will be discussed below, this configuration occasions some possible gains for international legal scholarship surrounding climate change, but it also potentially implies some losses.

[46] Shackley and Skodvin, 'IPCC Gazing', 180.

[47] Peel, for example, writes of a 'global culture of scientific rationality' and a 'scientific world-view [that] is a truly worldwide view', although she argues elsewhere that greater account needs to be taken of variability among the risk analysis tasks that international law calls upon scientists to undertake: Peel, *Science and Risk Regulation*, pp. 61, 63, 377, 380–383. For a somewhat countering viewpoint to that advanced by Peel, see Bruno Latour and Steve Woolgar, *Laboratory Life: The Construction of Scientific Facts* (Princeton University Press, 1986), p. 29: ('Scientists in our laboratory constitute a tribe whose daily manipulation and production of objects is in danger of being misunderstood, if accorded the high status with which its outputs are sometimes greeted by the outside world'). The reference to 'manipulation and production' should not be taken to imply malevolence. Rather, the claim Latour and Woolgar make is based on their painstaking ethnographic documentation of the mundane ways in which natural scientists actually work and generate knowledge (for their purposes, in the field of neuroendocrinology).

IPCC assessments as voices from beyond: catalyst, evidence, community

The work of the IPCC – its Assessment Reporting, in particular – has been the focus of extensive scholarly attention across the social sciences.[48] In international legal scholarship, however, attention to the IPCC and its work has for the most part been fleeting, as noted above.[49] In the momentary glimpses one is typically given of the IPCC and its work in international legal writings, there are three main, related ways in which its Assessment Reports tend to appear: as supra-legal precipitants of legal action; as supra-legal sources of evidence of unusually compelling status; and/or as expressions of some supra-legal, consensual community.

Catalyst

For international legal scholars, IPCC Assessment Reports are understood to have 'galvaniz[ed]' views 'now widely shared' concerning the need for 'urgent collective action' by international legal means.[50] The IPCC's work has reportedly 'catalyzed' understanding among international decision-makers, helping 'overcome policymakers' uncertainty' about the prospect of taking legal action, both domestic and international.[51] The work of the IPCC is said to have 'played a decisive role in creating the United Nations Framework Convention on Climate Change' (FCCC).[52] Its work is often characterised as the 'trigger that led to the FCCC and the Kyoto Protocol'.[53] In general, that work is

[48] Mike Hulme and Martin Mahony, 'Climate Change: What Do We Know About the IPCC?' (2010) 34 *Progress in Physical Geography* 705–718 (reviewing literature on the IPCC in 'science and technology studies, policy studies, political science, environmental sociology, philosophy of science and a few areas of academic geography').

[49] Exceptions include Peel, *Science and Risk Regulation*, pp. 320–332; Roda Verheyen, *Climate Change Damage and International Law: Prevention Duties and State Responsibility* (Leiden: Martinus Nijhoff Publishers, 2005), pp. 17–21; Plant, 'Institutional and Legal Responses to Global Warming'.

[50] Brunée and Toope, *Legitimacy and Legality*, p. 60.

[51] Jorge E. Vinuales, 'Legal Techniques for Dealing with Scientific Uncertainty in Environmental Law' (2010) 43 *Vanderbilt Journal of Transnational Law* 437–504 at 503; Babette Never, 'Regional Power Shifts and Climate Knowledge Systems in (Global) Climate Governance' (2010) 2 *Goettingen Journal of International Law* 311–333 at 324.

[52] Heide R. Lamirande, 'From Sea to Carbon Cesspool: Preventing the World's Marine Ecosystems from Falling Victim to Ocean Acidification' (2011) 34 *Suffolk Transnational Law Review* 183–217 at 192.

[53] Silke Beck, 'Moving Beyond the Linear Model of Expertise? IPCC and the Test of Adaptation' (2011) 11 *Regional Environmental Change* 297–306 at 298.

perceived as having been 'pivotal' to, and as exerting 'important and growing influence' over, global legal development relating to climate change.[54]

What is noteworthy in these accounts is the catalytic force with which the IPCC's work is imbued, beyond that which one might expect by reason of the subject matter of its work alone.[55] Global inter-governmental organisations often issue calls for action. These are frequently accompanied by predictions of imminent calamity and supported by global assemblages of scientific knowledge. In an October 2010 speech, for example, the Executive Secretary of the Convention on Biodiversity, Ahmed Djoghlaf, called upon state parties to that Convention to implement a strategic plan for the next decade. Djoghlaf warned that 'we shall soon reach a tipping point with irreversible and irreparable damage to the capacity of the planet to continue sustaining life on Earth'.[56] Reference was made, in this context, to the Global Biodiversity Outlook, a publication of the Secretariat of the Convention on Biodiversity that draws upon government reports, scientific literature and specially commissioned studies.[57]

Expertly informed predictions of imminent catastrophe like Djoghlaf's often feature in international legal literature.[58] Rarely, however, are these predictions attributed with independent causal impact to the degree that the IPCC's work seems to have been in international legal writing. The sense – shared by many – that 'something must be done' about global climate change is not generated solely by the IPCC Assessment Reports, let alone by international legal scholars'

[54] Peel, *Science and Risk Regulation*, pp. 328, 330.

[55] Cf. Babette Never's emphasis of the 'power' exerted by the IPCC: Never, 'Regional Power Shifts', 324.

[56] Ahmed Djoghlaf, 'Statement by Executive Secretary of the Convention on Biological Diversity at the Opening Session of the Tenth Meeting of the Conference of the Parties to the Convention', Nagoya (18 October 2010), www.cbd.int/doc/speech/2010/sp-2010-10-18-cop10-en.pdf (accessed 17 September 2012).

[57] www.cbd.int/doc/decisions/cop-10/cop-10-dec-02-en.pdf (accessed 17 September 2012). Statements made by Djoghlaf may also draw indirectly upon the work of the Intergovernmental Platform on Biodiversity and Ecosystem Services, a 'science-policy' platform endorsed by the Conference of the Parties to the Convention on Biological Diversity at its tenth meeting, UNEP/CBD/COP/DEC/X/11, 29 October 2010: www.cbd.int/doc/decisions/ cop-10/cop-10-dec-02.en.pdf (accessed 17 September 2012).

[58] See, for example, albeit one relating to different subject matter, Joseph S. Imburgia, 'Space Debris and Its Threat to National Security: A Proposal for a Binding International Agreement to Clean up the Junk' (2011) 44 *Vanderbilt Journal of Transnational Law* 589–641 at 631: ('Some experts predict … that space debris may cause the start of World War III').

representation of those Reports.[59] Nonetheless, IPCC Assessment Reports have been attributed with more or less autonomous effect in international legal scholarship.

In this sense, the status of IPCC Assessment Reports in international legal writing seems akin to that of pre-legal choice. As discussed in Chapter 4, legal writing and practice convey a sense that much international law is determined by the spontaneous, more or less autonomous choices of self-directing legal or natural persons. Persons and person-like entities of various kinds are imagined to formulate views about risks and risk appetites pre-legally, from which their subsequent legal choices are understood to flow. Scholarly analysis in international law often proceeds from the moment of a choice already having been made rather than inquiring into the conditions (and legal dimensions) of its making. Likewise the 'galvanizing' force with which IPCC Assessment Reports are attributed might be understood to arise from a pre-legal domain: from, that is, an exploratory and evaluative process that seemingly precedes the question of what to do, in international law, about its outcomes. The scientists have made decisions about the science or have found things out about the world and international law must act accordingly – this seems to be a common sequence.[60]

The correspondence with pre-legality explored in Chapter 4 is, however, limited. The IPCC Assessment Reports' 'galvanizing' force is not usually seen to arise from singular acts of choice continually taking place in the wings of international legal performance.[61] The imperatives with which the IPCC Assessment Reports are loaded (as they appear in

[59] Hans Corell, 'Sovereignty and Humanity: Reality and Possibility' (2007) 36 *Denver Journal of International Law and Policy* 1–7 at 5: ('The key conclusions of the Intergovernmental Panel on Climate Change (IPCC) are criticised by some but they constitute a clear warning that something must be done to stop the [*sic*] global warming').

[60] It is important to acknowledge, however, that international legal responses to, and perceptions of, scientific findings in this context are not uniform. Peel usefully highlights regional divergence among 'risk regulatory paradigms' contrasting a paradigm of 'sound science' championed in North America, especially in the United States, with a paradigm based on the precautionary principle that has achieved greatest prominence among European nations: Peel, *Science and Risk Regulation*, pp. 111–170.

[61] Counter-examples to this claim may be seen in some social scientific representations of the IPCC, as when the IPCC is imagined as an agent 'us[ing] its monopoly power' to particular ends or when the IPCC 'process' is imagined as 'decisive[ly] impact[ed]' by 'energy politics … the institutions of big science and the political North': Tol, 'Regulating Knowledge Monopolies', 830; Boehmer-Christiansen, 'Global Climate Protection Policy (Part 2)', 185.

international legal scholarship) have a far more sweeping, tidal quality. The Reports generate 'tipping point[s]' in global debate; they 'ground' international law as it is or should be.[62] Accordingly, the fact or prospect of international legal action is not attributed to decisive choice on the part of the IPCC Assessment Reports' many contributors in the same way that it is, in other contexts, traceable to agents enacting 'private' pre- or post-legal choice. Rather, when viewed as a single, univocal artefact (as is so often the case in international legal scholarship), an IPCC Assessment Report seems to generate a wake in international legal scholarship into which international law and international institutions are almost inevitably drawn. Reading much international legal scholarship – particularly that which touches on the IPCC only in passing – one gains a sense of the IPCC's release of an Assessment Report as something like a *force majeure* event.

Evidence

If the work of the IPCC exerts something like a *force majeure* effect in international legal scholarship, it is also called upon to 'deliver the *proof* to compel policy action'.[63] Yet, when imagined as evidence from this scholarly vantage point, IPCC Assessment Reports are not subjected to conventional measures of legal cogency applicable in international legal proceedings.[64] While some international legal scholars express views regarding the credibility or conservatism of IPCC predictions,[65] many seem (probably rightly) to presume themselves not competent

[62] Brunée and Toope, *Legitimacy and Legality*, p. 147; Oren Perez, 'Purity Lost: The Paradoxical Face of the New Transnational Legal Body' (2007) 33 *Brooklyn Journal of International Law* 1–58 at 26.

[63] Beck, 'Moving Beyond the Linear Model of Expertise?', 303. For illustrative representations of the IPCC in international legal scholarship as a source of evidence, or as having established certain facts for the purposes of attributing international legal liability, see Vinuales, 'Legal Techniques', 496; Christina Voigt, 'State Responsibility for Climate Change Damages' (2008) 77 *Nordic Journal of International Law* 1–22 at 9; Philippe Cullet, 'Liability and Redress for Human-Induced Global Warming: Towards an International Regime' (2007) 43A *Stanford Journal of International Law* 99–122 at 101; Maria Banda and John Opperman, 'Building a Latin American Coalition on Forests: Negotiation Barriers and Opportunities' (2011) 44 *Vanderbilt Journal of Transnational Law* 527–588 at 556.

[64] See generally Chester Brown, *A Common Law of International Adjudication* (Oxford University Press, 2007), pp. 92–102.

[65] For examples of international legal scholarship challenging, to some degree, the credibility or currency of IPCC predictions, see Angela Williams, 'Solidarity, Justice and Climate Change Law' (2009) 10 *Melbourne Journal of International Law* 493–508 at 494 (arguing that the IPCC's 'current scientific predictions' are '(if anything)

to evaluate the IPCC's work to determine its probative value to any applicable legal standard. Instead, the IPCC's work tends to be regarded as presumptively, even superlatively probative. This special status is justified (often tacitly) by reference to the IPCC's 'open[ness] to all scientists' as well as the peer review processes in which the 'scientific experts' concerned are understood to have taken part.[66] The framing of the IPCC's work as evidence may also be traced to a recurring sense, among international lawyers, that the system of which they are at once architects, ambassadors and foot soldiers should be made more like a domestic legal system, or more effectively linked up with domestic legal systems, by greater recourse to courts or court-like processes.[67]

Where the IPCC's competence as an evidence-producer *is* subjected to international legal scrutiny (if only by force of imagination), it frequently emerges super-charged. Although the IPCC does not purport to produce evidence for legal dispute resolution purposes,[68] at least one international legal scholar has entertained a fantasy of putting the IPCC, as it were, on the stand. Roda Verheyen speculates that 'it would be difficult indeed in a court of law to rebut conclusions made by the IPCC with single pieces of science originating [from climate change] sceptics'. According to Verheyen, the 'facts' of IPCC representativeness and peer review show 'at the very least that IPCC findings would be of very high evidentiary value in a court of law'. Verheyen goes on to imagine 'an IPCC scientist acting as an expert witness in accordance

conservative' and 'thus should be considered the very bare minimum of possible climactic change to be expected'); Siobhán McInerney-Lankford *et al.*, *Human Rights and Climate Change: A Review of the International Legal Dimensions* (Washington, DC: The World Bank, 2011) p. 1: ('[T]here is growing evidence that [the IPCC Fourth Assessment Reports'] conclusions underestimated both the scale and pace of global warming').

66 Verheyen, *Climate Change Damage and International Law*, pp. 19–20. Cf. Edwards and Schneider, 'Self-Governance and Peer Review in Science-for-Policy', p. 231, (discussing the 'often tacit' assumption that 'peer review acts as a kind of "truth machine," automatically separating "good" science from "bad"').

67 See generally Lan Cao, 'Culture Change' (2007) 47 *Virginia Journal of International Law* 357–412 at 376.

68 Edwards and Schneider characterise the IPCC's 'nominal goal' as one of 'represent[ing] fairly the full range of credible scientific opinion' and highlight that the IPCC's Summaries for Policymakers (SPMs, issued in conjunction with the release of IPCC Assessment Reports) tend to be replete with 'caveats about uncertainties and limitations of current understanding' even as the SPMs suggest, from the Second Assessment Report onwards, the 'beginning[s] [of] converge[nce] on a definitive answer' to the question of whether global warming should be attributed to human activity: Edwards and Schneider, 'Self-Governance and Peer Review in Science-for-Policy', pp. 220–221.

with ... Article 62 of the [International Court of Justice's] Rules of Procedure'. In such a role, Verheyen contends, the scientist in question 'would most certainly answer ... in the affirmative' the question of whether human activities have caused climate change. Eliding distinctions between the question of evidence's admissibility in particular proceedings and the question of its probative value, Verheyen continues: '[t]his kind of evidence would be permissible and persuasive' on the question of whether human activities caused climate change, since 'the weight of IPCC reviewed science rather than individual views ... would come to bear'.[69]

The imaginative scenario at work here is one of a single, representative IPCC scientist speaking before an international legal trier of fact. The weight with which the IPCC's work is attributed in international legal scholarship arises, however, from its chordal quality. It is precisely because it does not strike a single testimonial note – it does not, as Verheyen says, express 'individual views' – that the IPCC's 'evidence' is afforded supra-legal force. IPCC peer review processes, and the impact of individual persons and factors within them, can and have been probed in detail.[70] Yet, when translated into international legal scholarship, these processes tend to yield a single, colossal, more or less inscrutable product: 'the weight of IPCC reviewed science'.[71] Accordingly, in scholarly representations of 'transnational judicial dialogue', legal decision-makers are depicted 'interpret[ing] scientific data [including IPCC reports] directly rather than discuss[ing] how other courts [in relevant jurisdictions] have talked about [them]' or otherwise subjecting them to the sort of scrutiny that other evidence would typically weather.[72]

[69] Verheyen, *Climate Change Damage and International Law*, pp. 20, 263.

[70] Edwards and Schneider, 'Self-Governance and Peer Review in Science-for-Policy' (discussing the process of peer review adopted in relation to the IPCC's Second Assessment Report and, at p. 234, suggesting that it be conceived 'not [as] a truth machine but [as] a human technique for quality improvement, accountability, and community building'); Claudio Ho-Lem *et al.*, 'Who Participates in the Intergovernmental Panel on Climate Change and Why? A Quantitative Assessment of the National Representation of Authors in the Intergovernmental Panel on Climate Change' (2011) 21 *Global Environmental Change* 1308–1317. On scientific peer review practices more generally, see Daryl E. Chubin and Edward J. Hackett, *Peerless Science: Peer Review and US Science Policy* (Albany: SUNY Press, 1990).

[71] Verheyen, *Climate Change Damage and International Law*, p. 263.

[72] Hari M. Osofsky, 'Climate Change Litigation as Pluralist Legal Dialogue?' (2007) 43A *Stanford Journal of International Law* 181–238 at 193. See also Jacqueline Peel, 'Climate Change Law: The Emergence of a New Legal Discipline' (2008) 32 *Melbourne University*

The work of the IPCC is not, however, only imagined in this mode – as the utterances of an extraordinarily persuasive witness from some other realm. The IPCC simultaneously appears elsewhere in Verheyen's work as a non-appealable arbiter of disputed fact charged with producing some ruling on the 'scientific truth about climate change' in relation to unspecified, hypothetical disputes. The 'official system of reference' that Verheyen locates in the IPCC is said to 'closely resemble[ ] an impartial court hearing of arguments with a subsequent "finding of truth", which in the case of the IPCC is the scientific truth about climate change'. One could plausibly argue, Verheyen maintains, that 'no court of law could possibly deviate from IPCC findings, since any expertise put before the court would never be as inclusive as that inherent in the IPCC'.[73]

In both these instances, the international legal scholarship in question attributes to IPCC work qualities upon which neither the IPCC nor the social science literature surrounding the organisation insist. The work of the IPCC does not appear readied for consignment to some higher realm of more or less unquestionable truth. Nor does the IPCC's capacity to inform global policy development seem contingent upon such consignment. The tone of at least some of the IPCC's work product is engaged, contingent, even combative – consistent with its 'strongly intergovernmental nature'.[74] According to its guiding principles, the IPCC does aspire to remain 'neutral with respect to policy' in its handling of 'policy-relevant questions', as already noted.[75] Nonetheless, in some instances, the work of the IPCC addresses policy-relevant questions in a direct and overtly polemical way.

The Synthesis Report published alongside the Fourth Assessment Report, for instance, puts forward an unequivocal view that 'more extensive adaptation than is currently occurring is required to reduce vulnerability to climate change'. It suggests that 'a large shift in investment patterns' is required to reduce global energy-related carbon dioxide emissions and identifies certain emission mitigation technologies

Law Review 922–979 at 965: ('The majority of climate change cases in Australia have proceeded on the basis that climate change is a real and serious problem, often citing international documents such as the reports of the IPCC').

[73] Verheyen, *Climate Change Damage and International Law*, p. 20.

[74] Kal Raustiala and Natalie L. Bridgeman, 'Nonstate Actors in the Global Climate Regime', UCLA School of Law Research Paper No. 07–29, http://ssrn.com/abstract=1028603 (accessed 17 September 2012), p. 27.

[75] IPCC Principles.

characterised as 'key'. It singles out carbon pricing in particular, observing that '[a]n effective carbon-price signal could realise significant mitigation potential in all sectors'. It specifies a price range (between US$20 and US$80 per tonne) that may be consistent with carbon dioxide emission stabilisation, absent 'induced technological change'. It argues for 'expansion of market mechanisms' and for development that is 'more sustainable'.[76]

This is not the voice of some omnipotent super-witness or ultimate arbiter. It is one of the voices of an institution the work of which has, as Clark Miller emphasises, 'explicitly challenged the prior, local framing of climate change and mobilized the backing of the international scientific community behind a global framing'. The IPCC thereby 'boost[ed] the credibility of the claim that the Earth's climate system should be treated in international law as an ontologically unitary system that spans the entire globe' and 'helped organize a powerful epistemic community in support of policy action to reduce greenhouse gas emissions'. The credibility which the IPCC's work enjoys has, Miller observes, 'been hard won and acquired through dynamic epistemic disputes over the factual basis of global policymaking'.[77]

Marks of the IPCC's forays into such 'epistemic disputes' are plainly visible on its public record.[78] Nonetheless, the making of supra-legality in relation to the work of the IPCC depends upon an erasure of many of those marks. In international legal scholarship, the fate of a global policy agenda in relation to climate change is made to depend upon climate science being placed, as far as possible, beyond contention. To have the IPCC serve in the role of super-proof-provider or super-arbiter, international legal scholars prefer that the institution not be adorned in soiled battle fatigues. To have it so adorned would neuter its ability to advance the cause of robust action on climate change, or so much international legal scholarship seems to presume.

[76] International Panel on Climate Change (IPCC), *Climate Change 2007: Synthesis Report. Contribution of Working Groups I, II and III to the Fourth Assessment Report of the Intergovernmental Panel on Climate Change* (core writing team and eds Rajendra K. Pachauri and Andy Reisinger, Geneva: IPCC, 2007), pp. 14–18.

[77] Clark A. Miller, 'Democratization, International Knowledge Institutions, and Global Governance' (2007) 20 *Governance* 325–357 at 341, 349.

[78] Consider, for instance, IPCC Secretariat, 'The Role of the IPCC and Key Elements of the IPCC Assessment Process' (4 February 2010), www.ipcc.ch/pdf/press/role_ipcc_key_elements_assessment_process_04022010.pdf (accessed 17 September 2011). This document seems drafted in a way quite deliberately responsive to criticism. See generally *The Economist*, 'A Climate of Conflict'.

In these ways, international legal scholarship generates multiple, related ways of configuring the IPCC's work to 'inject' into international legal work surrounding climate change something of which it is perceived to be short.[79] These representations do not necessarily line up behind one another. The vision of the IPCC as supra-legal in a catalytic sense may be in tension with the idea of the IPCC as a supra-legal source of evidence, for instance. The latter may invite parsing of the IPCC's evidentiary inputs in a way likely to bring about some dissipation of that work's catalytic potential. The idea of the IPCC's work as catalytic of international legal order might also be in tension with a third representation of the IPCC's work circulating in international legal writing: that is, the depiction of the IPCC's work as a relatively stabilising or universalising point of reference by reason of its expression of communal consensus on a global scale.

Community

The evidentiary heft that the IPCC's work is made to carry in international legal scholarship arises not only from some sense of the nature, capacity or role of the institution itself. Crucially, the work of the IPCC gets tethered again and again in international legal writing to some larger aggregative unit or idea: 'community' in particular. It gets tethered, further, to an expectation of consensus-making within or in view of such aggregative units – that is, an expectation that 'dialogue will [or has] in some way minimize [or minimized] social division and controversy' in and around them.[80] In order to reconcile this dialogical picture of the IPCC's work with its quality of being (necessarily) beyond contention, however, the realisation of this consensus must always pre-date its registering in international legal writing. The dialogue understood to have produced it cannot appear ongoing on the terrain of international legal argument.

Accordingly, many international legal scholars seem to view the IPCC's work as an expression of some a priori community: a scientific community, an epistemic community, a community of 'the world's most prominent' experts in climate science, economics and risk analysis.[81]

[79] Brunée and Toope, *Legitimacy and Legality*, p. 138.

[80] Maja Horst and Alan Irwin, 'Nations at Ease with Radical Knowledge: On Consensus, Consensusing and False Consensus' (2010) 10 *Social Studies of Science* 105–126 at 106. See, for example, Osofsky, 'Climate Change Litigation as Pluralist Legal Dialogue?'.

[81] Joelin Lin and Charlotte Streck, 'Mobilising Finance for Climate Change Mitigation: Private Sector Involvement in International Carbon Finance Mechanisms' (2009) 10

Community here performs something of the anchoring and animating role played by the antinomian envelope-pusher in Chapter 2, the 'exceptional' decision-maker in Chapter 3, and the choice-making calculator in Chapter 4. However, as noted earlier in this chapter, the making of such 'persons' in those other argumentative contexts and the evocation of community with reference to the IPCC's work cannot be equated.[82] In relation to the IPCC's work, the referent community allows something more, namely, the enactment of a particular version of the 'consensus ideal'. At the same time, viewed in the reverse, the 'consensusing' of the IPCC's work allows for its constitutive evocation of community.[83]

The IPCC's 2007 Assessment Report is depicted, accordingly, as a 'current "go-to" document for the scientific consensus on climate change'.[84] For all its patent humanness (and for all the documentation of its twists and turns in social and political science literature),[85] this consensus tends to have a magical, found quality in much international legal scholarship in which it appears. 'Without actively engaging in either advocacy or policy formulation', one IPCC lead author has written in an international legal journal, 'the IPCC has been the key player in forming a consensus that action is necessary'.[86] Elsewhere, an international legal scholar has reported that, thanks to 'recent discoveries ... a scientific consensus now exists'.[87]

Melbourne Journal of International Law 70–101 at 78; Andrew Epstein, 'A New Approach to an Old Problem: Managing Fish Resources in the Beaufort Sea' (2011) 11 *Chicago Journal of International Law* 755–788 at 757; Never, 'Regional Power Shifts', 324.

82 Nevertheless, on the potential closeness of 'person' and 'community' when evoked as a metaphorical substrate for an international organisation, see Jan Klabbers, *An Introduction to International Institutional Law* (Cambridge University Press, 2002), pp. 58–59.

83 Horst and Irwin, 'Nations as Ease', 122.

84 Margaret Purdy and Leanne Smythe, 'From Obscurity to Action: Why Canada Must Tackle the Security Dimensions of Climate Change' (2010) 65 *International Journal* 411–433 at 413.

85 For an overview of the relevant social and political science literature, see Hulme and Mahony, 'What Do We Know About the IPCC?'. For an instance of international legal scholarship engaging that literature's accounts of the difficulties and contingencies of the IPCC's consensus-making, see Peel, *Science and Risk Regulation*, pp. 320–332 (emphasising, at p. 330, that the IPCC's work towards 'generating political consensus' has 'so far not yielded a binding international agreement').

86 R. T. Pierrehumbert, 'Climate Change: A Catastrophe in Slow Motion' (2006) 6 *Chicago Journal of International Law* 573–596 at 591.

87 Jennifer Kilinski, 'International Climate Change Liability: A Myth or a Reality?' (2009) 18 *Journal of Transnational Law & Policy* 377–418 at 381. For another example, see Lakshman Guruswamy, 'Climate Change: The Next Dimension' (2000) 9 *Journal*

Beyond the magic of 'discovery', no account is given of how that consensus came about or the degree to which it might remain a work-in-progress.

The ongoing efforts that consensus-making and consensus-projection entail, in and about the IPCC, are cast behind some thought-screen that international legal scholarship seems largely unwilling to penetrate. Most probably, this unwillingness is traceable to an unstated fear of calling that consensus into question and thereby undermining global policy-making on climate change. In this respect, international legal scholars seem attentive to the potential impact of their knowledge practices. What is curious, however, is that this attentiveness is not, by and large, combined with recognition of the wide range of powerful actions that international lawyers have taken in what might be termed post-consensual global policy-making settings. By 'post-consensual policy-making settings', I mean those in which policy-makers' claim-laying to global consensus has been fraught and widely contested, even as related institution-building and governance activities have proceeded in earnest.

Consider, for instance, contemporary international human rights law scholars' propensity to draw attention to the obstacles, conflicts and divergences plaguing the field in which they work, even as they celebrate and promote that field's ever-expanding reach.[88] In this context, where evocations of 'the international community' are routinely made, much international legal scholarship seems to have metabolised (albeit to varying degrees and in different ways) the sort of reminder that Martti Koskenniemi offers when he recalls that 'there is no representative of the whole that would not be simultaneously a representative of some particular'.[89] Yet international legal work in the human rights field rolls on regardless of this insight; to

of Transnational Law & Policy 341–382 at 349 (citing the IPCC's Second Assessment Report in support of the proposition that 'there is a strong general consensus among the international scientific community that some action should be taken now to limit or reduce atmospheric GHGs [greenhouse gases] on a global basis').

[88] See, for example, Henry Steiner *et al.*, *International Human Rights in Context: Law, Politics, Morals*, Third Edition (Oxford and New York: Oxford University Press, 2008), p. v (remarking on the 'major failures and inadequacies' of the post-Second World War human rights movement alongside its 'staying power and growth', the 'remarkably broad dissemination of its message' and the 'ever greater credibility' enjoyed by its 'claims of permanence').

[89] Martti Koskenniemi, 'International Law and Hegemony: A Reconfiguration' (2004) 17 *Cambridge Review of International Affairs* 197–218 at 199.

some extent, in debt to it.[90] In contrast, the global community consensus from or to which the IPCC's work is traced in international legal writing is attributed with an unadulterated naturalism of a sort often withheld from projections of a global, communal viewpoint in the international human rights law field.

Once again, the naturalistic, found quality of the scientific consensus underpinning the work of the IPCC – or the aspiration to generate or sustain it – is not everywhere considered useful to the global policy-making work to which the IPCC's work contributes. Nor is it a necessary outcome of international lawyers' recourse to 'science' in this context. Social scientific scholarship on the IPCC has much to say about the specific persons and contingent processes by which various forms of scientific consensus represented in the IPCC's work have been forged, so recourse to 'science' read as social science could well have a denaturalising effect on this consensus.[91] Moreover, social science seems to entertain a denaturalised account of climate-related scientific consensus without necessarily calling into question the importance of taking serious and urgent action to curtail the anthropogenic dimensions of climate change. Indeed, according to one account, the inscription of a consensus concerning climate change under 'one global signature' may be counter-productive as far as effective policy-making is concerned.[92]

[90] David Kennedy, 'Losing Faith in the Secular and the Culture of International Governance' in Marjorie B. Garber and Rebecca L. Walkowitz (eds.), *One Nation Under God? Religion and American Culture* (New York and London: Routledge, 1999), pp. 115–127 at pp. 118, 126: ('[T]he secular intelligentsia has a new sensibility about both political science and law. Political science takes a shine to law just as law embraces the worlds *both* of ethics, values, faith *and* of politics … But when we say they are "back", that law is back to politics, politics back to law … I'm afraid that we usually mean only that the same pieties are being woven from the other side').

[91] See, for example, Siebenhüner, 'How do Scientific Assessments Learn?'; Dennis Bray, 'The Scientific Consensus of Climate Change Revisited' (2010) 13 *Environmental Science and Policy* 340–350; Eleftheria Vasileiadou *et al.*, 'Exploring the Impact of the IPCC Assessment Reports on Science' (2011) 14 *Environmental Science and Policy* 1052–1061; Ho-Lem *et al.*, 'Who Participates in the Intergovernmental Panel?' For an instance of international legal scholarship taking account of social scientific understandings of scientific knowledge-production, see Peel, *Science and Risk Regulation*, pp. 341–343.

[92] Mike Hulme, 'Problems with Making and Governing Global Kinds of Knowledge' (2010) 20 *Global Environmental Change* 558–564 at 560 (arguing that 'collapsing human knowledge about climate change into one global signature hides far more than it discloses. It is psychologically sterile … It offers an inadequate and one-dimensional guide to policy … [a]nd it is increasingly recognised as severely limiting the

In contrast, many international legal scholars who touch on the IPCC's work seem to assume that representing that work under anything other than one global signature will, always and everywhere, serve to topple the global policy-making house of cards on which they see the fate of the planet resting.

Is 'science' (read as natural or physical science) or 'politics' carrying the day in this regard? That is, does international lawyers' apparent hesitancy to scrutinise too closely the consensus/community bequeathed them in the work of the IPCC (or to view that work other than in terms of such a bequest) reflect an international legal reflex of deference to scientific rationality (in the hope of accessing some 'impartial "interpret[ation] of reality"')?[93] Or does it reflect instead international lawyers' attunement to a perilous political reality (or reality effect) in which climate change sceptics,[94] 'energy interests',[95] the North,[96] the South (specifically, China and India)[97] or someone or other, seems to be holding all the cards while a 'slow motion catastrophe' unfolds?[98] Alternatively, is the signature under these supra-legal images characteristically that of 'law'? That is, are these tendencies to configure the IPCC supra-legally particular instantiations of a stylistic preference for 'smoky mirror[s]' and 'wilful blindness' (between science and/or politics, on one hand, and law on the other) characteristic of the prevailing culture of international legal governance?[99]

Why this supra-legal scaffolding gets constructed – the question of identifying key drivers, scientific, political or legal – ultimately seems less important than *how* this occurs and with what implications in particular instances. This chapter has shown how the IPCC's work has been given supra-legal effect in a particular setting: namely,

framing and goals of scientific enquiry' particular as regards 'other possible regional or local signatures of a changing climate').

93 Peel, *Science and Risk Regulation*, p. 68.

94 Stephen M. Gardiner, 'Ethics and Global Climate Change' (2004) 114 *Ethics* 555–600 at 560 n. 12, 566 n. 31, 569–570.

95 Boehmer-Christiansen, 'Global Climate Protection Policy (Part 2)', 185.

96 Never, 'Regional Power Shifts', 326.

97 Pierrehumbert, 'Catastrophe in Slow Motion', 593.

98 *Ibid.* Cf. Donald MacKenzie's argument that defence of a boundary between 'science' and 'politics' is a matter in which the IPCC has significant investments 'because it matters that action can be seen to be based on "sound science"': MacKenzie, 'Making Things the Same', 453.

99 David Kennedy, 'Losing Faith in the Secular', 119.

international legal scholarship concerned with climate change in which the IPCC appears. Let us now consider some possible ramifications of the IPCC's identification with supra-legality in international legal scholarship.

International legal work on climate change reaps gains from its evocation of some supra-legal sphere of science or politics with which the IPCC's work is identified. As indicated above, it gains from these sources impulsion, evidentness, commonalty and from these, potentially, assurance. Yet international legal work also incurs losses by reason of its supra-legal fixations. Evocations of supra-legality depicted in this chapter tend to encourage international lawyers to look somewhere beyond the here and now of their collective endeavour in order to experience these properties (of impulsion, evidentness and commonalty). In so doing, international legal scholars risk fostering a disposition of quiescent line-toeing - of answering calls understood to issue always from elsewhere, no more and no less - on climate change related questions.

Occupying international law on climate change

This chapter has suggested that supra-legal status is often conferred upon the work of the IPCC in international legal scholarship by recourse to three different narratives: a story about international legal change and how it may be brought about; a story about truth and how it may be established; and a story about community and the moderation of controversy.

Each of these stories carries with it a dark side. To tell a story of change centred on scientific catalysis is potentially to tell a story of international legal stasis and acquiescence, but for the pseudo-miraculous interventions of science. To relate a story about truth focused on the imaginative evocation of super-witnesses and super-arbiters is to contribute relatively little to the navigation of ongoing trans-disciplinary disputes surrounding climate change related resource redistribution; indeed, fantasies so evoked may make such mundane disputes more difficult to navigate. To propagate narratives that make effective action concerning climate change sound contingent upon the maintenance of near-immaculate consensus within one or other global whole may be to induce apathy or despair among international legal scholars and others working on climate change related initiatives.

What, then, might it entail to occupy or reoccupy the places and times of international legal work on climate change without routinised recourse to such supra-legal narratives or guarantees? Indications are immanently available. After all, international legal work on climate change is not always or everywhere so underwritten. In large part it remains unwritten, or in the process of being written. Shirley Scott has reminded us how much more is called for, in international legal work, than 'the design and implementation of mitigation measures', bearing in mind international law's 'complicit[y] in creating the climate change crisis' through its 'facilitation of an oil-based, capitalist, global economy'.[100] Harriet Bulkeley and others have drawn attention to the multiple sites at which this work is and may yet be ongoing.[101] Donald MacKenzie has highlighted a plenitude of 'existing and planned experiments in changing capitalism's bottom line': experiments which are 'heterogeneous, widely diffused worldwide, and involve many aspects – scientific, technological, political, accounting, sociological, anthropological, geographical [to which I would add, legal] – beyond economics as narrowly conceived'.[102] Timothy Duane has recorded some of the prolific 'policy innovation … [ongoing in] electricity sector regulation regardless of the outcome of international negotiations under the United Nations Framework Convention on Climate Change (UNFCCC) or the passage of new climate change legislation by the US Congress' or the national legislatures of other states.[103] Jerome Whitington has suggested that 'the diversity, range and intimacy of ways in which people associate with objects or things' – for present purposes, perhaps, the object or thing of a warming global climate – 'has produced an unprecedented

[100] Shirley V. Scott, 'Is the Crisis of Climate Change a Crisis for International Law: Is International Law too Democratic, too Capitalist and too Fearful to Cope with the Crisis of Climate Change?' (2008) 14 *Australian International Law Journal* 31–43 at 32, 35–36.

[101] Heike Schroeder and Harriet Bulkeley, 'Global Cities and the Governance of Climate Change: What is the Role of Law in Cities?' (2009) 36 *Fordham Urban Law Journal* 313–359; Michele M. Betsill and Harriet Bulkeley, 'Cities and the Multilevel Governance of Global Climate Change' (2006) 12 *Global Governance* 141–159.

[102] MacKenzie, 'Making Things the Same', 453.

[103] Timothy P. Duane, 'Greening the Grid: Implementing Climate Change Policy Through Energy Efficiency, Renewable Portfolio Standards, and Strategic Transmission System Investments' (2010) 34 *Vermont Law Review* 711–780 at 712.

creativity and dynamism', discernible in 'actual practices of politics and sciences in the contemporary'.[104] Occasions and openings may be made for 'writing dangerously' in international law on climate change (that is, pursuing scholarship and policy experimentation 'cut adrift from [any claim to knowledge] that one is in the right' and risking resistance to prevailing imperatives of service provision and outcome delivery, however pressing the demands).[105]

This chapter has foregrounded the making of that architecture of supra-legality which international legal scholarship on climate change labours variously to build, collapse, inhabit and flee.[106] In debate surrounding the sort of transformative structural changes of which climate change invites consideration, international legal work which intervenes and dwells for a time at the level of knowledge architecture – to ask questions of its crafting and explore possibilities for its remaking – is at least as important as work which strives to deliver urgently on the most prominent global policy deliverables, or so this chapter contends. More precisely, this chapter has called into question the orientation of international legal work on climate change around the would-be guarantorship of some global catalyst, evidence and/or community located above that work's terrain, such as that frequently identified with the work of the IPCC.

The architectures of assurance called into question by this chapter are not, however, solely built of spires and flying buttresses. They depend as much on the 'infra-' (that is, on the below, the inferior, the underneath and the within) as on the 'supra-' dimensions of international legal work.[107] The former dimension includes, for instance, the

[104] Jerome Whitington, 'Introduction – Science and its Politics' (2008) 14:3 *Parallax* 1–3 at 1.

[105] Fleur Johns, 'Address: On Writing Dangerously' (2004) 26 *Sydney Law Review* 473–480 at 480.

[106] The focus in this chapter has been on international legal scholarly tendencies to construct and seek to inhabit a split-level knowledge architecture in which the upper, supra-legal level is understood to be the preserve of science, politics or some hybrid of the two. It must be acknowledged, however, that international legal scholarship also routinely promotes some overcoming of this architecture partially of its own crafting. See, for example, Peel's canvassing of arguments for the 'democratisation' of scientific expertise within international institutions: Peel, *Science and Risk Regulation*, pp. 337–375.

[107] 'infra-, prefix': *Oxford English Dictionary Online*, www.oed.com (accessed 17 September 2012).

infra-legal conditioning of death through international legal work.[108] That is work to which the next chapter will turn.

[108] Ulrich Beck's writing alerts us (in passing, revealingly) to the ever-present force of death in thought and writing surrounding climate change, when he remarks upon the following: 'In the Christian conception of salvation, milk and honey flow in paradise; but on earth milk is supposed to lead straight to environmental death. The "climate killer" cow produces a couple of hundred litres of methane gas per day, the equivalent of almost a kilogram of carbon per litre of milk': Ulrich Beck, 'Climate for Change, or How to Create a Green Modernity?' (2010) 27 *Theory Culture Society* 254–266 at 263.

6 Death, disaster and infra-legality in international law

'Welcome US Marines. We need some help. Dead Bodies Inside.' So, according to media reports, read a hand-drawn sign posted in the hillside community of Nazon outside Port-au-Prince, Haiti, in January 2010.[1] In Haiti, in the wake of the earthquake of 12 January 2010 and ensuing aftershocks, dead bodies issued international invitations and elicited expertise of one kind or another. Foreign military might was summoned in the name of a generic and unidentified 'we' whose primary basis for claim consisted, it seemed, in the need for 'help' traceable to the immediate proximity of generic 'dead bodies'. Managerial and juridical authority has been widely evoked by death-bearing appeals along these lines and international law has, as it were, responded.[2] Prominent among those responses were those of international and regional institutions dedicated to the provision of humanitarian relief from disaster. Among those for whom such institutions undertook care were the dead and the living that were to perform the often-horrific work of retrieving and handling the dead.

More than 297,000 people were killed in 2010 in geophysical, meteorological, hydrological, climatological or biological 'disasters',

[1] Mike Esteri, 'After Delays, Water-Purification Tablets Arrive', *The Wall Street Journal*, 17 January 2010, p. 1; Ginger Thompson and Damien Cave, 'Officials Strain to Distribute Aid to Haiti as Violence Rises', *The New York Times*, 17 January 2010, p. 1; Manuel Roig-Franzia *et al.*, 'Anxiety Mounts in Lawless Haiti', *The Washington Post*, 18 January 2010, A01.

[2] There are some problems associated with thinking of disaster as a matter of call and response. International law and other disciplines implicated in disaster management do not simply respond to disasters. They also make disasters, making controversial decisions about resource allocation in the process. For a snapshot of some disagreements surrounding the making of 'disaster' as such, see E. L. Quarantelli (ed.), *What is a Disaster? A Dozen Perspectives on the Question* (London and New York: Routledge, 1998).

making it the third most deadly year, in these terms, of the preceding four decades. In 2011, natural disasters killed 30,773 people, but economic damages from natural disasters were said to have been the highest ever registered: estimated at US$366.1 billion.[3] Numbers – typically graphed against the 'normal' – matter in the business of disaster management. Dead bodies help to generate those numbers and, in the process, help to shape a field of operation for international institutions, international lawyers and others invoking international legal norms. This chapter explores the role of dead bodies in disaster situations as both catalysts to, and objects of, international regulation. It examines, in particular, a range of international 'soft law' instruments by which relief and regulatory actions concerned with the management of dead bodies have been guided, of late, around the world.[4]

This chapter places particular focus upon one widely circulated and adopted field manual on the management of dead bodies after disasters: *Management of Dead Bodies After Disasters: A Field Manual for First Responders*. This manual is now in its third edition but was first published in 2006 by the Pan American Health Organization (PAHO), the World Health Organization (WHO), the International Committee of the Red Cross (ICRC) and the International Federation of Red Cross and Red Crescent Societies (hereafter, *First Responders Manual*).[5] The stated aim of the *First*

[3] Debby Guha-Sapir *et al.*, *Annual Disaster Statistical Review 2010: The Numbers and Trends* (Brussels: Centre for Research on the Epidemiology of Disasters (CRED), 2011), http://cred.be/sites/default/files/ADSR_2010.pdf (accessed 17 September 2012), pp. 1, 21 (the greatest proportion of the 2010 deaths occurred in Haiti, but Russia also experienced 'excess mortality' attributed to extreme temperatures, floods and wildfires: p. 1); Debby Guha-Sapir *et al.*, *Annual Disaster Statistical Review 2011: The Numbers and Trends* (Brussels: CRED, 2012), http://cred.be/sites/default/files/2012.07.05.ADSR_2011.pdf (accessed 17 September 2012). The CRED defines 'disaster' as follows: 'a situation or event which overwhelms local capacity, necessitating a request to a national or international level for external assistance; an unforeseen and often sudden event that causes great damage, destruction and human suffering'. It only records disasters in which ten or more people are killed, 100 or more people are affected, there has been a declaration of a state of emergency and a request for international assistance has been made: p. 7.

[4] On 'soft law', see generally Anna di Robilant, 'Genealogies of Soft Law' (2006) 54 *The American Journal of Comparative Law* 499–554.

[5] Oliver Morgan *et al.* (eds.), *Management of Dead Bodies After Disasters: A Field Manual for First Responders* (Washington, DC: Pan American Health Organization, World Health Organization, International Committee of the Red Cross, 2006) (hereafter, *First Responders Manual*). The press release announcing publication of the *Manual* observed that 'the draft manual and forms were used in the field following the earthquake in Pakistan and mudslide in the Philippines': London School of Hygiene & Tropical Medicine Press Office, 'Handling Bodies After Disasters: Guidelines for First Responders', Press Release, 12 April 2006, www.lshtm.ac.uk/pressoffice/

Responders Manual is to promote the 'proper and dignified management of dead bodies' and to maximise their identification by regulating conditions and behaviours '[i]mmediately after a disaster'.[6] A related end of the *First Responders Manual*, in this chapter's account, is the generation of the infra-legal conditions for such 'management' involving, at the same, a problematisation of management in this mode.

As the previous chapter highlighted, the prefix 'infra-' denotes below, inferior to or underneath, but also within.[7] So, making infra-legality entails making that which lies at the edges of conventional international legal sightlines.[8] International guidelines concerned with the management of dead bodies help to evoke and inscribe generalised, surrounding circumstances which are understood to afford international institutions conditions for their action (or inaction) in the aftermath of disaster. Yet, for the most part, those conditions are not the target of institutional inquiry or concern, hence their marginality or 'infra-' status. The 'legality' of infra-legality indicates the normative or imperative force of these background conditions and the role of legal vocabularies and agents in generating them.[9]

press_releases/2006/manualdeadbodies.html (accessed 17 September 2012). The *Manual* was also referenced widely by relief agencies and governments in relation to the 2010 Haiti earthquake and the 2011 Japanese tsunami. See, for example, Do Dead Bodies in Haiti Pose a Health Risk?', *BBC News Magazine*, 19 January 2010, news.bbc.co.uk/go/pr/fr/-/2/hi/uk_news/magazine/8465464.stm (accessed 17 September 2012); World Health Organization, 'Health Action in Crises – Technical Guidance, Earthquake and Tsunami', www.who.int/hac/crises/jpn/en/ (accessed 17 September 2012).

6 Morgan *et al.*, *First Responders Manual*, p. 1.

7 'infra-, prefix': *Oxford English Dictionary Online*, www.oed.com (accessed 17 September 2012).

8 It is quite a common practice in the international legal field to ascribe a more or less singular disciplinary gaze to international law or a particular institution or sub-discipline of international law. See, for example, David Chandler, 'The Bureaucratic Gaze of International Human Rights Law' in Saladin Meckled-García and Başak Çali (eds.), *The Legalization of Human Rights: Multidisciplinary Perspectives on Human Rights and Human Rights Law* (Oxford: Routledge, 2006), pp. 108–123; Taslim Olawale Elias, *New Horizons in International Law* (Alphen aan den Rijn, The Netherlands: Sijthoff & Noordhoff, 1979), p. 140. The idea that law is invested with a particular gaze or line of vision is also a theme of legal theory more broadly, in which context it often owes its provenance to psychoanalytic theory (the work of Jacques Lacan in particular) or to Foucault's writing on the discipline of medicine: Michel Foucault, *The Birth of the Clinic: An Archaeology of Medical Perception* (trans. A. M. Sheridan Smith, London: Routledge, 2003). The ascription of a particular 'sightline' to international law here is indebted to the latter (Foucault) rather than the former (Lacan). Such a sightline is, inevitably, a fictional creation; see the discussion of the term 'fiction' in Chapter 1 of this book.

9 The making of infra-legality in international institutional manuals might be identified with what others have described as the making of 'blind spots' in international law. Literally, a blind spot is a spot on the human retina which is

The international manual on which this chapter focuses tries to equip people to pursue a range of activities concerning dead bodies (some of them almost unimaginably difficult) and to do so deliberately and with care. In many ways, the dead appear central in and to this text. The *First Responders Manual* is unequivocal in its insistence that the 'dead ... be respected at all times'.[10] Yet this text also, repeatedly, sets death and the dead aside as extraneous to international institutional work, albeit offering various justifications for doing so. This setting aside is justified in practical terms (there are more important things to do in the aftermath of disaster than worry about the dead).[11] This sidelining is articulated in disciplinary or jurisdictional terms (death may be cast as 'properly' within the purview of medical or religious counsellors or within the ambit of the family).[12] It is also expressed in temporal and/or spatial terms (many deaths have already happened at sites at which these manuals are brought to bear; international manuals' greatest concern is with preventing those yet to occur).[13]

This ambivalent marginality of mass death after disaster – the central-yet-peripheral locus of the dead – seems to induce constitutive and integrative impulses of a particularly insistent kind in the

insensible to light: 'blind spot, n.': *Oxford English Dictionary Online*, www.oed.com (accessed 17 September 2012). In international legal scholarship, the term has been used to denote certain questions, conditions or phenomena ostensibly lying within plain sight of international legal inquiry yet which the discipline on the whole seems nonetheless ill-inclined or ill-equipped to see. On 'blind spots' in international legal literature, see, for example, Balakrishnan Rajagopal, *International Law from Below: Development, Social Movements and Third World Resistance* (Cambridge University Press, 2003), pp. 197, 233; David Kennedy, *The Dark Sides of Virtue: Reassessing International Humanitarianism* (Princeton and Oxford: Princeton University Press, 2004), pp. 112, 114, 123, 235, 315. The rendering of such 'blindness' in infra-legal terms, however, suggests the shaping or conditioning of broad surrounding terrain, rather than isolated 'spots' of insensibility.

[10] Morgan *et al.*, *First Responders Manual*, p. 25.

[11] Caring for survivors should take priority over recovery of bodies, the *Manual* directs; '[t]he survivors need you more than the dead': *ibid.*, pp. 7, 28, 29.

[12] *Ibid.*, pp. 25–26: ('Families should be informed about findings and the identification of their loved ones before anyone else'; 'Advice and assistance from religious and community leaders should be sought to improve understanding and acceptance of the recovery, management, and identification of the dead bodies').

[13] The *First Responders Manual* generally expects the dead and the living to occupy different spaces and temporal zones and addresses itself overwhelmingly to the space and time of the living. '[T]he [living] public ... do not touch dead bodies', the *Manual* claims; ambulances should be reserved for 'help[ing] the living' rather than being occupied by the dead; burial sites should be 'separate ... from inhabited areas': *ibid.*, pp. 6, 8, 21.

First Responders Manual, suggesting the immanent problematisation of management practice to which I earlier alluded. The prospect of simply leaving the dead be, allowing them to cease to be (that is, to rot) unattended, or having them be or cease to be in some otherwise unforeseen or unruly fashion, are not prospects that the *First Responders Manual* and comparable texts readily entertain. Rather, in their infra-legal conditioning of death, the texts with which this chapter is concerned assemble – or can be made to assemble – a particular combination of governmental techniques.

The suggestion that the *First Responders Manual* and comparable texts enact 'governmental' assemblages merits some explanation. The first part of this chapter provides this explanation, after initially introducing the materials with which it is concerned. Next, and in this light, a close reading of the *First Responders Manual* is undertaken. This will be followed by a brief, comparative look at another international instrument concerned with management of the dead and messages surrounding the dead. The questions to which these readings will be directed are the following: what seems to happen to international institutions and those whom they would direct and organise when they take dead bodies as the object or a critical dimension of their work? What do the international guidelines in question make of those bodies and what, in turn, do those bodies make of international institutional authority? What, if anything, seems particular to the policy-making terrain surrounding the dead after disaster, as distinct, say, from international rules and policies concerned with bodies where death is attributable to violent conflict? Finally, this chapter will turn to the possible implications of tracking these international instruments' infra-legal preoccupations and effects, as distinct from some of their more familiar or central legal dimensions and concerns.

Field notes: reading the *First Responders Manual*

The *First Responders Manual*, on which this chapter focuses, was written under the co-editorship of three experts trained in health sciences: Oliver Morgan, then an Honorary Research Fellow at the London School of Hygiene and Tropical Medicine; Morris Tidball-Binz, Forensic Coordinator of the Assistance Division of the ICRC; and Dana Van Alphen, Regional Advisor in the PAHO/WHO.[14] These editors'

[14] Dr Van Alphen was trained as a medical doctor in the Netherlands and the UK and served as a medical coordinator within Médecins Sans Frontières before joining

collaboration, and that of the *Manual*'s contributors and reviewers, took place under the auspices of a cluster of international institutions: the PAHO,[15] the WHO[16] and the ICRC[17] (as well as the International

PAHO/WHO's programme on emergency preparedness and disaster relief: www.cdmha.org/conferences/interhands2003/bios/VanAlphen.pdf (accessed 17 September 2012). Dr Morris Tidball-Binz trained as a medical doctor in Argentina, pursued study in forensic anthropology and forensic medicine, and has been active in human rights organisations in Latin America and elsewhere: www.irct.org/Admin/Public/DWSDownload.aspx?File=%2fFiles%2fFiler%2fIPIP%2fFEAT%2fCV+Moris+Tidball-Binz.pdf (accessed 17 September 2012). Dr Oliver Morgan is an epidemiologist working, at the time of writing, with the US Centers for Disease Control and Prevention: http://cdczilla.com/cdc-employee/directory/ (accessed 17 September 2012).

15 http://new.paho.org (accessed 17 September 2012). The PAHO is an international public health agency founded in 1902 by member states of the Organization of American States. Under its 1947 Constitution, it serves thirty-five member states (and a number of participating, associate member and observer states) as well as serving as Regional Office for the Americas for the WHO. Given its status within the WHO, PAHO is recognised as a part of the United Nations system. See Héctor R. Acuña, 'The Pan American Health Organization: 75 Years of International Cooperation in Public Health' (1977) 92 *Public Health Reports* 537–544. The 1947 Constitution of PAHO (as amended) provides that its 'fundamental purposes' shall be 'to promote and coordinate efforts of the countries of the Western Hemisphere to combat disease, lengthen life, and promote the physical and mental health of the people': Constitution of the Pan American Health Organization in Pan American Health Organization (PAHO), *Basic Documents of the Pan American Health Organization*, Eighteenth Edition (Washington, DC: PAHO, 2012), Art. 1.

16 The WHO is a global health organisation and specialised agency of the United Nations established by agreement between sixty-one states in 1946 (which entered into force in 1948), whereupon it inherited the mandate and functions of the League of Nations Health Organization: www.who.int/about/history/en/index.html (accessed 17 September 2012); Walter R. Sharp, 'The New World Health Organization' (1947) 41 *American Journal of International Law* 509–530; League of Nations Information Section, *Health Organization* (1931), www.who.int/library/collections/historical/en/index2.html (accessed 17 September 2012). According to the WHO's Constitution, the objective of the Organization 'shall be the attainment by all peoples of the highest possible level of health' and its functions shall include acting 'as the directing and coordinating authority on international health work': Constitution of the World Health Organization, 14 UNTS 185, Arts. 1–2.

17 The ICRC is an international humanitarian organisation founded in 1863 by five individuals as an association under the Swiss Code, the status and functions of which have been recognised in a number of international treaties: David P. Forsythe, *The Humanitarians: The International Committee of the Red Cross* (Cambridge University Press, 2005). Under its Statutes, the ICRC is an element of the International Red Cross and Red Crescent Movement, also known as the International Red Cross, which comprises the National Red Cross and Red Crescent Societies, the ICRC and the International Federation of Red Cross and Red Crescent Societies: www.icrc.org/eng/resources/documents/misc/icrc-statutes-080503.htm#a1 (accessed 17 September 2012).

Federation of Red Cross and Red Crescent Societies with which the ICRC is associated).

As a product of cross-institutional collaboration on 'disaster management',[18] the *First Responders Manual* manifests an 'international disaster relief system' that has taken shape since the early 1970s.[19] A central feature of this has been the expanded humanitarian role assumed by the United Nations (with which both the PAHO and the WHO are affiliated, the latter as a United Nations specialised agency).[20] Expansion has also occurred in scholarly and expert publication on 'mass fatality planning' in the fields of disaster management and humanitarian relief.[21]

Succeeding and expanding upon a 2004 manual published by the PAHO (and an earlier, 'draft document' said to have been published in Spanish some time before then), the *First Responders Manual* reflected efforts by scholars and experts active in these burgeoning fields to extend guidance into a subject area in which 'historically, little information ha[d] been released'. This had, according to one of the *First Responders Manual*'s editors, undermined 'preparedness for mass fatality incidents'.[22]

Given the *First Responders Manual*'s complicated provenance and the multiple fields of research and practice to which it may be traced, it is important to highlight the limitations of this chapter's scope (and

[18] Tidball-Binz reports that the *Manual* was the 'result of a meeting held in Lima, Peru, in May 2005 and organised by PAHO and the ICRC, on lessons learnt on managing the dead in armed conflicts, disasters and catastrophes, including the 2004 tsunami in southeast Asia': Morris Tidball-Binz, 'Managing the Dead in Catastrophes: Guiding Principles and Practical Recommendations for First Responders' (2007) 89 *International Review of the Red Cross* 421–442 at 422.

[19] Randolph C. Kent, 'Reflecting Upon a Decade of Disasters: The Evolving Response of the International Community' (1983) 59 *International Affairs* 693–711 at 694.

[20] Randolph C. Kent, 'International Humanitarian Crises: Two Decades Before and Two Decades Beyond' (2004) 80 *International Affairs* 851–869.

[21] David Alexander, 'The Study of Natural Disasters, 1977–1997: Some Reflections on a Changing Field of Knowledge' (1997) 21 *Disasters* 284–304. The term 'mass fatality planning' comes from Martin A. Kalis, 'Management of Dead Bodies After Disasters: A Field Manual for First Responders' (2006) 3:3 *Journal of Homeland Security and Emergency Management* Article 9, 1–3 (reviewing the *First Responders Manual*).

[22] Oliver Morgan, 'Book Review: Management of Dead Bodies in Disaster Situations' (2005) 29 *Disasters* 288–289 at 288 (reviewing Pan American Health Organization, *Management of Dead Bodies in Disaster Situations*). According to Morgan, the PAHO's 2004 manual was '[w]ritten principally for disaster managers and medical professionals': at 288, and 'principally for the Latin American audience': at 289. The perception that the *First Responders Manual* was a 'follow up' to the PAHO's 2004 publication is made explicit by Kalis: Kalis, 'Management of Dead Bodies', 1.

to foreground thereby its own endeavours of elsewhere-making). The practices recommended in the *First Responders Manual* are traceable to at least three genres of literature and areas of practice with which this chapter is not, for the most part, concerned.

First, the *First Responders Manual* owes a great deal to the practice of issuing clinical guidelines in hospitals and government health services to guide medical personnel and others in the management of patient death.[23] Second, the *First Responders Manual* comprises part of, and draws from, a larger genre of disaster management and preparedness literature.[24] Third, the *First Responders Manual* is related to manuals concerned with armed forces' and others' handling of human remains in armed conflict or immediate post-conflict settings, about which some more will be said below.

Each of these three genres of literature has a distinct history or set of histories, each embraces considerable variation and disagreement, and each merits close attention in its own right. However, with the exception of the third of these categories (an example of which will be discussed later in this chapter), these related bodies of literature and associated practices will not be explored here. For the purposes of this chapter, it must suffice to note that international institutions' instructional texts on managing the dead after natural disaster draw upon practices and preoccupations cultivated in these various contexts.[25] If one were to approach the *First Responders Manual* from the perspective of the clinical guidelines literature, for example, one might be inclined

[23] See, for example, Sheffield NHS, *Care of the Deceased Person Policy (in relation to Infection Prevention and Control)* (2008), www.sheffield.nhs.uk/policies/resources/careofdeceasedpolicy.pdf (accessed 17 September 2012); NSW Health, *Deceased Persons In Health Facility Mortuaries & Management of Health Facility Mortuaries* (2007), www.health.nsw.gov.au/policies/pd/2007/PD2007_017.html (accessed 9 April 2012). See further Takuya Shinjo *et al.*, 'Care for the Bodies of Deceased Cancer Inpatients in Japanese Palliative Care Units' (2010) 13 *Journal of Palliative Medicine* 27–31; Jennifer Green and Michael Green (eds.), *Dealing with Death: A Handbook of Practices, Procedures and Law*, Second Edition (London and Philadelphia: Jessica Kingsley, 2006); Cynthia Ann Blum, '"Til Death Do Us Part?" The Nurse's Role in the Care of the Dead: A Historical Perspective: 1850–2004' (2006) 27 *Geriatric Nursing* 58–63; Susan Hughes and Alix Henley, *Dealing with Death in Hospital: Procedures for Managers and Staff* (London: King Edward's Hospital Fund for London, 1990). I am indebted to Shaun McVeigh for first drawing my attention to this literature.

[24] For an overview, see Emanuele Lettieri *et al.*, 'Disaster Management: Findings from a Systematic Review' (2009) 18 *Disaster Prevention and Management* 117–136.

[25] The three bodies of literature to which I have drawn attention do not comprise an exhaustive list. Also influencing practice in this area, for example, are professional guidelines on forensic investigation and evidence collection.

to notice things about it that are not given emphasis here. In their contemporary formulation and interaction all these genres of literature could, in Shaun McVeigh's words, 'be understood as establishing the repertoires of meaningful dying – that is, as an interest of government and government of the self'.[26]

Later, this chapter will explore how the *First Responders Manual* may be read to establish the dead body as an interest of government and government of the self in the aftermath of disaster. To preface that reading, let me explain briefly how 'government' is being understood for these purposes.

The *First Responders Manual* is concerned, at least in part, with dead bodies in generic or aggregate terms and with the promulgation of globally applicable recommendations in relation to those bodies.[27] So generalised, the dead are open to mobilisation, according to the *Manual*'s recommendations, towards the maximisation of a surviving population's capacity for life with and though disaster. In this respect, the *Manual*'s concern may be, at least in part, with 'security' in Michel Foucault's sense of the term: that is 'not so much [with] establishing limits and frontiers, or fixing locations, as, above all and essentially, making possible, guaranteeing, and ensuring circulations: the circulation of people, merchandise, and air, etcetera'.[28] Security, so understood, involves maintaining a population's sense of occupying a broad, global arena of 'freedom'.[29] In its preoccupation with securing life in these terms, the *First Responders Manual* may be read to counsel and exhibit those 'frugal' arts of government identified, in Foucault's work, with 'governmentality', 'normalization' and 'biopower'.[30]

[26] Shaun McVeigh, 'Subjects of Jurisdiction: The Dying, Northern Territory, Australia, 1995–1997' in *Jurisprudence of Jurisdiction* (Abingdon and New York: Routledge-Cavendish, 2007), pp. 202–221 at p. 206.

[27] In Foucualt's terms, the *Manual* 'intervene[s] at the level of generality' in the mode of generalities: Michel Foucault, *Society Must be Defended: Lectures at the Collège de France 1975–76* (ed. Mauro Bertani and Allessandro Fontana, trans. David Macey, London: Penguin Books, 2004), p. 246.

[28] Michel Foucault, *Security, Territory, Population: Lectures at the Collège de France 1977–1978* (ed. Michel Senellart, trans. Graham Burchell, New York: Palgrave Macmillan, 1997), p. 29.

[29] Foucault, *Security, Territory, Population*, pp. 48–49: ('[F]reedom is nothing else but the correlative of the deployment of apparatuses of security … no longer the exemptions and privileges attached to a person, but the possibility of movement, change of place, and processes of circulation of both people and things').

[30] Michel Foucault, *The History of Sexuality, Volume I: An Introduction* (trans. Robert Hurley, New York: Random House, 1978), pp. 133–159; Foucault, *Society Must Be Defended*, pp. 239–264; Foucault, *Security, Territory, Population*, pp. 87–114; Michel

In Foucault's writings, heterogeneous elements of governmental technology became, from the eighteenth century onwards, directed towards 'a series of specific finalities',[31] especially towards the management and maximisation of economy and population in a manner appropriate to the distinct properties with which these 'finalities' were ascribed. Despite some emphasis placed in this work upon the regression or recession of law,[32] legal or regulatory techniques of governance are pluralised in Foucault's telling, with particular importance becoming attached to the delineation of spheres of competence and the articulation of rights.[33] Foucault relates how the concern of laws – as well as the concerns of government otherwise – came to be 'allowing' things and populations to act according to their 'proper' function and sphere of interest or in line with a generalised condition of normality, as much as proscription and punishment. Modern governance of a population became, in Foucault's account, less a matter of saying 'no' to particular individual desires than of stimulating and managing the desire with which a population is seen 'naturally' to be ascribed, and recording and regularising the constants and variables by which a population is constituted as such.[34] It is in this mode, at least in part, that the *First Responders Manual* may be taken to enact governmental techniques.[35]

Foucault, *The Birth of Biopolitics: Lectures at the Collège de France 1978–79* (ed. Michel Senellart, trans. Graham Burchell, New York: Palgrave MacMillan, 2010) (hereafter *The Birth of Biopolitics*), pp. 27–73. On 'biopower', see especially Foucault, *Society Must Be Defended*, p. 249.

31 Foucault, *Security, Territory, Population*, p. 99.

32 See, for example, Foucault, *The History of Sexuality I*, p. 144; Foucault, *Security, Territory, Population*, p. 99.

33 Foucault, *The Birth of Biopolitics*, pp. 39–42, 56; Foucault, *Security, Territory, Population*, p. 66. For a compelling refutation of the claim that Foucault consistently expels or neglects law, see Ben Golder, 'Foucault and the Incompletion of Law' (2008) 21 *Leiden Journal of International Law* 747–763; Ben Golder and Peter Fitzpatrick, *Foucault's Law* (Oxford and New York: Routledge, 2009). This is not to say, however, that Foucault had a coherent theory of 'law' or that we should necessarily seek to ascribe one to him. Cf. Alain Pottage, 'Book Review: Foucault's Law by Ben Golder and Peter Fitzpatrick' (2011) 74 *Modern Law Review* 159–168 at 167: ('Foucault had no theory of law; he might have been interested in the process by which law has become such a generalised premise, but his starting point in exploring "world society" would not have been "law" but some form of *dispositif*').

34 Foucault, *Security, Territory, Population*, pp. 72–75.

35 It is important to emphasise, as Foucault does, the ongoing coexistence and recombination of different registers of power or government, as is evident in the PAHO/WHO/ICRC *Manual*. See *ibid.*, pp. 8–10.

To relate the infra-legal conditioning of the dead in the *First Responders Manual* to particular, historical assemblages of security and governmentality recorded in Foucault's work is not, however, to generate a moment of diagnostic revelation whereby some essential coordinates of 'international law' or the 'international legal condition' (or some such thing) are supposedly unveiled. Recourse to Foucault's work may assist but does not conclude or encompass the intervention in disaster-related scholarship and practice enacted and invited in this chapter. Likewise, this chapter does not give anything like full rein to the many, equivocal insights which may be drawn from Foucault's writings.

For the purposes of this chapter, it is salient that Foucault's work shows how governmental power may operate through the medium of the non-pertinent. Foucault's writings indicate how, in particular instances and ways, 'a nature that is not something on which, above which, or against which the sovereign must impose just laws' directly, may nonetheless be the contingent site and modality of 'techniques of power'. That is, with reference to the historical making of population as a 'set of elements' attributed with constants and regularities, Foucault writes, there is no longer so much of a call for 'authoritarian ... transformations' to seek to 'get a hold'. The sovereign is called upon, instead, to deploy 'procedures of government within this nature, with the help of it, and with regard to it'.[36]

Nonetheless, the *First Responders Manual* is not read here as a medium of generalised governmental technique – of this kind or any other – unfolding continuously or uniformly. Rather, in this chapter's account, the *First Responders Manual* is an enactment of 'specific iterations' of some techniques comparable to those represented in other historical

[36] *Ibid.*, p. 75. It could, perhaps, be assumed that Foucault's accounts of biopower are particularly telling for a study of international legal texts on mass death, given Foucault's characterisation of biopower as a 'power of regularization ... [that] consists in making live and letting die': Foucault, *Society Must Be Defended*, p. 247; see also Foucault, *The History of Sexuality I*, pp. 135–145. In at least some of Foucault's accounts, however, even as power becomes ever more oriented towards fostering and administering life, death is 'carefully evaded': Foucault, *The History of Sexuality I*, p. 138. Biopower may render death, Foucault suggests, that which comes to pass in private, becoming pertinent primarily as a matter of overall population measures (births, deaths, morbidity, hygiene): Foucault, *The History of Sexuality I*, pp. 138–139; Foucault, *Security, Territory, Population*, p. 96–97. Foucault's writings on biopower may be instructive, therefore, not so much for their focus on death or the dead as such, but for the tendency to sideline death that they highlight and, to some degree, explain. They may bring to light a contingent tendency to regularise death (at least death of certain types) infra-legally in the name of a central investment in life.

ensembles in Foucault's writing.[37] So fictionalised,[38] the *First Responders Manual* generates a rather different set of possibilities and questions to those which might have been suggested by a reading of this *Manual* as merely recommendatory or (at the other end of a familiar spectrum) as an effective instrument of Empire. Or so the final part of this chapter will endeavour to show.

Infra-legal death: a manual

How, then, might we read the *First Responders Manual* as speaking to and about the dead in the aftermath of disaster? And what would this text have us make of life in and through disaster – or disastrous life? Let me begin by making three observations concerning the *Manual*'s directions for the dead, with reference to some Foucauldian renderings of security discussed above. These pertain to circulation, serialisation and need.

In relation to dead bodies and otherwise, the concern of the *First Responders Manual* is less with fixing locations or establishing boundaries (although it does that too)[39] than with ensuring continued circulation. Primary emphasis is placed in the *Manual* upon coordination between agencies and related flows of data and authority. The untrammelled passage of information is a major concern.[40] 'Local' information centres should, the *First Responders Manual* stipulates, serve as 'focal points for collection and consolidation of information on the dead'. A national system for information management should then 'centralize' that information with the assistance of international agencies. 'Data should flow in both directions between the national and local level' the *Manual* stresses, such that the 'population' may be 'promptly and clearly informed'. Information should, however, be released 'in a

[37] Pottage, 'Book Review: Foucault's Law', 167.

[38] See the discussion of the 'fictioning' of history, politics and, by extrapolation, law at note 79 of Chapter 1.

[39] Consider, for instance, the *First Responders Manual*'s characterisation of the 'local' and the 'national' as more or less fixed points between which data should be encouraged to flow: Morgan *et al.*, *First Responders Manual*, p. 19. Consider also the *Manual*'s stipulations concerning the location of graves and their distance from each other, from water sources and the water table, and from affected communities: pp. 21–22.

[40] The untrammelled circulation of people is not, however, given equal encouragement. No mention is made in the *First Responders Manual* of the possibility that the 'local' people might wish to leave the site of disaster, with or without taking their dead with them.

managed way', the *Manual* directs, to minimise rumour, stress and misinformation. In the *First Responders Manual*, the dead and missing are repositories of '[a] large amount of information'.[41] This is one of dead bodies' primary functions in the text – to generate data. When continually circulated, these data serve to sustain complex networks of authority and expertise, alongside more intimate networks of mourning, memorialisation and claim-making.

These data come, in part, from the human attachments that the dead are presumed to have maintained. The *First Responders Manual* indicates that information taken from a body must be matched with information received about individuals who are missing or presumed dead. A loss must have registered among the living for a dead body's informational potential to be realised. Yet, once registered, these bonds with the living are, for the most part, set aside in the *Manual*. 'Visual recognition of cadavers or their photographs by acquaintances of the deceased is', the *Manual* states, 'the simplest form of identification', but 'can result in mistaken identification'. Whenever possible it is to be complemented with other means of forensic identification: autopsies, fingerprinting, dental examinations, DNA. To this end, instructions are given in the *First Responders Manual* as to the proper means of a body's storage, preservation and disposal. Yet the professed goals of these measures are 'forensic evidence' or 'future forensic investigation' and an act of identification judged 'valid' through its minimisation of 'emotional stress'.[42] The physical body is to be preserved in order for its re-composition into data points to be realised all the more effectively.

The information so generated is, nevertheless, subject to a 'persistent undertow of decay'.[43] The *First Responders Manual* seems to anticipate that the flow of data emanating from dead bodies will be 'continually decaying and recomposing'.[44] 'Sooner is better for victim identification', the *Manual* advises, just as the 'population' must be kept 'promptly … informed'.[45] Moreover, this occurs, it seems, not primarily by virtue of processes of disproof. It occurs, largely, as a consequence of the passage of time.[46] This information decay is related to processes

[41] Morgan *et al.*, *First Responders Manual*, pp. 19, 24. [42] *Ibid.*, pp. 13–17, 21, 28.

[43] Karin Knorr Cetina, 'Financial Analysis: Epistemic Profile of an Evaluative Science' in Camic *et al.*, *Social Knowledge in the Making*, pp. 405–441 at 410 (writing of information generated for purposes of financial analysis).

[44] *Ibid.* [45] Morgan *et al.*, *First Responders Manual*, pp. 13, 19.

[46] As Knorr Cetina observes, this is at odds with the characterisation of 'true knowledge [as] a specific commodity that does not decay'. 'Information knowledge

of physical decomposition: 'early opportunities to identify bodies may be lost as the bodies decompose'.[47] Yet there are other factors informing this temporalisation as well. The *Manual* hints at the possibility, for instance, that living people may abandon their search after some time. With or without evidence of decomposition, the body is presumed to lose much of its data-generating capacity over time. Hence 'unidentified bodies' become subject, after an unspecified period, to 'long-term storage' and 'disposal'.[48]

This is one way in which the dead are constituted in the interests of governance: through their breakdown into temporalised bits of data and their merger with other bits in endless circulation. Involved in this process of circulation is the continuous shedding of decaying data and the related devaluing, revaluing and repositioning of bodies. This data circulation is vital. It is the stuff of which a surviving population, as such, may be made in the aftermath of disaster.

In the course of promoting this data flow, the *First Responders Manual* serialises the aleatory event of mass death, making it thereby both exceptional and normal. The chance event of disastrous death, and the countless dead bodies that attest to it, are made, according to the *Manual*'s recommendations, aberrant or transitory in relation to a global arena of life. The prevalence of wellbeing among living populations is cast as the norm. This entails, as Foucault observes, a splitting of that chance event.[49] Conditions making it extremely difficult to survive

decay', she continues, 'does not result from … critical examination, disproof, or any other form of evaluation. It is not a process of discarding a piece of knowledge that for some reason is found wanting … It is rather that the information loses its clout after some time and is then considered to be no longer informative': Knorr Cetina, 'Financial Analysis', 412–413. Because of the *First Responders Manual*'s assumption that the dead derive virtually all their meaning and value from identification and a consequent reconnection with the living, the solitary dead body fairly rapidly 'loses its clout' as Knorr Cetina describes.

47 Morgan *et al.*, *First Responders Manual*, p. 13.

48 *Ibid.*, p. 21.

49 Against an uncertain phenomenon, an apparatus is sought 'for arranging things, so that, by connecting up with the very reality of these fluctuations, and by establishing a series of connections with other elements of reality, the phenomenon is gradually compensated for, checked, finally limited, and, in the final degree, cancelled out, without it being prevented or losing any of its reality'. Grain scarcity, for instance (encompassing high grain prices, difficulty in buying grain and associated hunger) subsists. This is understood to affect a multiplicity of individuals from time to time. Yet at the level of the population as a whole, scarcity all but disappears because there are presumed to be market mechanisms available by which it may gradually be corrected. 'The scarcity-scourge disappears, but scarcity that causes the death of individuals not only does not disappear, it must not disappear': Foucault, *Security, Territory, Population*, pp. 37–38, 42.

subsist and are understood to affect a multiplicity of individuals. Yet at the level of any particular population, the imminence of random death is made to all but disappear – it is made, as Foucault says, a 'chimera' – because there are understood to be mechanisms available by which the unpredictability of its occurrence may be mitigated over time.[50] In anticipating 'future forensic investigation' presumed to be more powerful and revealing than current investigative capacities, the *First Responders Manual* evokes a progress-oriented view of science whereby the uncertainty and incapacity attendant upon disaster might gradually be allayed over time.[51] In this way, it comes to be that the multiplicity's daily confrontations with death may no longer be pertinent – the population is, or the population's life and wellbeing as such is.[52]

Even so, readers of the *First Responders Manual* (and those otherwise instructed by it) must remain aware of these no-longer-pertinent events of mass fatality in order for sense to be made of the specific circuitry of governance it inscribes.[53] The manifold dead must remain visible but not worthy of undue concern. The extreme difficulty of sustaining life for many in poverty and the recurrence of mass death in natural disaster (especially among those otherwise maintaining a brink-of-death existence)[54] are, accordingly, given the status of natural conditions. They are rendered as 'physical processes, which could be called natural processes, and which we could also call elements of reality'.[55] They are made, in other words, normal as well as aberrant.[56] According to Foucault, these 'techniques of normalization develop

[50] *Ibid.*, p. 38 (quoting Louis-Paul Abeille, *Lettre d'un négociant sur la nature du commerce des grains* (1763), p. 4).

[51] Morgan *et al.*, *First Responders Manual*, pp. 1, 21.

[52] Foucault, *Security, Territory, Population*, p. 42.

[53] *Ibid.*, p. 45: ('The function of security is to rely on details that are not valued as good or evil in themselves, that are taken to be necessary, inevitable processes, as natural processes in the broad sense, and it relies on these details, which are what they are, but which are not considered to be pertinent in themselves, in order to obtain something that is considered to be pertinent in itself because situated at the level of the population').

[54] Neumayer and Plümper report 'widespread agreement that the poor are more adversely hit by the impact of natural disasters than are those more well-off': Eric Neumayer and Thomas Plümper, 'The Gendered Nature of Natural Disasters: The Impact of Catastrophic Events on the Gender Gap in Life Expectancy, 1981–2002' (2007) 97 *Annals of the Association of American Geographers* 551–566 at 555.

[55] Foucault, *Security, Territory, Population*, pp. 65–66.

[56] Mechanisms of security operate through a process of normalisation characterised by the collectivisation and zonal distribution of risks across a population and the categorisation of sudden intensifications of risk as crises or, for our purposes, disasters: *ibid.*, pp. 60–61.

from and below a system of law, in its margins and maybe even against it'.[57] In other words, it is precisely at the level of infra-legality that the natural seriality of the taking-place of mass death (and thereby its no-longer-pertinence) is sustained.[58]

In so far as the *First Responders Manual* mobilises these governmental techniques, it does so especially in its tallying and indexation of death on a global scale. Projected onto a global plane, mass death is made routine – the stuff of quotidian life. 'Globally', the *Manual* observes on its rear cover, 'disasters claim thousands of lives each year'. The cover of the *Manual* features scattered autumn leaves as though to highlight the annual seasonality of mass death in disaster. Yet, to ameliorate the prospect of this terrible tirage, attention is again directed towards life. Mass death is thus naturalised in the name of life, for while reference is made in the *Manual* to 'care of the deceased', priority is given throughout to 'care of the living and injured'. 'Recovery of bodies should not', the *Manual* insists, 'interrupt other interventions aimed at helping survivors'. Medical personnel and ambulances should not be dedicated to disaster relief as such or to body recovery, the *Manual* cautions, since their proper place is among the living.[59]

The dead are made doubly so through an insistence upon their remoteness from this generalised arena of living. 'Most infectious organisms do not survive beyond 48 hours in a dead body', the *Manual* reassures. And '[t]he risk to the public is negligible because they do not touch dead bodies'. The dead do not, it seems, comprise part of 'the public'. And because living people do not touch them – because there is no allowance for intimacy between the living and the dead – they are not part of the private either. They are ephemera: it is the 'fecal material', 'body fluids' and 'gases' emanating from a dead body by which the *Manual* is mainly worried. No matter how precarious daily life may, in fact, be for the surviving population, it is expertly supported life or

[57] *Ibid.*, p. 56. Normalisation involves the 'plotting ... of different curves of normality, and ... establishing an interplay between these different distributions of normality', p. 63.

[58] Working with an apparatus of security largely entails abstention from the matter of separating the permitted from the forbidden. Instead, with such an apparatus, one seeks to 'grasp the point at which things are taking place, whether or not they are desirable' which is to 'grasp them at the level of their nature ... or ... their effective reality' and respond to that reality in such a way as to cancel out or regulate it: *ibid.*, pp. 46–47.

[59] Morgan *et al.*, *First Responders Manual*, pp. 3, 8, rear cover.

wellbeing that is made to appear the norm, while the dead become gas, body fluid, waste and data.[60]

In this erasure of death and associated shaping of life, the *First Responders Manual* exercises power partially in a pastoral mode; a mode of caring, responsiveness and necessity. It does not adopt the near-ubiquitous language of rights, nor does it otherwise seem explicitly steeped in a culture of legality.[61] The *Manual* does arrogate to itself – or rather the institutions and agents that it would authorise and endorse – quite extraordinary powers. The *Manual* issues directions concerning the appointment of persons to be 'in charge' within particular jurisdictions or spheres of competence. It regulates the denial or acceptance of 'claim[s]' to a dead body made by the living: bodies should only be released 'by the responsible authority', must be documented, and release should only be permitted once 'identification is certain' and after the name and contact details of the claimant have been recorded against the body's 'unique reference number'. Yet the word 'right' does not appear in the *First Responders Manual*; it speaks instead of 'promoting better treatment'.[62]

The directions issued by the *First Responders Manual* are framed, on its rear cover, as 'simple recommendations for non-specialists' and as 'suggestions'. The acceptance of these is expressly predicated on their 'useful[ness]' and 'relevan[ce]' for those engaged in planning exercises

[60] *Ibid.*, pp. 5, 6, 27.

[61] In this regard, it is important to emphasise that the named contributors to the PAHO/WHO/ICRC *Manual* are scientists (forensic scientists, for the most part), public health officials and experts in disaster management and emergency response. Persons with similar credentials were identified as among the peer reviewers of the *Manual*, with the exception of a 'human rights specialist from ICRC' mentioned as one of the reviewers. The press release announcing publication of the *Manual* observed that '[t]he Manual has undergone an extensive peer review process. We have received comments from 8 technical reviewers: the chair of INTERPOL's DVI committee, the Head Forensic Pathologist at the Home Office in the UK, a forensic specialist in Sri Lanka, two disaster managers in the Caribbean, an academic disaster expert in the UK, a human rights specialist from ICRC and an international disaster professional. In addition, the manual has also been reviewed by attendees of a meeting of forensic specialists in Colombia, 15 Public Health leaders from 9 Asian countries at a regional meeting about mass fatality management, and forensic experts from Jordan who participated in an ICRC workshop': London School of Hygiene & Tropical Medicine Press Office, 'Handling Bodies After Disasters: Guidelines for First Responders', Press Release (12 April 2006), www.lshtm.ac.uk/pressoffice/press_releases/2006/manualdeadbodies.html (accessed 17 September 2012).

[62] Morgan *et al.*, *First Responders Manual*, pp. v, 3, 4, 16, 17, 29.

or exercising authority at a local, regional or national level, even as it is acknowledged that the principles outlined in the *Manual* are being 'implemented and promoted' worldwide by the institutions responsible for its publication.[63]

This is, then, an apparatus directed not towards the salvation of the individual or individuals' investiture with rights, but towards the population as such. And the signature gesture sought from the population – by way of grant of power or legitimacy – is its demonstration of need. Need is the currency in which disaster management trades; the *First Responders Manual*'s is not a constitutional vision in conventional terms, but a jurisdictional assemblage built upon trauma and desire, with the latter cast in part as a need to know, to see, to identify. Hence the *First Responders Manual* places emphasis upon the 'need for relatives to view the bodies of their loved ones as part of the grieving process'; the 'overwhelming desire of relatives from all religions and cultures … to identify their loved ones' and the need for 'support', primarily psycho-social support, to mitigate 'profound and long-lasting effect on the mental health of survivors and communities' and to prevent them being 'traumatize[d]' further. Among these needs are explicitly legal, compensatory ones: the Foreword to the *Manual* highlights the 'legal significance for inheritance and insurance' of 'correct identification of the dead' with mismanagement carrying the risk of 'impact on families and relatives for many years after the disaster'.[64]

Given its recasting of trauma as a need to know, to see and to identify, the main way in which the *First Responders Manual* answers (as it were) is with information: written, image-based and embodied. Need authorises the collection, consolidation and management of information; need also authorises the active quelling of alternative sources or forms of information. Such alternative sources and forms are repeatedly derided throughout the *Manual* as 'rumour', 'incorrect information' or 'conflicting information'. It is the 'reduc[tion]' or 'defus[ing]' of these rumours and the 'political pressure' and 'stress' they supposedly found towards which the *First Responders Manual* is principally directed. Jurisdictional power here depends upon maintaining a circular movement between need (read primarily as informational need) and 'correct' information.[65] The living are equipped for survival in part by their expertly supported acquisition of knowledge of their dead. Their

[63] *Ibid.*, rear cover. [64] *Ibid.*, pp. v, 25, 26, 28, 29.
[65] *Ibid.*, pp. 5, 23, 24.

survival is to be a knowing survival rather than one secured through insulation from danger. If 'criminality has become a more or less global trope of undoing', as the legal anthropologists Jean and John Comaroff have suggested, then misinformation and mismanagement are, at least in disaster settings, important counterparts to it.[66]

The lawful management of the dead after disaster is, however, by no means a matter of complete information or monopoly in the *First Responders Manual*. This is another dimension of the infra-legal status of the dead in the *Manual*: the dead are not characterised as wholly within the grasp of the *Manual* or the activities it contemplates. Among the operations at work in the *First Responders Manual* that are oriented around the dead, there is much beyond the work of the international, regional, national and local agencies that it names. The *Manual* does not, it announces in its introduction, 'provide a comprehensive framework'. Upon a body's identification, for instance, the prospect of retaining that body as a data source seems to be more or less relinquished in the face of other lawful rites and vocabularies. 'All identified dead bodies should be released to relatives or their communities for disposal according to local custom and practice', the *Manual* stipulates.[67]

There are, nevertheless, some familiar tropes at work in the *Manual*, to which dead bodies are sometimes tethered. The presumptive centrality of 'family' is asserted throughout. '[T]raditional' burial and grieving practices are recognised, albeit mainly within the frame of averting 'mental health issues' latent within the population. The native informant is tapped for 'advice and assistance' aimed at 'improv[ing] understanding and acceptance of the recovery, management, and identification of … dead bodies'; the *Manual* recommends that religious and community leaders be consulted for this purpose. Familiar appeals are made to the presumed finalities of 'needs, culture, and context'.[68]

Yet also registered within the *Manual* is lawful terrain not so forthcoming in these terms, including unidentified 'local coping mechanisms', open-ended reference to 'funeral rituals' and the suggestion that '[s]pecial legal provisions for those affected' might have been or might yet be negotiated.[69] Indeed, there may be implicit recognition of this unresolved yet effectual legal terrain in the *First Responders Manual*'s

[66] John L. Comaroff and Jean Comaroff, 'Reflections on the Anthropology of Law, Governance and Sovereignty' in Franz von Benda-Beckmann *et al.* (eds.), *Rules of Law and Laws of Ruling* (Farnham and Burlington: Ashgate, 2009), pp. 31–60 at p. 54.

[67] Morgan *et al.*, *First Responders Manual*, pp. 1, 21.

[68] *Ibid.*, pp. 25, 29, 26. [69] *Ibid.*, pp. 26, 3–4.

insistence that its readers '[a]s soon as possible ... identify an agency and name a person to serve as local coordinator with full authority and responsibility' (suggesting, by way of example, a local Governor, Police Chief, Military Commander or Mayor).

Recognition of lawfulness in other modes and by other means could also underpin the *Manual*'s deferrals to nationhood, such as its emphatic attribution of 'primary responsibility for the proper handling of ... the dead' to 'State authorities' and its instruction that '[f]oreign consulates and embassies should be informed and INTERPOL contacted' in order for the bodies of 'foreigners' to be duly 'managed'. The alternative, the *Manual* suggests, is for body recovery efforts and related practices to persist that are 'usually chaotic and disorganized', involve '[m]any different people or groups' and are often done 'spontaneously by a large number of individuals'. The threat of this 'chao[s]' emanates not only from people, groups and individuals identified as local; Annex 6 of the *Manual* alludes also to 'the chaos that often results from the massive influx of international aid'.[70]

For all its insistence upon dead bodies' 'proper and dignified management', the *First Responders Manual* cannot wholly overwrite the places and bodies to which it seeks to give meaning. For all its emphasis upon the generation and circulation of accurate information, the *First Responders Manual* cannot manage the leaking, blurring or remaking of its message that is ongoing. Nor does it seek to do so in any complete way, for it is the prospect of this lawful and non-lawful message-making – identified in the *First Responders Manual* with rumour, chaos, 'political pressure', 'religious and cultural sensitivities' and 'overwhelming desire' – that sustains institutions' and experts' presumptive authority to manage on a global scale.[71]

Managing the dead: redux

Circulation, serialisation and ubiquitous need are features of life after disaster on which the *First Responders Manual* appears to insist through its recommendations for handling the dead. However, the *First Responders Manual* is just one manual of its kind, albeit a widely used one. There are other indicia of international institutions' practice in managing dead bodies.

[70] *Ibid.*, pp. 19, 29, 7, 44. [71] *Ibid.*, pp. 1, 5, 26.

I noted earlier that practices relating to dead bodies after disaster are guided by at least three other genres of literature, one of which concerns the conduct of military forces and others in post-conflict settings. For a snapshot of this literature, one might compare the *First Responders Manual* with another widely circulated field manual: the manual published in 2004 under the title *Operational Best Practices Regarding the Management of Human Remains and Information on the Dead by Non-Specialists for All Armed Forces; for all Humanitarian Organisations* (the *ICRC Manual*).[72] The *ICRC Manual* was the outcome of a project launched by the ICRC in cooperation with 'representatives of families of missing persons and a variety of experts' as an '[a]ction to resolve the problem of people unaccounted for as a result of armed conflict or internal violence and to assist their families'.[73]

In the *ICRC Manual*, mass death is also a record and sometime harbinger of chaos, albeit in quite a different sense. In the *ICRC Manual*, the dead comprise, in the aggregate, a 'festering wound' that impedes 'closure' or 'mov[ing] on to personal or community rehabilitation or reconciliation'. This threat extends into the future. This wound, the *ICRC Manual* warns, 'can rot the fabric of society' and 'undermine relations between persons, groups and nations'. The idea of persons, groups and nations 'moving on' from and through death emerges as a central theme.[74]

The most pressing dangers to a population emboldened to 'move on', in the *ICRC Manual*, are those of recurrent violence rather than those of misinformation. Whereas dead bodies in the *First Responders Manual* are described as being 'recovered' from amid 'debris', the *ICRC Manual*

[72] ICRC, *Operational Best Practices Regarding the Management of Human Remains and Information on the Dead by Non-Specialists for All Armed Forces; for all Humanitarian Organisations* (Geneva: International Committee of the Red Cross, 2004), www.icrc.org/eng/resources/documents/publication/p0858.htm (accessed 17 September 2012). The ICRC reportedly promotes use of the *First Responders Manual* in contexts of armed conflict and violence in combination with other guidelines aimed at such contexts, including the ICRC Manual: Tidball-Binz, 'Managing the Dead in Catastrophes', 423.

[73] ICRC Manual, inside front cover.

[74] *Ibid.*, p. 3. The emphasis that the ICRC Manual places on having persons and communities 'move on' probably reflects increased prominence of the idea of 'resilience' in scholarship and practice concerned with humanitarian operations, and in global governance more broadly. See Siambabala Bernard Manyena, 'The Concept of Resilience Revisited' (2006) 30 *Disasters* 433–450; Pat O'Malley, 'Resilient Subjects: Uncertainty, Warfare and Liberalism' (2010) 39 *Economy and Society* 488–509.

envisages their 'collect[ion] from the battlefield'.[75] The *ICRC Manual*'s orientation is, accordingly, towards rites and vocabularies of appeasement: the 'honour[ing] [of] memor[ies]', the assurance of 'accountability' and the attribution of 'responsibility'. Emphasis is placed too upon the risk of the dead being 'despoiled', 'desecrate[ed]' or 'mutilat[ed]'. The residual agency of the dead is, in this sense, more potent and enduring in the *ICRC Manual* than the *First Responders Manual*; in the former, the dead are more readily bundled with the living. The *ICRC Manual* groups the dead with others deserving of special international legal attention by reason of impairment of their integration within community: 'the wounded, sick, shipwrecked … protected persons deprived of their liberty, children whose identity is in doubt and persons who have been reported missing'.[76]

Yet, for all its emphasis upon 'repatriation', 'redress' and the recruitment of the dead for pedagogic functions – having commemoration of the dead serve, that is, 'as an instructive reminder' for the living – the *ICRC Manual* also strives to demarcate its own limits, or to acknowledge that its deployment may be limited in practice, just as the *First Responders Manual* does. At times, it resorts to proffering general rules about specific legalities beyond its grasp. 'As a general rule', the *ICRC Manual* observes, 'death and the practices associated with death are specific to each local culture'. To obstruct those practices or seek to temper them too much would, the *ICRC Manual* cautions, be ill-advised as a matter of risk management: 'To prevent funerals and other mourning practices is to make the dead and the living incur a risk.'[77]

The most that the *ICRC Manual* seems inclined to do is to try to cabin these specific legalities within conceptions of locality and culture, categories that inevitably (and, indeed, by design) overflow their purported bounds. As in the *First Responders Manual*, that potential overflowing remains essential to the authority of international institutions. For without the prospect of 'anxiety' and 'resentment' emerging regarding 'the proper handling of the remains of those who die in direct or indirect relation to an armed conflict or internal violence', as the *ICRC Manual* anticipates, what are all the 'experts' and uniformed 'non-specialists' to which the *ICRC Manual* refers doing messing about with the dead?[78]

[75] Morgan *et al.*, *First Responders Manual*, p. 8; ICRC Manual, p. 11.

[76] ICRC Manual, pp. 3, 9–10, 51, 7. [77] *Ibid.*, pp. 10, 18, 16.

[78] *Ibid.*, pp. 3, 6, 4.

Dead bodies do not, then, remain among the background conditions to international institutional management. It is as if the dead kept thrusting themselves or being thrust into the foreground of international institutional decision and practice and, in their waywardness, providing occasion for beleaguered rule, at once sacred and profane. By way of illustration of this, let us return to a scene of disaster, or rather its aftermath, in Haiti and examine yet another form of international institutional initiative obliquely concerned with the dead.

In June 2010, *The New York Times* reported on a UN-sponsored programme of making and screening soap operas to and about those displaced by the earthquake in Haiti, with a view to keeping those inhabiting temporary camps both entertained and informed. Jacques Roc, 'who left Haiti when he was 14 and spent most of his career in New York directing commercials and writing jingles' was charged with directing the series. The goal of this programme was clear. '[O]rganizers say the programs will fill in for a government that has failed to communicate effectively, letting rumors and schemes spread', *The New York Times* reported. The UN spokesperson in Haiti, David Wimhurst, was quoted as follows: 'We need to get them good information, not disinformation ... We have a lot to tell them.'[79]

At least one camp inhabitant, however, seemed to encounter a heteronomy on the screen quite distinct from that which the UN apparently sought to project. Fifty-four-year-old Ameniz Auxide told *The New York Times* journalist, as she sang and prayed before the soap opera, her face 'lit by the screen': 'If you listen and watch ... you feel like God is with us.'[80]

In this remark, Auxide may have fingered some dimension of the *First Responders Manual*, and of work under its auspices, which the preceding discussion has not grasped or acknowledged. There seems, after all, much more than governance in the *First Responders Manual* and the often horrifying work that it would have its readers undertake. For instance, there is, at least potentially, something approaching grace in that work: the giving of favour without deservedness, claim or entitlement.[81] One can register that sense of grace in the *Manual* and the

[79] Damien Cave, 'Haiti's Displaced See Their Stories on TV', *The New York Times*, 9 June 2010, www.nytimes.com/2010/06/10/world/americas/10haiti.html (accessed 17 September 2012).

[80] *Ibid.*

[81] The reference to 'grace' here is made with agnosticism as to whether the gestures and labours in question are experienced by those who undertake them as worldly

work it guides even as one observes, as Latour has done (in relation to legal work of a very different kind), that '[t]here are no angels, demons or supermen here'.[82] Consider, for instance, the role which the *First Responders Manual* contemplates volunteers playing in the meticulous, individualised burial of unnamed (and in many cases unnameable) dead bodies.[83] For all the *Manual*'s enumeration and data-management, contingency remains at the forefront of the sorts of unimaginably difficult tasks and interactions for which it provides.

The UN and other international legal agencies may have 'a lot to tell' Haitians about the 'proper and dignified' management of life and death, but the prospect endures that those would-be listeners will continue to engage otherwise. A wide range of these engagements, tellings and retellings are involved in generating, sustaining and securing the 'thick natural[ness]' that is, in Foucault's account, a living population's characteristic way of appearing as such.[84] Even so, there remains much that is unnatural and unforeseeable about such a population's encounter with mass death. There can be no assurance that meaningfulness

acts or as acts channelling some divine source. The literature on the Classical and Hellenistic Greek notion of *charis* and literature on the related 'doctrine' of grace in Christian theology is voluminous. For a glimpse of the latter, see Ian A. McFarland, 'Grace' in Ian A. McFarland *et al.* (eds.), *The Cambridge Dictionary of Christian Theology* (Cambridge University Press, 2011), pp. 201–3. Also extensive is the body of scholarship exploring translations of and analogies to grace in secular literature. See, for example, Thelma J. Shinn, 'Flannery O'Connor and the Violence of Grace' (1968) 9 *Contemporary Literature* 58–73; Jackson Campbell Boswell, 'Milton and Prevenient Grace' (1967) 7 *Studies in English Literature, 1500–1900* 83–94; A. S. P. Woodhouse, 'Nature and Grace in the Faerie Queene' (1949) 16 *ELH* 194–228; Wallace Fowlie, 'Racine, Poet of Grace' (1939) 12 *The French Review* 391–400. There are, of course, also other secular understandings of grace which owe little or nothing to the theological notion of unmerited favour, but they are not being evoked here.

[82] Bruno Latour, *The Making of Law: An Ethnography of the Conseil d'État* (trans. Marina Brilman and Alain Pottage, Cambridge and Malden: Polity Press 2010), p. 69: ('There are no angels, demons or supermen here ... The quality of the work here consists entirely in bodies, mouths and voices, processes of writing and archiving, regularly maintained conversations, and the meticulous fattening of files').

[83] Morgan *et al.*, *First Responders Manual*, p. 10 (depicting white plastic-clad workers carrying out the temporary burial of dead bodies in Thailand following the 'tsunami disaster' of 26 December 2004) and p. 29 (emphasising that volunteers assisting with the recovery and disposal of the dead 'first need to be briefed, advised, equipped, and supported for this difficult task').

[84] Foucault, *Security, Territory, Population*, pp. 71–72.

will flow from the repertoires outlined in the *First Responders Manual*, or exactly what their meanings might be.

If, nevertheless, the *First Responders Manual* and other materials discussed in this chapter are helping to establish contemporary 'repertoires of meaningful dying' (and through that, repertoires for a disastrous life), then of what do those repertoires consist?[85] In closing this section, let me highlight four features of the repertoire of meaningful dying that emerge from the foregoing reading of the *First Responders Manual*.

First, as already noted, death is serialised. Less emphasis is placed on the singularly terminal experience of dying than upon its potential meaning as part of a sequence or index of global disaster. It is said in the *Manual* to be a matter of long-standing knowledge that natural disasters 'cause a large number of deaths' and 'frequently overwhelm local systems'.[86]

Second, dying is, for want of a better term, futurised. Dead bodies are less carriers of a lived past and means for its memorialisation than a possible vehicle for 'future forensic investigation' and a basis for the forging of familial and communal futures: hence the concern that bodies' mishandling might have an adverse 'impact on families and relatives for many years after the disaster'.[87]

Third, dying is made inchoate and needy of informational overlay. Yet this need is not concerned with long-entrenched, material want. As Andrew Lakoff writes of disaster planning more generally, 'the poverty rate and the percentage of people without health insurance are not salient indicators of readiness or of the efficacy of response'.[88] 'The survivors need you more than the dead', the *Manual* counsels disaster management volunteers, but even then priority is given to survivors' non-material needs. Needs in question in the *First Responders Manual* are needs for information, coordination, 'practical guidance', 'respect' and 'psycho-social support'.[89]

Fourth and finally, dying is given weight and value in the aggregate and in more or less fungible terms.[90] Regardless of particular

85 McVeigh, 'Subjects of Jurisdiction'.

86 Morgan *et al.*, *First Responders Manual*, p. v.

87 *Ibid.*, pp. 21, v.

88 Andrew Lakoff, 'Preparing for the Next Emergency' (2007) 19 *Public Culture* 247–271 at 271.

89 Morgan *et al.*, *First Responders Manual*, pp. 29, v, 24, 25.

90 This is not to deny that the *First Responders Manual* places great emphasis on the goal of identifying dead bodies individually by attribution to every body or body part of a 'unique reference number'. It seeks, similarly, to ensure that unidentified bodies

experiences or understandings of death (regardless, for instance, of whether death resulted from crushing in a crowd of evacuees, the collapse of some public or private building, the deceased's futile attempt to save another, or the coincidence of natural disaster and terminal illness, and regardless also of whether dying is understood as passage to another life or otherwise), dying is said to give rise to a 'psychological burden on survivors' and, to a far lesser extent, a 'burden of disease'.[91] Disaster management is, accordingly, oriented towards this burden's disbursement through circulation: above all, the managed circulation of data. Dying as productive of de-sacralised burdens signals an actual or potential arresting of global flows. To manage mass death according to international institutions' 'practical guidance' is to clear the way for such flows to begin again.

Marginal notes: the critical possibilities of infra-legal inquiry

The foregoing analysis of the 'practical guidance' offered in the *First Responders Manual* carries, for the most part, only a suggestion of critique. At this point, let me make some dimensions of that critique explicit.

In the devastating scenarios for which the *First Responders Manual* provides, the *Manual*'s focus on policy acceptance and implementation seems troubling. While the *Manual* instructs readers to 'be professional' and to '[r]efer to the mass fatality section of your disaster response plan or major incident procedures manual',[92] so many unanswered questions are likely to linger around the dead: about contributing factors unconsidered, responsibilities unassumed, appeals unheeded, inequities unnoticed and unaddressed. Perhaps, in the *First Responders Manual*'s time-scape, a time will come, after the efforts of 'first responders' give way to those of other experts and non-experts, for these questions to be given due attention. (The *Manual* anticipates the prospect of 'future … investigation' and does not prescribe how or by whom that might be conducted.[93]) Just as possible, however, seems a scenario in which a succession of always-more-pressing matters absorb the energy and attention of those who would manage the aftermath

are buried in such a way that individual identification might be possible in the future: *ibid.*, pp. 14, 17, 21.

[91] *Ibid.*, pp. 7, 45. [92] *Ibid.*, pp. 4, 30. [93] *Ibid.*, p. 21.

of disaster and those whom they would manage, leaving little time for the most confronting of questions to be explored.[94]

It seems problematic too, in such circumstances, that the *Manual* propagates a sense of the aberrance of death in disaster, as I suggested above that it does. How aberrant is mass death in natural disaster really for many people? Numerous scholars have shown that natural disasters do not strike people equally or at random.[95] Poor people in the Third World experience most of the suffering arising from natural disasters.[96] This, then, prompts a further question: how aberrant is the perception of the non-Western world, especially the equatorial zone, as inherently unsafe? Might the *Manual*, in its very insistence upon survivors' routine wellbeing and security, be peddling an historical discourse that has long depicted 'large parts of the globe ... [as] unsafe and then progressively safer' thanks to the interventions of Western governments and institutions?[97] Either way, the *Manual*'s rendering of 'security' as the norm for a surviving population disregards the material and the discursive conditioning of that population's survival.

In this connection, it is noteworthy that the *Manual* might authorise or validate architectures of rule familiar from colonial and post-colonial settings. For all its rhetorical deference to 'local custom and practice', the *Manual* reinforces a small number of central authority figures located at the pinnacle of one or other bureaucratic hierarchy: the 'local Governor, Police Chief, Military Commander, Mayor'.[98] As Brian Smith writes of colonialism in general, the *Manual* seems 'more

[94] Such matters could include, for instance: outbreaks of disease and/or violence in camps accommodating the displaced; dwindling resources; hazardous waste-containment concerns; etc.

[95] The social science literature on 'vulnerability' in the context of natural disaster has challenged the idea that the greater incidence of mass fatality due to environmental hazards in the non-Western world is primarily a matter of geography. It is, this literature has argued, peoples' vulnerability (arising from a combination of factors including economic resources, class, gender and ethnicity) that determines whether a hazard will become a disaster. See Benjamin Wisner *et al.*, *At Risk: Natural Hazards, People's Vulnerability and Disasters*, Second Edition (London and New York: Routledge, 2004).

[96] Terry Cannon, 'Vulnerability Analysis and the Explanation of "Natural' Disasters' in Ann Varley (ed.), *Disasters, Development and Environment* (Chichester: John Wiley & Sons, 1994), pp. 13–30 at p. 27 (highlighting, nonetheless, that 'it may not be the case that all the poor suffer' and '[n]or is it only the poor who suffer').

[97] Gregory Bankoff, 'Rendering the World Unsafe: "Vulnerability" as Western Discourse' (2001) 25 *Disasters* 19–35 at 21.

[98] Morgan *et al.*, *First Responders Manual*, pp. 21, 3–4.

interested in the power of officials in relation to society than in the power of representative assemblies, political parties, pressure groups and other organizations representative of different sections of society'.[99] Indeed, 'political pressure' is among the forces that the *Manual* is concerned to quell.[100]

In promoting the discourse of management and the offices of certain, familiar authority figures, the *Manual* expresses an assumption that the wellbeing of 'survivors and communities' would not be well served by casting into doubt the pre-existing order – or rather, the order that the *Manual* presumes to have pre-existed disaster. The *Manual*'s goal is to bring 'order to ... chaos' by ensuring that the 'chaotic and uncoordinated' fields of life and death within its purview get conditioned for management.[101] Yet surely the elements, structure and style of any 'order' to be affirmed by the *Manual* may be open to debate in particular instances among 'survivors and communities' and people imagined otherwise. For all its overtones of centrist competence, or indeed *because* of those overtones, 'management' is not benign.[102] Vesting a 'local coordinator' with 'full authority and responsibility for the management of dead bodies' and, through that, the governance of people, their connections and their futures, as the *First Responders Manual* envisages: can one be so sure that this amounts, universally and uniformly, to 'best practice'?[103]

99 B. C. Smith, *Understanding Third World Politics: Theories of Political Change and Development* (Bloomington: Indiana University Press, 2003), p. 161.

100 Morgan *et al.*, *First Responders Manual*, p. 5: ('The political pressure brought about by ... rumors causes authorities to use unnecessary measures such as rapid mass burials and spraying so-called "disinfectants"' and otherwise engage in 'mismanagement'). Efforts to centralise authority and stabilise political shifts in the immediate aftermath of disaster – and the invocation of disaster as a rationale for these efforts, whether temporarily or on a longstanding basis – are not only identifiable with colonial and post-colonial power. Consider, for instance, the effect upon Rudolf Giuliani's political standing of the events of 11 September 2001. See Sandra Silberstein, *War of Words: Language, Politics and 9/11* (London and New York: Routledge, 2002), pp. 91–106.

101 Morgan *et al.*, *First Responders Manual*, pp. v, 3, 44.

102 Cf. David Kennedy, 'The Turn to Interpretation' (1985) 58 *Southern California Law Review* 251-276 at 254–255: ('This management [referring to discursive management of the perceived difference between truth and power within 'liberal discourse'] occurs from a plateau above the fray of discourse ... for some reason, the open and humble acknowledgment of diverse interpretive possibilities is transformed into a self-conscious defense of the center ... a politics of the center appears inevitable').

103 Morgan *et al.*, *First Responders Manual*, p. 3. A concern with 'best practice' is implicit in the *First Responders Manual* but explicit in the *ICRC Manual*: in the title of the latter, for instance.

In these respects and others, the governance work that the *First Responders Manual*'s would have its readers carry out on and through the dead bodies that litter its (largely) peripheral vision is contentious and worthy of contention. Even so, the *Manual* evidences no agenda of rule being surreptitiously slipped in from the sidelines. The infra-legal conditions and constructions to which this chapter has drawn attention may be sidelined, but they remain in plain view.

The normative conditioning of dead bodies in the *First Responders Manual* is not, moreover, solely a matter of making infra-legality, or conditioning backgrounds, surroundings and sidelines. Other modes of non-legality explored in this book are also operative. Characterisations of illegality, for instance, animate and justify disaster management work. The UN-sponsored soap opera mentioned above 'focused mainly on one issue: con men in the camps'. The thrust of one episode was as follows: 'After a slick villain in dark sunglasses tried to sell registration cards to the show's main characters, claiming falsely that they could be redeemed for cash, officials with the International Organization for Migration suddenly appeared to save the day.'[104] Likewise, the *First Responders Manual*'s inattention to the otherwise ubiquitous language of rights might be read as a consequence of its characterisation of disaster zones as extra-legal.[105]

The making of infra-legality – and the critical representation of that work – is no more decisive of prospects for change than it is all revealing. To the extent that the practices and presumptions manifest in the *First Responders Manual* bear the mark of bias (against the Third World or anyone else), it is entirely within the contemplation of 'operational best practices' that they be discarded and improved upon.[106] Persistent tweaking is a frequent corollary of 'management'. Hence neither a charge of bias nor the sorts of concerns just raised would likely unhinge or derail the management practices that the *Manual* engenders. The point of stabilising momentarily the infra-legal terrain of the dead in the *First Responders Manual* is not, accordingly, to try to expose what is 'really going on' in the *Manual* in anticipation of some total delegitimation and demobilisation.

[104] Cave, 'Haiti's Displaced See Their Stories on TV'.

[105] See, for example, Matthew Jude Egan, 'A Legal Typology for Disaster Response Operations: Public Lawyering in the State of Emergency', 5 September 2010, http://ssrn.com/abstract=1672204 (accessed 17 September 2012).

[106] The reference to 'operational best practices' is drawn from the title of the ICRC Manual.

The point of this chapter's assemblage, rather, is to foreground a dimension of power within international institutions' work that remains open to tactical engagement in particular instances (in the sense discussed in Chapter 1) yet has not, by and large, attracted critical attention. Here, that possibility rests with the infra-legal making of dead bodies as contingent vehicles for globalised management practice and sites for the forging of particular types of communal vision of and among 'surviving populations' as such. Contrary to the *First Responders Manual*'s instruction, the public *do* touch the dead and the dead *do* touch the public.[107] Many among the living are touched and sometimes respond with grace towards those with whom they have no connection or prospect of connection. The practice of making and remaking a public in and through the *First Responders Manual* assembles the dead together with those who would manage and attend to the dead. The public so assembled includes the international institutions that respond – ever more frequently, extensively and influentially, it seems – to disaster.[108] Those institutions comprise part of the public assembled through disaster and they also give shape to those publics, guided in part by the *First Responders Manual*. If disaster-response work so guided – and the configuration of the public to which it would give effect in particular instances – are to be opened to critical question, then the dead bodies lying at the side of habitual institutional routes ('heard' partially through the voices and postures that the *First Responders Manual* ascribes to them) may have as much to contribute as anyone.

[107] Morgan *et al.*, *First Responders Manual*, p. 6.

[108] According to Bankoff, 'United Nations experts calculate that the number of disasters rose on average 6 per cent each year between 1962 and 1992 ... and that they affected an average of 200 million people each year during the 1990s, a fourfold increase from the late 1960s': Bankoff, 'Rendering the World Unsafe', 19 (references omitted). In 2004, reflecting upon at least three decades of practice in international disaster relief, Kent reported that '[t]he "humanitarian enterprise" occupies the attention of more and more bilateral, multilateral and non-governmental organizations and finds itself a relative "growth industry"': Randolph C. Kent, 'International Humanitarian Crises: Two Decades Before and Two Decades Beyond' (2004) 80 *International Affairs* 851–869 at 851 (references omitted).

Conclusion

Nearly ten years ago, I developed a sense that there was something telling – and possibly something wrong – in the way that much international legal scholarship approached those instances of violence, injustice, excess and dysfunction by which it seemed most captivated. That intuition formed the basis initially for work on international legal depictions of Guantánamo Bay – work now comprising Chapter 3 of this book. It has since been metabolised into a series of intuitions pursued in this book. These may be enumerated as follows:

1. The repertoire of contemporary international legal work pursued in a mode of managerialism may be far less meagre than much international legal scholarship currently registers, or it is capable of being so experienced.
2. Realisation of the potential range of this repertoire might be more likely if some of the more familiar concerns of contemporary international legal scholarship could be bypassed and closer attention paid to the patterned practices in which international legal scholars (and others invoking international legal norms) in a range of specialties engage, and to the ways in which those practices relate to one another.
3. There may be as much to be gained – in ways international lawyers commonly think about 'gains' today – from a focus on the negative spaces around or against which international legal work is pursued, as is gained from a relentless focus on the positives that international legal work seeks to generate.

These concluding pages sketch what each of these intuitions might imply for those interested in any or all of the debates with which this book's various chapters are concerned.

Expanding the repertoire

Each of the debates with which this book's chapters are concerned tends to generate a familiar range of policy proposals in international legal scholarship: tendencies that might be identified in part with the prevalence of a 'managerialist mindset' discussed in this book's opening chapter.[1] Writing on the theme of torture – taken up in Chapter 2 – frequently revolves around the imperative of strengthening international legal prohibitions to minimise ambiguity, narrow exceptions and increase the prospect of responsible individuals' criminal prosecution.[2] International legal scholarship concerned with Guantánamo Bay – with which Chapter 3 was concerned – has largely focused on means of pressuring the United States and its allies to acknowledge and give fuller effect to their obligations with respect to detainees under international human rights law and international humanitarian law.[3] When writing about multinational corporations' conduct, especially corporate activities in the Third World, international legal commentary has tended to argue either for tempering the power of unalloyed corporate choice through regulatory circumscription on a global scale, or affording corporations freer rein to choose among available legal regimes (while pursuing some harmonisation of the latter).[4] This was made apparent in Chapter 4. In debate surrounding global climate change, a snapshot of which was presented in Chapter 5, international lawyers have generally gravitated towards some version of an international liability regime.[5] With respect to the 'management'

[1] Martti Koskenniemi, 'Constitutionalism as Mindset: Reflections on Kantian Themes about International Law and Globalization' (2007) 8 *Theoretical Inquiries in Law* 9–36 at 9.

[2] See, for example, John T. Parry, *Understanding Torture: Law, Violence and Political Identity* (Ann Arbor: University of Michigan Press, 2010), pp. 15–43.

[3] See, for example, Helen Duffy, *The 'War on Terror' and the Framework of International Law* (Cambridge University Press, 2005), pp. 379–442.

[4] See, for example, M. Sornarajah, *The International Law on Foreign Investment*, Third Edition (Cambridge University Press, 2010), p. 63; Larry Catá Becker, 'Multinational Corporations, Transnational Law: The United Nations' Norms on the Responsibilities of Transnational Corporations as a Harbinger of Corporate Social Responsibility in International Law' (2006) 37 *Columbia Human Rights Law Review* 287–390, at 288–291, 317–321, 374–375, 383–384; Jürgen Basedow, '*Lex Mercatoria* and the Private International Law of Contracts in Economic Perspective' in Jürgen Basedow and Toshiyuki Kono (eds.), *An Economic Analysis of Private International Law* (Tübingen: Mohr Siebeck, 2006), pp. 57–72.

[5] See, for example, Philippe Cullet, 'Liability and Redress for Human-Induced Global Warming: Towards an International Regime' (2007) 43 *Stanford Journal of International Law* 99–121; Michael G. Faure and André Nollkaemper, 'International Liability as

of dead bodies in the immediate aftermath of natural disaster, Chapter 6 showed that international institutions have favoured a recommendatory, 'best practice'-oriented governance approach aimed at reconstituting the surviving population in a particular image of public wellbeing.

As evidenced by its recurrence in contemporary writings, this repertoire of international legal projects and preoccupations is far from exhausted. The foregoing chapters have not, accordingly, sought to dispense with this repertoire altogether. On the contrary, I would hope that this book has recorded many labours in which international lawyers today remain engaged with care and, in many respects, admiration. Each chapter of this book has, nonetheless, sought to make of those familiar international legal moves an unlikely iteration – to throw them off centre in some way – so as to interrupt, if only momentarily, the return to familiar ground for yet another round of international legal making and doing. In each case, this tactical engagement has been with a view to expanding – or inviting some prospective expansion of – the contemporary international legal repertoire of ideas and actions.[6]

To engage in areas of contemporary global concern with a view to an expanded repertoire of international legal moves is not to promise that some magical array of as-yet-unrecognised policy solutions can now be made to appear. I do not have global fixes for torture, counter-terrorist abuse, economic inequity, human-induced climate change or the horrors of mass death ready to pull out from some textual back pocket, nor do I expect any version of international law offered here or elsewhere to make such fixes available. What I do nevertheless wish to make of contemporary international legal practice in the tactical readings presented in this book is something richer, more ambivalent and more apparent in its accommodation of the beyond-the-pale, than has typically been allowed by prevailing 'usable knowledge' of and about international law.[7]

an Instrument to Prevent and Compensate for Climate Change' (2007) 43 *Stanford Journal of International Law* 123–179; Roda Verheyen, *Climate Change Damage and International Law: Prevention Duties and State Responsibility* (Leiden and Boston: Martinus Nijhoff Publishers, 2005), pp. 339–343, 364.

[6] On tactical engagement, see Chapter 1.

[7] The highly migratory idea of 'usable knowledge' is traceable to the work of Peter Haas, who characterises it as 'accurate information that is of use to politicians and policy-makers': Peter Haas, 'When Does Power Listen to Truth? A Constructivist Approach to the Policy Process' (2004) 11 *Journal of European Public Policy* 569–592 at 574.

I want to dispense with the word 'just' in the claim that international legal work aspires increasingly 'just to operate some technical rules' and the associated reading down of the possibilities embedded in international legal work in a managerial mode.[8] If a person with a hammer sees every problem as a nail,[9] then a person with an architectural blueprint sees every problem as a foundation and every hammer-carrier as a 'mere' labourer implementing some architect's vision. Even when performed as little more than call-answering, in a service-provision capacity (perhaps *especially* when operating in such a mode), international legal work entails the projection of controversial, varied and impactive visions of the personal and the political, and the foreclosure of other visions to comparable effect. This book brings to the fore how much those who invoke international legal norms do, and insist upon not doing, in the mode of responding to imperatives issued from non-legal sources, in part through legal configuration of the non-legal sources in question.

Tracking trans-disciplinary practices

Despite this book's insistence upon immanent tactical engagement, many of the practices to which it draws attention are not those on which conventional policy discussions focus, as will already be apparent. Debate surrounding what to do in the wake of a natural disaster does not typically dwell on the particular version of public wellbeing that international institutions bring to bear through their work with the dead, as Chapter 6 does. International legal conversations about torture do not usually address what operative international legal norms make of the tortured, or of the international legal professionals envisaged rushing to their aid, as Chapter 2 does. Attention to these practices – to the 'how' rather than the 'what' or 'why' of international legal work – largely bypasses routes traversed by much contemporary international legal writing.

Many of those routes of argument, inquiry and initiative currently trodden by international legal scholarship are laid out pursuant to meta-worries concerning the discipline as a whole. Prominent among

[8] Martti Koskenniemi, 'International Law: Constitutionalism, Managerialism and the Ethos of Legal Education' (2007) 1 *European Journal of Legal Studies* 1–18 at 4.

[9] David Kennedy, 'Tom Franck and the Manhattan School' (2003) 35 *New York University Journal of International Law and Politics* 397–435 at 399; *ibid.*, 5.

these of late is a worry about the fragmentation of international law and the international legal profession. International lawyers are concerned that those who work in the various areas of specialty represented in this book - international environmental law, international human rights law or international economic law, for example - do not understand international law in the same way. The international legal work represented in this book's various chapters is being pursued, it seems to many, by recourse to increasingly discrete and divergent bodies of international norms. It can 'easily be assumed', Gerhard Hafner warned the International Law Commission in 2000, 'that presently, there exists no homogenous system of international law' because of that system's expansion and increasing heterogeneity in recent decades. The Commission should, Hafner recommended, 'seek ways and means to overcome the possible detrimental effects of such fragmentation'. This might be accomplished, Hafner suggested, by endowing central institutions with expanded monitoring functions, or through the elaboration of new global guidelines.[10]

Prevailing worries about the fragmentation of international legal order - and the imperative of remedying this at the level of doctrine and/or institutional design - seem to translate into a preoccupation with isolating and encircling outliers and bringing them home, so to speak, to international law. This emerged in different ways in Chapters 2 (on torture), 3 (on Guantánamo Bay) and 4 (on transnational corporate dealings). Worries of this kind may also inform understandings of

[10] Gerhard Hafner, 'Risks Ensuing From Fragmentation of International Law', in International Law Commission (ILC), *Report on the Work of its Fifty-Second Session*, Official Records of the General Assembly, Fifty-fifth Session, Supplement No. 10 (A/55/10), 19 January 2001, Annex: Syllabuses on Topics Recommended for Inclusion in the Long-Term Programme of Work of the Commission, http://untreaty.un.org/ilc/reports/2000/english/annex.pdf#page=9 (accessed 17 September 2012), pp. 143–150 at 143, 144, 149. The ILC accepted Hafner's recommendation by convening a Study Group to address the dilemmas posed by fragmentation. For General Assembly acknowledgement of the ILC's inclusion of this topic within its programme of work, see United Nations General Assembly, A/RES/57/21, 21 January 2003, http://untreaty.un.org/ilc/documentation/english/a_cn4_l682.pdf (accessed 17 September 2012). The Study Group so convened promulgated a series of 'Conclusions' in 2006: International Law Commission (ILC), 'Conclusions of the Work of the Study Group on the Fragmentation of International Law: Difficulties Arising from the Diversification and Expansion of International Law'. *Report on the Work of its Fifty-Eighth Session*, Official Records of the General Assembly, Sixty-first Session, Supplement No. 10 (A/61/10, para 251), 4 December 2006, http://untreaty.un.org/ilc/texts/instruments/english/draft%20articles/1_9_2006.pdf (accessed 17 September 2012) (hereafter 'Conclusions of the Study Group').

wrongdoing in which international lawyers currently trade. It is often easier to attribute wrongdoing to a paucity of international legal principle, or its relative lack of influence at specific sites, than to envisage and tackle it in terms of conflict between contending legal orders. The former proclivity was discernible in Chapters 2 and 3.

Concern that an ever more unwieldy international legal order lacks plausibly common points of reference might also help to foster tendencies to project commonalty elsewhere in international legal writing, placing the commonalty in question at some remove from legal scrutiny, as in Chapter 5 (on climate change).[11] Anxiety about international law's recent breakdown into irreconcilable fragments (presuming, of course, that things were once otherwise) might also inspire prevailing practices of governing by recommendation, in a posture of normative modesty and power-disavowal, as was apparent in Chapter 6 (on dead bodies' management post-disaster). At the same time, a sense that '[a]nswers to [international] legal questions [have] become dependent on whom you ask, [and on] what rule-system is your focus',[12] might be encouraging international lawyers to fixate, more and more, on a relatively narrow set of questions. Who may be liable and before which tribunal may they be brought? This is the sort of question that has tended to dominate policy discussion surrounding torture, Guantánamo Bay and climate change, as discussed in Chapters 2, 3 and 5, respectively.

In the interests of expanding the repertoire of ideas, actions and ways of being that may be enacted through international legal work, it seems timely[13] to bracket prevailing tendencies to equate 'bad things', globally speaking, with a deficit of international law or its isolated

[11] David Kennedy characterises this as a practice of 'denying abroad what we know to be true at home', observing that '[t]he realm to which reference is made is projected far more stably than it might appear to scholars tilling its fields': David Kennedy, 'A Rotation in Contemporary Legal Scholarship' in Christian Joerges and David M. Trubek (eds.), *Critical Legal Thought: An American-German Debate* (Baden Baden: Nomos Verlagsgesellschaft, 1989), pp. 353–396 at 360, 362.

[12] International Law Commission (ILC), 'Fragmentation of International Law: Difficulties Arising from the Diversification and Expansion of International Law', Report of the Study Group of the International Law Commission, Finalised by Martti Koskenniemi, A/CN.4/L.682, 13 April 2006, http://untreaty.un.org/ilc/documentation/english/a_cn4_l682.pdf (accessed 17 September 2012), p. 245 (hereafter 'Report of the Study Group').

[13] On the contrary, this suggestion and the one in the following paragraph could well be thought of as untimely or out of step in the sense of Nietzsche's 'Untimely Meditations': Friedrich Nietzsche, *Untimely Meditations* (trans. Reginald John Hollingdale, Cambridge and New York: Cambridge University Press, 1983).

inoperancy. As the preceding chapters have shown, it is possible to read many of the global deficits and excesses by which international lawyers are most concerned today as outcomes of international legal work, at least in part. Such readings give pause to the idea that international lawyers today are concerned above all with the elaboration and reconciliation of 'networks of international rules and instruments that for all practical purposes ... are treated as single "wholes" or "regimes"'.[14] The international lawyers depicted in the pages of this book are concerned as much with the projection of 'holes' and the elaboration of 'anti-regimes' in their respective fields of work.

It seems timely too to bracket prevailing worries about fragmentation in the international legal order, as well as any sense that one should aspire to overcome this fragmentation, once and for all, through some further augmentation of the ambit of international legal work.[15] This book's focus on trans-disciplinary practices of making the non-legal puts paid to the notion that '[t]he whole complex of inter-regime relations is presently a legal black hole' in the international legal field.[16] International lawyers already mobilise an extensive, shared repertoire of mediants, chords, proxies and archetypes spanning multiple international regimes, even if these resonate in different ways within different arrangements.

We may think of this trans-disciplinary repertoire in terms of its protagonists: Chapter 2's antinomian envelope-pusher and Chapter 4's pre- or post-legal choice-maker are repeat players, for instance, and highly versatile. We might think of this repertoire in terms of the sorts of spaces with which it is frequently identified: the empty cell of exception, emergency or 'pure' political (or economic) decision that featured so prominently in Chapter 3, for example, appears in many different

[14] ILC, 'Report of the Study Group', p. 252.

[15] The Conclusions of the Study Group are distinguishable, in this respect, from the Report of the Study Group finalised by the Study Group Chairman, Martti Koskenniemi. Compare, for example, the Conclusions' insistence that '[c]onflicts between rules of international law should be resolved in accordance with the principle of harmonization' and '[i]n case this is not possible, the superior norm will prevail', with the Report's observation that '[t]he very effort to canvass a coherent legal-professional technique on a fragmented world expresses the conviction that conflicts between specialized regimes may be overcome by law ... Yet ... [p]ublic international law does not contain rules in which a global society's problems are, as it were, already resolved. Developing these is a political task': ILC, Conclusions of the Study Group, para. 42; ILC, 'Report of the Study Group', pp. 245–247.

[16] ILC, 'Report of the Study Group', p. 253.

areas of international legal work as a mechanism for exoneration, rallying, explanation and justification. We saw it at work again in Chapter 4. We could think of this repertoire in terms of some of its characteristic invitations: the calling forth of ultimata (such as those which 'science' or 'politics' are made to issue in international legal debates surrounding climate change, discussed in Chapter 5) and the gentle guidance towards a governable life discernible in Chapter 6: invitations of this kind are issued in many different fields of international legal work, often eliciting welcome answers (however provisional or problematic) to that interminable question: what is to be done?

As they navigate normative conflict within, between and across areas of distinct international legal specialisation, international lawyers deploy these characters and gestures promiscuously. Attention to patterned practices of representation, argument and explanation across a variety of international legal issue areas allows us to see the richness of this existing repertoire and to recognise what may be at stake in its variable deployment.

Accentuating the negative

To focus on this repertoire of practices surrounding international legal norms' unmaking by reference to something else – whether the 'something else' in question is understood as another normative order or characterised by a violation, rejection or suspension of norms – is to pursue a project that will likely strike some readers as odd.[17] International law is, this book has made plain, vitally concerned with making non-legal phenomena. Nonetheless, lingering with these phenomena is not something international lawyers routinely do. For all the unsought suffering that they confront, international lawyers like, by and large, to accentuate the positive. It is out of recognition of – indeed, respect for – international lawyers' persistent capacity to

[17] One might anticipate a reaction like that of the narrator and the Other Professor in Lewis Carroll's *The Story of Sylvie and Bruno*: 'The Other Professor ... suddenly brightened up again, and addressed the Professor. "There's nothing more to be done *now*, is there?" "Well, there's the dinner to finish", the Professor said with a bewildered smile ... "I hope you'll enjoy the dinner – such as it is; and that you won't mind the heat – such as it isn't". The sentence *sounded* well, but somehow I couldn't quite understand it; and the Other Professor seemed to be no better off. "Such as it isn't *what*?" he peevishly enquired': See Lewis Carroll, *The Story of Sylvie and Bruno* (Whitefish, Montana: Kessinger Publishing, 2007), p. 298.

strike an upbeat note that I turn now to the question of gains that might be reaped from accentuating the negative, as this book does.

Some positive repercussions that may flow from such an accentuation of the negative have already been anticipated. An expansion in the international legal repertoire – an expansion, that is, in the range of ideas, actions and ways of being that may be enacted through international legal work: this seems like a gain, doesn't it (framing gains, here, in terms familiar to those who do international legal work – in terms of greater freedom, for instance)? Perhaps not; as anyone who has surveyed a dizzying display of cereals or mutual funds knows intuitively, there is no necessary correlation between an expanded number of options and a heightened experience of freedom. Nevertheless, I do wish to persist with the claim that it might be gainful to try to make of international legal work more than prevailing scholarship mostly registers of and about it.

Why, for instance, should it be regarded as the privy of the executive branches of certain governments – and others whose core business is politics in a popular sense – to craft extra-legal orders in which novel transmutations of ordinary legal norms and institutions are understood to prevail? Why shouldn't international lawyers concerned about global poverty, for instance, and interested in experimental ways of addressing it, add this to their proverbial toolbox? Why shouldn't international legal scholarship include leaders of global criminal networks, suspected terrorist detainees, and other tainted and unruly types among the pantheon of law-makers to whose norm-generating endeavours it pays close attention? Why should international lawyers belabour the birthing of new global treaties (on, say, multinational corporate conduct or climate change) – and agonise when these labours fail – when so many governing and governable beings and things, at least in part of international legal provenance, are already hard at work recommending, valuing, modelling, expertising? Why read down the capacities of international legal technicians as monolingual managerialism if one is interested in showing how 'many things are open for re-definition and innovation inside the [specialised] vocabularies themselves' and in their complicities and conflicts?[18]

An accentuation of international law's negative spaces – attention, that is, to international legal makings of the non-legal – could embolden

[18] Martti Koskenniemi, 'The Politics of International Law – 20 Years Later' (2009) 20 *European Journal of International Law* 7–19, at 13.

the sort of experimentation these questions imply without necessary recourse to some higher or lower ground of assurance or initiative. Here and now the endlessly cross-pollinating fields of contemporary international legal specialisation remain to be tilled or 'fictioned' in the sense discussed in Chapter 1.[19] Consider this book but one turning of the sods.

[19] See Chapter 1, note 79.

Bibliography

Abi-Saab, Georges, 'Namibia and International Law: An Overview' (1993) 1 *African Yearbook of International Law* 3–12.

Abramovsky, Abraham, 'Extraterritorial Abductions: America's "Catch and Snatch" Policy Run Amok' (1991) 31 *Virginia Journal of International Law* 151–210.

Ackerman, Bruce, 'The Emergency Constitution?' (2004) 113 *Yale Law Journal* 1029–1093.

Ackerman, Bruce, Mark D. Agrast *et al.*, 'Lawyers' Statement on Bush Administration's Torture Memos, Open Letter Addressed to President George W. Bush, Vice President Richard B. Cheney, Secretary of Defense Donald Rumsfeld, Attorney General John Ashcroft and Members of Congress', 4 August 2004, www.sfcityattorney.org/Modules/ShowDocument.aspx?documentid=507 (accessed 17 September 2012).

Acuña, Héctor R., 'The Pan American Health Organization: 75 Years of International Cooperation in Public Health' (1977) 92 *Public Health Reports* 537–544.

Agamben, Giorgio, *Homo Sacer: Sovereign Power and Bare Life* (trans. Daniel Heller-Roazen, Stanford University Press, 1998).

State of Exception (trans. Kevin Attell, Chicago University Press, 1998).

Agrawala, Shardul, 'Context and Early Origins of the Intergovernmental Panel on Climate Change' (1998) 39 *Climactic Change* 605–620.

'Structural and Process History of the Intergovernmental Panel on Climate Change' (1998) 39 *Climactic Change* 621–642.

Alexander, David, 'The Study of Natural Disasters, 1977–1997: Some Reflections on a Changing Field of Knowledge' (1997) 21 *Disasters* 284–304.

Alston, Philip, *Report of the Special Rapporteur on Extrajudicial, Summary or Arbitrary Executions*, United Nations General Assembly, Human Rights Council, 28 May 2010, A/HRC/14/24/Add.6, www2.ohchr.org/english/bodies/hrcouncil/docs/14session/A.HRC.14.24.Add6.pdf (accessed 17 September 2012).

Althusser, Louis, *For Marx* (trans. Ben Brewster, London and New York: Verso, 1977).

Alvarez, José E., 'Torturing the Law' (2006) 37 *Case Western Reserve Journal of International Law* 175–233.

Amann, Dianne Marie, 'Guantánamo' (2004) 42 *Columbia Journal of Transnational Law* 263–348.

American Civil Liberties Union, *Index of Bush-Era OLC Memoranda Relating to Interrogation, Detention, Rendition and/or Surveillance*, www.aclu.org/pdfs/safefree/olcmemos_2009_0305.pdf (accessed 17 September 2012).

Amin, Ash and Patrick Cohendet, *Architectures of Knowledge: Firms, Capabilities, and Communities* (Oxford University Press, 2004).

Amnesty International, *Beyond Abu Ghraib: Detention and Torture in Iraq* (Amnesty International, 2006), www.amnesty.org/en/library/info/MDE14/001/2006 (accessed 17 September 2012).

Andrew, Edward G., 'Hobbes on Conscience Within The Law and Without' (1999) 32 *Canadian Journal of Political Science* 203–225.

Appelbaum, Richard P., William L. F. Felstiner and Volkmar Gessner (eds.), *Rules and Networks: The Legal Culture of Global Business Transactions* (Oxford: Hart Publishing, 2001).

Arias, Enrique Desmond, *Drugs and Democracy in Rio De Janeiro: Trafficking, Social Networks and Public Security* (Chapel Hill: The University of North Carolina Press, 2006).

Askin, Kelly Dawn, *War Crimes Against Women: Prosecution in International War Crimes Tribunals* (The Hague: Martinus Nijohff Publishers, 1997).

Atiyah, Patrick S., *The Rise and Fall of Freedom of Contract* (Oxford University Press, 1979).

Bailey, Richard, 'Up Against the Wall: Bare Life and Resistance in the Camp' (2009) 20 *Law and Critique* 113–132.

Banda, Maria and John Opperman, 'Building a Latin American Coalition on Forests: Negotiation Barriers and Opportunities' (2011) 44 *Vanderbilt Journal of Transnational Law* 527–588.

Bankoff, Gregory, 'Rendering the World Unsafe: "Vulnerability" as Western Discourse' (2001) 25 *Disasters* 19–35.

Barents, René, *The Autonomy of Community Law* (The Hague: Kluwer Law International, 2004).

Barnes, Julian E. and Evan Perez, 'Clarity Sought on Detainees', *The Wall Street Journal*, 12 August 2011, online.wsj.com/article/SB10001424053111904823804576502331882663322.html (accessed 17 September 2012).

Basedow, Jürgen and Toshiyuki Kono (eds.), *An Economic Analysis of Private International Law* (Tübingen: Mohr Siebeck, 2006).

Bast, Carol, 'A Short History of Boilerplate' (1994) 5 *Scribes Journal of Legal Writing* 155–157.

BBC News Magazine, 'Do Dead Bodies in Haiti Pose a Health Risk?', *BBC News Magazine*, 19 January 2010, news.bbc.co.uk/go/pr/fr/-/2/hi/uk_news/magazine/8465464.stm (accessed 17 September 2012).

Beck, Silke, 'Moving Beyond the Linear Model of Expertise? IPCC and the Test of Adaptation' (2011) 11 *Regional Environmental Change* 297–306.

Beck, Ulrich, 'Climate for Change, or How to Create a Green Modernity?' (2010) 27 *Theory Culture Society* 254–266.

Becker, Larry Catá, 'Multinational Corporations, Transnational Law: The United Nations' Norms on the Responsibilities of Transnational Corporations as a Harbinger of Corporate Social Responsibility in International Law' (2006) 37 *Columbia Human Rights Law Review* 287–390.

Beckett, Jason, 'Rebel Without a Cause? Martti Koskenniemi and the Critical Legal Project' (2006) 7 *German Law Journal* 1045–1088.

Bekoe, Ama S., 'The Illusory Choice: Examining the Illusion of "Choice" in Choice of Law Provisions – A Country Study Exploring One Aspect of Foreign Investment in the Caribbean' (1999) 42 *Howard Law Journal* 505–534.

Benkler, Yochai, 'A Free Irresponsible Press: Wikileaks and the Battle Over the Soul of the Networked Fourth Estate' (2011) 46 *Harvard Civil Rights-Civil Liberties Law Review* 311–398.

Berg, Laurie, 'At the Border and between the Cracks: The Precarious Position of Irregular Migrant Workers Under International Human Rights Law' (2007) 8 *Melbourne Journal of International Law* 1–34.

Berman, Nathaniel, ''Legitimacy through Defiance: From Goa to Iraq' (2005) 23 *Wisconsin International Law Journal* 93–125.

'Privileging Combat? Contemporary Conflict and the Legal Construction of War' (2004) 43 *Columbia Journal of Transnational Law* 1–72.

Berman, Paul Schiff, 'From International Law to Law and Globalization' (2005) 43 *Columbia Journal of Transnational Law* 485–556.

Bessendorf, Ari, 'Games in the Hothouse: Theoretical Dimensions in Climate Change' (2005) 28 *Suffolk Transnational Law Review* 325–357.

Betsill, Michele M. and Harriet Bulkeley, 'Cities and the Multilevel Governance of Global Climate Change' (2006) 12 *Global Governance* 141–159.

Bilder, Richard B., 'On Being an International Lawyer' (2006) 3 *Loyola International Law Review* 135–147.

Bilder, Richard B. and Detlev F. Vagts, 'Speaking Law to Power: Lawyers and Torture' (2004) 98 *American Journal of International Law* 689–695.

Blasco, Paloma Gay y and Huan Wardle, *How to Read Ethnography* (Abingdon and New York: Routledge, 2007).

Blum, Cynthia Ann, '"Til Death Do Us Part?" The Nurse's Role in the Care of the Dead: A Historical Perspective: 1850–2004' (2006) 27 *Geriatric Nursing* 58–63.

Bodansky, Daniel, 'The Legitimacy of International Governance: A Coming Challenge for International Governance' (1999) 93 *American Journal of International Law* 596–624.

Boehmer-Christiansen, Sonja, 'Global Climate Protection Policy: The Limits of Scientific Advice (Part 1)' (1994) 4 *Global Environmental Change* 140–159.

'Global Climate Protection Policy: The Limits of Scientific Advice (Part 2)' (1994) 4 *Global Environmental Change* 185–200.

Bonell, Michael Joachim, 'Soft Law and Party Autonomy: The Case of the UNIDROIT Principles' (2005) 51 *Loyola Law Review* 229–252.

Boswell, Jackson Campbell, 'Milton and Prevenient Grace' (1967) 7 *Studies in English Literature, 1500–1900* 83–94.

Bourdieu, Pierre, *Distinction: A Social Critique of the Judgment of Taste* (trans. Richard Nice, London: Routledge, 1984).

In Other Words: Essays Towards a Reflexive Sociology (trans. Matthew Adamson, Stanford University Press, 1990).

Outline of a Theory of Practice (trans. Richard Nice, Cambridge University Press, 1977).

Boyle, Francis A., 'The Irrelevance of International Law: The Schism Between International Law and International Politics' (1980) 10 *California Western International Law Journal* 193–219.

Bravin, Jess, 'Pentagon Report Set Framework for Use of Torture', *The Wall Street Journal*, 7 June 2004, www.informationclearinghouse.info/article6288.htm (accessed 17 September 2012).

Bray, Dennis, 'The Scientific Consensus of Climate Change Revisited' (2010) 13 *Environmental Science and Policy* 340–350.

Brilmayer, Lea, 'Rights, Fairness, and Choice of Law' (1989) 98 *Yale Law Journal* 1277–1320.

Broadhead, Philip J., 'Guildsmen, Religious Reform, and the Search for the Common Good: The Role of the Guilds in the Early Reformation in Augsburg' (1996) 39 *The Historical Journal* 577–597.

Brower, Charles N. and Jeremy K. Sharpe, 'International Arbitration and the Islamic World: The Third Phase' (2003) 97 *American Journal of International Law* 643–655.

Brown, Chester, *A Common Law of International Adjudication* (Oxford University Press, 2007).

Brownlie, Ian, *Principles of Public International Law*, Seventh Edition (Oxford University Press, 2008).

Brudney, Victor, 'Corporate Governance, Agency Costs, and the Rhetoric of Contract' (1985) 85 *Columbia Law Review* 1403–1444.

Brunée, Jutta and Stephen J. Toope, *Legitimacy and Legality in International Law: An Interactional Account* (Cambridge University Press, 2010).

Burchell, Graham, Colin Gordon and Peter Miller (eds.), *The Foucault Effect: Studies in Governmentality* (University of Chicago Press, 1991).

Butler, Judith, *Gender Trouble: Feminism and the Subversion of Identity* (New York and London: Routledge, 2006).

Precarious Life: The Powers of Mourning and Violence (London and New York: Verso, 2004).

Camic, Charles, Neil Gross and Michèle Lamont (eds.), *Social Knowledge in the Making* (University of Chicago Press, 2011).

Cao, Lan, 'Culture Change' (2007) 47 *Virginia Journal of International Law* 357–412.

Carbonneau, Thomas E. (ed.), *Lex Mercatoria and Arbitration: A Discussion of the New Law Merchant*, Revised Edition (New York: Juris Publishing, 1998).

Carrington, Damian, 'In Defence of the IPCC: Critics Ignore the Real Scandal', *Damian Carrington's Environment Blog*, 28 July 2011, *Guardian*, www.guardian.co.uk/environment/damian-carrington-blog/2011/jul/28/ipcc-climate-change-science-pachauri (accessed 17 September 2012).

Carroll, Lewis, *The Story of Sylvie and Bruno* (Whitefish, Montana: Kessinger Publishing, 2007).

Cave, Damien, 'Haiti's Displaced See Their Stories on TV', *The New York Times*, 9 June 2010, www.nytimes.com/2010/06/10/world/americas/10haiti.html (accessed 17 September 2012).

Chaffee, Devon, 'Military Commissions Revived: Persisting Problems of Perception' (2011) 9 *University of New Hampshire Law Review* 237–260.

Cheng, Tai-Heng, 'Power, Authority and International Investment Law' (2005) 20 *American University International Law Review* 465–520.

Chesney, Robert M., 'Boumediene v. Bush' (2008) 102 *American Journal of International Law* 848–853.

Cheung, Steven N. S., 'The Contractual Nature of the Firm' (1983) 26 *Journal of Law and Economics* 1–22.

Choi, Stephen J. and G. Mitu Gulati, 'Contract as Statute' (2006) 104 *Michigan Law Review* 1129–1174.

Christodoulidis, Emilios, 'Strategies of Rupture' (2009) 20 *Law and Critique* 3–26.

Chubin, Daryl E. and Edward J. Hackett, *Peerless Science: Peer Review and US Science Policy* (Albany: SUNY Press, 1990).

Chukwumerije, Okezie, *Choice of Law in International Commercial Arbitration* (Westport: Quorum Books, 1994).

Churchill, Robin and David Freestone (eds.), *International Law and Global Climate Change* (London and Boston: Graham & Trotman/Martinus Nijhoff, 1991).

Cirielli, Stefano E., 'Arbitration, Financial Markets, and Banking Disputes' (2003) 14 *American Review of International Arbitration* 243–284.

Clark, Kathleen, 'Ethical Issues Raised by the OLC Torture Memorandum' (2005) 1 *Journal of National Security Law and Policy* 455–472.

Clegg, Stewart, 'Weber and Foucault: Social Theory for the Study of Organizations' (1994) 1 *Organization* 149–178.

Clifford, James, *The Predicament Of Culture: Twentieth-Century Ethnography, Literature and Art* (Cambridge, MA: Harvard University Press, 1998).

Cole, David, 'The Priority of Morality: The Emergency Constitution's Blind Spot' (2004) 113 *Yale Law Journal* 1753–1801.

Conchiglia, Augusta, 'Dans le trou noir de Guantanamo', *Le Monde Diplomatique*, January 2004, pp. 1, 20 and 23, www.monde-diplomatique.fr/2004/01/CONCHIGLIA/10996 (accessed 17 September 2012).

Condorelli, Luigi and Pasquale De Sena, 'The Relevance of the Obligations Flowing from the UN Covenant on Civil and Political Rights to US Courts Dealing with Guantánamo Detainees' (2004) 2 *Journal of International Criminal Justice* 107–120.

Cook, Walter Wheeler, '"Contracts" and the Conflict of Laws: "Intention" of the Parties' (1938) 32 *Illinois Law Review* 899–920.

'"Contracts" and the Conflict of Laws: "Intention" of the Parties: Some Further Remarks' (1939) 34 *Illinois Law Review* 423–432.

'The Logical and Legal Bases of the Conflict of Laws' (1924) 33 *Yale Law Journal* 457–488.

The Logical and Legal Bases of the Conflict of Laws (Cambridge, MA: Harvard University Press, 1942).

Cooper, Davina, 'Institutional Illegality and Disobedience: Local Government Narratives' (1996) 16 *Oxford Journal of Legal Studies* 255–274.

Cooperman, Alan, 'Bush's References to God Defended by Speechwriter: President Does Not Claim Divinity is on His Side, Gerson Contends', *The Washington Post*, 12 December 2004, p. A.06.

Corell, Hans, 'Sovereignty and Humanity: Reality and Possibility' (2007) 36 *Denver Journal of International Law and Policy* 1–7.

Crabbe, Kelly Charles, 'The Reality of Extra-legal Barriers to Mergers and Acquisitions in Japan' (1987) 21 *International Lawyer* 97–128.

Cramton, Roger C., David P. Currie and Herma H. Kay (eds.), *Conflict of Laws: Cases, Comments, Questions*, Third Edition (Minnesota: West Publishing Company, 1981).

Cullet, Philippe, 'Liability and Redress for Human-Induced Global Warming: Towards an International Regime' (2007) 43A *Stanford Journal of International Law* 99–122.

Curtin, Deirdre, *Executive Power of the European Union: Law, Practices and the Living Constitution* (Oxford University Press, 2009).

Cutler, A. Claire, *Private Power and Global Authority: Transnational Merchant Law in the Global Political Economy* (New York: Cambridge University Press, 2003).

Dahlstrom, K. Elizabeth, 'The Executive Policy Toward Detention and Trial of Foreign Citizens at Guantánamo Bay' (2003) 21 *Berkeley Journal of International Law* 662–682.

Dalhuisen, Jan H., 'Legal Orders and Their Manifestation: The Operation of the International Commercial and Financial Legal Order and its Lex Mercatoria' (2006) 24 *Berkeley Journal of International Law* 129–191.

Daly, Kathleen, 'Women's Pathways to Felony Court: Feminist Theories of Law-breaking and Problems of Representation' (1992) 2 *Southern Californian Review of Law and Women's Studies* 11–52.

Dan-Cohen, Meir, 'Responsibility and the Boundaries of the Self' (1992) 105 *Harvard Law Review* 959–1003.

Danner, Mark, 'The Red Cross Torture Report: What it Means', *The New York Review of Books*, 30 April 2009, www.nybooks.com/articles/archives/2009/apr/30/the-red-cross-torture-report-what-it-means (accessed 17 September 2012).

Torture and Truth: America, Abu Ghraib, and the War on Terror (New York Review of Books, 2004).

'US Torture: Voices from the Black Sites', *The New York Review of Books*, 9 April 2009, www.nybooks.com/articles/archives/2009/apr/09/us-torture-voices-from-the-black-sites/?pagination=false (accessed 17 September 2012).

Daston, Lorraine and Katharine Park, *Wonders and the Order of Nature, 1150–1750* (New York: Zone Books, 1998).

Dean, Jodi, 'Why the Net is not a Public Sphere' (2003) 10 *Constellations* 95–112.

de Certeau, Michel, *The Practice of Everyday Life* (trans. Steven Rendall, Berkeley: University of California Press, 1984).

Dekker, Ige, 'Declaration on the Fight Against Terrorism and the Protection of Human Rights – A Resolvable Conflict' (2003) 14 *Helsinki Monitor* 321–327.

De Ly, Filip, 'The Place of Arbitration in the Conflict of Laws of International Commercial Arbitration: An Exercise in Arbitration Planning' (1991) 12 *Northwestern Journal of International Law and Business* 48–85.

Dembour, Marie-Bénédicte, 'Human Rights Talk and Anthropological Ambivalence: The Particular Context of Universal Claims' in Olivia Harris (ed.), *Inside and Outside the Law: Anthropological Studies of Authority and Ambiguity* (London and New York: Routledge, 1996), pp. 19–40.

Denbeaux, Mark P. and Jonathan Hafetz (eds.), *The Guantánamo Lawyers: Inside a Prison Outside the Law* (New York and London: New York University Press, 2009).

Derrida, Jacques, *Acts of Religion* (ed. Gil Anidjar, New York: Routledge Press, 2002).

The Post Card: From Socrates to Freud and Beyond (University of Chicago Press, 1987).

Diaz, Lt. Cmdr. Matthew, 'Ex-Navy Lawyer Explains Guantanamo Leak', *All Things Considered*, National Public Radio broadcast interview transcript, 10 April 2008, www.npr.org/templates/story/story.php?storyId=89538109 (accessed 17 September 2012).

Dibadj, Reza, 'Reconceiving the Firm' (2005) 26 *Cardozo Law Review* 1459–1534.

di Robilant, Anna, 'Genealogies of Soft Law' (2006) 54 *The American Journal of Comparative Law* 499–554.

Drumbl, Mark A., 'Guantánamo, Rasul, and the Twilight of Law' (2004–2005) 53 *Drake Law Review* 897–922.

Duane, Timothy P., 'Greening the Grid: Implementing Climate Change Policy Through Energy Efficiency, Renewable Portfolio Standards, and Strategic Transmission System Investments' (2010) 34 *Vermont Law Review* 711–780.

Duff, R. Antony, *Answering for Crime: Responsibility and Liability in the Criminal Law* (Oxford: Hart Publishing, 2007).

Duffy, Helen, *The 'War on Terror' and the Framework of International Law* (Cambridge University Press, 2005).

Dufresne, Todd, *Tales from the Freudian Crypt: The Death Drive in Text and Context* (Stanford University Press, 2000).

Durkheim, Emile, *Suicide: A Study in Sociology*, Second Edition (London: Routledge, 2002).

Duxbury, Neil, *Patterns of American Jurisprudence* (Oxford University Press, 1995).

Dyzenhaus, David, 'The Puzzle of Martial Law' (2009) 59 *University of Toronto Law Journal* 1–64.

'Schmitt v. Dicey: Are States of Emergency Inside or Outside the Legal Order?' (2006) 27 *Cardozo Law Review* 2005–2040.

Ebel, Robert E., 'Politics Before Business: A Study in Risk Analysis by a Multinational Corporation' (1989) 11 *University of Pennsylvania Journal of International Business Law* 453–468.

The Economist, 'A Climate of Conflict: A New Row about the IPCC', 25 June 2011, p. 72.

Egan, Matthew Jude, 'A Legal Typology for Disaster Response Operations: Public Lawyering in the State of Emergency', 5 September 2010, http://ssrn.com/abstract=1672204 or http://dx.doi.org/10.2139/ssrn.1672204 (accessed 17 September 2012).

Eggleston, Simon, Leandro Buendia, Kyoko Miwa, Todd Ngara and Kiyoto Tanabe (eds.), *2006 IPCC Guidelines for National Greenhouse Gas Inventories* (Hayama, Japan: Institute for Global Environmental Strategies, 2006), www.ipcc-nggip.iges.or.jp/public/2006gl/index.html (accessed 17 September 2012).

Eisenberg, Melvin A., 'The Conception that the Corporation is a Nexus of Contracts, and the Dual Nature of the Firm' (1999) 24 *Journal of Corporation Law* 819–836.

Elias, Taslim Olawale, *New Horizons in International Law* (Alphen aan den Rijn, The Netherlands: Sijthoff & Noordhoff, 1979).

Epstein, Andrew, 'A New Approach to an Old Problem: Managing Fish Resources in the Beaufort Sea' (2011) 11 *Chicago Journal of International Law* 755–788.

Esteri, Mike, 'After Delays, Water-Purification Tablets Arrive', *The Wall Street Journal*, 17 January 2010, p. 1.

European Parliament, *Report on the Alleged Use of European Countries by the CIA for the Transportation and Illegal Detention of Prisoners*, 30 January 2007, European Parliament Document A6-0020/2007, www.europarl.europa.eu/sides/getDoc.do?type=REPORT&reference=A6-2007-0020&language=EN (accessed 17 September 2012).

Fadahunsi, Akin and Peter Rosa, 'Entrepreneurship and Illegality: Insights from the Nigerian Cross-Border Trade' (2002) 17 *Journal of Business Venturing* 397–429.

Fatovic, Clement, *Outside the Law: Emergency and Executive Power* (Baltimore: Johns Hopkins University Press, 2009).

Faure, Michael G. and André Nollkaemper, 'International Liability as an Instrument to Prevent and Compensate for Climate Change' (2007) 43 *Stanford Journal of International Law* 123–179.

Fawcett, James (ed.), *Reform and Development of Private International Law: Essays in Honour of Sir Peter North* (Oxford University Press, 2002).

Feldman, Robin, *The Role of Science in Law* (Oxford University Press, 2009).
Finn, Peter, 'Obama Seeks Halt to Legal Proceedings at Guantánamo', *The Washington Post*, 21 January 2009, p. A.2.
Fisher, William W. III, Morton J. Horwitz and Thomas A. Reed (eds.), *American Legal Realism* (New York: Oxford University Press, 1993).
Fleischer, Victor, 'Brand New Deal: The Branding Effect of Corporate Deal Structures' (2006) 104 *Michigan Law Review* 1581–1638.
'Deals: Bringing Corporate Transactions into the Law School Classroom' (2002) *Columbia Business Law Review* 475–498.
Fletcher, George P., 'Black Hole in Guantánamo Bay' (2004) 2 *Journal of International Criminal Justice* 121–232.
Flood, John, 'Doing Business: The Management of Uncertainty in Lawyers' Work' (1991) 25 *Law and Society Review* 41–72.
Forcese, Craig, 'The Myth of the Virtuous Torturer: Two Defences of the Absolute Ban on Torture' (2008) 46 *Osgoode Hall Law Journal* 853–870.
Forsythe, David P., *The Humanitarians: The International Committee of the Red Cross* (Cambridge University Press, 2005).
Foucault, Michel, *The Birth of Biopolitics: Lectures at the Collège de France 1978–79* (ed. Michel Senellart, trans. Graham Burchell, New York: Palgrave Macmillan, 2010).
The Birth of the Clinic: An Archaeology of Medical Perception (trans. A. M. Sheridan Smith, London: Routledge, 2003).
Ethics: Subjectivity and Truth. Essential Works of Foucault 1954–1984, Volume One (ed. Paul Rabinow, London: New Press, 1997).
The History of Sexuality, Volume I: An Introduction (trans. Robert Hurley, New York: Random House, 1978).
Madness and Civilization: A History of Insanity in the Age of Reason (trans. Richard Howard, New York: Vintage Books, 1988).
The Order of Things: An Archaeology of the Human Sciences (London: Tavistock Publications, 1970).
Power: The Essential Works of Michel Foucault 1954–1984, Volume Three (ed. James D. Faubion, trans. Robert Hurley, Baltimore: Penguin Books, 2000).
Power/Knowledge: Selected Interviews and Other Writings 1972–1977 (ed. Colin Gordon, New York: Pantheon Books, 1980).
Security, Territory, Population: Lectures at the Collège de France 1977–1978 (ed. Michel Senellart, trans. Graham Burchell, New York: Palgrave Macmillan, 1997).
Society Must be Defended: Lectures at the Collège de France 1975–76 (ed. Mauro Bertani and Allessandro Fontana, trans. David Macey, London: Penguin Books, 2004).
The Use of Pleasure: Volume 2 of The History of Sexuality (trans. Robert Hurley, New York: Vintage Books, 1985).
Foucault, Michel and Maurice Blanchot, *Foucault/Blanchot* (trans. Jeffrey Mehlman and Brian Massumi, New York: Zone Books, 1987).

Fowlie, Wallace, 'Racine, Poet of Grace' (1939) 12 *The French Review* 391–400.

Franck, Thomas M., 'After Austerlitz: The International System in the Age of Rampant American Unilateralism', (2003) 8 *Austrian Review of International and European Law* 35–48.

Freud, Sigmund, *The Freud Reader* (ed. Peter Gay, London: Vintage, 1995).

Freund, James C., *Lawyering: A Realistic Approach to Legal Practice* (New York: Law Journal Seminars-Press, 1979).

Fried, Barbara H., *The Progressive Assault on Laissez Faire: Robert Hale and the First Law and Economics Movement* (Cambridge, MA: Harvard University Press, 1998).

Gamble, John King and Charlotte Ku, 'International Law – New Actors and New Technologies: Centre Stage for NGOs?' (2000) 31 *Law and Policy in International Business* 221–262.

Garber, Marjorie B. and Rebecca L. Walkowitz (eds.), *One Nation Under God? Religion and American Culture* (New York and London: Routledge, 1999).

Gardiner, Stephen M., 'Ethics and Global Climate Change' (2004) 114 *Ethics* 555–600.

Geltzer, Joshua Alexander, 'Decisions Detained: The Courts' Embrace of Complexity in Guantánamo-Related Litigation' (2011) 29 *Berkeley Journal of International Law* 94–131.

Gibbs, Nancy with Viveca Novak, 'Inside "The Wire"', *Time Magazine*, 30 November 2003, www.time.com/time/magazine/article/0,9171,552060,00.html (accessed 17 September 2012).

Gilson, Ronald J., 'Value Creation by Business Lawyers: Legal Skills and Asset Pricing' (1984) 94 *Yale Law Journal* 239–313.

Glazier, David, 'A Self-Inflicted Wound: A Half-Dozen Years of Turmoil over the Guantánamo Military Commissions' (2008) 12 *Lewis & Clark Law Review* 131–204.

'Still a Bad Idea: Military Commissions Under the Obama Administration', Loyola-LA Legal Studies Paper No. 2010-32, ssrn.com/abstract=1658590 (accessed 17 September 2012).

Golden, Tim, 'Naming Names at Gitmo', *The New York Times Magazine*, 21 October 2007, www.nytimes.com/2007/10/21/magazine/21Diaz-t.html?pagewanted=all (accessed 17 September 2012).

Golder, Ben, 'Foucault and the Incompletion of Law' (2008) 21 *Leiden Journal of International Law* 747–763.

Golder, Ben and Peter Fitzpatrick, *Foucault's Law* (Oxford and New York: Routledge, 2009).

Goldsmith, Jack, *The Terror Presidency: Law and Judgment Inside the Bush Administration* (New York: W. W. Norton, 2007).

Goldsmith, Jack Landman and Eric A. Posner, 'Moral and Legal Rhetoric in International Relations: A Rational Choice Perspective' (2002) 31 *Journal of Legal Studies* 115–139.

Goldstein, Judith O., Miles Kahler, Robert O. Keohane and Anne-Marie Slaughter, 'Introduction: Legalisation and World Politics' (2000) 54 *International Organization* 385–399.

Green, Jennifer and Michael Green (eds.), *Dealing with Death: A Handbook of Practices, Procedures and Law*, Second Edition (London and Philadelphia: Jessica Kingsley, 2006).

Greenberg, Karen J. and Joshua L. Dratel (eds.), *The Torture Papers: The Road to Abu Ghraib* (Cambridge University Press, 2005).

Greenstein, Richard K., 'Why the Rule of Law?' (2005) 66 *Louisiana Law Review* 63–94.

Gross, Oren, 'Chaos and Rules: Should Responses to Violent Crises Always be Constitutional?' (2003) 112 *Yale Law Journal* 1011–1134.

'The Normless and Exceptionless Exception: Carl Schmitt's Theory of Emergency Powers and the "Norm-Exception" Dichotomy' (2000) 21 *Cardozo Law Review* 1825–1868.

Gross, Oren and Fionnuala Ní Aoláin, *Law in Times of Crisis: Emergency Powers in Theory and Practice* (Cambridge University Press, 2006).

Guha-Sapir, Debby, Femke Vos and Regina Below with Sylvain Ponserre, *Annual Disaster Statistical Review 2010: The Numbers and Trends* (Brussels: Centre for Research on the Epidemiology of Disasters (CRED), 2011), http://cred.be/sites/default/files/ADSR_2010.pdf (accessed 17 September 2012).

Annual Disaster Statistical Review 2011: The Numbers and Trends (Brussels: CRED, 2012), http://cred.be/sites/default/files/2012.07.05.ADSR_2011.pdf (accessed 17 September 2012)

Guruswamy, Lakshman, 'Climate Change: The Next Dimension' (2000) 9 *Journal of Transnational Law & Policy* 341–382.

Haas, Peter, 'When Does Power Listen to Truth? A Constructivist Approach to the Policy Process' (2004) 11 *Journal of European Public Policy* 569–592.

Hale, Robert L., 'Bargaining, Duress, and Economic Liberty' (1943) 43 *Columbia Law Review* 603–628.

'Labor Legislation as an Enlargement of Individual Liberty' (1925) 15 *American Labor Legislation Review* 155–160.

'Law Making by Unofficial Minorities' (1920) 20 *Columbia Law Review* 451–456.

'Our Equivocal Constitutional Guaranties' (1939) 39 *Columbia Law Review* 563–594.

'Value and Vested Rights' (1927) 27 *Columbia Law Review* 523–529.

Hardt, Michael and Antonio Negri, *Empire* (Cambridge, MA: Harvard University Press, 2000).

Harris, Olivia (ed.), *Inside and Outside the Law: Anthropological Studies of Authority and Ambiguity* (London and New York: Routledge, 1996).

Hay, Bruce L., 'Conflicts of Law and State Competition in the Product Liability System' (1992) 80 *Georgetown Law Journal* 617–652.

He, Xin, 'Why Do They Not Comply with the Law? Illegality and Semi-Legality among Rural-Urban Migrant Entrepreneurs in Beijing' (2005) 39 *Law & Society Review* 527–562.

Heyman, Josiah McC. (ed.), *States and Illegal Practices* (Oxford: Berg, 1999).

Hobbes, Thomas, *Leviathan: Parts I and II* (ed. A. P. Martinich, Peterborough, Ontario: Broadview Press, 2005).

Ho-Lem, Claudio, Hisham Zerriffi and Milind Kandlikar, 'Who Participates in the Intergovernmental Panel on Climate Change and Why? A Quantitative Assessment of the National Representation of Authors in the Intergovernmental Panel on Climate Change' (2011) 21 *Global Environmental Change* 1308–1317.

Honig, Bonnie, *Emergency Politics: Paradox, Law, Democracy* (Princeton University Press, 2009).

'The Miracle of Metaphor: Rethinking the State of Exception with Rosenzweig and Schmitt' (2007) 37:2–3 *Diacritics* 78–102.

Hope, David, 'Torture' (2004) 53 *International and Comparative Law Quarterly* 807–832.

Horst, Maja and Alan Irwin, 'Nations at Ease with Radical Knowledge: On Consensus, Consensusing and False Consensus' (2010) 10 *Social Studies of Science* 105–126.

Horton, Scott, 'Legal Ethics and the War on Terror: The Role of the Government Lawyer - Ethics Lawyers and the Torture Memoranda' (2005) 99 *American Society of International Law Proceedings* 301–306.

Hughes, Susan and Alix Henley, *Dealing with Death in Hospital: Procedures for Managers and Staff* (London: King Edward's Hospital Fund for London, 1990).

Hulme, Mike, 'Problems with Making and Governing Global Kinds of Knowledge' (2010) 20 *Global Environmental Change* 558–564.

Hulme, Mike and Martin Mahony, 'Climate Change: What Do We Know About the IPCC?' (2010) 34 *Progress in Physical Geography* 705–718.

Human Rights Watch, 'By the Numbers: Findings of the Detainee Abuse and Accountability Project' (2006) 18 *Human Rights Watch* no. 2(G), hrw.org/reports/2006/ct0406/ (accessed 17 September 2012).

'"No Blood, No Foul": Soldiers' Accounts of Detainee Abuse in Iraq' (2006) 18 *Human Rights Watch* no. 3(G), www.hrw.org/reports/2006/us0706/ (accessed 17 September 2012).

Hunt, Jane and Simon Shackley, 'Reconceiving Science and Policy: Academic, Fiducial and Bureaucratic Knowledge' (1999) 37 *Minerva* 141–164.

Hussain, Nasser, *The Jurisprudence of Emergency: Colonialism and the Rule of Law* (Ann Arbor: University of Michigan Press, 2006).

Imburgia, Joseph S., 'Space Debris and Its Threat to National Security: A Proposal for a Binding International Agreement to Clean up the Junk' (2011) 44 *Vanderbilt Journal of Transnational Law* 589–641.

Intergovernmental Panel on Climate Change (IPCC), *Climate Change 2007: Mitigation of Climate Change: Contribution of Working Group III to the Fourth Assessment Report of the Intergovernmental Panel on Climate Change* eds.

Bert Metz, Ogunlade Davidson, Peter Bosch, Rutu Dave and Leo Meyer, (Cambridge and New York: Cambridge University Press, 2007).

Climate Change 2007: Synthesis Report. Contribution of Working Groups I, II and III to the Fourth Assessment Report of the Intergovernmental Panel on Climate Change (core writing team and eds. Rajendra K. Pachauri and Andy Reisinger, Geneva: IPCC, 2007).

International Committee of the Red Cross, 'Guantanamo Bay: Overview of the ICRC's Work for Internees', 30 January 2004 Operational Update, www.icrc.org/eng/resources/documents/misc/5qrc5v.htm (accessed 17 September 2012).

'ICRC Report on the Treatment of Fourteen "High Value Detainees" in CIA Custody', Regional Delegation for the United States and Canada, Washington, 14 February 2007, WAS 07/76, www.nybooks.com/icrc-report.pdf (accessed 17 September 2012).

'Interpretive Guidance on the Notion of Direct Participation in Hostilities under International Humanitarian Law' (2008) 90 *International Review of the Red Cross* 991–1047, www.icrc.org/eng/assets/files/other/irrc-872-reports-documents.pdf (accessed 17 September 2012).

'Persons Detained by the US in Relation to Armed Conflict and the Fight Against Terrorism – the Role of the ICRC', 9 January 2012, www.icrc.org/eng/resources/documents/misc/united-states-detention.htm (accessed 17 September 2012).

'Report of the International Committee of the Red Cross (ICRC) on the Treatment by the Coalition Forces of Prisoners of War and Other Protected Persons by the Geneva Conventions in Iraq During Arrest, Internment and Interrogation', February 2004, www.globalsecurity.org/military/library/report/2004/icrc_report_iraq_feb2004.pdf (accessed 17 September 2012).

International Court of Justice, 'Advisory Opinion of 21 June 1971: Legal Consequences for States of the Continued Presence of South Africa in Namibia (South West Africa) Notwithstanding Security Council Resolution 276' (1970) *International Court of Justice Reports* 16–345, www.icj-cij.org/docket/files/53/5595.pdf (accessed 17 September 2012).

'Advisory Opinion of 22 July 2010: Accordance with International Law of the Unilateral Declaration of Independence in Respect of Kosovo', 22 July 2010, General List no. 141, www.icj-cij.org/docket/files/141/15987.pdf (accessed 17 September 2012).

'Advisory Opinion of 8 July 1996: Legality of the Threat or Use of Nuclear Weapons' (1996) *International Court of Justice Reports* 226–593, www.icj-cij.org/docket/files/95/7495.pdf (accessed 17 September 2012).

International Law Commission (ILC), *The International Law Commission's Articles on Responsibility of States for Internationally Wrongful Acts: Introduction, Text and Commentaries* (ed. James Crawford, Cambridge University Press, 2002).

Jackson, Aaron R., 'The White House Counsel Torture Memo: The Final Product of a Flawed System' (2006) 42 *California Western Law Review* 149–182.

Jackson, Dick, 'Introductory Note to Executive Order 13567: Periodic Review of Individuals Detained at Guantánamo Bay Naval Station Pursuant to the Authorization for Use of Military Force and Accompanying Presidential Fact Sheet: New Actions on Guantánamo and Detainee Policy' (2011) 50 *International Legal Materials* 928–936.

James, Louis C., 'Effects of the Autonomy of the Parties on Conflict of Laws Contracts' (1959) 36 *Chicago-Kent Law Review* 34–59.

Jasanoff, Sheila, *Science at the Bar: Law, Science, and Technology in America* (Cambridge, MA and London: Harvard University Press, 1995).

(ed.), *States of Knowledge: The Co-Production of Science and the Social Order* (London: Routledge, 2004).

Jensen, Michael C. and William H. Meckling, 'The Theory of the Firm: Managerial Behavior, Agency Costs, and Ownership Structure' (1976) 3 *Journal of Financial Economics* 305–360.

Jinks, Derek and David Sloss, 'Is the President Bound by the Geneva Conventions?' (2004) 90 *Cornell Law Review* 97–202.

Joerges, Christian and David M. Trubek (eds.), *Critical Legal Thought: An American-German Debate* (Baden Baden: Nomos Verlagsgesellschaft, 1989).

Johns, Fleur, 'Address: On Writing Dangerously' (2004) 26 *Sydney Law Review* 473–480.

'Financing as Governance' (2011) 31 *Oxford Journal of Legal Studies* 391–415.

'Guantanamo Bay and the Annihilation of the Exception' (2005) 16 *European Journal of International Law* 613–635.

'Performing Party Autonomy' (2008) 71 *Law & Contemporary Problems* 243–271.

'Performing Power: The Deal, Corporate Rule, and the Constitution of Global Legal Order' (2007) 34 *Journal of Law and Society* 116–138 reprinted in Stewart Motha (ed.), *Democracy's Empire: Sovereignty, Law, and Violence* (Oxford: Blackwell, 2007), pp. 116–138.

Johns, Fleur, Richard Joyce and Sundhya Pahuja, *Events: The Force of International Law* (London: Routledge-Cavendish, 2011).

Johnson, Carrie, 'Judge Invited to Testify about Role in Interrogation Memos', *The Washington Post*, 30 April 2009, A07.

Jolls, Christine, Cass R. Sunstein and Richard Thaler, 'A Behavioral Approach to Law and Economics' (1998) 50 *Stanford Law Review* 1593–1608.

Jones, LTG Anthony R. and MG George R. Fay, 'Article 15–6 Investigation of the Abu Ghraib Prison and 205th Military Intelligence Brigade', 23 August 2004, http://slate.com/features/whatistorture/pdfs/FayJonesReport (accessed 17 September 2012).

Juenger, Friedrich K., 'American Conflicts Scholarship and the New Law Merchant' (1995) 28 *Vanderbilt Journal of Transnational Law* 487–502.

'The Lex Mercatoria and Private International Law' (2000) 60 *Louisiana Law Review* 1133–1150.

Kahan, Marcel and Michael Klausner, 'Standardization and Innovation in Corporate Contracting (or "The Economics of Boilerplate")' (1997) 83 *Virginia Law Review* 713–770.

Kalis, Martin A., 'Management of Dead Bodies After Disasters: A Field Manual for First Responders' (2006) 3:3 *Journal of Homeland Security and Emergency Management* Article 9, 1–3.

Kalyvas, Andreas, *Democracy and the Politics of the Extraordinary: Max Weber, Carl Schmitt, and Hannah Arendt* (Cambridge University Press, 2008).

Kaplan, Amy, 'Where is Guantánamo?' (2005) 57 *American Quarterly* 831–858.

Kennedy, David, 'Challenging Expert Rule: The Politics of Global Governance' (2005) 27 *Sydney Law Review* 5–28.

'Comparative Approaches to the Theory of International Law: Remarks' (1986) 80 *American Society of International Law Proceedings* 161–169.

The Dark Sides of Virtue: Reassessing International Humanitarianism (Princeton and Oxford: Princeton University Press, 2004).

'The Disciplines of International Law and Policy' (1999) 12 *Leiden Journal of International Law* 9–133.

'International Law in the Nineteenth Century: History of an Illusion' (1995) 65 *Nordic Journal of International Law* 385–420.

'The International Style in Postwar Law and Policy' (1994) *Utah Law Review* 7–104.

'The Last Treatise (Project and Person)' (2006) 7 *German Law Journal* 982–992.

'The Move to Institutions' (1987) 8 *Cardozo Law Review* 841–988.

'New Approaches to Comparative Law: Comparativism and International Governance' (1997) 2 *Utah Law Review* 545–638.

'A New Stream of International Law Scholarship' (1988) 7 *Wisconsin International Law Journal* 1–49.

'A New World Order: Yesterday, Today, and Tomorrow' (1994) 4 *Transnational Law and Contemporary Problems* 329–376.

'One, Two, Three, Many Legal Orders: Legal Pluralism and the Cosmopolitan Dream' (2007) 31 *New York University Review of Law & Social Change* 641–660.

'When Renewal Repeats: Thinking Against the Box' (2000) 32 *New York University Journal of International Law and Politics* 335–500.

'The Sources of International Law' (1987) 2 *American University Journal of International Law and Politics* 1–96.

'Theses About International Discourse' (1980) 23 *German Yearbook of International Law* 353–390.

'Tom Franck and the Manhattan School' (2003) 35 *New York University Journal of International Law and Politics* 397–435.

'The Turn to Interpretation' (1985) 58 *Southern California Law Review* 251–276.

Of War and Law (Princeton University Press, 2006).

Kennedy, Duncan, *A Critique of Adjudication (Fin de Siècle)* (Cambridge, MA: Harvard University Press, 1998).

'The Disenchantment of Logically Formal Legal Rationality, or Max Weber's Sociology in the Genealogy of the Contemporary Mode of Western Legal Thought' (2004) 55 *Hastings Law Journal* 1031–1076.

'Freedom and Constraint in Adjudication: A Critical Phenomenology' (1986) 36 *Journal of Legal Education* 518–562.

The Rise and Fall of Classical Legal Thought (Washington, DC: Beard Books, 2006).
Kent, Randolph C., 'International Humanitarian Crises: Two Decades Before and Two Decades Beyond' (2004) 80 *International Affairs* 851–869.
'Reflecting Upon a Decade of Disasters: The Evolving Response of the International Community' (1983) 59 *International Affairs* 693–711.
Kessler, Friedrich, 'Contracts of Adhesion – Some Thoughts About Freedom of Contract' (1943) 43 *Columbia Law Review* 629–642.
Kilinski, Jennifer, 'International Climate Change Liability: A Myth or a Reality?' (2009) 18 *Journal of Transnational Law & Policy* 377–418.
Klabbers, Jan, *An Introduction to International Institutional Law* (Cambridge University Press, 2002).
'The Relative Autonomy of International Law or The Forgotten Politics of Interdisciplinarity' (2005) 1 *Journal of International Law & International Relations* 35–48.
Klausner, Michael, 'Corporations, Corporate Law, and Networks of Contracts' (1995) 81 *Virginia Law Review* 757–852.
Knop, Karen, 'Here and There: International Law in Domestic Courts?' (2000) 32 *New York University Journal of International Law and Politics* 501–535.
Koh, Harold Hongju, 'On American Exceptionalism' (2003) 55 *Stanford Law Review* 1479–1528.
'America's Offshore Refugee Camps' (1994) 29 *University of Richmond Law Review* 139–174.
'The Case Against Military Commissions' (2002) 96 *American Journal of International Law* 337–344.
'The Future of Lou Henkin's Human Rights Movement' (2007) 38 *Columbia Human Rights Law Review* 487–498.
'Review Essay: Why Do Nations Obey International Law?' (1997) 106 *Yale Law Journal* 2599–2660.
'A World Without Torture' (2005) 43 *Columbia Journal of Transnational Law* 641–662.
Koskenniemi, Martti, *From Apology to Utopia: The Structure of International Legal Argument*, Reissue with Epilogue (Cambridge University Press, 2005).
'Constitutionalism as Mindset: Reflections on Kantian Themes About International Law and Globalization' (2007) 8 *Theoretical Inquiries in Law* 9–36.
'The Fate of Public International Law: Between Technique and Polis' (2007) 70 *Modern Law Review* 1–30.
The Gentle Civilizer of Nations: The Rise and Fall of International Law 1870–1960 (Cambridge University Press, 2001).
(ed.), *International Law* (Aldershot: Dartmouth, 1992).
'International Law: Constitutionalism, Managerialism and the Ethos of Legal Education' (2007) 1 *European Journal of Legal Studies* 1–18.
'International Law and Hegemony: A Reconfiguration' (2004) 17 *Cambridge Review of International Affairs* 197–218.
'The Politics of International Law – 20 Years Later' (2009) 20 *European Journal of International Law* 7–19.

Koskenniemi, Martti (ed.), *Sources of International Law* (Aldershot: Dartmouth, 2000).

Kreitner, Roy, 'Speculations on Contract, or How Contract Law Stopped Worrying and Learned to Love Risk' (2000) 100 *Columbia Law Review* 1096–1138.

Lakoff, Andrew, 'Preparing for the Next Emergency' (2007) 19 *Public Culture* 247–271.

Lamirande, Heide R., 'From Sea to Carbon Cesspool: Preventing the World's Marine Ecosystems from Falling Victim to Ocean Acidification' (2011) 34 *Suffolk Transnational Law Review* 183–217.

Lando, Ole, 'The Lex Mercatoria in International Commercial Arbitration' (1985) 34 *International and Comparative Law Quarterly* 747–768.

Larson, Jane E., 'Informality, Illegality, and Inequality' (2002) 20 *Yale Law & Policy Review* 137–182.

Latour, Bruno, *The Making of Law: An Ethnography of the Conseil d'État* (trans. Marina Brilman and Alain Pottage, Cambridge and Malden: Polity Press, 2010).

We Have Never Been Modern (trans. Catherine Porter, Cambridge, MA: Harvard University Press, 1993).

Latour, Bruno and Steve Woolgar, *Laboratory Life: The Construction of Scientific Facts* (Princeton University Press, 1986).

Lawlor, Leonard, 'Un Ecart Infime (Part I): Foucault's Critique of the Concept of Lived-Experience (Vécu)' (2005) 35 *Research in Phenomenology* 11–28.

Lazar, Nomi Claire, *States of Emergency in Liberal Democracies* (Cambridge University Press, 2009).

Lederman, Lawrence, *Tombstones: A Lawyer's Tales from the Takeover Decades* (New York: Farrar, Straus and Giroux, 1992).

Leigh, David, James Ball, Ian Cobain and Jason Burke, 'Guantánamo Leaks Lift Lid on World's Most Controversial Prison', *Guardian*, 25 April 2011, www.guardian.co.uk/world/2011/apr/25/guantanamo-files-lift-lid-prison (accessed 17 September 2012).

Leopold, Jason, 'CIA Interrogation Tapes Predated Torture Memo', *The Public Record*, 11 April 2009, pubrecord.org/torture/264/cia-interrogation-tapes-predated-torture-memo (accessed 17 September 2012).

Lerner, Craig S., 'Calling a Truce in the Culture Wars: From Enron to the CIA' (2006) 17 *Stanford Law and Policy Review* 277–302.

Lessig, Lawrence, 'The Law of the Horse: What Cyberlaw Might Teach' (1999) 113 *Harvard Law Review* 501–549.

Lettieri, Emanuele, Cristina Masella and Giovanni Radaelli, 'Disaster Management: Findings From a Systematic Review' (2009) 18 *Disaster Prevention and Management* 117–136.

Levinson, Sanford (ed.) *Torture: A Collection* (Oxford and New York: Oxford University Press 2004).

Lewis, Neil A., 'Detainees from the Afghan War Remain in a Legal Limbo in Cuba', *The New York Times*, 24 April 2003, www.nytimes.com/2003/04/24/us/aftereffects-prisoners-detainees-afgha

n-war-remain-legal-limbo-cuba.html?pagewanted=allandsrc=pm (accessed 17 September 2012).

Lewis, William S., 'The Under-Theorization of Overdetermination in *Hegemony and Socialist Strategy*' (2005) 4:2 *Borderlands E-Journal*, www.borderlands.net.au/vol4no2_2005/lewis_overdetermination.htm (accessed 17 September 2012).

Likosky, Michael (ed.), *Transnational Legal Processes: Globalisation and Power Disparities* (London: Butterworths, 2002).

Lilley, Ian (Coordinator), *Early Human Expansion and Innovation in the Pacific: ICOMOS Thematic Study* (Paris: International Council on Monuments and Sites, 2010), www.international.icomos.org/world_heritage/TS_Pacific_20101210_final.pdf (accessed 17 September 2012).

Lin, Joelin and Charlotte Streck, 'Mobilising Finance for Climate Change Mitigation: Private Sector Involvement in International Carbon Finance Mechanisms' (2009) 10 *Melbourne Journal of International Law* 70–101.

Lindahl, Hans, 'Border Crossings by Immigrants: Legality, Illegality, and Alegality' (2008) 14 *Res Publica* 117–135.

Lipman, Jana K., *Guantánamo: A Working-Class History Between Empire and Revolution* (Berkeley and Los Angeles: University of California Press, 2008).

Lipshaw, Jeffrey M., 'Contingency and Contracts: A Philosophy of Complex Business Transactions' (2005) 54 *DePaul Law Review* 1077–1146.

Llewellyn, Karl N., 'Some Realism About Realism – Responding to Dean Pound' (1931) 44 *Harvard Law Review* 1222–1264.

Lopez, Marisa, 'Professional Responsibility: Tortured Independence in the Office of Legal Counsel' (2005) 57 *Florida Law Review* 685–716.

Lowenfeld, Andreas F., 'International Litigation and the Quest for Reasonableness' (1994) 245 *Recueil des Cours* 9–320.

Luban, David, 'Conscientious Lawyers for Conscientious Lawbreakers' (1991) 52 *University of Pittsburgh Law Review* 793–814.

'Lawfare and Legal Ethics in Guantánamo' (2008) 60 *Stanford Law Review* 1981–2026.

Luck, Edward C., Anne-Marie Slaughter and Ian Hurd, 'Stayin' Alive – The Rumors of the UN's Death Have Been Exaggerated *Response*' (2003) 82 *Foreign Affairs* 4, 201–205.

Lukács, Georg, *History and Class Consciousness* (trans. Rodney Livingstone, London: Merlin Press, 1971).

Lynch, Colman, 'Indonesia's Use of Capital Punishment for Drug-Trafficking Crimes: Legal Obligations, Extra-legal Factors, and the Bali Nine Case' (2009) 40 *Columbia Human Rights Law Review* 523–594.

Macaulay, Stewart, 'Elegant Models, Empirical Pictures, and the Complexities of Contract' (1977) 11 *Law and Society Review* 507–528.

MacKenzie, Donald, 'Making Things the Same: Gas, Emission Rights and the Politics of Carbon Markets' (2009) 34 *Accounting, Organizations and Society* 440–455.

Maclean, Janet, 'Divergent Legal Conceptions of the State: Implications for Global Administrative Law' (2005) 68:3/4 *Law and Contemporary Problems* 167–188.

Malloy, Michael P., 'International Project Finance: Risk Analysis and Regulatory Concerns' (2004) 18 *Transnational Lawyer* 89–106.

Maniruzzaman, Abul F. M., 'The Lex Mercatoria and International Contracts: A Challenge for International Commercial Arbitration?' (1999) 14 *American University International Law Review* 657–734.

Mansfield Jr., Harvey C., *Taming the Prince: The Ambivalence of Modern Executive Power* (New York: The Free Press, 1989).

Manyena, Siambabala Bernard, 'The Concept of Resilience Revisited' (2006) 30 *Disasters* 433–450.

Marcus, George E., *Ethnography Through Thick and Thin* (Princeton University Press, 1998).

Marcuse, Herbert, *One-Dimensional Man* (Boston: Beacon Press, 1964).

Margulies, Peter, 'Putting Guantanamo in the Rear-View Mirror: The Political Economy of Detention Policy' (2010) 32 *Western New England Law Review* 339–372.

'When to Push the Envelope: Legal Ethics, the Rule of Law, and National Security Strategy' (2007) 30 *Fordham International Law Journal* 642–72.

Marks, Susan, 'Four Human Rights Myths', Remarks at Human Rights: Old Dichotomies Revisited Conference, Sydney Law School, 25–26 November 2011; revised version to be published in David Kinley, Wojciech Sadurski and Kevin Walton (eds.), *Human Rights: Old Problems, New Possibilities* (Cheltenham: Edward Elgar Publishing, forthcoming).

Maton, John and Carolyn Maton, 'Independence Under Fire: Extra-Legal Pressures and Coalition Building in WTO Dispute Settlement' (2007) 10 *Journal of International Economic Law* 317–334.

Mayerfeld, Jamie, 'Playing by Our Own Rules: How US Marginalization of International Human Rights Law Led to Torture' (2007) 20 *Harvard Human Rights Journal* 89–140.

Mazzetti, Mark and Scott Shane, 'Interrogation Memos Detail Harsh Tactics by the CIA', *The New York Times*, 16 April 2009, www.nytimes.com/2009/04/17/us/politics/17detain.html?_r=1> (accessed 17 September 2012).

McBarnet, Doreen, 'Transnational Transactions: Legal Work, Cross-Border Commerce and Global Regulation', in Michael Likosky (ed.), *Transnational Legal Processes: Globalisation and Power Disparities* (London: Butterworths, 2002), pp. 98–133.

McCallum, Daniel F., 'Why GTMO?', National Security Strategy Process Research Paper, National War College Report, National Defense University, 2003, www.dtic.mil/cgi-bin/GetTRDoc?AD=ADA442074%27andLocation=U2anddoc=GetTRDoc.pdf (accessed 17 September 2012).

McCormick, John P., *Carl Schmitt's Critique of Liberalism: Against Politics as Technology* (Cambridge University Press, 1999).

'The Dilemmas of Dictatorship: Carl Schmitt and Constitutional Emergency Powers' (1997) 10 *Canadian Journal of Law and Jurisprudence* 163–188.

McDonald, Avril, 'The Year in Review' (2005) 8 *Yearbook of International Humanitarian Law* 211–264.

McFarland, Ian A., David S. Fergusson, Karen Kilby and Ian R. Torrance (eds.), *The Cambridge Dictionary of Christian Theology* (Cambridge University Press, 2011).

McInerney-Lankford, Siobhán, Mac Darrow and Lavanya Rajamani, *Human Rights and Climate Change: A Review of the International Legal Dimensions* (Washington, DC: The World Bank, 2011).

McMahan, Jeff, *Killing in War* (Oxford University Press, 2009).

McVeigh, Shaun (ed.), *Jurisprudence of Jurisdiction* (Abingdon and New York: Routledge-Cavendish, 2007).

Meckled-García, Saladin and Başak Çali (eds.), *The Legalization of Human Rights: Multidisciplinary Perspectives on Human Rights and Human Rights Law* (Oxford: Routledge, 2006).

Mégret, Frédéric, '"War?" Legal Semantics and the Move to Violence' (2002) 13 *European Journal of International Law* 361–399.

Merry, Sally Engle, 'Legal Pluralism' (1988) 22 *Law and Society Review* 869–896.

'New Legal Realism and the Ethnography of Transnational Law' (2006) 31 *Law and Social Inquiry* 975–995.

Michaels, Ralf, 'EU Law as Private International Law? Reconceptualising the Country-of-Origin Principle as Vested-Rights Theory' (2006) 2 *Journal of Private International Law* 195–242.

'The Re-state-ment of Non-State Law: The State, Choice of Law, and the Challenge from Global Legal Pluralism' (2005) 51 *Wayne Law Review* 1209–1260.

Miller, Clark A., 'Democratization, International Knowledge Institutions, and Global Governance' (2007) 20 *Governance* 325–357.

'Hybrid Management: Boundary Organizations, Science Policy, and Environmental Governance in the Climate Regime' (2001) 26 *Science Technology Human Values* 478–500.

Miller, Clark A. and Paul N. Edwards (eds.), *Changing the Atmosphere: Expert Knowledge and Environmental Governance* (Cambridge, MA: MIT Press, 2001).

Miller, Ruth A., *Law in Crisis: The Ecstatic Subject of Natural Disaster* (Stanford University Press, 2009).

Minow, Martha, 'Breaking the Law: Lawyers and Clients in Struggles for Social Change' (1991) 52 *University of Pittsburgh Law Review* 723–752.

Mintz, John, 'Chaplain Clashed with Officials over Guantánamo Detainees', *The Washington Post*, 24 October 2003, www.community.seattletimes.nwsource.com/archive/?date=20031024&slug=chaplain24 (accessed 17 September 2012).

Mitchell, Andrew D., 'Does One Illegality Merit Another? The Law of Belligerent Reprisals in International Law' (2001) 170 *Military Law Review* 155–177.

Mitchell, Timothy, 'The Work of Economics: How a Discipline Makes its World' (2005) 46 *Archives Européennes de Sociologie* 297–320.

Montague, Robert L. III, 'A Brief Study of Some of the International Legal and Political Aspects of the Guantánamo Bay Problem' (1962) 50 *Kentucky Law Review* 459–523.

Moore, Sally Falk (ed.), *Law and Anthropology: A Reader* (London: Blackwell, 2005).

Morgan, Oliver, 'Book Review: Management of Dead Bodies in Disaster Situations' (2005) 29 *Disasters* 288–289.

Morgan, Oliver, Morris Tidball-Binz and Dana Van Alphen (eds.), *Management of Dead Bodies After Disasters: A Field Manual for First Responders* (Washington, DC: Pan American Health Organization, World Health Organization, International Committee of the Red Cross, 2006).

Mouffe, Chantal, 'Carl Schmitt and the Paradox of Liberal Democracy' (1997) 10 *Canadian Journal of Law and Jurisprudence* 21–34.

Mundis, Daryl A., 'The Use of Military Commissions to Prosecute Individuals Accused of Terrorist Acts' (2002) 96 *American Journal of International Law* 320–328.

Nariman, Fali S., 'Courts and Arbitrators: Paradigms of Arbitral Autonomy' (1997) 15 *Boston University International Law Journal* 185–190.

Neuman, Gerald L., 'Anomalous Zones' (1996) 48 *Stanford Law Review* 1197–1234.

'Closing the Guantánamo Loophole' (2004) 50 *Loyola Law Review* 1–66.

Neumayer, Eric and Thomas Plümper, 'The Gendered Nature of Natural Disasters: The Impact of Catastrophic Events on the Gender Gap in Life Expectancy, 1981–2002' (2007) 97 *Annals of the Association of American Geographers* 551–566.

Never, Babette, 'Regional Power Shifts and Climate Knowledge Systems in (Global) Climate Governance' (2010) 2 *Goettingen Journal of International Law* 311–333.

The New York Times, 'The Guantánamo Docket', projects.nytimes.com/guantanamo (ongoing, accessed 17 September 2012).

'The Prison that Won't Go Away', 8 March 2011, Editorial, www.nytimes.com/2011/03/09/opinion/09wed2.html (accessed 17 September 2012).

Nietzsche, Friedrich, *Basic Writings of Nietzsche* (trans. Walter Arnold Kaufmann, New York: The Modern Library, Random House, 2000).

The Gay Science: With a Prelude in German Rhymes and an Appendix of Songs (trans. Josefine Nauckhoff and Adrian Del Caro, New York: Cambridge University Press, 2001).

Untimely Meditations (trans. Reginald John Hollingdale, Cambridge and New York: Cambridge University Press, 1983).

Writings from the Late Notebooks (trans. Kate Sturge, ed. Rudiger Bittner, Cambridge University Press, 2003).

Nowak, Manfred, 'What Practices Constitute Torture? US and UN Standards' (2006) 28 *Human Rights Quarterly* 809–841.

Nygh, Peter E., *Autonomy in International Contracts* (Oxford and New York: Clarendon Press and Oxford University Press, 1999).

O'Hara, Erin A., 'Opting Out of Regulation: A Public Choice Analysis of Contractual Choice of Law' (2000) 53 *Vanderbilt Law Review* 1549–1604.

O'Hara, Erin A. and Larry E. Ribstein, 'From Politics to Efficiency in Choice of Law' (2000) 67 *University of Chicago Law Review* 1151–1232.

O'Leary, Timothy, 'Foucault, Experience, Literature' (2008) 5 *Foucault Studies* 5–25.

Foucault and Fiction: The Experience Book (London and New York: Continuum, 2009).

O'Malley, Pat, 'Resilient Subjects: Uncertainty, Warfare and Liberalism' (2010) 39 *Economy and Society* 488–509.

O'Neill, John, 'The Disciplinary Society: From Weber to Foucault' (1986) 37 *British Journal of Sociology* 42–60.

Ong, Aihwa and Stephen J. Collier (eds.), *Global Assemblages: Technology, Politics, and Ethics as Anthropological Problems* (Oxford: Blackwell, 2005).

O'Reilly, Karen, *Key Concepts in Ethnography* (London: Sage, 2009).

Orford, Anne, 'Muscular Humanitarianism: Reading the Narratives of the New Interventionism' (1999) 10 *European Journal of International Law* 679–711.

Osofsky, Hari M., 'Climate Change Litigation as Pluralist Legal Dialogue?' (2007) 43A *Stanford Journal of International Law* 181–238.

Owen, David, *Maturity and Modernity: Nietzsche, Weber, Foucault and the Ambivalence of Reason* (London: Routledge, 1994).

Pan American Health Organization (PAHO), *Basic Documents of the Pan American Health Organization*, Eighteenth Edition (Washington, DC: PAHO, 2012).

Parry, John T., *Understanding Torture: Law, Violence and Political Identity* (Ann Arbor: University of Michigan Press, 2010).

Paust, Jordan J., *Beyond the Law: The Bush Administration's Unlawful Responses in the 'War' on Terror* (New York: Cambridge University Press, 2007).

'Post-9/11 Overreaction and Fallacies Regarding War and Defense, Guantánamo, The Status of Persons, Treatment, Judicial Review of Detention, and Due Process in Military Commissions' (2004) 79 *Notre Dame Law Review* 1335–1364.

'War and Enemy Status After 9/11: Attacks on the Laws of War' (2003) 28 *Yale Journal of International Law* 325–336.

Peel, Jacqueline, 'Climate Change Law: The Emergence of a New Legal Discipline' (2008) 32 *Melbourne University Law Review* 922–979.

Science and Risk Regulation in International Law (Cambridge University Press, 2010).

Perez, Oren, 'Purity Lost: The Paradoxical Face of the New Transnational Legal Body' (2007) 33 *Brooklyn Journal of International Law* 1–58.

Perrigo, Sarah and Jim Whitman (eds.), *The Geneva Conventions Under Assault* (London and New York: Pluto Press, 2010).

Physicians for Human Rights, 'Break Them Down: Systematic Use of Psychological Torture by US Forces' (authored by Gretchen Borchelt, Jonathan Fine and Christian Pross, Cambridge, MA: Physicians for Human Rights, 2005), www.williambowles.info/iraq/2005/psych_torture-1.pdf (accessed 17 September 2012).

Pierrehumbert, R. T., 'Climate Change: A Catastrophe in Slow Motion' (2006) 6 *Chicago Journal of International Law* 573–596.

Pilkington, Ed, 'Obama Lifts Suspension on Military Terror Trials at Guantánamo Bay', *Guardian*, 7 March 2011, www.guardian.co.uk/world/2011/mar/07/guantanamo-military-terrorism-trials-resume (accessed 17 September 2012).

Pillard, Cornelia, 'Unitariness and Myopia: The Executive Branch, Legal Process, and Torture' (2006) 81 *Indiana Law Journal* 1297–1312.

Porth, Jacquelyn S., 'Pentagon Creates New Policy Office to Review Detainee Issues', *Washington File*, Bureau of International Information Programs, U.S. Department of State, 16 July 2004, www.iwar.org.uk/news-archive/2004/070-16.htm (accessed 17 September 2012).

Posner, Richard A., *Economic Analysis of Law*, Second Edition (Boston and Toronto: Little Brown & Co., 1977).

Pottage, Alain, 'Book Review: Foucault's Law by Ben Golder and Peter Fitzpatrick' (2011) 74 *Modern Law Review* 159–168.

Project Finance Magazine, 'Latin American Oil and Gas Deal of the Year 2011: OSX 2', 1 March 2012, www.projectfinancemagazine.com/Article/2985460/Latin-American-Oil-and-Gas-Deal-of-the-Year-2011-OSX-2.html (accessed 17 September 2012).

Purdy, Margaret and Leanne Smythe, 'From Obscurity to Action: Why Canada Must Tackle the Security Dimensions of Climate Change' (2010) 65 *International Journal* 411–433.

Quarantelli, E. L. (ed.), *What is a Disaster? A Dozen Perspectives on the Question* (London and New York: Routledge, 1998).

Rabel, Ernest, *The Conflict of Laws: A Comparative Study*, Second Edition (Michigan: Michigan Legal Studies, 1960).

Rajagopal, Balakrishnan, *International Law from Below: Development, Social Movements and Third World Resistance* (Cambridge University Press, 2003).

Ramraj, Victor V. (ed.), *Emergencies and the Limits of Legality* (Cambridge University Press, 2008).

Raustiala, Kal, 'The Geography of Justice' (2005) 73 *Fordham Law Review* 2501–2560.

Raustiala, Kal and Natalie L. Bridgeman, 'Nonstate Actors in the Global Climate Regime' UCLA School of Law Research Paper No. 07-29, http://ssrn.com/abstract=1028603 (accessed 17 September 2012).

Reid-Henry, Simon, 'Exceptional Sovereignty? Guantánamo Bay and the Re-colonial Present' (2007) 39 *Antipode* 627–648.

Ribstein, Larry E., 'Choosing Law by Contract' (1993) 18 *Journal of Corporation Law* 245–300.

Riles, Annelise, 'The Anti-Network: Private Global Governance, Legal Knowledge, and the Legitimacy of the State' (2008) 56 *American Journal of Comparative Law* 605–630.

Collateral Knowledge: Legal Reasoning in the Global Financial Markets (Chicago and London: University of Chicago Press, 2011).

The Network Inside Out (Ann Arbor: University of Michigan Press, 2000).

'A New Agenda for the Cultural Study of Law: Taking on the Technicalities' (2005) 53 *Buffalo Law Review* 973–1034.

'The View From the International Plane: Perspective and Scale in the Architecture of Colonial International Law' (1995) 6 *Law and Critique* 39–54.

Roig-Franzia, Manuel, Mary-Beth Sheridan and Michael E. Ruane, 'Anxiety Mounts in Lawless Haiti', *The Washington Post*, 18 January 2010, A01.

Rosen, Jeffrey, 'The Nation; The Struggle Over the Torture Memos', *The New York Times*, 15 August 2004, www.nytimes.com/2004/08/15/weekinreview/15rose.html (accessed 22 February 2012).

Rosenberg, Carol, 'New Chief Brings Guantánamo Up to Date', *Miami Herald*, 25 October 2003, A15.

Ross, James, 'Black Letter Abuse: The US legal Response to Torture Since 9/11' (2007) 89 *International Review of the Red Cross* 561–590.

Rotunda, Kyndra, 'Halting Military Trials in Guantánamo Bay: Can the President Call a Time-Out?' (2010) 19 *Michigan State University College of Law Journal of International Law* 95–104.

Saar, Erik and Viveca Novack, *Inside the Wire: A Military Intelligence Soldier's Eyewitness Account of Life at Guantánamo* (New York: Penguin Press, 2005).

Sachs, Stephen E., 'From St. Ives to Cyberspace: The Modern Distortion of the Medieval "Law Merchant"' (2006) 21 *American University International Law Review* 685–812.

Sadat, Leila Nadya, 'Extraordinary Rendition, Torture and Other Nightmares from the War on Terror' (2007) 75 *George Washington Law Review* 1200–1248.

Sahni, Isher-Paul, 'Max Weber's Sociology of Law: Judge as Mediator' (2009) 9 *Journal of Classical Sociology* 209–233.

Salacuse, Jeswald W., 'Renegotiating International Business Transactions: The Continuing Struggle of Life Against Form' (2001) 35 *International Lawyer* 1507–1542.

Samuels, Warren J., 'The Economy as a System of Power and its Legal Bases: The Legal Economics of Robert Lee Hale' (1973) 27 *University of Miami Law Review* 261–371.

Sands, Philippe, 'Torture Team: The Responsibility of Lawyers for Abusive Interrogation' (2008) 9 *Melbourne Journal of International Law* 365–381.

Torture Team: Rumsfeld's Memo and the Betrayal of American Values (Hampshire: Palgrave Macmillan, 2008).

Sarat, Austin and Thomas R. Kearns (eds.), *Law's Violence* (Ann Arbor: University of Michigan Press, 1992).

Sassòli, Marco, 'Is There a Status of "Unlawful Combatant"?' (2006) 80 *International Law Studies* 57–68.

Saul, Ben, *Defining Terrorism in International Law* (Oxford University Press 2006).

Savvides, Sawakis, 'Risk Analysis in Investment Appraisal' (1994) 9 *Project Appraisal Journal* 3–18.

Scarry, Elaine, *The Body in Pain: The Making and Unmaking of the World* (Oxford and New York: Oxford University Press, 1987).

Scharf, Michael P., 'International Law and the Torture Memos' (2009) 42 *Case Western Reserve Journal of International Law* 321–358.

Scharf, Michael P. and Paul R. Williams, *Shaping Foreign Policy in Times of Crisis: The Role of International Law and the State Department Legal Adviser* (Cambridge University Press, 2010).

Schauer, Frederick, 'Exceptions' (1991) 58 *University of Chicago Law Review* 871–900.

Scheuerman, William, 'American Kingship? Monarchical Origins of Modern Presidentialism' (2005) 37 *Polity* 24–53.

Between the Norm and the Exception: The Frankfurt School and the Rule of Law (Cambridge, MA: MIT Press, 1997).

'Globalization, Exceptional Powers, and the Erosion of Liberal Democracy' (1999) 93 *Radical Philosophy* 14–23.

Schmitt, Carl, *The Concept of the Political*, Expanded Edition (trans. George Schwab, John P. McCormick and J. Harvey Lomax, Chicago and London: University of Chicago Press, 1996).

Political Theology: Four Chapters on the Concept of Sovereignty (trans. George Schwab, Cambridge, MA: MIT Press, 1985).

Schmitt, Eric, 'U.S. Shifts, Giving Detainee Names to the Red Cross', *The New York Times*, 22 August 2009, A1, www.nytimes.com/2009/08/23/world/middleeast/23detain.html (accessed 17 September 2012).

Schroeder, Heike and Harriet Bulkeley, 'Global Cities and the Governance of Climate Change: What is the Role of Law in Cities?' (2009) 36 *Fordham Urban Law Journal* 313–359.

Schulte-Bockholt, Alfredo, *The Politics of Organized Crime and the Organized Crime of Politics: A Study in Criminal Power* (Lanham: Lexington Books, 2006).

Schwarcz, Steven L., 'Explaining the Value of Transactional Lawyering' (2007) 12 *Stanford Journal of Law, Business and Finance* 486–535.

Scott, Shirley V., 'Is the Crisis of Climate Change a Crisis for International Law: Is International Law too Democratic, too Capitalist and too Fearful to Cope with the Crisis of Climate Change?' (2008) 14 *Australian International Law Journal* 31–43.

Shackley, Simon, 'The Intergovernmental Panel on Climate Change: Consensual Knowledge and Global Politics' (1997) 7 *Global Environmental Change* 77–79.

Shackley, Simon and Tora Skodvin, 'IPCC Gazing and the Interpretative Social Sciences' (1995) 5 *Global Environmental Change* 175–180.

Sharp, Walter R., 'The New World Health Organization' (1947) 41 *American Journal of International Law* 509–530.

Shaw, Alison and John Robinson, 'Relevant but not Prescriptive? Science Policy Models within the IPCC' (2004) 48: Supplement *Philosophy Today* 84–95.

Shelton, Dinah (ed.), *Commitment and Compliance: The Role of Non-binding Norms in the International Legal System* (New York and Oxford: Oxford University Press, 2000).

Shinjo, Takuya, Tatsuya Morita, Mitsunori Miyashita, Kazuki Sato, Satoru Tsuneto and Yasuo Shima, 'Care for the Bodies of Deceased Cancer Inpatients in Japanese Palliative Care Units' (2010) 13 *Journal of Palliative Medicine* 27–31.

Shinn, Thelma J., 'Flannery O'Connor and the Violence of Grace' (1968) 9 *Contemporary Literature* 58–73.

Sica, Alan, *Max Weber and the New Century* (New Jersey: Transaction Publishers, 2004).

Siebenhüner, Bernd, 'The Changing Role of Nation States in International Environmental Assessments – The Case of the IPCC' (2003) 13 *Global Environmental Change* 113–123.

'How do Scientific Assessments Learn? Part 1. Conceptual Framework and Case Study of the IPCC' (2002) 5 *Global Environmental Change* 411–420.

Silberstein, Sandra, *War of Words: Language, Politics and 9/11* (London and New York: Routledge, 2002).

Simpson, Gerry, *Law, War and Crime: War Crimes Trials and the Reinvention of International Law* (Cambridge and Malden: Polity, 2007).

Singer, Joseph William, 'A Pragmatic Guide to Conflicts' (1990) 70 *Boston University Law Review* 731–820.

Smith, B. C. *Understanding Third World Politics: Theories of Political Change and Development* (Bloomington: Indiana University Press, 2003).

Smith, Clive Stafford, 'America's Legal Black Hole', *Los Angeles Times*, 5 October 2007, available at articles.latimes.com/2007/oct/05/opinion/oe-smith5 (accessed 17 September 2012).

Bad Men: Guantánamo Bay and The Secret Prisons (London: Weidenfeld & Nicolson, 2007).

Smith, D. Gordon, 'The "Branding Effect" of Contracts' (2007) 12 *Harvard Negotiation Law Review* 189–200.

Solan, Lawrence M., 'The Written Contract as Safe Harbor for Dishonest Conduct' (2001) 77 *Chicago-Kent Law Review* 87–120.

Sornarajah, M., *The International Law on Foreign Investment*, Third Edition (Cambridge University Press, 2010).

Spivak, Gayatri Chakravorty, 'Terror: A Speech After 9–11' (2004) 31:2 *Boundary 2* 81–111.

Stanford, Peter, 'Can Prof Rajendra Pachauri Really Survive "Glaciergate"? The Head of the UN Panel on Climate Change, Prof Rajendra Pachauri, is Still Adamant that One Famously Exaggerated Report Should Not Cost Him His Job', *The Daily Telegraph* (UK), 26 July 2011, www.telegraph.co.uk/earth/environment/climatechange/8660714/Can-Prof-Rajendra-Pachauri-really-survive-Glaciergate.html (accessed 17 September 2012).

Stark, Tina L., *Negotiating and Drafting Contract Boilerplate* (New York: ALM Publishing, 2003).

Stein, Jeremy B., 'The Necessary Language of Exceptions: A Response to Frederick Schauer's "Exceptions"' (2007) 63 *New York University Annual Survey of American Law* 99–138.

Steiner, Henry, Philip Alston and Ryan Goodman, *International Human Rights in Context: Law, Politics, Morals*, Third Edition (Oxford and New York: Oxford University Press, 2008).

Steyn, Johan, 'Guantánamo Bay: The Legal Black Hole', 27th F. A. Mann Lecture, 25 November 2003, www.statewatch.org/news/2003/nov/guantanamo.pdf (accessed 17 September 2012).

Suchman, Mark C., 'The Contract as Social Artifact' (2003) 37 *Law and Society Review* 91–142.

Sullivan, Scott and Joshua Colangelo-Bryan, 'Closing the Loop on Guantánamo' (2010) 19 *Tulane Journal of International & Comparative Law* 247–260.

Sulloway, Frank J., *Freud, Biologist of the Mind: Beyond the Psychoanalytical Legend* (New York: Basic Books, 1979).

Sweeney, Joseph C., 'Guantánamo and U.S. Law' (2007) 30 *Fordham International Law Journal* 673–779.

Symeonides, Symeon C., 'The American Choice of Law Revolution in the Courts: Today and Tomorrow' (2002) 298 *Recueil des Cours* 9–448.

'Contracts Subject to Non-State Norms' (2006) 54 (Supplement) *American Journal of Comparative Law* 209–232.

Szakolczai, Árpád, *Max Weber and Michel Foucault: Parallel Life-Works* (London: Routledge, 1998).

Tamanaha, Brian Z., 'The Folly of the "Social Scientific" Concept of Legal Pluralism' (1993) 20 *Journal of Law and Society* 192–217.

'Understanding Legal Pluralism: Past to Present, Local to Global' (2008) 30 *Sydney Law Review* 375–411.

Teitz, Louise Ellen, 'The Hague Choice of Court Convention: Validating Party Autonomy and Providing an Alternative to Arbitration' (2005) 53 *American Journal of Comparative Law* 543–558.

Thompson, Ginger and Damien Cave, 'Officials Strain to Distribute Aid to Haiti as Violence Rises', *The New York Times*, 17 January 2010, p. 1.

Tidball-Binz, Morris, 'Managing the Dead in Catastrophes: Guiding Principles and Practical Recommendations for First Responders' (2007) 89 *International Review of the Red Cross* 421–442.

Tol, Richard S. J., 'Regulating Knowledge Monopolies: The Case of the IPCC' (2011) 108 *Climactic Change* 827–839.

Toope, Stephen J., *Mixed International Arbitration: Studies in Arbitration Between States and Private Persons* (Cambridge: Grotius Publications, 1990).

Tribe, Laurence H. and Patrick O. Gudridge, 'The Anti-Emergency Constitution' (2004) 113 *Yale Law Journal* 1801–1870.

Trubek, David M., Yves Dezalay, Ruth Buchanan and John R. Davis, 'Global Restructuring and the Law: Studies of the Internationalization of Legal Fields and the Creation of Transnational Arenas' (1994) 44 *Case Western Reserve Law Review* 407–498.

Turner, Stephen P. (ed.), *The Cambridge Companion to Weber* (Cambridge University Press, 2000).

Turner, Stephen P. and Regis A. Factor, *Max Weber: The Lawyer as Social Thinker* (London: Routledge, 1994).

United Nations Office of Legal Affairs (ed.), *Collection of Essays by Legal Advisers of States, Legal Advisers of International Organizations and Practitioners in the Field of International Law* (New York: United Nations, 1999), www.un.org/law/books/CollectionOfEssaysByLegalAdvisers.pdf (accessed 17 September 2012).

Utset, Manuel A., 'A Model of Time-Inconsistent Misconduct: The Case of Lawyer Misconduct' (2005) 74 *Fordham Law Review* 1319–1352.

Valverde, Mariana, *Law's Dream of a Common Knowledge* (Princeton and Woodstock: Princeton University Press, 2003).

van Boven, Theo, 'The Torture Papers: The Road to Abu Ghraib' (2006) 53 *Netherlands International Law Review* 149–152.

Varley, Ann (ed.), *Disasters, Development and Environment* (Chichester: John Wiley & Sons, 1994).

Vasileiadou, Eleftheria, Gaston Heimeriks and Arthur C. Petersen, 'Exploring the Impact of the IPCC Assessment Reports on Science' (2011) 14 *Environmental Science and Policy* 1052–1061.

Vega, Arturo Olvera, 'Risk Allocation in Infrastructure Financing' (1997) 3:2 *Journal of Project Finance* 38–42.

Verheyen, Roda, *Climate Change Damage and International Law: Prevention Duties and State Responsibility* (Leiden and Boston: Martinus Nijhoff Publishers, 2005).

Verkaik, Robert, 'Exclusive: Caught in America's Legal Black Hole', *Independent*, 9 August 2010, www.independent.co.uk/news/world/americas/exclusive-caught-in-americas-legal-black-hole-2047307.html (accessed 17 September 2012).

Vierucci, Luisa 'Is the Geneva Convention on Prisoners of War Obsolete? – The Views of the Counsel to the US President on the Application of International Law to the Afghan Conflict' (2004) 2 *Journal of International Criminal Justice* 866–871.

Vinuales, Jorge E., 'Legal Techniques for Dealing with Scientific Uncertainty in Environmental Law' (2010) 43 *Vanderbilt Journal of Transnational Law* 437–504.

Voigt, Christina, 'State Responsibility for Climate Change Damages' (2008) 77 *Nordic Journal of International Law* 1–22.

von Benda-Beckmann, Franz, Keebet von Benda-Beckmann and Julia Eckert (eds.), *Rules of Law and Laws of Ruling* (Farnham and Burlington: Ashgate, 2009).

Waelde, Thomas W. and George Ndi, 'Stabilizing International Investment Commitments: International Law Versus Contract Interpretation' (1996) 31 *Texas International Law Journal* 215–268.

Wai, Robert, 'Transnational Liftoff and Juridical Touchdown: The Regulatory Function of Private International Law in an Era of Globalization' (2002) 40 *Columbia Journal of Transnational Law* 209–274.

Waldron, Jeremy, 'Torture and Positive Law: Jurisprudence for the White House' (2005) 105 *Columbia Law Review* 1681–1750.

Weber, Max, *Economy and Society: An Outline of Interpretive Sociology* (ed. Guenther Roth and Claus Wittich, Berkeley: University of California Press, 1978).

From Max Weber: Essays in Sociology (ed. H. H. Gerth and C. Wright Mills, Oxford University Press, 1946).

Max Weber on Law in Economy and Society (ed. Max Rheinstein, Cambridge, MA: Harvard University Press, 1954).

Wedgwood, Ruth, 'Al Qaeda, Terrorism and Military Commissions' (2002) 96 *American Journal of International Law* 328–337.

Weinstein, Henry, 'Prisoners May Face "Legal Black Hole"', *Los Angeles Times*, 1 December 2002, articles.latimes.com/2002/dec/01/nation/na-detainees1 (accessed 17 September 2012).

Welling, James C., 'The Law of Torture: A Study in the Evolution of Law' (1892) 5 *American Anthropologist* 193–216.

Wendel, W. Bradley, 'Legal Ethics and the Separation of Law and Morals' (2005) 91 *Cornell Law Review* 67–128.

'Professionalism as Interpretation' (2005) 99 *Northwestern University Law Review* 1167–1234.

Whimster, Sam and Scott Lash (eds.), *Max Weber, Rationality and Modernity* (London: Allen & Unwin, 1987).

Whincop, Michael J. and Mary Keyes, *Policy and Pragmatism in the Conflict of Laws* (Aldershot: Ashgate/Dartmouth Publishing, 2001).

'Putting the "Private" Back into Private International Law: Default Rules and the Proper Law of the Contract' (1997) 21 *Melbourne University Law Review* 515–543.

White, Morton, *Social Thought in America: The Revolt Against Formalism* (London and New York: Oxford University Press, 1976).

Whitington, Jerome, 'Introduction – Science and its Politics' (2008) 14:3 *Parallax* 1–3.

Whitman, Jim and Sarah Perrigo (eds.), *The Geneva Conventions Under Assault* (London: Pluto Press, 2010).

Wilde, Ralph, 'Legal "Black Hole"?: Extraterritorial State Action and International Treaty Law on Civil and Political Rights' (2005) 26 *Michigan Journal of International Law* 739–806.

'Casting Light on the "Legal Black Hole": Some Political Issues at Stake' (2006) 5 *European Human Rights Law Review* 552–557.

Williams, Angela, 'Solidarity, Justice and Climate Change Law' (2009) 10 *Melbourne Journal of International Law* 493–508.

Williams, George, 'Guantanamo: Legal Black Hole', 30 November 2010, www.amnesty.org.au/hrs/comments/24286/ (accessed 17 September 2012).

Wilson, Richard J., 'A Long, Strange Trip: Guantánamo and the Scarcity of International Law', WCL Research Paper No. 2009-12, American University, ssrn.com/abstract=1368420 (accessed 17 September 2012).

Wisner, Benjamin, Piers Blaikie, Terry Cannon and Ian Davis, *At Risk: Natural Hazards, People's Vulnerability and Disasters*, Second Edition (London and New York: Routledge, 2004).

Wittes, Benjamin, Robert Chesney and Rabea Benhalim, 'The Emerging Law of Detention: The Guantanamo Cases as Lawmaking', University of Texas Law, Public Law Research Paper No. 165, 22 January 2010, www.ssrn.com/abstract=1540601 (accessed 17 September 2012).

Wolcott, Harry F., *Ethnography: A Way of Seeing* (Lanham: AltaMira Press, 2008).

Wolfendale, Jessica, *Torture and the Military Profession* (Basingstoke and New York: Palgrave Macmillan, 2007).

Wood, Donald C. (ed.), *Choice in Economic Contexts: Ethnographic and Theoretical Enquiries* (Oxford, Amsterdam and San Diego: Elsevier JAI, 2007).

Woodhouse, A. S. P., 'Nature and Grace in the Faerie Queene' (1949) 16 *ELH* 194–228.

Yoo, John C., 'War and the Constitutional Text' (2002) 69 *University of Chicago Law Review* 1639–1684.

Zachary, Shlomy, 'Between the Geneva Conventions: Where Does the Unlawful Combatant Belong?' (2005) 38 *Israeli Law Review* 378–419.

Zumbansen, Peer, 'Transnational Legal Pluralism' (2010) 1 *Transnational Legal Theory* 141–190.

Index

CAMBRIDGE STUDIES IN INTERNATIONAL AND COMPARATIVE LAW

Books in the series

Non-Legality in International Law: Unruly Law
Fleur Johns

Armed Conflict and Displacement: The Protection of Refugees and Displaced Persons under International Humanitarian Law
Mélanie Jacques

Foreign Investment and the Environment in International Law
Jorge Viñuales

The Human Rights Treaty Obligations of Peacekeepers
Kjetil Larsen

Cyberwarfare and the Laws of War
Heather Harrison Dinniss

The Right to Reparation in International Law for Victims of Armed Conflict: The Role of the UN in Advocating for State Responsibility
Christine Evans

Global Public Interest in International Investment Law
Andreas Kulick

State Immunity in International Law
Xiaodong Yang

Reparations and Victim Support in the International Criminal Court
Conor McCarthy

Reducing Genocide to Law: Definition, Meaning, and the Ultimate Crime
Payam Akhavan

Decolonizing International Law: Development, Economic Growth and the Politics of Universality
Sundhya Pahuja

Complicity and the Law of State Responsibility
Helmut Philipp Aust

State Control over Private Military and Security Companies in Armed Conflict
Hannah Tonkin

'Fair and Equitable Treatment' in International Investment Law
Roland Kläger

The UN and Human Rights: Who Guards the Guardians?
Guglielmo Verdirame

Sovereign Defaults before International Courts and Tribunals
Michael Waibel

Making the Law of the Sea: A Study in the Development of International Law
James Harrison

Science and the Precautionary Principle in International Courts and Tribunals: Expert Evidence, Burden of Proof and Finality
Caroline E. Foster

Legal Aspects of Transition from Illegal Territorial Regimes in International Law
Yaël Ronen

Access to Asylum: International Refugee Law and the Globalisation of Migration Control
Thomas Gammeltoft-Hansen

Trading Fish, Saving Fish: The Interaction between Regimes in International Law
Margaret Young

The Individual in the International Legal System: State-Centrism, History and Change in International Law
Kate Parlett

The Participation of States in International Organisations: The Role of Human Rights and Democracy
Alison Duxbury

'Armed Attack' and Article 51 of the UN Charter: Evolutions in Customary Law and Practice
Tom Ruys

Science and Risk Regulation in International Law: The Role of Science, Uncertainty and Values
Jacqueline Peel

Theatre of the Rule of Law: The Theory, History and Practice of Transnational Legal Intervention
Stephen Humphreys

The Public International Law Theory of Hans Kelsen: Believing in Universal Law
Jochen von Bernstorff

Vicarious Liability in Tort: A Comparative Perspective
Paula Giliker

Legal Personality in International Law
Roland Portmann

Legitimacy and Legality in International Law: An Interactional Account
Jutta Brunnée and Stephen J. Toope

The Concept of Non-International Armed Conflict in International Humanitarian Law
Anthony Cullen

The Challenge of Child Labour in International Law
Franziska Humbert

Shipping Interdiction and the Law of the Sea
Douglas Guilfoyle

International Courts and Environmental Protection
Tim Stephens

Legal Principles in WTO Disputes
Andrew D. Mitchell

War Crimes in Internal Armed Conflicts
Eve La Haye

Humanitarian Occupation
Gregory H. Fox

The International Law of Environmental Impact Assessment: Process, Substance and Integration
Neil Craik

The Law and Practice of International Territorial Administration: Versailles, Iraq and Beyond
Carsten Stahn

Cultural Products and the World Trade Organization
Tania Voon

United Nations Sanctions and the Rule of Law
Jeremy Farrall

National Law in WTO Law: Effectiveness and Good Governance in the World Trading System
Sharif Bhuiyan

The Threat of Force in International Law
Nikolas Stürchler

Indigenous Rights and United Nations Standards
Alexandra Xanthaki

International Refugee Law and Socio-Economic Rights
Michelle Foster

The Protection of Cultural Property in Armed Conflict
Roger O'Keefe

Interpretation and Revision of International Boundary Decisions
Kaiyan Homi Kaikobad

Multinationals and Corporate Social Responsibility: Limitations and Opportunities in International Law
Jennifer A. Zerk

Judiciaries within Europe: A Comparative Review
John Bell

Law in Times of Crisis: Emergency Powers in Theory and Practice
Oren Gross and Fionnuala Ní Aoláin

Vessel-Source Marine Pollution: The Law and Politics of International Regulation
Alan Tan

Enforcing Obligations Erga Omnes *in International Law*
Christian J. Tams

Non-Governmental Organisations in International Law
Anna-Karin Lindblom

Democracy, Minorities and International Law
Steven Wheatley

Prosecuting International Crimes: Selectivity and the International Criminal Law Regime
Robert Cryer

Compensation for Personal Injury in English, German and Italian Law: A Comparative Outline
Basil Markesinis, Michael Coester, Guido Alpa, Augustus Ullstein

Dispute Settlement in the UN Convention on the Law of the Sea
Natalie Klein

The International Protection of Internally Displaced Persons
Catherine Phuong

Imperialism, Sovereignty and the Making of International Law
Antony Anghie

Necessity, Proportionality and the Use of Force by States
Judith Gardam

International Legal Argument in the Permanent Court of International Justice: The Rise of the International Judiciary
Ole Spiermann

Great Powers and Outlaw States: Unequal Sovereigns in the International Legal Order
Gerry Simpson

Local Remedies in International Law
C. F. Amerasinghe

Reading Humanitarian Intervention: Human Rights and the Use of Force in International Law
Anne Orford

Conflict of Norms in Public International Law: How WTO Law Relates to Other Rules of Law
Joost Pauwelyn

Transboundary Damage in International Law
Hanqin Xue

European Criminal Procedures
Edited by Mireille Delmas-Marty and John Spencer

The Accountability of Armed Opposition Groups in International Law
Liesbeth Zegveld

Sharing Transboundary Resources: International Law and Optimal Resource Use
Eyal Benvenisti

International Human Rights and Humanitarian Law
René Provost

Remedies Against International Organisations
Karel Wellens

Diversity and Self-Determination in International Law
Karen Knop

The Law of Internal Armed Conflict
Lindsay Moir

International Commercial Arbitration and African States: Practice, Participation and Institutional Development
Amazu A. Asouzu

The Enforceability of Promises in European Contract Law
James Gordley

International Law in Antiquity
David J. Bederman

Money Laundering: A New International Law Enforcement Model
Guy Stessens

Good Faith in European Contract Law
Reinhard Zimmermann and Simon Whittaker

On Civil Procedure
J. A. Jolowicz

Trusts: A Comparative Study
Maurizio Lupoi

The Right to Property in Commonwealth Constitutions
Tom Allen

International Organizations Before National Courts
August Reinisch

The Changing International Law of High Seas Fisheries
Francisco Orrego Vicuña

Trade and the Environment: A Comparative Study of EC and US Law
Damien Geradin

Unjust Enrichment: A Study of Private Law and Public Values
Hanoch Dagan

Religious Liberty and International Law in Europe
Malcolm D. Evans

Ethics and Authority in International Law
Alfred P. Rubin

Sovereignty Over Natural Resources: Balancing Rights and Duties
Nico Schrijver

The Polar Regions and the Development of International Law
Donald R. Rothwell

Fragmentation and the International Relations of Micro-States: Self-determination and Statehood
Jorri Duursma

Principles of the Institutional Law of International Organizations
C. F. Amerasinghe